VIGILANTE

THE BACKLASH AGAINST CRIME IN AMERICA

Also by William Tucker
*Progress and Privilege: America in the Age
    of Environmentalism*

VIGILANTE

THE BACKLASH AGAINST CRIME IN AMERICA

William Tucker

STEIN AND DAY/Publishers/New York

First published in 1985
Copyright © 1985 by William Tucker
All rights reserved, Stein and Day, Incorporated
Designed by Louis A. Ditizio
Printed in the United States of America
STEIN AND DAY/*Publishers*
Scarborough House
Briarcliff Manor, N.Y. 10510

Library of Congress Cataloging-in-Publication Data

Tucker, William, 1942–
   Vigilante, the backlash against crime in America.

   Bibliography: p.
   1. Vigilance committees. 2. Crime prevention—
United States—Citizen participation. I. Title.
HV7431.T92   1985   364.4′0973   85-40520
ISBN 0-8128-3070-9

To my mother and father

Acknowledgments

First I should like to pay an intellectual debt. The inspiration for this book came from Thomas Sowell and his landmark work, *Knowledge and Decisions.* I read it five years ago and it has served almost as a blueprint for my work since that time. As a journalistic entrepreneur I am constantly looking for circumstances where there is a wide gap between what is actually happening in a situation and what people think *should* be happening. Sowell's brief twenty-page section on crime was my first introduction to how astonishingly wide that gap has become in the criminal justice system. Much of this book has evolved out of Sowell's brief but powerful treatment of the problem.

On the financial side, I must offer sincere thanks to the Reason Foundation and its director, Robert Poole, Jr., for supporting this effort for a year and for making the book possible. Bob has also been extremely helpful in offering ideas, both in personal correspondence and through his own prolific writing in *Reason* and other publications. I can only hope that this work meets the Reason Foundation's expectations.

Several people have read the manuscript to offer ideas and criticism. Frank Carrington, former policeman and now an attorney with Americans for Effective Law Enforcement, has been a constant source of information. His own work in this field is monumental. James Q. Wilson, at Harvard, offered much advice, much of which has been incorporated.

Victor Aranow, an old friend and an excellent defense attorney, has offered considerable comment. James Arehart, an older friend and an excellent federal prosecutor, has also been helpful with his advice. And Nick Allis, a talented attorney and perhaps my oldest friend, has been extremely helpful, particularly in warning me candidly of some of the withering criticism portions of this book are likely to evoke from within the legal profession.

Although all these people have offered their advice, the views presented are strictly my own.

At Stein and Day, Sol Stein has been a stern taskmaster and a wellspring of ideas. The title of the book and much of its general direction are his. Pat Day has been an exacting editor and Benton Arnowitz a steady source of countenance. Dawn Horstman and Daphne Hougham have helped shepherd the project through a breakneck schedule.

Peter McCabe helped considerably in shaping earlier versions of much of this material, as did Ben Cheever, of *Reader's Digest,* and Gerry Marzorati, of *Harper's.* Fred Kapner has been an excellent researcher and a steady source of friendly criticism. My parents, William and Grace Tucker, have also been most helpful in their support, both specific and general, over the years.

I would also like to thank my son Kevan for being a good boy while Daddy spent long, long hours at the computer. And finally, I would like to thank my wife, Sarah, for all her contributions and inspiration. Only she knows the true meaning of it.

One additional acknowledgment is also due. I cannot finish without expressing my deep sympathy and admiration for the many victims of crime, and surviving families of crime victims, who have been brave enough to suppress their grief and take the trouble to tell their story to a reporter. They are the emotional center of this book. Time and again I have felt an overwhelming admiration for their suffering and bravery that is almost too deep to express.

This book is the expression of that admiration.

Contents

Of course, the criminal who revolts against society hates it, and almost always considers himself in the right and society in the wrong. Moreover, he has already endured punishment at its hands, and for that reason almost considers himself purged and quits with society. There are points of view, in fact, from which one is almost brought to justify the criminal. But in spite of all possible points of view everyone will admit that there are crimes which always and everywhere from the beginning of the world, under all legal systems, have unhesitatingly been considered crimes, and will be considered so as long as man remains human. Only in prison have I heard stories of the most terrible, the most unnatural actions, of the most monstrous murders told with the most spontaneous, childishly merry laughter.

—Dostoevski, *The House of the Dead*

"Crime? Gee, I don't know what the crime was here. I just know the case law."
—a deputy state attorney general

Part I

What Went Wrong

VIGILANTE 1

ON THE UNSEASONABLY warm afternoon of December 22, 1984, a mild-mannered electronics engineer named Bernhard Goetz boarded a southbound IRT in Manhattan and headed for the Wall Street district. Before the car had reached the next station, a group of four black youths surrounded him and asked him for five dollars. Goetz reached into his coat, pulled out an unlicensed .38-caliber pistol he had been carrying with him for six months, and shot all four of them.

The shooting incident touched off one of the most remarkable spontaneous displays of public support in New York City history. When New York City police set up a hotline for information about the mysterious attacker, they found themselves deluged with phone calls praising his actions. New York City's Mayor Edward Koch made some cautious remarks about the dangers of "taking the law into your own hands" and received calls and letters from around the country running 80-to-1 in support of the gunman.

Newspaper reporters, rounding up the usual suspects, were astonished to find Roy Innes, director of the Congress of Racial Equality and one of the country's most venerable civil rights leaders, offering to pay all the gunman's legal expenses. When the newspapers looked into Innes's personal history the reasons became apparent. Innes had already lost one son to street crime and had another nearly beaten to death in a vicious mugging.

The Guardian Angels, the largely black and Puerto Rican subway vigilante organization, announced their full support of the "subway vigilante." They urged Mayor Koch to offer amnesty to the gunman in exchange for his identity. When shy, soft-spoken Bernhard Goetz turned himself in to New Hampshire police a week later, he was already a national celebrity.

Goetz seemed fearful of the press and public. He called the press "vultures" and was obviously still feeling like a criminal. "If you corner a rat and you're about to butcher it, OK? The way I responded was viciously and savagely, just like a rat," he told a friend from New York in a secret phone conversation.[1] He told New Hampshire police, "I know it's a disgusting thing to say, but once I started shooting, it was so goddamn easy."

The hero's welcome that greeted him in New York apparently came as a complete surprise. Dozens of people—including comedienne Joan Rivers and several former mugging victims—offered to help put up his $50,000 bail. Lawyers were falling over each other to represent him.

Longstanding liberal press commentators led a chorus of support. Mike Royko, veteran columnist for the Chicago *Tribune,* once the scourge of Mayor Richard Daley's law-and-order administration, had only recently found himself staring down a gun barrel:

> As some of you may recall, a few months ago a couple of young men, seeking to increase their net worth, put a gun to my nose. That wasn't the first time I was robbed or mugged, but it was the closest I've come to croaking—either from a twitch of a trigger finger or my own fright.
>
> So as a recent victim, I have a different perspective than that of a reporter . . .
>
> It goes like this: To hell with the questions. I'm glad Goetz shot them. I don't care what his motives were or whether he has all of his marbles. The four punks looked for trouble and they found it. Case closed.[2]

Even more outspoken was New York *Daily News*'s outstanding liberal columnist, Lars-Erik Nelson. Comparing Goetz's volley to "the first shot fired at Lexington and Concord," Nelson called on the American public to exercise its "revolutionary right to dismember and overthrow" the "absolute despotism of the criminal justice system." Nelson wrote perceptively:

> If Goetz had shot youths attempting to murder him, he would have been a momentary celebrity. What has made him a hero is that he shot four insufferable thugs attempting a routine petty ripoff—the kinds the cops and courts laugh at . . .

Goetz has shown that people are not prepared to live as constant cringers before daily, petty, bullying assaults by rowdies, toughs, skylarking hoodlums—who when caught say innocently, "We were just fooling, man. We didn't mean to hurt the guy."[3]

What was most remarkable, however, was the grueling testimony that appeared day after day in the letters columns of New York's newspapers. Everybody, it seemed, had a story to tell about crime.

Take, for example, this letter from California:

On July 5, 1982, my brother-in-law, a middle-aged widower, was robbed at knifepoint and then terribly beaten and mutilated by four young hoodlums, one block from the Pierre Hotel in Manhattan, just after dark.

Without protest, he handed over his wallet and $3,000 in traveler's checks to the hoods. Then they beat him to the ground, slashing him through his suit coat, around his arms and shoulders. He was protecting his face. He wasn't protective enough. At a New York hospital, his left eye had to be removed. There were witnesses but none came forward.

My brother-in-law is a gentle, kind man. In the Korean War he served as a combat medic with the 24th Infantry because he refused to bear arms against another human. He was wounded twice, and decorated with the Silver Star.

That assault has changed his personality completely. He carries a pistol with him now at all times. Business takes him to New York four or five times a year. He walks along dark streets at night hoping someone will attempt to mug him again.

I've tried to reason with him, warning him that he might kill an innocent person. His bitterness and rage have consumed him. When I heard about the shooting on the subway, I was afraid he might be the guilty one.

Or this one to the *Daily News*:

A little over a year ago on a train in New York, I was sitting with a friend of mine next to three white youths going to school. Across the way was an elderly couple minding their own business, being harassed by two black youths. Everyone on that train made believe they didn't know what was going on. A white youth went over to the black youths and told them to leave the elderly couple alone. No sooner were the words out of his mouth than he fell to the floor from a knife wound. Was Bernhard Goetz correct in his actions? You'd better believe it.

Or this from a Manhattan man:

As a religious man I feel guilty because I cannot get myself to feel any sympathy for the four wounded muggers.

I wonder if one of the screwdrivers (not considered a lethal weapon) was used to stab my son, in broad daylight in Central Park, because he wouldn't give up his camera.

The mugger threatened to kill him. Fortunately the screwdriver wouldn't go through his thick coat, but he let him have it through the jaw and in back of his ear.

We must show more compassion for the victims instead of the muggers and reward the heroes.

Or this one:

On July 7, two such vermin burst into my office and mugged and almost slaughtered me.

One holding a sawed-off shotgun to my head, the other almost piercing my neck with a hunting knife, they robbed me of my watch, money, and antique Masonic ring.

They also ripped out the phones and made a shambles of my office, taking everything they could carry.

Before leaving, one of them said, "I think I'll kill this old bastard." They other said, "Nah, I'd rather go up for robbery, instead of murder, if they catch us."

Since then, I have been living under the trauma of humiliation and degradation to have been so degraded by two subhumans, unable to sleep or function properly.

I fault Goetz for only one thing—that his aim was inaccurate.

And while the newspapers at first tried to portray the whole affair as just another "racial incident," it was obvious that black people were just as fed up with crime as white people. A poll by *The New York Times* taken shortly after the shooting showed a plurality of black people supporting

Goetz—44-to-33 percent, as opposed to 56-to-26 percent among whites. Moreover, blacks felt crime was worse in New York than whites did.

A writer in the *Voice* reported this conversation with a black friend, whose husband had been robbed at gunpoint in front of their apartment on 160th Street in Manhattan only a few months before. The woman told him:

> When I first heard about the shooting, I was glad. I thought it served them right. I was actually happy for a few days, and the mood in the subway cars was a kind of camaraderie I had never felt before. Everybody seemed closer. It was like we all had won one. Nobody said anything, but you could feel it. It didn't have anything at all to do with race. Everybody was in agreement. Goetz had done something for *all* of us.[4]

The day of the Goetz shooting, one 23-year-old Puerto Rican explained his reaction to the Goetz incident:

> Sure, I'm supporting him. My father was mugged on the subway last year for fifty cents. When they found that's all the money he had, they nearly beat him to death. You should have seen my father's eye when they were through with him. It was hanging out the side of his head. And all that for fifty cents, can you believe that—fifty cents!

Other letters expressed the same feelings:

> Let's stop this nonsense about police brutality in New York. Look at our courtrooms and jails and see who makes up the majority of criminals in custody. The minorities in this city will not face up to the fact that minority crime is making our city a ghost town. I'm black, and I was mugged twice by punks in Mt. Morris Park going to church services. What is a person to do when they can't even go to church without getting assaulted? It's time the decent citizens of all races stop this crime problem and give the police a helping hand.

Or this letter from Westchester County:

> I'm a black woman. I have been robbed twice, both times by blacks.

I didn't feel safe because they were black boys or the fact that I recognized one of them and thought maybe they wouldn't hurt me.

I didn't even see black boys. What I saw was fear.

Fear has no color. The only color you see is not the color of skin, but the color of being scared to death.

Bernhard Goetz didn't see black boys. He saw the color of fear, the color of his life being at stake. Fear has no color.

Another *New York Times* poll showed that black people were actually more afraid of gangs of black youths than they were afraid of similar gangs of white youths and that blacks' concern for crime was higher than that of whites.

Even some responses that were critical of Goetz hardly reflected well on American society. Said one writer:

A few months ago I was riding the subway about two in the morning on a week night. Three blacks strolled into the car as the train was moving. Two carried short pieces of pipe, wrapped with electrician's tape at one end. One carried a child's baseball bat. They were shouting and teasing the passengers in the car. They reached a quiet black man, fairly well-dressed, reading a newspaper. I don't know if they began harassing him, or if he beat them to the punch—it happened very quickly. He pulled out a large revolver and began screaming at the boys. He ordered them off the train as we were pulling into 42nd Street. The boys muttered and cursed, but didn't give the appearance of wanting to stay and argue.

Recalling the incident, I can't help but think that Bernhard Goetz was not really reacting properly to his situation; perhaps he was acting out a fantasy. Shooting all four youths was surely excessive.

In America in 1984, it wasn't a question of whether you should carry a gun to protect yourself from crime. The only ethical question was when you should use it. It wasn't exactly what George Orwell had imagined. Maybe it was a lot worse.

Whether a jury ultimately finds Bernhard Goetz guilty or innocent of the charges is in many ways immaterial. The important question concerns the rents in the social fabric that the subway shooting incident has uncovered.

People have lost faith in the justice system. There is, obviously, widespread support for individual, vigilante actions. In fact, vigilantism has been on the rise in recent years, and the public response has been almost identical to the outpouring of support that came for Bernard Goetz's actions. For example:

—less than a week after the Goetz shooting, Harold Brown, a 68-year-old Chicago plumber, was attacked on the street as he was returning home with a bag of groceries. Two black youths threw him to the ground, one putting a knife to his throat, while the other put a gun in his ear. Brown, who is black, was carrying a gun. He managed to fire it, killing one of the youths. His actions were widely praised in Chicago, and no charges were pressed against him.

—In Buffalo, N.Y., in 1983, Willie E. Williams, a 35-year-old truck driver, learned that his 10-year-old daughter had been kidnapped for ten hours and sexually molested by a man in the same housing project. Although Williams did not know it at the time, the man had a record of similar offenses. Williams gathered a group of friends, and together they beat the man and stabbed him in the stomach. The action was caught by television news cameras that happened to be cruising in the area.

Williams was arrested for assault and inciting to riot but was congratulated by police officers in his cell and received supportive letters from all over the country. A Buffalo city councilman led the campaign to raise his bail. When he was returned to his neighborhood, he was given a hero's welcome. Williams eventually pleaded guilty to a lesser charge.

—Roberta Leonard, a 67-year-old, partially blind grandmother was forced to come to New York in 1983 to tend her sick brother. In only a few weeks of living in New York, she was mugged and robbed of $140.

After returning to Alabama, she was forced to come back again to New York two months later. She got into the Port Authority Bus Terminal at eleven o'clock at night. Even before making it to the subway, she was set upon by a gang of teenage muggers—one only twelve—led by a 40-year-old woman the police called a "female Fagin."

This time, however, she was prepared. She quickly pulled out an unloaded, unlicensed pistol and held the muggers at bay until police arrived. The muggers were corraled, but she was placed under arrest for carrying an unlicensed gun.

When the story of the "pistol-packing grandma" made the newspapers the next day, there was an outpouring of public support. As with Goetz, lawyers fell over themselves to handle her case. Charges were dropped the next day, and she was hailed as a heroine. Unfortunately, the muggers got off easy as well. Because they had been unable to complete the robbery—and because she didn't want to stay in New York for court proceedings—charges were dropped against them, too.

—In South Carolina in 1978, Tony Cimo found his mother and stepfather brutally murdered after a robbery of their small grocery store. Rudolph Tyner, nineteen, was arrested a few hours later. A shotgun shell in his pocket tied him to the murder. He confessed and was sentenced to death in August, 1978.

Inevitably, civil liberties groups and liberal lawyers rushed to prevent the execution. In 1979, the state supreme court overturned the sentence, ruling that the prosecutor had made a mistake in his closing arguments. State officials were ordered to go through the sentencing part of the conviction again. Cimo and his family would once again have to undergo the ordeal of testifying. Meanwhile, word filtered back that Tyner was bragging about the killings in jail, joking of how Cimo's parents had begged for their lives before he shot them.

Finally, Cimo couldn't stand it anymore. He contacted Donald (Pee Wee) Gaskins, the state's most notorious mass murderer, who was serving several life sentences in a cell near Tyner's. With Cimo's help, Gaskins rigged up an explosive device and told Tyner it was a radio. When Tyner put it to his ear and hooked the wires into the wall, it detonated, blowing his head off.

Cimo, the father of two children, subsequently pleaded guilty to withholding knowledge of a felony and conspiracy to murder. In 1983, he began serving a eight-year sentence.

"I'm not advocating vigilantism," said Cimo, "but I don't feel as bad about killing Tyner as I would killing a rabid dog. It's just something that should have been done, and now it's over. I had to do it for my peace of mind."

For years now, public frustration about crime has been mounting to a flash point. No issue has raised such persistent anxiety over the decades. Since the late 1960s, crime has ranked as one of the top three worries among Americans. The Vietnam War came and went, the energy crisis came and went, but still America's high crime rates remain.

Vigilantism has become the symbol of that fear and frustration. People are announcing that they will not allow themselves to be harassed and intimidated forever. The social contract that says we will forswear private vengeance and allow the state to defend us in criminal matters is only that—a social contract. If there is widespread feeling that the state is no longer holding up its end of the bargain, then people will start "taking the law back into their own hands"—which is where it was in the first place. The right to self-protection, after all, is one of those "unalienable rights" of "life, liberty, and the pursuit of happiness" that Jefferson wrote about in the Declaration of Independence.

Still, vigilantism creates its own problems. A vigilante is someone who tries to enforce the law by breaking the law. His efforts are contradictory and likely to be self-defeating. He may settle a score or "do justice" in a particular instance, but his effort will become a precedent that can only lead to further social disintegration.

Private vengeance may seem to offer swift and efficient satisfaction to the victim, but it allows everyone to become the judge of his own case. There are always personal motives involved, and situations are often entangled enough so that it is difficult to decide where the real crime lies. One of the best reasons for taking punishment out of the hands of individuals and spreading the responsibility over the entire society is that it offers the greatest potential for filtering out personal motives and giving the situation a "fair trial."

But this arrangement remains only a mutual agreement between society and its individual members. People always feel a personal sense of vengeance and submit to the decisions of the state because the state agrees to shoulder the responsibility of policing crime and punishing criminals.

Most of us have mentally incorporated this contract so completely that we do not even think that things could be any different. When we feel threatened or in danger, we almost automatically turn to the police. When a dispute arises, we reflexively think of going to court. We expect the police to protect us, district attorneys to bring charges, judges to make wise decisions, and a jury to deliver a fair and impartial verdict. When the word begins to filter down that these things are no longer happening, we begin to feel a nagging sense of frustration and anxiety. It is only after many years that these frustrations may build until they explode into broad public support for vigilante actions.

Self-protection and vigilantism form a strong thread running through American history. Because we were building a new country from the ground up, we often saw the social contract forming right before our eyes. Without an organized state to enforce law and order, people often took on the responsibility themselves.

In the early days of the Gold Rush, for example, San Francisco was governed by "vigilance committees" composed of the city's leading citizens. At one point these organizations boasted membership of over seven thousand. The vigilance committees chartered police patrols similar to the "crime watch" groups that have arisen in many communities today. People were arrested, brought before informal judicial counsels, tried and punished, all without the benefit of an officially sanctioned state apparatus. Considering the tremendous pressures San Francisco was under from the influx of the Forty-Niners, the vigilance committees created a fairly well-ordered community.

During the nineteenth century, vigilante efforts were often seen as part of the "can-do" American spirit. They even received some general approval from scholars and academics. As legal historian Andrew Karmen writes:

> The vigilante credo was accepted by legal scholars, judges, and lawyers, as well as by men of action, during the late 1800s and early 1900s. On the whole, the legal illuminati granted qualified approval to vigilantism as a rational response to the inadequacies of the criminal justice system.[5]

As far back as the Revolutionary War, a group of Virginians under Colonel Edward Lynch had set up their own criminal courts to try and punish suspected Tories. These "lynch mobs" administered public whippings and drove people from the community but did not hang people, as their name later came to imply. They acted while the nation was at war and because there were no established courts nearby.

In 1767, farmers in remote rural areas of South Carolina, besieged by robber gangs roving the frontier, formed a vigilante group called the "Regulators" that carried on a bloody, two-year campaign against banditry. Their efforts tended toward excess, however, and they were soon opposed by another counter-vigilante group called the "Moderators."

At other times, outbreaks of vigilantism have occurred when people were suspicious of corruption or generally disillusioned with law enforcement.

In Montana from 1863 to 1865, violence swept over the territory when a sheriff was suspected of being in league with horse thieves. About thirty people were killed. There was another outbreak in 1884, when thirty-five people branded as outlaws were hung by armed posses.

Where vigilantism has gotten a bad name is in its inevitable tendency toward excess. Vigilante groups notoriously deliver bad judgment or embody the biases of the community. *The Ox-Bow Incident,* written in the 1940s, is a moving account of a nineteenth-century Western vigilante posse that hangs an innocent man.

The unavoidable problem of vigilantism is that it draws its sanction from only a portion of the community. Vigilantes may win widespread support, but they are inherently self-selective. Their deliberations do not have the built-in check of randomness that comes from selecting twelve members from the community by lot to serve as the ultimate decision-makers—the jury. Vigilantes are almost inevitably that portion of the community that has already made up its mind.

From the point of view of community safety, there are other safeguards to the jury system as well. Juries are convened temporarily and then dissolved. Vigilantes are self-appointed and tend to stick around. They may soon develop their own private interests. The Mafia, after all, began as a vigilante group that protected Sicilian peasants from the rapacious nobility. They have since moved on to other things.

Thus, it isn't surprising that vigilantism eventually got a bad name in American history. The main offender has been the Ku Klux Klan, which suppressed blacks and enforced white supremacy in the South. Whereas in 1885 there were 110 whites and 74 blacks lynched across the country, mob violence soon became an almost entirely Southern phenomenon. During the 1930s, 103 blacks but only 11 whites were victims of lynchings, almost all of them by Southern mobs. The federal anti-lynching laws finally brought an end to the practice.

In the light of the historical record, one question that immediately comes to mind is whether the isolated outbreaks we are seeing today are really "vigilantism" at all. There is not too much resemblance to the historical phenomenon. We do not yet have vigilante committees organizing whole communities. Nor do we have armed mobs hunting down accused criminals, trying to supplant the efforts of the courts and police.

What we have instead are lone individuals who are suddenly taking the law into their own hands.

One plausible explanation that has been offered is that today's vigilantism is simply the old frontier anarchy bursting forth again. In truth, part of the American tradition has always been a mild distaste for law enforcement. The American "can-do" tradition has often produced a willingness to do without judges and police altogether.

Visiting Montgomery, Alabama, in 1813, Alexis de Tocqueville met an attorney who gave him the following account of early Southern justice:

"Our magistrates are completely incompetent," the attorney told de

Tocqueville, "so no one is disposed to appeal to regular justice... There is no one here but carries arms under his clothes. At the slightest quarrel, knife or pistol comes to hand."

But aren't people brought to trial when such things happen? asked de Tocqueville.

"He is always brought to trial and always acquitted by the jury ... I cannot remember seeing a single man who was a little known pay with his life for such a crime... Each juror feels that he might, on leaving the court, find himself in the same position as the accused, and he acquits.

"Besides, I have been no better myself than another in my time; look at the scars that cover my head," added the attorney, showing de Tocqueville several deep scars. "Those are knife blows I have been given."

But didn't you go to the law? asked de Tocqueville.

"My God! No," replied the attorney. "I tried to give as good in return."[6]

All this has led some people to argue that today's outbreaks of vigilantism are nothing more than the old frontier lawlessness in a new guise. Commenting on vigilantism at a recent college graduation, Federal District Judge Harold Greene said:

> There is also in this country a strain of violence and vigilantism apart
> from the law, which stems from the civilizing of the wilderness not long
> ago as historical time is measured. If all these forces are not to tear the
> nation apart, there must be centers of gravity apart from the shifting
> political majorities. The law, as represented by its guardians, the
> judges and lawyers, is one such fixed star.[7]

But this cannot be the complete explanation for what is happening in American society today. In the situation described by de Tocqueville, for example, people had entered into a kind of informal understanding not to punish each other through law-enforcement agencies. Instead, there was a tacit agreement to settle their differences among themselves. As de Tocqueville's informant told him, "juries never convict."

Today we have just the opposite. Juries convict all the time. The vast majority of the public has an almost passionate desire for law enforcement. Defense attorneys I have interviewed say they have never encountered a citizenry with less tolerance for crime.

Yet these efforts are continually frustrated. Appeals courts in particular are constantly overturning jury convictions and undermining public decisions by adhering to procedural rules and minutia that are often totally irrelevant to the substance of the case. Some of these hairsplitting exercises make medieval scholasticism look like a broad-minded pursuit.

Lost in the minutia of the law, the judges have forgotten the end product that the system is supposed to deliver—justice. When the system is unable to produce satisfactory results—when people finally give up all hope that the courts and the state apparatus can deliver what they expect of it—then people turn to vigilantism. This happens not because they prefer to settle their differences privately, but because they see no other recourse in protecting themselves from crime.

Thus, today's situation is definitely *not* a recapitulation of the American frontier. In those times, the public could be fairly blamed for the anti-authoritarian attitudes toward the justice system. Today, things are different. Much of the anti-authoritarianism is coming from the judiciary itself.

The roots of today's vigilantism lie within our experience with the judiciary and the courts. The vast majority of Americans are no longer untamed frontier people ready to join lynch mobs or settle their differences with dueling pistols. The overwhelming majority of Americans have a thirst for law enforcement. They just aren't getting it from the system.

Something has gone wrong within the American justice system. In a remarkable case of historical amnesia, justice officials awoke at one point in the 1960's and said, "Who are all these unfortunate criminal defendants society keeps bringing before us? Can't anything be done besides punishing them? How can we expect these unfortunate individuals to defend themselves against the overwhelming powers of the state?"

Thus, in a series of crucial reforms over the past twenty-five years, the criminal justice system has been completely transformed. Perhaps the most remarkable of these changes is the metamorphosis of criminal trials themselves. Although few people realize it, we no longer live in a system where the guilt or innocence of the criminal defendant is the *sole* issue of a criminal trial. Instead, the justice system has become a forum where the criminal defendant can "put the state on trial" himself. All this has been instituted to give an accused criminal a "sporting chance" to defend himself against the "overwhelming powers of the state."

There is, however, one small problem with this equation. The state may have overwhelming powers, but it also has overwhelming *responsibilities.* The state has to protect everybody. The criminal defendant only has to protect himself.

Thus, while the system now bends over backward and ties itself in knots worrying about the "rights of the defendant," the issue that has been almost completely forgotten is the rights of the *public* in being *protected* from crime. It is this loss of faith in the criminal justice system that has led us at last to self-protection and the vigilante syndrome.

That is one result of the reforms of the past twenty-five years. Another consequence, however, has been that the people who run the system—the judges and attorneys—are left with far more decision-making power, while the public has less and less. In fact, the public servants who run the system now tend to see the public as an irrelevant nuisance.

This was brought home to me again recently in a conversation with a New York City attorney about the indictment of Bernhard Goetz. I said I thought the action by the second grand jury had been positive because it would give the public a forum in which it could resolve the knotty issue of vigilantism and self-protection. He insisted that the second grand jury was wrong. It was a bad precedent, he said, that could easily be used to indict innocent blacks in the South.

Sensing that I was once again being bludgeoned by a moral issue that had little relevance to the question, I persisted. Didn't he think that the public was entitled to a full-dress discussion of the issues? Shouldn't the public be able to participate in the full-scale drama of a courtroom trial?

"I think the public should participate in Wingo games," he suddenly exploded. (Wingo is a popular newspaper game in New York.) "They should leave the justice system to us."

That's just the problem. To a very large degree, the justice system is now run for the benefit of the people who are *always* in court—lawyers, judges, and accused criminals. The public's only avenue of participation—the jury—is being constantly circumscribed so that the public has less and less to say about what comes out of the system.

There is a great danger in this. Legal thinking is basically a self-enclosed system, based on precedents and logical deductions from fixed principles. Small incremental steps add up, and small incremental *mistakes* can eventually add up to a social disaster. In the end, criminal procedure can become a web of subtleties that lawyers will admire and spend hours and hours debating, yet will be completely lacking in common sense.

Public opinion is the only thing that can reign in this climate. Twelve jurors relying on common sense are ultimately a better decision-making body than a judge who can be so entangled in procedural niceties that the question of actual wrongdoing is often the furthest thing from his mind. Yet most of the "reforms" of the past twenty-five years have been a carefully orchestrated effort to keep both information and decision-making power out of the hands of juries. The result is that the justice system has soon departed from common sense.

Strange as it may seem, the Constitution and the Bill of Rights—which have been used so often to push the public out of the system—were actually written to do the opposite.

"The Founding Fathers were very suspicious of judges and lawyers," said Professor Raoul Berger, Professor Emeritus of American Legal History at Harvard Law School. "They knew that lawyers inevitably become entangled in their own subtleties, and that their deductive logic eventually carries them further and further away from common sense.

"A jury is chosen for its very *ignorance* of the law. The jurors are brought into the courtroom for their practical wisdom. That is why the Founding Fathers wrote so many provisions into the Constitution and the Bill of Rights trying to protect the powers of juries.

"But American judges and attorneys have been able to circumvent these restrictions over the past twenty-five years," he added. "Procedural triviali- ties have come to dominate the system—the kind of things only lawyers understand or care about. Decision making has been taken out of the hands of juries and put in the hands of appellate judges. Although most people seem to have forgotten, this is precisely what the Bill of Rights was written to prevent."

The question will probably be raised, of course, what can all this possibly matter? At a time when murder rates have skyrocketed, when burglaries are soaring, when hordes of teenage gangs roam the streets robbing and mugging people, what possible difference can it make whether a few juries get to make reasonable decisions in the trivial number of cases that actually go to trial? Full-dress trials, after all, are just a sideshow in the great auction of plea bargaining that dominates the criminal justice system.

I think it does make a difference, and showing why it makes a difference is the theme of this book.

Crime is not controlled only in the courts. It is controlled in the streets and, above all, in people's minds. We all carry around an invisible concept called "justice" in our heads.

When the justice system no longer reinforces people's sense of right and wrong—when what comes out of the courts no longer corresponds with what people are thinking—then public standards of morality begin to erode. This produces two results. First, it emboldens people who harbor criminal tendencies. Second, it demoralizes the public and makes people afraid to stand up and fight crime *through* the justice system. A justice system that no longer has public support can no longer really perform its responsibilities.

What judges and attorneys often seem to forget is that the criminal justice system is more than just a method for dealing with criminals. The system is also a public stage upon which the continuing drama of public morality is enacted. As Robert Frost put it bluntly: "Society can never think things out. / It has to see them acted out by actors, / Devoted actors at a sacrifice."

The thesis of this book, then, is that the public matters. We have a system of self-government that is supposed to allow us to construct a justice system that reflects our public values. When that system is distorted so that it no longer reflects the public will, but the views of the minority that runs the system, then regardless of how beautiful it all may seem to the legal professionals, we are in trouble. As Oliver Wendell Holmes said, "The life of the law is not logic, but experience."

In going around the country attending conventions and meetings of lawyers, judges, criminologists, and justice reform groups, I heard three groups criticized so uniformly and consistently that I began to think of them as the "three p's." They were "the public, the press, and the politicians." According to the justice professionals, all the problems of the system occur because "the public, the press, and the politicians" want to interfere with the system.

After seeing how the judges and lawyers have painted themselves into corners on so many issues, I have a different interpretation of the problem. I think the public, the press, and the politicians are the only thing that can save the lawyers from themselves.

What we need, then, are citizens armed not with guns, but with facts and ideas. We have a wonderful system of government—one that should have no trouble producing public justice. We have gotten only a little bit off the track. But we need to rediscover some of the forgotten principles of our Constitutional system to make things work again.

Judges and lawyers are continually reminding us that majoritarian government has its dangers and that we need the "fixed star" of the law, as interpreted by its "guardians," the judges and lawyers, to keep us on course. But we must also remember that these "guardians of the law" can also develop their own fixations. We generally call a tyrannical system of government "draconian," without often remembering that Draco was a seventh-century B.C. lawyer who tried to govern Athens with a beautiful set of laws that everyone found intolerable.

Government ultimately comes from the consent of the governed. If the public is upset about crime, if they feel endangered, then it doesn't do for the judges and lawyers to argue that "the public doesn't understand the system," or that "there is nothing anyone can do about it." As de Tocqueville himself said:

> In the constitutions of all nations, a certain point exists at which the legislator must have recourse to the good sense and the virtue of his fellow citizens. . . . There is no country in which everything can be provided for by the laws, or in which political institutions can prove a substitute for common sense and public morality.[8]

AMERICA'S CRIME WAVE

2

TWO MONTHS AFTER the Bernhard Goetz shooting, *New York Daily News* columnist Bill Reel wrote an encouraging column stating that perhaps crime in New York wasn't as bad as everyone was saying.

A few days later he received a long letter from a woman in Brooklyn, recounting her lifetime with crime. "I love New York," she said. "But things aren't just as bad as everyone says they are. They're a lot worse."

> I was born in a three-family house on Eastern Parkway in 1928. My father painted signs. We lost the house, for want of a mortgage payment, when I was ten. Times were tough. Poverty was a part of life. But nobody in our neighborhood ever locked a door. Muggings were unheard of. Murder? That was done by Murder Incorporated. They lived in Brownsville, and those guys only killed each other.
>
> I was supposed to go to Brooklyn College, but my father got sick, so I had to work as a filing clerk in Manhattan. For years I walked home from dances at the Club 28 on Eastern Parkway and never gave a thought to safety.
>
> But something changed in Brownsville in the 1950s. Street crime became a problem. I got married and my husband and I moved to East New York. We lived in the projects. On hot summer nights we used to go out and sleep on the roof.
>
> Then, in the 1960s, crime became much more common. My husband was viciously mugged one night in the project. We had to flee—everybody was leaving.
>
> We moved to a nicer part of East New York. It was fine for a while, but one day a rock crashed through the window while our two young

sons were playing on the floor. We found out later it was the way the local burglars checked to see if you were home.

We left and moved into a modest apartment in Flatbush, where I lugged groceries and laundry up four flights. The area was the jewel of the city—Prospect Park, the Botanical Gardens, the Brooklyn Museum.

But fear invaded Flatbush in the '70s. Street crime became commonplace. My friends and I quit visiting stores and going to movies at night. Returning from work one evening in 1975, I saw three teenage boys walking toward me. I knew what was going to happen, but I was trapped. They tore the handbag right off my arm.

On Election Day, 1976, I was mugged in the lobby of my own building. The kid threw me down on the floor and put a knife to my heart. I was traumatized for months. Fear began to rule my life. I lived in constant dread of violence. I'd take the car service just the few blocks from the subway stop to my building every night. One night, a dozen kids, none of them older than twelve, surrounded me in front of my building. They demanded my bag. One kid said to me, "How do you know I don't have a gun?" I became hysterical. I was shaking so badly, I had to be helped home.

We felt we were running for our lives. We left Flatbush and moved out to Sheepshead Bay. Today I'd like to take college courses at night, but I'm afraid to ride the bus after dark. When I studied speedwriting for six months at a business school, my husband walked me home every night after class. I'm terrified every time I get on the subway. My heart pounds, and my throat goes dry.

I don't want to leave New York. I love my city. I think of it as an old dowager that's down on her luck. But where can we turn? The politicians don't give a damn about people like us. We're ignored. The district attorneys and the judges let the muggers prey on us.

And don't say I'm filled with hate. I don't hate anybody. I'm filled with indignation.[1]

For years voices such as this were exactly the ones that were ignored. For almost a decade the experts dismissed fear of crime as merely a disguised form of racial hostility. The first sentence of the introduction of the report published by the 1968 President's Commission on Law

Enforcement and Administration of Justice suggests that concern about "crime in the streets" may be a "euphemism for racism."[2]

Meanwhile, most experts simply refused to believe that crime was rising. For almost the entire late 1960s, criminologists and leading academic experts pooh-poohed public fears as popular hysteria.

In particular, it was long fashionable among criminologists to argue that the FBI Uniform Crime Statistics were cooked-up figures that the police manipulated at will. As one report of the time put it:

> Crime statistics have always been an inside joke, a near-absurdity to criminologists, sociologists, and like cognescenti. Across the years law enforcement officials have orchestrated the figures and then played them as a fabulous concerto in numbers that served varying purposes depending on the occasion.[3]

Many criminologists liked to believe that local police departments could inflate or deflate crime statistics depending on which elected superiors were in or out of their favor. If a popular incumbent were up for reelection, crime statistics would fall; if the police wanted the man in office replaced, crime statistics would jump.

There was, of course, a degree of underlying condescension toward the police in all this. Agencies all over the country are independently responsible for reporting statistics in similar ways. Some of this data may be fudged and some not. But there is no obvious reason for singling out the police on this issue. In any case, if figures were manipulated here and there for local reasons, much of this would cancel itself out. There was little reason to believe that a long-term rise in crime such as appeared in the mid-sixties was the result of police manipulations. Nevertheless, this was the common interpretation for a long while.

So the public got it from both sides. First, they were told that fear of crime was purely imaginary. Second, if people persisted in expressing a fear of crime, it had to be disguised racism. Either way, mounting public anxiety could be dismissed.

Only when the U.S. Census Bureau and the Law Enforcement Assistance Administration started asking people in the 1970 census whether they had been crime victims, did the truth begin to emerge. In fact, the trends showed by the FBI statistics had been essentially accurate for what they were measuring. If there was a major flaw in the data it was in the *understatement* of crime rates. Crime was actually about double the FBI estimates. The reason was fairly simple. A great many crimes are never reported to the police.

Almost twenty-five years later it is possible to get a very firm idea of exactly what happened to crime rates beginning in the early 1960s. Public fears, it turns out, were not exaggerated.

From 1940 to 1960, crime in America steadily *declined.* This trend began in the Depression—a telling point against the argument that only "poverty causes crime." It continued into the postwar era and through the rising affluence of the 1950s.

In 1950, the national murder rate was 5.3 per 100,000. By the late 1950s, it had sunk to 4.5, and by 1964 stood at 5.1. Although this was an era in which "juvenile delinquency" was regarded as a vexing social problem, crime rates—even among youth—hardly moved during the decade. Among black males, for example, the rate of homocide victimization *decreased* 22 percent from 1950 to 1960—even though there was a 24 percent increase among the number of blacks living in cities, where murder rates are generally higher.

By the early 1960s, it would have been easy to predict that we were going to be living in an ever-more-affluent and civilized society. This prediction, however, would have been wrong.

Beginning in 1963, crime rates began to take off in what soon became an unprecedented upswing. Within a few short years, we were living in the midst of what could only be called a "crime explosion."

After 1963, subway robberies in New York City began increasing at a rate of 50 percent *per year.* In Washington, D.C., burglaries and robberies jumped 20 percent from 1967 to 1968 alone. By 1969, America's population had risen 13 percent since 1960, while violent crime had grown 131 percent.

The figures continued to rise by fits and starts throughout the 1970s, leveling off only in 1980. In the past few years they have been inching downwards. Even so, violent crime has reached a plateau that is *two-and-a-half times* higher than it was in 1960. Property crimes—burglary and theft—have also nearly tripled since that time.[4]

Once it finally became obvious in the 1970s that crime was rising at an unprecedented rate, the experts soon came up with another easy explanation. Crime was increasing, they said, because of a demographic shift. Most crimes are committed by young males, 15 to 24 years of age. As the "baby boomers," born between 1946 and 1961, reached these crime-prone years, crime rates naturally began to surge.

Thus, it was argued, crime was purely a statistical phenomenon. It had nothing to do with public morality or the workings of the criminal justice system. Instead, it was purely a matter of demographics—there were more young people around.

Even Charles Silberman, author of *Criminal Violence, Criminal Justice* and a liberal revisionist on crime, found this argument too contrived to tolerate. Writing in 1977, he pointed out that while the population of crime-prone young males had increased 50 percent between 1960 and 1975, the number of crimes had risen *200 percent*:

> The change in the age distribution of the population thus accounts for only 25 percent of the increase; the rest is due to the greater frequency with which members of every age group, but particularly the young, commit serious crimes.[5]

James Q. Wilson, perhaps the country's leading expert on crime, makes the same point. In *Thinking About Crime,* he noted that between 1960 and 1970 the crime-prone youth population of Washington, D.C., increased in numbers by 32 percent. At the same time, serious crime rose 400 percent, welfare rates rose 200 percent, and heroin addiction, by some estimates, increased almost 1,000 percent.

In Detroit, the murder rate *quintupled* from 1960 to 1970, while the youth population rose only about 35 percent. An MIT study showed that murder rates in several large cities rose *ten times* what would have been expected if the "youth boom" were the only contributing factor.

"Apparently much more complex forces are at work in almost all large cities," Wilson concluded.[6]

And so we are brought back, once again, to an irreducible fact. Our skyrocketing rate of crime has been a cultural phenomenon, unrelated to any historical accidents or changing statistical characteristics.

America now has the highest crime rate in the industrial world. We also rank right among the leaders in the *non*industrialized world. Only Mexico and a few South American countries have slightly higher murder rates.

Murder is generally considered the most reliable indicator of overall levels of violent crime. Murders rarely go unreported and the statistics are essentially complete. Murder is also considered a good indicator of the level of violent assaults, since murder is often considered "an assault that didn't stop in time." American murder rates have doubled since the 1950s and now stand at 9.7 per 100,000. In Japan and all western European countries, the figure hovers around 1.0 per 100,000.

When calculated over the average person's lifetime, these figures become even more compelling. At current rates, *one out of every 21 black men will be murdered.* For the overall American population, the figure is one out of 133. The average American living his or her entire life in a large city now has a better chance of being murdered than the average American soldier had of being killed in combat during World War II.[7]

If murder is the most reliable reading, street robberies have become almost a signature of American crime. "Mugging" is an old British word that seems to have originally meant "to punch someone in the face." It gradually evolved into an "assault with the intent to rob." In America, its operational definition now seems to be "an armed robbery committed by a teenager."

Americans visiting aboard are amazed at the ease with which Europeans walk their streets at night. The level of fear that Americans live with simply doesn't exist in many parts of the world. A *Washington Post* reporter, recently returning from Lebanon, said that one of the most striking impressions about battle-torn Beirut was how much more comfortable women are walking the streets than they are in Washington, D.C.[8]

A family of Cambodian refugees who recently migrated to the Flatbush section of Brooklyn after escaping the Khmer Rouge fled again in a few months. They said conditions there were worse than in Cambodia. Walid Jumblatt, leader of Lebanon's Druze, whose great-grandfather, grandfather, and father have been killed in that country's ongoing sectarian warfare, told *Playboy* magazine, "I would not dare go on the New York City subway."[9]

A Brooklyn tailor was recently discussing Nazi concentration camps on a radio call-in show when a gang of fleeing subway muggers broke into his shop and held him hostage. He escaped only when the talk-show host called police headquarters and sent them to the rescue. "I was in Auschwitz and was on intimate terms with Dr. Joseph Mengele," the tailor said. "But I'll tell you, the crime in my neighborhood scares me more."[10]

All this has happened almost completely independent of the supposed "causes" and "cures" for crime—jobs, schooling, better housing, and better living conditions. James Q. Wilson notes that while in 1950 the median level of schooling among Washington, D.C.'s black population was 8.8

years, it had risen to 11.4 in 1970. Black median family income, adjusted for inflation, *tripled* over those two decades. In 1970, the unemployment rate for black adult men was only 4.5 percent, and for adult women only 3.6 percent—practically the lowest levels in history. Yet crime rates at the end of the two decades were almost three times higher.[11]

Moreover, it isn't just crime *rates* that have been skyrocketing. It is the changing *nature* of crime that is truly shocking. Crime is becoming much more random, violent, and senseless in its brutality.

Until the 1960s, sociologists argued convincingly that murder was a "crime of passion," committed almost entirely between people who knew each other. In almost 90 percent of all murders, there was some known relationship between the killer and the victim.

Today, in *30 percent* of all killings, the victim and the killer are *complete strangers.* This means victims are being chosen more or less at random. Usually this murder is part of a rape or robbery attempt. But in a growing number of instances the murder is completely "senseless"—committed with no apparent motive at all.

Rape has shown the same movement toward "stranger" confrontations. In 1967, half of all rapists were at least casually known to their victims. They were estranged husbands, friends, lovers, relatives, or slight acquaintances. Today, despite a greater propensity to report "date rapes," two-thirds of all rapes are committed by complete strangers. Seventy percent of rape victims are assaulted in streets, parking lots, schools, or residential buildings, while only 30 percent are victimized in their own homes. Moreover, this vast jump in "stranger rapes" accounts for the *entire 140 percent increase in rape over the past eighteen years.*[12]

Nor does it appear that this upward spiral of violence has yet reached its peak. While "acquaintance murders" have been dropping in the past few years, "stranger murders" are still on the rise. In fact, in the ever-evolving subculture of street crime, "killing your victim" has become something of a popular fad.

Claude Brown, author of *Manchild in the Promised Land,* recently spent the better part of three years revisiting the Harlem of his youth, gathering material for a book on the effect of heroin on black culture. He was frankly appalled at what he found:

> For more than a year, I was thoroughly baffled by the apparently senseless, and often maniacal, rampant killings of mugging and robbery victims. According to what I had gathered . . . it was as though

shooting the victim had become an integral part of the crime. Sometimes, it seemed to occur with the incredible casualness of an insignificant afterthought, an "Oh, I forgot to shoot him," bang.

    I had been talking to young men in prisons and on the ghetto streets
. . . but I wasn't comprehending what they were telling me. Perhaps
what I was hearing was too mind-boggling, too ghastly to understand:
"Murder is in style now."[13]

Talking casually with youths on streetcorners, Brown discovered that
the killing of mugging victims no longer has anything to do with whatever
resistance they might offer. Instead, victim-murder has become a way of
signing your name to a crime—of proving that you "have heart."

    Manchild 1984 is the product of a society so rife with violence that
killing a mugging or robbery victim is now fashionable.

    "That's what they do now," the 16-year-old Harlemite said.

    "That's what who does now?" I asked, not understanding.

    "You know, you take their stuff and you pop (shoot) them."

    "You mean shooting the victim is in style now, like wearing a pair of
Pony jogging shoes or a Pierre Cardin suit?"

    "Yeah, it's wrong to kill somebody. But you gotta have dollars,
right?"[14]

Here is a sampling of the kind of murders that are "in style" today, drawn
randomly from the pages of New York's newspapers over the course of
a year:

—Jacqueline McKail, an 18-year-old high-school graduate, holding
down two jobs and planning to study medicine, was sitting with her
boyfriend in a parked car. Two teenage boys carrying a high-power rifle
smashed the window of their car and searched them for money and jewels.
Finding nothing, they shot McKail in the stomach, killing her.

—James Johnson, 18, of Brooklyn, was visiting his girlfriend in a
housing project when two teenage boys approached him and demanded
his box radio. He apparently offered no resistance. They shot and killed
him anyway.

—Robert Tabib, an Iranian immigrant, ran a Brooklyn jewelry store
with his family. They were closing up one night when they were
approached by two robbers in ski masks. When Tabib tried to toss a
suitcase full of jewelry to a family member to make a getaway, the robbers
shot and killed him.

—Alfred Riddick, 23, of Brooklyn, was riding on an IRT subway car at eleven o'clock at night when he was approached by two young men. They demanded his gold chains. When Raddick refused, one pulled a gun and killed him.

—Frankie Lane Martin, 20, of Brownsville, Brooklyn, was walking down the street, when a man with a .22 jumped out of a Cadillac and forced Martin against a wall. After ripping one gold chain from his neck, he shot Martin in the back of the head, killing him.

—Joel Ungar, 59, the owner of a factory in Flatbush, surprised one of his employees, a 19-year-old, robbing his offices after hours. Ungar was beaten to death with a hammer. The police finally caught up with the killer in his home neighborhood a week later. When he tried to escape, a score of people helped chase him down. When the police led him away, the neighborhood crowd expressed its approval with "riotous applause."

—Ping-To Chang, 55, a Chinese immigrant with one son on a Westinghouse scholarship at Yale and another at Bronx High School of Science, ran a Bronx liquor store while teaching at Pace University. Ping-To regularly wore a bulletproof vest after being robbed three times. When he tried to resist a fourth hold-up, the robber shot him between the eyes and killed him.

—Kevin Perry, 24, a former Brooklyn football player and supervisor at a small computer firm in Manhattan, was shopping in a Bedford-Stuyvesant supermarket when he found a dollar on the floor. A moment later, two youths walked up and said it was theirs. A mild dispute ensued. When Perry turned to walk away, one of the youths stabbed him in the back, killing him.

None of these incidents are unique to New York. In fact, in terms of murder, New York City now ranks in thirteenth place on a per-capita rate. (New Orleans, Houston, St. Louis, Detroit, and Cleveland lead in that order.) Nor is this random sampling unrepresentative of the national norms. The median victim here is a 23-year-old black male. The median murder victim nationwide is a 25-year-old black male.

Time magazine, taking a nationwide sampling of the 400 murders committed in one week in 1981, came up with the same dreary catalogue:[15]

—Kenny Black, 20, a steelworker in Charlotte, North Carolina, was shot and killed by four muggers while walking through a housing project.

—Margaret Dudley, a 61-year-old Detroit secretary, was beaten to death by a 17-year-old robber in a church basement.

—Alejandro Freyre, a 25-year-old Oakland uniformed security guard, was leaving his apartment for work one night when he was shot through the heart by strangers.

—Thomas Mounce, a 51-year-old Memphis businessman, was robbed in the parking lot outside his wallpaper store and shot to death.

—Lyric Davis, a 27-year-old Los Angeles office worker, and her five-year-old son were stabbed to death by an intruder.

—Ronald Fitzer, a 31-year-old Seattle dentist, got lost driving in a downtown area at two in the morning. He apparently stopped to ask directions, and someone shot him fatally in the chest.

According to the Gallup Poll, one out of every four Americans now knows someone who was mugged or assaulted *in the preceding year.* One out of five Americans has been burglarized in the past year. One out of every twenty-five Americans can expect to be the victim of a mugging or violent assault in the next two years.[16]

Are Americans taking all this lying down? Of course not. People are learning to adjust their entire lives in order to deal with crime. But the unfortunate results often make you wonder what a "police state" would really be like.

At the parking lots of the New Jersey Bell Telephone Company in Newark, a cordon of private security guards rings the building every night at 5 P.M. People are instructed to leave on time. Uniformed officers stand every 25 yards for three blocks, forming a safe corridor through which commuters can reach the nearby railroad station. Rapes, muggings, and robberies of company personnel have made all this necessary.

Jacksonville, Florida, was recently hit by a series of brutal rapes. The police actively urged women to start carrying guns. They even offered extensive target practice. Rapes immediately plummeted to only 5 percent of their former rate.

Claude Brown describes the style of life he discovered in his old haunts:

> In Harlem, elderly people walking their dogs in the morning cross the street when they see some young people coming. They try to act casual, but of course they aren't. They are very aware of those young people—you can almost feel the tension as the youngsters get closer. And what those elderly men and women have in the paper bags they're carrying is not just a pooper scooper—it's a gun. And if those youngsters cross that street, somebody's going to get hurt—you're going to hear it. Everybody knows this.[17]

In many places, people's daily routines are becoming dominated by the fear of victimization. The Figgie Report on the Fear of Crime—commissioned by a businessman whose brother had been killed in a street mugging—found that 60 percent of Americans have altered their lives for fear of crime, and 75 percent are now afraid to walk in their own neighborhoods at night.[18]

"We have allowed ourselves to degenerate to the point where we're living like animals," said Houston Police Chief B. K. Johnson. "We live behind burglar bars and security locks on top of security locks. We set all the alarms at night and lay down with a shotgun next to the bed. It's a ridiculous way to live."

Americans now spend $18 billion a year on *private* security, as opposed to only $15 billion on public police forces. Karate clubs flourish, guard dogs become household pets, mace and stun-guns are sold over the counter. The burglar-alarm industry has been one of the fastest growing sectors of the economy over the past ten years.

"It's the Matt Dillon Syndrome," said Jack Wright, Jr., a criminologist at Loyola University in New Orleans. "People no longer believe the forces of law and order can protect them."

Gordon Tullock, professor of economics at George Mason University, undertook a study to find out what would happen if we just gave up altogether and repealed the laws forbidding theft. He found that people would spend lots more time trying to steal from each other, but they would also spent lots more time defending themselves. There would be an "arms race" of the kind we are beginning to see today.[19]

"Even without moral considerations, there is very good economic reason for enforcing the laws against thefts," Tullock concluded. "Society suffers a huge loss in productive activity when people are left alone to defend themselves."

Unfortunately, the turn toward private defense works only for those who can afford it. Luxury high-rise apartments and suburban subdivisions now openly advertise their elaborate security systems. Exclusive homes in the southwest now come with bars on the windows and eight-foot walls that make them feel like prison compounds. Burglar alarms, private guards, closed-circuit television monitors— all cost money. Crime statistics reflect this. A woman making less than $3,000 per year is four times more likely to be raped than a woman making more than $25,000.

In theory, at least, public police protection extends to everyone. But private security is available only to those who can afford it. Politics and social influence also end up playing a part. In New York City, for example, strict gun-control legislation has limited gun ownership to a small minority, among whom the rich and well-connected are well represented. John Lindsay, the former mayor; Arthur Ochs Sulzburger, publisher of *The New York Times*; and Michael Korda, editor-in-chief of Simon and Schuster, all have gun permits, even though they rarely visit dangerous neighborhoods or ride the subways. Yet two out of three applicants for gun permits are turned down.

One of them was Bernhard Goetz.

How did all this happen? Throughout this crime epidemic, one amazing statistic stands out. By 1975, all forms of violent crime in the United States—murder, rape, and armed robbery—had increased as much as 200 percent around the country. Yet the prison population was actually 10 percent *lower* in 1975 than it was in 1960.

To a large extent, we stopped punishing people for crimes in the early 1960s. For a variety of reasons, law enforcement started becoming more lenient. A number of factors contributed to this social trend.

First, there were new theories floating around among criminologists and other specialists, theories that tended to *legitimize* criminals and to call into question whether what they did was really all that bad. Although the public is rarely aware of the influence of these "policy-makers" and purveyors of ideas, they often have an enormous impact on public policies.

Second, there was an invasion of the justice system by the psychiatric profession. Leading psychiatrists and psychologists argued convincingly that crime was really a "disease" that could be cured with the proper treatments. Interestingly, some parts of the legal profession mounted what might be seen as a counterattack by arguing that mental patients have "civil rights" and that psychiatrists should not be allowed to hospitalize disturbed or uncontrollable people without a legal hearing. As a result of these "turf wars," psychiatrists now frequently give the key testimony in determining the guilt or innocence of criminal defendants, while now judges and lawyers have the last word in committing people to mental hospitals.

Beyond this, there was an obvious general public sentiment throughout the late sixties and early seventies to understand the plight of the down-trodden and to improve their condition. Unfortunately, this effort often tended to focus on the minority of the poor who commit crimes. This was done without taking any notice that the victims of these crimes are usually poor as well. During that period, crime was often characterized as an upwelling of class or racial consciousness that would eventually redeem poor neighborhoods. Instead, crime was usually destroying them.

Finally, there was the revolution in the criminal justice system led by the U.S. Supreme Court under Chief Justice Earl Warren. This effort made radical changes in the interpretation of the Bill of Rights and fundamentally transformed criminal justice procedure. The effect of these changes— although they may not have been intended that way—was to make it harder to convict criminals and easier for people to get away with crimes.

Each of these changes has exacted a small but cumulative price in the normal moral revulsion that people everywhere feel toward crime. As a result of increasingly perfectionist standards imposed on police and prosecutors, many guilty people are set free without punishment. As the rules of trial have become more complex and difficult to observe, prosecutions are delayed and court backlogs mount. This often leads to a counterattack by defendants who demand a "speedy trial" (even though one of the most effective ways to avoid conviction is to delay prosecution as long as possible). Faced with these conflicting demands, district attorneys are forced to bargain away cases by accepting pleas at much lower charges. The situation is complicated by an ever-more-refined appeals process, in which convicted criminals can challenge technical aspects of their trials for years on end. Meanwhile, federal judges are busy closing down jails and prisons on the grounds that their conditions "violate the Constitution." As a result of all this, the justice system is often so overloaded that it eventually spins dangerous people back into the street just to get rid of them.

All of this has had a tremendous impact on the public morale in the battle against crime. After all, it is not *just* the criminal justice system that holds crime in check. The public plays an indispensable role. If people are made fearful by the results of the justice system, however, they become unwilling to cooperate with the police and afraid to get involved. Once this happens, there is little the police and the courts can do by themselves.

In a sense, the public is the body of the system, and the court is the head. The head may want to move, but it can do little if the body will not function. At the same time, the body may feel the impulse to act, but it can do little without direction from the head. If the courts become hopelessly entangled in dotting "i's" and crossing "t's," or if they lose the will to punish people, then public revulsion against crime cannot be organized in a sensible fashion. Retreat and self-protection become the only alternative.

In going around the country talking about crime, I have heard police and prosecutors say one thing over and over again. The most difficult task in law enforcement, they say, is *getting people to come forward and testify*.

People do not unhesitatingly take a stand on crime. They do so only when they believe it is relatively safe. When they see the courts turning criminals loose on procedural technicalities, or spinning the revolving door of reduced charges, they lose all faith that the justice system can protect them. Under these circumstances, people are no longer willing to step forward and make a stand for themselves.

One story from a pair of New York City policemen tells it all:

> We had an old man in this neighborhood who was robbed and beat up on the street. He could identify the guy who did it, but he was afraid to go into court and testify against him. We worked with him for months, telling him we'd protect him and that we had a good chance of getting the guy convicted. Finally, he went to court and testified, and the guy got put away on an assault charge.
>
> About seven months later, the old man comes running up to us one day and says, "Hey, what happened? I saw the guy on the street the other day." We thought about it a minute, and said, "Well, it's been seven months now. We only got him on assault, so he's probably out on parole already."
>
> The old man couldn't believe it. "Seven months?" he said. "Are you kidding? He beats me up and robs me on the street, and he only gets seven months? To hell with this, I'm going back to Puerto Rico!" And that's the last we ever saw of him.
>
> The guy who beat him up is still around, though. We see him every day.

The real cost of lenient law enforcement has been that *it has made the public more afraid to speak out or act against crime.* Psychiatrists would call this a "neurotic repression" of fear and anxiety. Ordinarily, these feelings would be worked out through the normal functioning of the justice system. But if the judges start playing Hamlet about punishing criminals, or if court proceedings become dominated by technical quibbles rather than central questions of guilt or innocence, the public can no longer find a normal outlet for its moral reaction against crime. Instead, these feelings will be repressed until they erupt unexpectedly in "vigilante" actions—and in the enormous outpourings of public approval that greet them.

"What we need is not vigilantes, but vigilant citizens," said FBI director

William Webster recently. This is true. Outbreaks of individual violence or mob action will not end crime. They only lead to greater social chaos. Arming the citizenry and allowing every man and woman to enforce the law according to his or her own judgment only takes us further down the road we are already traveling.

The best way to fight crime is the old-fashioned way—through a justice system that vigorously embodies the public's instinctive sense of right and wrong. We need forthright cooperation with the police, bravery from individual citizens, and judges who value their responsibility to the community at least as much as their "judicial independence."

For too long, crime experts have held out the hope that crime can be cured by making the justice system more responsive to the needs of criminals. This simply does not work. For too long, the judiciary has cast itself as a neutral party, blandly calling balls and strikes while "arbitrating disputes" between law-abiding citizens and the people who prey on them. In fact, the judiciary has a responsibility to supervise a system that does not become hopelessly absorbed in "law for law's sake," but remembers that exhilarating case law also involves real, live human beings.

In fact, the key to producing a vigilant citizenry may lie in a broad rediscovery of the concept of justice itself.

NEW IDEAS ABOUT CRIME   3

I N THE EARLY 1960s, psychiatrist Karl Menninger, head of the Menninger Foundation in Topeka, Kansas, was on a world tour with his wife and another psychiatrist. In Italy one night they parked their car in front of the hotel. When they came down the next morning, the police informed them they had to go down to the police station. Someone had tried to break into the car. The police had caught him. The Menningers and their friend would have to stay for the trial, which might not be for a few days.

The Americans, fumbling in weak French and Italian, were naturally frustrated. They didn't care whether the prisoner was tried or not. Describing the scene a few years later in his book *The Crime of Punishment,* Menninger wrote:

> We began to be desperate. We said we knew no prisoner, we had seen no molester, we had suffered no damage, we had made no charge. So far as we knew, nothing had happened. Again, we painfully "explained" and sought to leave.
>
> Ah, but if the alert and clever police had not *seen* the marauder *about to open the Americans' car* and pounced upon him instantly, the Americans would have indeed suffered loss. But bravo! the *police!*
>
> All right. Fine! Alert policemen, crime prevented. No crime. No trial. So, now, let's go!
>
> Unfortunately not possible.
>
> But why?
>
> "Ah" (solemnly), *"Guistizia! Giustizia!* (Justice! Justice!) . . .
>
> The abstract concept of justice never seemed to me so ridiculous . . .
>
> Justice was not invented, as we think, to protect the weak but to

protect the King's Peace; it was belatedly applied . . . to the protection
of (some of) the King's subjects.[1]

It is certainly easy to sympathize with Menninger's predicament and the
absurdity of the situation. (He finally got out of it when the other psychiatrist produced a sheriff's badge he had earned by serving as a consultant to a
California court.)

But Menninger quickly threw out the baby with the bath. Justice, he
argued, was a "childish" concept, an "ancient, savage ritual" left over from
the Middle Ages. Science—particularly the modern science of psychiatry—had arrived to vanquish the superstitious practice of punishment and
to put the treatment of criminals on a firm *medical* footing.

> People no longer have to rely on common sense. . . . Science has
> discovered better ways by the use of *uncommon* sense. The common-
> sense time to go to bed is when it gets dark; the uncommon sense of
> artificial illumination has changed all that. Crime problems have been
> dealt with too long with only the aid of common sense. Catch criminals
> and lock them up; if they hit you, hit them back. This is common sense,
> but it does not work.[2]

Dr. Menninger was only one of thousands of social scientists in the
1960s who decided that he had a "better idea" for dealing with criminals.
In fact, the woods were full of such theorists. Together they pulled off an
enormous revolution in the American criminal justice system in a very
short time. Their essential reform was to "deprisonize" the justice system.

The first instance that brought these new experts together on a "policy-
making" level was President Johnson's Commission on Law Enforcement
and the Administration of Justice, organized in 1966 to study the already
burgeoning problem of crime. Although the commission was equally
weighted with law-enforcement officers and seasoned prosecutors, the
academics quickly began to dominate the proceedings.

Among them was Lloyd E. Ohlin, of the New York School of Social
Work at Columbia University. In 1960, Ohlin and Richard A. Cloward,
also of Columbia, had written an enormously influential little book entitled
Delinquency and Opportunity.[3] In it they argued that young people who
joined juvenile gangs were really pursuing "legitimate goals by illegitimate
means." Delinquents are not abnormal or sick people. They had the same
goals as anybody else. They simply had fewer legitimate opportunities.

Ohlin and Cloward did not offer any specific suggestions for solving crime, except for a vague call to "reorganize slum communities." But one thing they were certain of was that punishing people for committing crimes didn't help. Delinquents, after all, were not doing anything that *they* saw as wrong themselves. They were merely victims of circumstance, who "learned" criminal behavior from peers who also did not see anything wrong with it. Therefore, punishment was unfair, if only because it was not likely to be understood.

In truth, Ohlin and Cloward seem to have understood crime better than most criminologists. They argued, for example, that lower-class delinquents have essentially rejected middle-class values. Therefore, if the dominant society begins to criticize itself as "unfair," they said, this will not necessarily encourage delinquent groups to accept its values. Instead, it may be interpreted as a justification for *more intensive* criminal activity. This seems to have been exactly what happened during the 1960s.

Still, Ohlin and Cloward could not bring themselves to the idea that punishment could play a part in an attempt to limit these delinquent subcultures. While a member of the President's Commission, Ohlin later said, "The criminal justice system should be used only as a last resort in the control of undesirable conduct."[4]

Ohlin became one of the four associate directors of the President's Commission. There, he was joined by many other academic criminologists who had "grave doubts" about the old-fashioned methods of dealing with crime by putting people in jail. Working skillfully in small committees, the academics were able to shape the commission's work to their own ideas.

The chief recommendation was a "deprisonization" of American society. The criminologists confidently talked about "rehabilitation," "alternate sentencing," and "community-based corrections" that would replace conventional prisons. To a degree that surprised even the academics, these new approaches became part of the commission's general recommendations.

By the time the report had made itself felt, however, there had been a considerable change in the political climate of the country. The Johnson presidency had been replaced by the Nixon administration, which had campaigned on a platform of crime control. President Nixon quickly rejected the proposals of the Crime Commission—to much loud complaint from the academic community. However, the matter did not end there.

As James Q. Wilson, a dissenting member on the President's Crime Commission, has noted, "deprisonization" was already being instituted by the judges themselves. There was, he reports, a "growing belief among some judges that since prisons apparently do not rehabilitate, it is wrong to send criminals to them." Thus:

> During the 1960s, while crime rates were soaring, there was no significant increase in the amount of prison space, and there was an actual decline in the number of prisoners, state and federal, from about 213,000 in 1960 to 196,000 in 1970. In New York State the chances of the perpetrator of a given crime going to prison fell during this period by a factor of *six*. . . . In Los Angeles, only 6 percent of those charged with burglary, who had a serious prior record, were sent to prison; only 12 percent of those charged with burglary who had already *been* in prison were sent back.[5]

By 1975, the average murderer in Massachusetts was spending two-and-a-half years in jail. California alone had six times as many robbers as England, yet there were more people in jail for robbery in England than in California.[6]

Several other currents of academic and professional thought were all converging into one mainstream of opinion during this era. The general tenor was that the whole question of crime was not as clear-cut as people often thought. One of the most powerful of these ideas was the theory of "deviance."

Deviance theory, first introduced in the early sixties, suggested that what is called "crime" is largely determined by social conventions. In Puritan societies, for example, dancing was labeled as deviant. In strict Moslem societies, wearing blue-jeans and t-shirts—the standard uniform of any American teenager—would be considered deviant. In the Soviet Union, doing plumbing for your neighbor is deviant because it is free enterprise, done without sanction of the state.

All social rules and morality are essentially relative, said deviance theorists. What is tolerated in one society—or in one situation—is punished or disapproved in another. We condemn people for committing murder on the street, but we praise it during warfare. We reward a business individual for outsmarting a competitor, but we condemn a safecracker when he outsmarts the bank's security system. As Howard Becker, one of the leading deviance theorists expressed it:

[D]eviance is not a simple quality, present in some kinds of behavior and absent in others. Rather, it is the product of a process which involves responses of other people to the behavior. The same behavior may be an infraction of the rules at one time and not at another; may be an infraction when committed by one person, but not when committed by another; some rules are broken with impunity, others are not. In short, whether a given act is deviant or not depends in part on the nature of the act (that is, whether or not it violates some rule) and in part on what other people do about it. . . . Deviance is not a quality that lies in behavior itself, but in the interaction between the person who commits an act and those who respond to it.[7]

Instead of looking for intrinsic "rightness" and "wrongness" in actions, then, deviance theorists began to look at the *people who made the rules.* Certain people, it was argued, had the power to condemn *other people's* actions. Everyone's natural inclination, of course, is to condemn the things that other people do and excuse the things they do themselves. Thus, there is, by implication, something vaguely illegitimate about what rule-makers themselves do.

Deviance theorists developed the concept of "moral entrepreneurs" to describe the people who *make* the rules. These are people who may be a little "uptight" and who spend a lot of time worrying about other people's behavior. The temperance crusaders who imposed Prohibition on America, for example, are a prime example of moral entrepreneurship at work.

It was also suggested, in a vague way, that the "normal" people who do not break the rules, but who punish others for doing so, take a special sort of satisfaction in seeking out wrongdoers and labeling them as "deviants."

"Labeling" was perhaps the key concept in deviance theory. People only felt secure in their communities and their own personalities, it was argued, when they could make clear distinctions between themselves and "outsiders." Any deviant group—homosexuals, bookworms, beatniks, foreigners, or (importantly) criminals—was likely to be "labeled" as "deviant."

Kai Erikson, of Yale, a leading deviance theorist, wrote, "It may well be, that without this ongoing drama at the outer edges of group space, the community would have no sense of identity and cohesion."[8]

Crime, then, the deviance theorists suggested, was not something bad in itself, but only a "label" *imposed* on the actions of certain people by the majority. Since no one wants to be labeled a criminal, the ones who end up

suffering it are likely to be the weak, the stupid, the disadvantaged—
outcast individuals who aren't clever enough to escape the labeling process.
Wrote Becker:

> To be labeled a criminal one need only commit a single criminal
> offense. . . . A man who has been convicted of housebreaking and
> thereby labeled criminal is presumed to be a person likely to break into
> other houses; the police, in rounding up known offenders for investiga-
> tion after a crime has been committed, operate on this premise.
> Further, he is considered likely to commit other kinds of crimes as well,
> because he has shown himself to be a person without "respect for the
> law." Thus, apprehension for one deviant act exposes a person to the
> likelihood that he will be regarded as deviant or undesirable in other
> respects . . .
>
> Treating a person as though he were generally rather than specifi-
> cally deviant produces a self-fulfilling prophecy. It sets in motion
> several mechanisms which conspire to shape the person in the image
> people have of him. . . [T]he popular diagnosis of why he is that way,
> and the treatment itself, may likewise produce increasing deviance.[9]

The label of criminal, suggested deviance theorists, is something people
impose on others in society. Criminals are simply people whom *other*
people say have done something wrong. They are the unfortunate victims
of the process—hapless losers whose actions are labeled "deviant" by the
powerful majority.

Karl Menninger was one leading psychiatrist who absorbed and embel-
lished the ideas of deviance theory. Using the concept of the labeling
process, Menninger quickly condemned *all* efforts to punish criminals as
"barbaric."

How does a person become a criminal? Menninger asked in the best-
selling *The Crime of Punishment*:

> Now and then—like the rest of us—he feels under pressure and
> takes a shortcut. It is a risk; but it seems at the moment to be a justified
> or necessary one. He exceeds his bank balance. He runs a red light. He
> "borrows" a car. Nine times out of ten he escapes detection.
>
> But every once in a while—in fact, *every minute or two*—
> somewhere in this country one of these unimportant people does one
> of these forbidden things and *does not* get away with it. He may have

been careless or impulsive or greedy; he may have been drunk, or only very angry; he may have been jealous, embittered, frightened, or just plain hungry. He may have been head-over-heels in an insoluble complication of commitments, indebtedness, and despair. He gets caught. He becomes involved with the "system."[10]

Once "the system" gets a hold of people, it turns them into "real criminals." They are abandoned by society, subject to the cruelties of prison life. They turn hostile and bitter and are educated into crime.

> The prisons . . . grimy lockups, are full of people—not, for the most part, vicious, violent men who have done dreadful things, nor yet penitent, hand-wringing breast-beating men who wish they had not robbed the bank. They are full of men labeled *criminal* because they got caught at something and convicted of something forbidden. But they are mostly poor, inadequate, incompetent, frustrated misfits— young failures, or lifelong failures, offenders who could not even make a success at crime![11]

As a trained psychiatrist, accustomed to ferreting out people's innermost motives, Menninger turned the whole deviance idea back upon the public:

> The inescapable conclusion is that society secretly *wants* crime, *needs* crime, and gains definite satisfactions from the present mishan- dling of it! . . . The crime and punishment ritual is a part of our lives. We need crimes to wonder at, to enjoy vicariously, to discuss and speculate about, and to publicly deplore. We need criminals to identify ourselves with, to secretly envy, and to strongly punish. Criminals represent our alter egos—our "bad" selves—rejected and projected. They do for us the forbidden, illegal things we *wish* to do and, like scapegoats of old, they bear the burdens of our displaced guilt and punishment—the "inequities of us all."[12]

And so, Menninger carried the whole concept of deviance and the labeling process to its logical conclusion. The *public* is the real criminal. Everyone commits crimes, but only certain people are labeled as criminals. Once we have identified these scapegoats, we punish them for *our* guilt:

> And there is one crime we all keep committing, over and over. I accuse the reader of this—and myself, too—and all the nonreaders.

We commit the crime of damning some of our fellow citizens with the label "criminal." And having done this, we force them through an experience that is soul-searching and dehumanizing. In this way we exculpate ourselves from the guilt *we* feel and tell ourselves that we do it to "correct" the "criminal" and make us all safer from crime. We commit this crime every day that we retain our present stupid, futile, abominable practices against detected offenders . . .

"Doesn't anybody care about the victims?" cry some demagogues, with melodramatic flourishes. "Why should all this attention be given to the criminals and none to those they have beaten or robbed?"

This childish outcry has an appeal for the unthinking.[13]

As a popularization of academic ideas of crime and imprisonment, Menninger's book had enormous impact. Ann Landers, a trustee of the Menninger Foundation, still refers to it constantly. Recently, one of her readers wrote:

Why is everybody so dumb about crime? I unknowingly befriended a drug pusher. The first I knew about his illegal activities was when he was sent back to prison. . . I couldn't believe it. Three meals a day, a nice library, shops, fishing, TV, extension courses, medical and dental services—you name it. They had everything but work . . .

After he got out of the stir he told me life inside was so terrific he wouldn't mind going back. He said he missed the guys . . .

Why is our penal system so nutty? The criminals on the inside who get sent to minimum security places have a better life than honest, hard-working people like my husband.

At the opposite pole, we read horror stories about men who were sent in for minor offenses and came out hardened criminals. There's a lot of talk about gang rapes of young boys, and sometimes there are murders . . .

Landers recommended Menninger's *The Crime of Punishment.*[14]

At the heart of the labeling concept was the notion, popular among academics, that *most criminals don't get caught.* Looking at crime figures, crime experts noted that only about one in every ten armed robberies is ever solved. Therefore, nine out of ten armed robbers must be getting away.

Thus, they argued, it is only the most incompetent criminals—the "stumblers and bumblers"—who wind up in the hands of the law. In this context, the punishment inflicted on these few poor souls is almost by definition "cruel and unusual." In punishing those who are caught, we are only taking vengeance against nine unapprehended criminals by inflicting ten times the punishment on the one poor soul who is detected. Said Menninger, reflecting the consensus of academic thought:

> [W]hile an army of men across the country tries to serve our interests and safety by turning the wheels of this internal machine for the grinding up of a minority of the easily-caught offenders and administering to them the futile ritual of punishment, a horde of known but immune predatory professional criminals grows fat and famous in front of our eyes.[15]

Thus, the labeling argument contained two major premises: 1) real criminals don't go to prison, and 2) the "stumblers and bumblers" who do go to prison are turned into worse people.

The conclusion was inescapable: *"Don't send anyone to prison."* Since the real criminals don't get caught anyway, and since the stumblers and bumblers only become worse behind bars, emptying the prisons can reasonably be expected to *reduce crime.* It was on the cumulative weight of these various arguments that the nation's judiciary set about the "deprisonization" of the justice system during the late sixties and early seventies.

Around 1965, a young Harvard Fellow named Bruce Jackson left academia for a while and made a tour of several Texas prisons. There he did a long series of interviews with several dozen inmates. His work was later published in a book entitled *In the Life.*

Jackson himself was a confirmed "labelist," as he declared in his introduction:

> Sometimes I find crime a lot like door-to-door selling: it seems easy, it seems to require little talent, yet few people ever do it well, and few manage to stick with it very long. In both fields there are mobs of amateurs trying to make it, many because there seems nothing else to do; there are also losers who haven't made it doing anything else. But door-to-door selling and crime are hard work. To do either well requires intelligence, adaptability, and perseverance. Not many people have those qualities in abundance, and most of those who do have

them find remunerative employment with more job security than either crime or door-to-door selling has to offer.

Most people who do well at criminal activity are called business-men; they are called businessmen because that is what they are. We don't call them criminals because, for a variety of reasons, they escaped the labeling process. More and more I have come to believe that a criminal is not someone who has done any act, however gross or heinous or grabbing, but rather someone who somewhere along the way has been *named* a criminal, who has had the Finger pointed at him and the Magic Marker make its perfectly indelible X in the center of his brow.[16]

Yet ten pages later, when Jackson introduces his first pair of Texas bank robbers, something seemed amiss. Here are the two men, whom Jackson called "Bob" and "Ray," recounting their entrance into crime:

BOB: I've never had any trouble getting a job. Anybody can work, but of course I don't dig working. I mean, not that type of manual work. And then when we got together and talked it over and decided that in order to get the amount of money we wanted in the shortest time, that crime was the way to get it . . .

When we decided to go into crime, we were both what you might call inexperienced criminals at the time, so we decided that to decide what branch we wanted to go into we should first do as much research as we could and find out which made the most money the fastest, and percentage-wise was the safest.

I think you'll find that every public library in the city has the statistics on the number of crimes committed the previous year, approximate value of each crime, and you could figure out from the number or amount stolen the number of crooks caught, the number of convicted, all types of things, what was best for you. We spent four days at the public library and researched, and we came up with armed robbery as the best.

Now you've got to take into consideration: there are crimes that are pulled and got away with, but one man might have pulled twenty armed robberies before he's caught, so they got him on one and there's nineteen unsolved. Statistics-wise it looks like everybody's getting away, but actually they're not. And you've got to take that into consideration when you check into it.

RAY: We found that armed robbery is by far the best as far as getting away with it is concerned. Unlike burglary, or breaking and entering, you don't take anything that you have to convert into cash, thereby putting something into somebody else's hands, and you're taking nothing but money, which is spendable any damn place. I don't care where you go, that money's going to be good. And unlike stealing cars, you don't have to worry about transporting the car to wherever you're going to sell it, and unlike strong-armed robbery—which I tried once—you don't have to worry about knocking some sonofagun in the head and maybe causing him a hell of an injury or maybe even killing him when you didn't even intend to. But still, there is always that chance.

BOB: There's that possibility in armed robbery, too. Of having to shoot somebody.

RAY: We discussed this a great deal. What we would do, if and when. And luckily, in all this time, there's only been one or two slight instances where we've had to worry about it. And I think we came out with flying colors. We could have very easily killed a couple of people, but we never did.[17]

Not every convict, of course, is Bob or Ray. Few are as articulate or objective in analyzing their profession. Still, it seemed as if, somewhere along the line, labeling theory had missed something.

It soon began to dawn upon many crime experts that there might be something wrong with the picture of criminals as mild-mannered stumblers and bumblers "forced" into a life of crime by "the system."

Charles Silberman, the veteran author who was heading the Ford Foundation's Study of law and justice, was one of the first to deal with the problem. He quickly realized that Bob and Ray—whom he called "The Bobbsey Twins"—had given a much more accurate portrayal of the criminal life than the criminologists had done themselves.

In his 1978 classic, *Criminal Violence, Criminal Justice,* Silberman acknowledged that the conventional wisdom about crime was almost entirely wrong. "For a career criminal, doing time is simply an unavoidable cost of doing business," he wrote. "Sooner or later, almost everyone who persists in crime gets caught."

> To assert that almost everyone gets caught is to run counter to the conventional wisdom among criminologists, which holds that only

incompetent offenders are arrested and convicted, and that prison
inmates thus are not representative of the criminal population as a
whole. Since most crimes go unsolved, the reasoning goes, there must
be a great many highly skilled criminals who operate with impunity.
Superficially, at least, the crime statistics seem to support this view.[18]

Silberman noted, however, that this superficial analysis—which was the
view of the crime experts—was wrong. "The Bobbsey Twins," Silberman
said, were right. The great number of unsolved crimes is *not* evidence of a
vast horde of unapprehended criminals. In fact almost anyone who stays in
crime for even a short time almost invariably ends up in the hands of the
law. As Roger Starr, of *The New York Times* editorial board, once
summed it up, "Criminals are people whom the police catch committing
other crimes."

In interviewing professional criminals, Silberman found a unanimous
consensus that there is no such thing as the "real criminal" who never gets
caught. "I don't care how good you are," one experienced convict told him.
"You'll end up in the slammer sooner or later. The law of averages is
against you."

Indeed, none of the criminals I interviewed knew, or had ever heard
of, anyone who had been a criminal for any length of time without
having been imprisoned.[19]

Other independent studies soon began to confirm this observation. One
criminologist calculated that, although a person has only a 20 percent
chance of being caught committing an armed robbery, the chances of being
caught after ten robberies are 90 percent, and after twenty-one are 99
percent.[20]

A Rand Corporation study of New York City subway crime found that,
for all the thousands of robberies committed each year, there were probably no more than *ten* regular muggers among New York's seven million
people who had never been in the hands of the police.[21]

And so, by the mid-1970s, the criminologists and academic experts
found themselves in a rather embarrassing situation. For more than a
decade, they had been encouraging judges and law-enforcement officials to
"deprisonize" the system on the grounds that "the real criminals never get
caught."

Now they were staring at a rather horrifying realization. *The people we catch ARE the real criminals.* There are no shadowy "other criminals" deftly eluding the police while the stumblers and bumblers end up in jail. Moreover, by the time the real criminals get caught, they have probably already committed a long string of crimes. The law of averages is just catching up with them.

The people we had been turning loose for almost a decade in order to avoid "labeling" them as criminals *were the real criminals in the first place.* Moreover, they were using their new-found freedom to commit crimes that went far beyond the benign "juvenile delinquency" that had been at the heart of the theory. Magically disguised as stumblers and bumblers by academic theory, these criminals were out producing the biggest crime wave in American history.

The justice system quickly recovered its equilibrium. Officials started pouring old wine into new bottles. They came up with the new label— "career criminal"—and began putting the bad guys back in jail again.

In fact, inmate populations have risen steadily since 1975, and now stand close to 380,000—the highest they have ever been in our history. This reversal of "deprisonization" is probably the reason that crime rates leveled off in 1980, and have since begun slightly dropping.

Far from accepting these simple facts about crime and punishment, however, the criminologists have fallen back on another argument. Even though they were now willing to admit that the people in jail probably are the "real criminals," academic experts *still* argue against punishment and imprisonment on the grounds that "deterrence doesn't work."

Just why criminologists believe that deterrence doesn't work is one of the great sociological mysteries of our time. Nearly all criminologists seem to believe it, and very few people *except* criminologists believe it. In fact, it might be fair to say that one plausible definition of a criminologist is "a person who believes that punishing criminals doesn't work."

As James Q. Wilson points out, criminologists never even began *studying* the deterrence issue until around 1966—even though the science of criminology has been around for more than a century. When the study of crime and deterrence was finally undertaken, it was done mostly by economists.

Nearly all the research has found that deterrence does have an impact on crime. In an extensive review of several studies, George E. Antunes, of Rice University, and A. Lee Hunt, of the University of Houston, found that the *certainty* of punishment deters all crimes, while the *severity* of punishment has an effect only on murder. Isaac Ehrlich, of the University of Chicago, found, on the other hand, that both the certainty of capture and longer prison sentences lowered crime in several states.[22]

In fact, criminals seem to have a very finely tuned sense of what they can get away with and what they can't. One comparison of jailed inmates in Texas and California showed that the perceptions of both groups about what a crime was "worth" corresponded almost exactly to the comparative punishment placed on these crimes in the two states.

Thus, there is probably still some question as to whether certainty or severity is more important—whether the death penalty, for example, deters murder as much as life imprisonment. Still, as James Q. Wilson comments, "[R]econciling these various studies is less important, and perhaps less difficult, than persuading informed persons to take them seriously. What is remarkable is that so few knowledgeable persons, especially among the ranks of many professional students of crime, are even willing to entertain the possibility that penalties make a difference."[23]

Ignoring the statistics, criminologists usually rely on their own personal constructs of the criminal personality. Criminals are "impulsive," it is argued, and "don't calculate the costs of their actions." "Most criminals do not even plan their escape route from the scene of the crime, and they are certainly not planning their trial tactics," says one defense attorney, echoing the common wisdom.[24] ("But their attorneys are," should be the answer.) Since criminals are so impulsive and uncontrollable, it doesn't make sense to try to punish them anyway.

Strangely enough, often all of this merely results in a very condescending viewpoint that criminals are *too stupid* to absorb the lesson of punishment. As James Q. Wilson says in addressing his fellow academics:

> [W]e have almost succeeded in persuading ourselves that criminals are radically different from ordinary people—that they are utterly indifferent to the costs and rewards of their activities, and are responding only to deep passions, fleeting impulses, or uncontrollable social forces.[25]

Despite the fancies of criminologists, there is every indication that even the most "impulsive" street criminals are acutely aware of the "costs and benefits" of their activities, and that they are constantly making rational calculations.

Listen, for example, to John Allen, a Washington, D.C., street criminal with a long history of muggings and armed robberies who was finally paralyzed from the waist down in a shootout with police in 1972. In his oral autobiography, *Assault with a Deadly Weapon,* Allen said:

> When I was around fourteen a couple of things happened that stopped me from doing little things and started me doing bigger things. I found out that people with little or nothing try harder to keep what they have . . .
>
> Say I felt like going out and robbing something, and there's a bank on one corner and there's a gas station on the other corner. Now you see the man pumping gas all day long, and he got a big old roll in his pocket. Which one would you rob? The bank, of course. Why? Less risk. The man been pumping gas all day long, he tired, he been working hard, and he's not going to give that money up as easy as a bank teller would. A bank teller in a bank behind the cage counting somebody else's money out to him or taking somebody else's money in, they not going to get hurt for their scratch. They going to give it up. But the gas station attendant, that's his money most of the time, and he'll take a loss if he's robbed. Sometimes he may even have to pay back what's been taken in a robbery. Most of the time, that's all he has. So I would rather walk into the bank any day with all their cameras and security officers and silent alarms and loud alarms and secret alarms and pushbutton flowers and all that stuff. I would rather go facing the camera and the FBI than rob a gas station. Not only will the guy in the gas station buck on you, but he will pull a gun and shoot somebody.
>
> Robbing is an art, and the whole art of robbing is fear, and the main reason for robbing is to get what you came after—the money—and to get away. You don't go there to hurt people. Sometimes you have to. Sometimes you do it in self-defense or because a person is trying to protect their property, but most of the time that somebody gets hurt is when somebody bucks: "I'm not giving you nothing. If you want it from me, then you have to kill me." I heard that a lot of times, but you really don't have to do that. If you instill the fear the moment that the robbery started to take place, then you got more than half the battle won. When you succeed in getting away—find a good escape route— then that's the whole battle right there.[26]

The ability of even the most "uneducated" and "impulsive" criminals to make careful calculations about punishment has also been tragically revealed through the juvenile justice laws. In order to "protect" young criminals from being "labeled" by the system, many states adopted laws that said that no one under a certain age (usually eighteen) can be punished for *any* crime under the adult system. Even murder will bring only a few years in the reformatory. In many states, juvenile records are even destroyed once an offender turns eighteen, in order to avoid giving a young offender "a bad reputation."

As a result, violent juvenile offenders rightly concluded that any crime committed before one turns eighteen is essentially "free." In New York City, groups of armed robbers often bring along an underage juvenile to "carry the gun." "They think, 'I can kill because I'm 14,'" is the way one magazine story put it.[27]

Juvenile criminals often seem to understand the results of the system better than the crime experts themselves. "You don't have to worry about anything you do before you're eighteen, because all that is covered by the juvenile laws," one young felon told Charles Silberman. Silberman, sadly missing the point, dismissed the youth as a "cynic."

In fact, interviews with young criminals often reveal that very little *except* rational calculations of crime and punishment enter their deliberations. New York City teenage thrill-killer Willie Bosket, when asked whether he had any feelings for two people he had murdered "just for the experience," told a reporter, "I didn't care about those people because I knew I could only get about two years for it."

Ken Auletta, in his book *The Underclass,* asked one 20-year-old ex-mugger if he would have shot someone during a robbery. He replied:

> I can't say. That was like four years ago. It all depends. If I thought they was strutting it big, maybe. At that time I felt I was invincible. I thought, you know, at that time guys were killing people and doing three months. I was fifteen, sixteen, man, and people were doing like three months for things like that.[28]

Unfortunately, there is only one inescapable conclusion to all this. *Almost all criminals value their crimes by the punishment that society places on them.* While it would be nice to believe that every human being comes into the world with an inborn respect for the life and well-being of others, the evidence is very much to the contrary. Particularly among young criminals—and 20 percent of the violent crime in the country is now committed by people under eighteen—the value placed on other people's life, liberty, and property seems to be *exactly the price society places on it in terms of punishing crime.*

In brief, the "understanding" and "humane" approach to crime has not worked. It is not that understanding and humanity are not noble virtues. The problem is that people who purported to be understanding of criminals actually understood very little about them. Their "humaneness" ignored some very basic realities about human nature.

It was not that these ideas weren't given a chance. In fact, "the establishment" was often surprisingly willing to experiment.

At Illinois Statesville Prison, for example, a Special Programs Unit was created in the late 1960s to try to implement some of the new humane approaches with some of the prison's most incorrigible inmates. Charles Silberman describes the results:

> The idea backfired: for violent gang members, assignment to SPU became a status symbol—evidence that they were indeed the "baddest motherfuckers" of all. Lest anyone doubt their credentials, SPU residents tore down the wire mesh, then the heavier bars with which the mesh was replaced, and hurled porcelain and metal missiles, as well as urine and feces, at guards and other officials (including Dr. Karl Menninger, who served as special consultant to the unit). [The] inmates' defiance of authority simply overwhelmed the prison's capacity for punishment and exposed reform administrations' inability to create a humane and effective approach to governance.[29]

Unfortunately, while these new ideas were being fairly well discredited in practice, they were simultaneously being institutionalized in a series of remarkable decisions being handed down by the U.S. Supreme Court. While many of the new theories about criminology have faded, those Supreme Court decisions have created the criminal justice system we still have today.

THE COURTS 4
AND JUSTICE

A
MERICANS generally assume that we live in a government "of, by, and for the people." We are, after all, a democracy, with elected officials acting in response to the public at almost every level of government. What few Americans realize, however, is that there is another strong, countervailing theory of American government that says that the stability of our system does not necessarily lie in majority rule, but in the more permanent wisdom embodied in the nation's courts.

This strain of opinion prevails most strongly in the legal profession and in certain sections of the academic community. It serves as a justification for the interventions that courts frequently undertake in overriding legislatures and defying majority opinion. To a great degree, this argument says, majorities tend to be wrong: they are easily swept away by popular passions, conformist, and indifferent to the rights of minorities and individuals. Courts, on the other hand, represent a permanent, fixed star.

The danger of democracy is usually described as the "tyranny of the majority," a phrase coined by de Tocqueville. Another common formulation says that legislatures are only responsive to the whims of "shifting majorities." The courts, on the other hand, are wedded to those more permanent principles and ideals embodied in "the law." Among the nation's judiciary, lawyers, law school professors, and civil libertarians, it has become almost an article of faith that the "tyranny of the majority" makes all branches of the government except the judiciary somewhat suspect.

Here, for example, is the way Stephen Gillers, a New York City attorney, expressed it in a 1971 book called *Getting Justice,* a "citizens' guide" to dealing with the police:

It is essentially antidemocratic to allow nine men [the Supreme Court] to decide what rules the remainder of the population will have to obey. Other things being equal, it would seem fairer for Congress or state legislatures to hold this power. A legislative body is more representative of the people than is the Supreme Court, whose appointed members serve for life. But the power does lie with the Court, not with Congress; one of the reasons this is preferable is that the Court is better able to protect the rights of minorities in face of majority antagonisms. Momentary but intense emotional feeling, coupled with a legislative majority, has too often resulted in emasculation of the rights of a minority that happens to be on the "out." The court, however, is expected to remain cool and act as a restraint on the corner-cutting that often accompanies self-righteousness.[1]

This argument is pivotal in understanding the problems the public has in dealing with crime. Ordinarily, one would expect that, in a democracy, public fears about crime would prompt legislative efforts that would work to curtail it. But this is not necessarily so. Because most criminal matters are settled in the courtroom, judges feel it is their particular sphere of influence to have the last word with matters concerning crime and criminals.

The public, it is argued, may be upset about crime, but that should not induce "panic" in the justice system. While the public may want to crack down on criminals, it is the responsibility of the judges to protect individual rights. Otherwise we risk a police state. Legislatures may respond to public pressures demanding longer sentences or a death penalty, but it is the business of the courts to stand firm against majority passions, particularly when these matters involve "due process of law."

Thus, an apparent division of labor has evolved within our system. Because legislatures are assumed to represent the "will of the majority," courts feel compelled to offset this tendency to some degree by taking the side of the minority and unpopular individuals. Crime, on the other hand, is almost inevitably a matter of "the majority versus a small minority." Only a very small minority of people commits serious crimes, and the vast majority of people is always opposed to them. As a result of all this, the courts often seem compelled to view crime and punishment from the perspective of the criminal—or, as it is often phrased, "the individual pitted against the overwhelming powers of the state."

This would not be so bad except for another aspect of our system of government. Unlike judicial systems in most parts of the world, courts in America almost always have the last word.

A full-dress disquisition of this Constitutional division of labor was offered recently by Supreme Court Justice William Brennan in a widely quoted 1985 speech. Brennan, the only remaining member of the 1960s Warren majority, feels that in the last few years the Court has once again turned away from its historical mission.

"Increasingly," Brennan lamented, "the Court these days [is] becoming primarily concerned with vindicating the will of the majority and less interested in its role as a protector of the individual's constitutional rights."[2]

Justice Brennan noted that, while the Supreme Court had sustained "Constitutional claims" in 86 percent of the cases presented to it in 1963, the Court had only upheld 14 percent of similar claims in 1983. This is not an inaccurate figure. Between 1960 and 1968 the Supreme Court struck down 80 percent of all criminal convictions brought before it for review. All these appeals, of course, involved "individuals seeking redress against the government."

Quoting an article entitled "The Era of Aggressive Majoritarianism: A Court in Transition," by a University of Chicago law professor, Brennan noted:

> When government fails in its job to preserve and protect the rights of those who . . . are threatened by the policeman and the jailer, it is for the Supreme Court—the essential "guardian of those rights"—to serve as the "impenetrable bulwark" of our Constitution.

Brennan also favorably quoted a press release by the American Civil Liberties Union that warned:

> When, as occurred [in the 1983 term], the Supreme Court functions, not as a vigorous guardian of the individual, but as a cheerleader for the government, individual constitutional rights cease to have independent meaning.

How are we to evaluate this interpretation of the Constitution that seems to suggest that the Supreme Court is not doing its duty unless it pits itself against the will of the majority?

First, it should be noted that even though Justice Brennan sees his task as upholding "the individual against the government," he himself is part of the government. He is an associate justice of the Supreme Court, holding a far more powerful government office than all but a handful of Americans can ever hope to achieve.

Characterizing the Court's responsibilities as involving "the individual versus the government," is obviously a shorthand expression. What he really means to say is "the individual versus *other branches of the government besides the courts.*" Just what these other branches are likely to be is indicated by the Chicago law professor, who specifically cites "the policeman and the jailer."

Justice Brennan's reference to "the Constitution" is also a kind of shorthand. When he refers to "the Constitution," he is almost inevitably referring to a portion of the Constitution called the "Bill of Rights."

The Constitution, it should be noted, is the document that chartered self-government for the American people. It has many aspects to it, of which the Bill of Rights is but one part. The purposes the Founding Fathers had in mind in drawing up the Constitution and submitting it to the people for ratification by the majority are outlined in the Preamble. It is appropriate to quote this portion of the Constitution in full because it gives a good indication of just what the Founding Fathers and the majority of Americans had in mind when they wrote and ratified that document:

> We, the People of the United States, in order to form a more perfect Union, establish justice, insure domestic tranquility, provide for the common defense, promote the general welfare, and secure the blessings of liberty to ourselves and our posterity, do ordain and establish this Constitution of the United States of America.

Two phrases immediately stand out with relation to criminal matters: "establish justice" and "insure domestic tranquility." They imply the creation and maintenance of a criminal justice system that works toward these ends. They are also part of the oath of office that Justice Brennan and all other federal officials swear to uphold.

Thus, the Constitution is not a document *simply* empowering people *against* their government. The Constitution is the charter by which we, the American people, govern ourselves. Emphasizing only those portions that protect people's rights "against the government" is a very narrow interpretation of the Constitution.

Courts have become remarkably more aggressive in recent years about intervening in the decisions of *other* portions of the government and even in transactions between private parties. Under the general mandate that the courts have given themselves, there are very few events in society that cannot somehow be interpreted as a matter of "Constitutional rights," and therefore within the decision-making powers of the courts. This has often been referred to as "government by judiciary."[3]

The most general mandate the courts have used is one sentence that occurs in the Fourteenth Amendment, which says, "nor shall any State deprive any person of life, liberty, or property, without due process of law; nor deny to any person within its jurisdiction the equal protection of the laws."

Most Constitutional scholars admit that these two phrases are so vague that, if the courts are so disposed, they can be used by the judiciary to intervene almost anywhere, anytime, in the workings of society. As Richard Neely, Chief Justice of the West Virginia Supreme Court of Appeals, candidly admits:

> Courts are the final arbiters of what the federal and state constitutions mean, and since every conceivable political question can theoretically be stated in Constitutional terms (usually within the confines of the vague "due process" or "equal protection" clauses), courts essentially can define their own role in the political structure.[4]

During most of American history, the Supreme Court used its autocratic power to intervene on behalf of *property* rights. Business owners, creditors, and landlords are, after all, almost inevitably a *voting* minority. When state legislatures adopted "social legislation" at the behest of the majority, it usually involved what could be interpreted as taking property or restricting the rights of property owners. Therefore, the Supreme Court almost invariably portrayed its intervention as a matter of "upholding the rights of the minority against majority passions." As the Court expressed it once in overturning an Arizona statute that required employers to be partly responsible for on-the-job injuries suffered by their employees:

> In the last analysis, it is for us [the Court] to determine what is arbitrary of oppressive . . . [A] man's liberty and property [are] under the protection of [the Constitution] and not subordinate to whims or

caprices or fanciful ideas of those who happen for the day to constitute the legislative majority.[5]

This pattern continued until the Supreme Court tried to veto *federal* social legislation: the New Deal adopted during the administration of Franklin Roosevelt. Then the results were different. President Roosevelt fought back, and the attempted Court-packing episode of 1937 ensued. Although the structure of the Supreme Court remained intact, its membership and political direction quickly yielded to majority opinion.

Thus, after 1937, the Court abandoned its sole concern with "property rights" and began looking in other directions. In particular, there was a strong current of opinion among academic liberals for greater protection on behalf of "civil liberties."

Writing in 1955, Professor Fred Rodell, of Yale Law School, outlined an agenda that was very close to the one pursued by the Warren majority five years later. Rodell drew up a list of those whom he thought to be protected from "majoritarian passions." At the top he placed intellectuals and purveyors of unpopular opinion. "The Jacobeans of 1799 and the Communists of 1949" obviously stood in danger of having their rights to free speech overrun by "alien and sedition laws" or "loyalty oaths." The McCarthy era, of course, had given intellectuals and academics a bad scare and had left them extremely sensitive to majority passions.

Next came racial and ethnic minorities. Blacks in the South, and Japanese and Mexicans on the West Coast, were listed as frequent targets of restrictive legislation by "democratically chosen state governments." What but the "autocratic power" vested in the Supreme Court, asked Rodell, could protect these groups?

Finally Rodell listed criminal defendants:

> If, as probably happens daily somewhere in the U.S., a confession is wrung from a suspect by third-degree methods, or his home is searched without a search warrant, or his so-called trial, as in an espionage or kidnapping case, with public opinion inflamed for revenge and a prejudiced judge and jury, more nearly resembles a formalized lynching—what but an autocratic power can reverse, in the name of the Constitution, the popularly approved acts of overzealous law-enforcement officials. In short, if there is any place in a near-democracy for the proper use of ultimate political power by an

autocratic group like the nine justices, that place is in protecting the few against the legalized tyrannies, major or minor, of the many?[6]

Thus, more than most academics would care to admit, the "autocratic power" the court has wielded on behalf of minority and individual rights is the same power the court wielded so unpopularly on behalf of property rights in the 19th century.

There, was of course, some justification for much of this agenda. School segregation in the South was one obvious example of minority oppression that the Court was already beginning to address. The internment of Japanese during World War II was commonly cited—as it still is today—as an example of runaway majority passion.

But as for criminals and accused criminal defendants, there were certain small shortcomings in the argument. Although these three groups—unpopular radicals, ethnic minorities, and criminal suspects—could be lumped together in some respects, in others they are quite different.

Purveyors of unpopular opinion, for example, may offend the majority, but there is an underlying justification for their actions. They are almost always trying to win others to their point of view. One of the basic justifications for freedom of speech, after all, is to ensure the free flow of ideas and information in a society.

At the same time, when racial and ethnic minorities are singled out for repression, they are selected for *qualities that they do not specifically choose.* The thing that makes them "minorities" is life's lottery, or the shifting tide of history, which puts certain people in a minority in certain arbitrarily defined characteristics. It is patently against the spirit of a democracy to single people out for "second-class citizenship" on the basis of racial or ethnic characteristics that they do not choose themselves—or for characteristics that they are entitled to choose themselves, such as a religious belief.

In addition, there is the underlying presumption that different racial, ethnic, and religious groups should be able to get along and participate in a democratic society on an equal basis. People should not be defined or excluded for superficial or inconsequential characteristics.

But neither of these justification fully applies to *criminals.* Criminals are not trying to proselytize their fellow citizens or persuade people to adopt their behavior. Indeed, their success depends on everybody *else* observing the rules while they make exceptions for themselves.

Neither are criminals defined by superficial and meaningless characteristics. They are defined by their *behavior*—a behavior that they choose voluntarily and that victimizes other people and deprives those people of *their* basic rights. It is precisely a people's need to protect themselves against such actions that makes the formation of a "minimal state" necessary in the first place.[7]

There is a difference, of course, between criminals and criminal *suspects.* But the public also has a right to *suspect* people of crimes and to follow through with these suspicions to the point of conducting a fair trial. This fundamental right of the majority of the law-abiding public to protect itself and enforce the laws against crime is so ancient and unimpeachable that the Founding Fathers saw very little need to spell it out in any great detail in the Constitution.

Thus, the "rights" of criminals and criminal suspects are distinctly circumscribed in ways that are qualitatively different from those of unpopular radicals, or racial, religious, and ethnic minorities. There is no prima facie reason that can be made for curtailing freedom of speech—except, of course, for falsely "shouting 'Fire' in a crowded theater," which is itself a crime. Nor is there any rational justification that can be accepted that a person of certain racial, religious, or ethnic background should be singled out on the grounds of that identification.

But the rights of criminals and criminal suspects must necessarily be weighed against the rights of the majority to protect themselves and be safe from crime. Joseph Weintraub, former Chief Justice of the New Jersey Supreme Court, injected a clearheaded view into the debate in 1968:

> There is no right to escape detection. There is no right to commit a
> perfect crime or to an equal opportunity to that end. The Constitution
> is not at all offended when a guilty man stubs his toe. On the contrary,
> it is decent to hope that he will.[8]

Unfortunately, the notion that everyone's civil liberties can be enhanced by protecting unpopular radicals or other minorities has often degenerated into the notion that the more rights we give to criminal suspects, the happier, freer, and less subject to government tyranny we all will be. This argument takes on an even more compelling attraction when the person who is being showered with "rights" is demonstrably *guilty* of something. "If we can let this person off," the argument seems to go, "then none of us will ever have to fear oppression from the government." Unfortunately, the government is not the only agency in society that can harm people.

"The rights of criminals are the rights of all Americans," is the way Tom Wicker, of *The New York Times,* once put it. It would be more correct to say: "The rights of all Americans are also the rights of criminals." Certainly, criminals are entitled to "equal protection under the law." But that does not mean they should be given *special* protections, or that we should create rights that benefit *only* criminals and do not give any reward to the average citizen *unless and until they have actually committed a crime.* That is what we have been doing for the past twenty-five years.

This basic rivalry between courts and legislatures is by no means recent or peculiar to our history. It is endemic in all systems that have developed a separation of powers. Judges have always "made law" in vague competition with legislatures.

In historical terms, popular legislatures are relatively new institutions. Centuries before people started electing their lawmakers, judges were already handing down decisions that served as the equivalent of today's legislation. Donald Horowitz reminds us in The Courts and Social Policy:

> The common law of England was judge-made law, law forged in the course of contested cases. The statute was a rather late and occasional interloper. In medieval England, legislation was often regarded as simply confirming what was already established as customary law. For a considerable time, statutes met with hostility at the hands of lawyers and judges.[9]

When the British legal tradition came to America, this conflict came with it. American legal historian Lawrence Friedman notes:

> Legislation, whatever its subject, was a threat to [the judges] primordial function, molding and declaring the law. Statutes were brute intrusions, local in scope, often shortsighted in principle or effect. They interfered in a legal world that belonged, by right, to the judges. Particularly after 1870, judges may have seen themselves more and more as guardians of a precious and threatened tradition.[10]

The battle over primacy between judicial law and legislative law has long engaged legal scholars. Roscoe Pound, one of the great jurists of the twentieth century, argued that judicial law is superior because it "works with concrete cases and generalizes only after a long course of trial and error," while legislation "involves the difficulties and perils of prophecy."[11]

In criminal law in particular, where the courts are the central forum, most of the system's procedural structure has now been determined by judicial fiat, with only the most peripheral discussion or participation by the majority. Although legislatures define crimes and punishments, it is the judges who determine how the law will be put into practice.

Some of the provisions of the law, of course, are very old and should not be changed. When attempts are made—such as abolishing the insanity defense—judges almost invariably strike them down as violating "due process" by taking away rights or procedures that are "traditional."

But even the judges do not always honor tradition. The Supreme Court itself has been the most radical innovator of criminal procedure in recent decades. Under Earl Warren the Court radically transformed the functions of criminal trials from a procedure in which only the guilt or innocence of the defendant was at issue to one in which the state can also be "put on trial" for its conduct in bringing prosecution. When the justices themselves impose these sweeping innovations on the justice system, they usually argue that criminal justice standards are "evolving," or that all these changes can be "discovered" in the Constitution.

All of this leaves the majority in a rather awkward position. Kierkegaard wrote of how the poet usually cries out in the depths of his anguish, only to have people hear him and exclaim: "What beautiful music!" The public now finds itself in a very similar situation. The more the public chafes and complains about the effects the changes in the justice system are having on crime rates, the more the judges smile to themselves and say, "Ah, the public doesn't like this. That means we must be doing the right thing."

The key question, then, is whether law enforcement can be successfully viewed solely as a matter of "individuals versus the government," or whether there are other factors involved. In the narrow framework, criminals are inevitably portrayed as the lone individuals and therefore the beneficiaries of the courts' concerns. The public, on the other hand—trapped by the unanimity of its opinion—is cast in the role of the "oppressive majority." Expressing majority frustration does little good—it only confirms the judges' certitude that they must act to forestall "majority passions." In the end, the public is left asking itself: Is it necessary for the community of law-abiding people to split up into lone "vigilantes" before they can become the beneficiaries of "individual rights?"

The response seems obvious. The premise that the courts must be *solely* concerned with "individuals in opposition to the government" is an extremely narrow interpretation of the Constitution. The courts should be neither cheerleaders for the majority nor blocking backs for the criminal minority. Instead, they should try to adhere to the broadest possible interpretations of the Constitution and represent the broadest interests of American society.

People who belong to majorities have rights, too. A person should not begin to lose his rights simply because he finds himself in agreement with large numbers of other people.

Vigilante violence has been very much the result of this disarming of majority opinion within the criminal justice system.

It is often argued that we have to "tolerate a little extra crime in our society in order to preserve our civil liberties." This is nonsense. The right to be relatively safe and secure in your home and on the street is just as much a "civil liberty" as the right to a grand jury indictment or a fair trial. And the right to *choose* between degrees of safety and security on the one hand, and extreme civil libertarianism on the other, is an even more basic right of a free people.

In the end, casting criminal justice as "the individual versus the government," when added to an overzealous pursuit of individual rights as "symbolized" by criminals, has done much more than forestall the "tyranny of the majority." It has led us back to an even older and more dreaded form of tyranny—the tyranny of the minority.

SEARCH AND SEIZURE

5

O N MAY 5, 1979, Boston police discovered the badly burned body of 25-year-old Sandra Boulware in a vacant lot in the Roxbury section. A brief investigation led police to her boyfriend, 45-year-old Osborne Sheppard. When asked to account for his actions the night of the murder, Sheppard said he had spent the whole night in a gaming house.

Sheppard's alibi didn't pan out, however, and the police obtained a warrant to search his home. There they found several articles of Boulware's bloodstained clothing and wire matching some wire that had apparently been used to strangle her. Sheppard was tried and convicted of murder.

Two years later, the Massachusetts Supreme Court overturned the conviction. The problem was that police had gone to a local judge for a search warrant on a Sunday when the courthouse was closed. Neither the police nor the judge had a key or a proper warrant form. So they used another form designed for drug cases. The judge made some changes indicating that the warrant was not to be used to search for drugs. But in the end, he forgot to staple together the improvised warrant and the police affadavit indicating what the police would be looking for in Osborne's home.

This failure to staple the police affadivit to the search warrant was judged a "violation of Sheppard's Constitutional rights." In compensation for this violation of his rights, Sheppard was excused for committing a murder.

In August 1981, police in Burbank, California, received an anonymous tip from a person who said that five months previously he had bought cocaine from a man and a woman, named "Armando" and "Patsy," who were selling drugs out of their home. Police confirmed that two people of that name lived at the stated address. They also found that Armando had a previous drug record. They launched an extensive surveillance operation.

During the course of a month they saw several people, including at least one known drug offender, visiting the house and leaving with small packages. The investigation also led to the residence of several other individuals known to be involved with drug smuggling. At one point, Patsy and Armando made a trip to Miami. When their luggage was searched on the return flight, a small quantity of marijuana was discovered.

One month later, after extensive consultation with several district attorneys, the police obtained a warrant and made a search. A simultaneous raid on all three dwellings turned up large quantities of cocaine.

Several months later a federal district judge ruled that the activities police had observed were "as consistent with innocence as with guilt," that the original tip had been "close to" being "stale," and that, as a result, there was no "probable cause" for issuing the search warrant. Therefore, all the drugs seized in the raid could not be used in court as evidence.[1]

Although few Americans were aware of it, by the early 1980s we were living with a criminal justice system in which it was possible that a mass murderer could get away completely free because a police secretary made a typing error on a search warrant.

District attorneys, the police, and some judges continually tore their hair at the situation and said that criminal justice in America had become a mockery. Civil libertarians, criminal defense attorneys, and other judges, however, argued that this was all necessary to "protect the Constitution."

The public has rarely understood the issues—not because people don't care, but because the whole situation is so incredibly complicated and hard to believe that it generally escapes public apprehension. The end results, however, are well known. Since the Supreme Court changed the functioning of the Constitution, beginning in 1961, "criminals getting off on technicalities" has become an American way of life.

At the center of this ongoing absurdity is something called the "exclusionary rule" or, more precisely, "the exclusionary rule to the Fourth Amendment." That amendment protects citizens from "unreasonable searches and seizures." The exclusionary rule, which was set up by the Supreme Court to "enforce" the Fourth Amendment, says something more complicated. It says that if evidence is seized by the police in violation of the Fourth Amendment, it cannot be used in court.

It is very likely that the Warren Court never anticipated just how absurd the results of the exclusionary rule would eventually become. But that is exactly what happened. Police errors are taken as the equivalent of crimes, no matter how trivial the procedural mistake nor how heinous the criminal act. The "tainted" evidence can be anything from dead bodies to illegal guns to millions of dollars in confiscated drugs. The "Constitutional violations" can be as insignificant as a set of mixed-up digits on a license plate to a misspelled name or a typing error. It does not matter. All are subject to what Chief Justice Warren Burger calls the "universal capital punishment" of the exclusionary rule.

The story begins on May 23, 1957. On that day, three Cleveland police officers came to the door of Dolree Mapp, a black woman whom police had been told was harboring a suspect from a bombing incident; they were also told that she was running an illegal numbers operation.

When confronted with the police, Miss Mapp called her lawyer, who instructed her to refuse entry without a search warrant. The officers departed. Three hours later, they returned with reinforcements. This time they waved a piece of paper in front of her face, which they said was a warrant, and demanded entry.

Mapp grabbed the paper and stuffed it into her dress. The police grabbed her, wrestled the paper away from her, and put her into handcuffs. Her attorney had arrived on the scene but was not allowed to talk with Mapp or gain admittance to the house. The police ransacked Miss Mapp's dwelling, but they found neither the fugitive nor evidence of any numbers operation. In the basement, however, police discovered a suitcase that Miss Mapp said belonged to a friend. In the suitcase, they found four pamphlets, a couple of photographs, and a pencil doodling that were alleged to be pornographic.

Miss Mapp was charged with possession of pornographic material under an Ohio statute. She was convicted and sentenced to 2-to-7 years in prison.

The Fourth Amendment to the Constitution reads as follows:

> The right of the people to be secure in their persons, houses, papers, and effects, against unreasonable searches and seizures, shall not be violated, and no warrants shall issue, but upon probable cause, supported by oath or affirmation, and particularly describing the place to be searched, and the persons or things to be seized.

The intent of the Amendment is clear. The police are not allowed to go around breaking down people's doors and rummaging through their houses and belongings looking for things that can be used to charge them with crimes. Neither are they allowed to obtain a warrant to search your home without presenting a good reason. Random, expeditionary searches are obviously the target of the Fourth Amendment. Thus, it would be hard to find a *better* example of what the Fourth Amendment was designed to prevent than what happened to Dolree Mapp in 1957.

Unfortunately, enforcement of the Fourth Amendment had been impeded by the ongoing controversy over whether the Bill of Rights applied only to the federal government, or to the state governments as well. As we shall see later, much of American Constitutional history has revolved around this question.

In 1960, in a rather antiquated remnant of early Federalism, the Fourth Amendment had not yet been generally applied to the state governments. Most states had adopted their own bills of rights, and many had also adopted provisions against unreasonable searches and seizures. But even where state restraints had been in place, they often went unenforced. Ohio was one of the worst. Until 1960, the city of Cincinnati had issued only a few search warrants in its entire history.

As early as 1914, however, the Supreme Court had reacted to the habit of the FBI and other agencies of making searches without warrants in violation of the Fourth Amendment and using the evidence anyway.

In 1914, a man named Weeks, living in Kansas City, had been running a mail fraud. While he was at work one day, FBI officials went to his house, borrowed a key from his neighbor, and collected evidence. Weeks was convicted. When the case came to the Supreme Court for appeal, however, the Court threw out the conviction. In the process, they attached an "exclusionary rule" to the Fourth Amendment. This said that any evidence gathered through a search that violated the Fourth Amendment could not be used in court against the individual. It was argued that the inadmissibility of such evidence would deter the police from unconstitutional conduct.

Despite the strictures of the rule, *Weeks v. United States* did not have much impact on law enforcement. The Constitution says that: "The trial of all crimes . . . shall be held in the State where the said crimes shall have been committed," and about 90 percent of all criminal trials are handled by state and local governments. FBI participation is limited to certain "federal cases"—kidnappings, bank robberies, some drug cases, and crimes that cross interstate lines.

From 1914 to 1960, FBI officials largely avoided the exclusionary rule through the "silver platter" method. State police officers, who were not restricted by the federal Constitution, would often collect evidence without warrants and turn it over to federal authorities "on a silver platter," saving federal authorities the problems of dealing with the Fourth Amendment. About half the states did have exclusionary rules of their own, but these were not as strictly enforced as the federal rule.

Witnessing all this, the Supreme Court eventually got tired of watching the federal exclusionary rule circumvented through the silver-platter syndrome. And so the new majority, headed by Chief Justice Earl Warren, decided it was time to crack down.

When *Mapp v. Ohio* reached the Supreme Court in 1960, Dolree Mapp's attorneys were actually appealing on the grounds that Ohio's pornography laws violated free speech. Both the Warren majority and the American Civil Liberties Union, however, saw it as a good opportunity to expand the exclusionary rule. In the final written arguments, the Ohio Civil Liberties Union—possibly acting on a cue from somewhere in the Court itself—attached a footnote asking the Court to consider overturning the conviction on the grounds of illegal search-and-seizure and applying the exclusionary rule to the states.

Justice John Harlan, who was soon to emerge as the most scholarly dissenter on the Warren Court, smelled a rat. He complained that the Court was slapping the exclusionary rule on the states "without full-dress argument." Justice Potter Stewart thought that Miss Mapp's conviction should be overturned on the pornography grounds, but he agreed that the Warren majority was cutting corners by not fully exploring the implications of the exclusionary rule in a formal courtroom debate.

Still, the Warren majority had five votes. On July 19, 1961, the Warren Court, in its first important ruling in criminal law, announced the "incorporation" of both the Fourth Amendment and its hybrid child, the exclusionary rule, into the vast criminal-justice apparatus of all fifty states. From now on, any evidence seized in searches that later proved to violate the Fourth Amendment would no longer be admissible in American courtrooms.

On the face of it, there was a strong case for doing *something* to deter unrestrained police behavior. Expeditionary searches like the one that convicted Miss Mapp were fairly common. In many parts of the country, judicial oversight was almost nonexistant. The police often had a free hand to go wherever they wanted, using whatever evidence they turned up to bring charges that would justify the search after the fact.

Both criminal and civil proceedings had tried to curtail such practices, but did not prove successful. Almost universally it was found that juries would not convict the police or award civil damages. Jurors were especially offended when the complainant was a previously convicted criminal claiming that his Constitutional rights had been violated in seizing the evidence that led to his conviction.

Nor were local prosecutors likely to be very diligent about pursuing such cases. They had to work with the police and did not feel very comfortable about bringing officers up on charges. Sometimes the district attorneys even participated in these searches or at least gave their tacit approval. With no popular support for cracking down on the police, local prosecutors were not giving the matter very high priority.

Since that time, the pressure brought from the exclusionary rule has brought vast changes. Many administrative procedures are now in place that punish the police and give considerable strength to the protections of the Fourth Amendment. In New York City, for example, patrolmen are fired for making illegal searches—one of the few ways a policeman can lose his job. But in 1960 there were very few such mechanisms.

Thus, there was good reason and ample justification for the Supreme Court to step in and try to clean up state procedures. The Fourth Amendment was in danger of becoming an historical curiosity. Unfortunately, the mechanism that the Court chose to enforce the Amendment—the exclusionary rule—had serious logical flaws. Although these flaws had heretofore been disguised, the uniform imposition of the exclusionary rule upon all fifty states soon brought those faults into the glaring light of courtroom reality.

On the face of it, the idea of attaching a deterrent to the Fourth Amendment makes sense. Criminologists, after all, are the only people who don't believe in deterrence, and even they make an exception for the police. The problem is, however, that the exclusionary rule is a bit roundabout in its deterrent effect, and a bit off the mark when it lays its punishment.

It is hard to say that the police are really "punished" by the exclusionary rule. There is no direct penalty, either for the individual patrolman or for the police department, for making an illegal search. There is frustration and disappointment but no direct sanctions. Instead, the rule tries to "remove the incentive" for these searches by making the evidence inadmissible in court. If the police know the evidence can't be used in court, so the reasoning goes, then why make searches in the first place?

But what if the police make them anyway or if a search that they assumed to be legal turns out not to be? Someone will indeed be punished, but it will not be the police. Instead, it is the *public* that is punished by having a guilty criminal turned loose upon them.

In a way, it is as if a judge were to try to deter a bank robber by saying, "Every time you commit a crime, I'm going to beat this small child." Although the police are the offenders, they do not suffer any direct pain. The brunt of the punishment is received by the public.

But that was only the beginning. What completely escaped the attention of the judges was that the exclusionary rule does more than just "enforce" the Fourth Amendment. It significantly *narrows* its scope as well. Specifically, the Fourth Amendment, as amended by the exclusionary rule, no longer protects the average citizen from unreasonable searches in any meaningful way. There may be some vague general protections for the public at large, but the specific benefits of the rule fall on only one specific class of people—*guilty criminals*.

Let me illustrate how this works. Suppose the police come to your house, break down your door, wreck your furniture, scatter your papers, ravage your belongings, and *don't* find any incriminating evidence. What does the exclusionary rule do to enforce your Fourth Amendment rights? Nothing. There is no evidence to be held against you. Therefore you cannot be "compensated" for having your rights violated by having evidence thrown out of court. Your protections against unreasonable searches are essentially what they were without the exclusionary rule.

But suppose the police come to your house and do the same thing and they find evidence proving that you *are* guilty of something. Now the exclusionary rule works to "protect your rights." Whatever evidence the police find cannot be used against you. Without the evidence, you are more likely to be acquitted or avoid being charged. Supreme Court Justice Benjamin Cardozo memorialized the phenomenon in 1926 when he rejected the exclusionary rule as New York State's chief justice: "The criminal goes free because the constable has blundered."

This lack of enhanced protection for the innocent by the exclusionary rule extends to all cases. Say, for example, we have two people, George and Isaac. George is guilty and Isaac is innocent. If the police illegally search George and find evidence of his guilt, then the evidence must be dismissed. If they illegally search Isaac and find nothing, nothing happens.

But consider a third possibility. Suppose they illegally search Isaac and find evidence of George's guilt. Then, the judges have ruled, the evidence *is* admissible because *George's* rights have not been violated. Thus, George cannot benefit from an illegal search of Isaac.

But there is another implication here as well. *Isaac has no rights under any circumstances.* He is not guilty of anything, and therefore he has no protections. The exclusionary rule doesn't do anything to enhance your Fourth Amendment rights *until you have done something wrong.*

One would think that anything as broad as one of the guarantees in the Bill of Rights should apply to all citizens. One of the strictures of the Fourteenth Amendment, which ranks with the Bill of Rights in importance, is that there should be "equal protection under law."

But when the exclusionary rule is attached to the Fourth Amendment, the Amendment no longer provides "equal protection." Its protections extend only to one narrow constituency—*people who have actually committed crimes.* No one else receives any additional reward or safeguard under the exclusionary rule. Moreover, the protection takes only one form—excusing guilty people of their crimes.

It is often charged that the Warren Court was "more concerned with the right of the criminal than the rights of the defendant." That is not quite right. What the Warren Court did was *create rights that work only for guilty criminals.* The Fourth Amendment, originally a broad mandate that was supposed to protect everyone, has been turned into a narrower rule that only protects the guilty.

Prior to *Mapp,* the standard for judging the Constitutionality of searches and seizures—and of all criminal matters—had been the doctrine of "fundamental fairness."

The fundamental fairness doctrine was a rule of thumb, similar to Justice John Paul Stevens's famous definition of pornography: "I may not be able to define it, but I know it when I see it."

Under the fundamental fairness doctrine, the judges looked at a whole criminal proceeding and asked the simple question, "Did the defendant really get a fair trial?" The unspoken question, of course, was this: "Are we railroading an innocent man here, or is it simply that there have been a few procedural flaws that did not really make a crucial difference?" The fundamental fairness doctrine allowed the justices to use common sense, instead of becoming bound to a hard and fast rule that could be quickly overwhelmed by technical quibbles.

Implicit in the fundamental fairness doctrine was the idea that the *public* has an interest in a fair trial. A criminal proceeding is not just a sporting contest between "the individual and the state." The public also has a stake in the outcome. It has the right to see guilty people punished and justice done. Under fundamental fairness, the guilt or innocence of the defendant remained the core question of every criminal proceeding.

There was at the same time a recognition that a violation of the defendant's rights could be so gross and obvious that the state had "played an ignoble part." Evidence was excludable when it was gathered in a method that "shocked the conscience." The phrase originally was used in a case in which the police had pumped a man's stomach after he had swallowed morphine in order to avoid being arrested for possession. Obviously, there were things the police could do that surpassed the bounds of "fundamental fairness," even where a guilty person was involved. But that did not mean that *any* procedural violation, no matter how small, could become sufficient to dismiss evidence that suggested a person was guilty.

All this changed with the introduction of the exclusionary rule. *The guilt or innocence of the defendant is now no longer the overriding consideration* at a trial procedure. Instead, trials have been turned into more "adversarial" proceedings, where the state tries to prove the defendant has done something wrong while the defendant tries to prove the state has done something wrong. If both sides prove their case, then these two "wrongs" cancel each other out, and the defendant does not have to be judged by the evidence.

Justice Harlan, in his eloquent *Mapp* dissent, caught this right away. Inserting the exclusionary rule into trial procedures, he said, would "use [trial] procedures as an incidental means of pursuing other ends than the correct resolution of the controversies before it." Evidence should be admitted, said Justice Harlan, "regardless of how it was obtained, if it is relevant to the one issue with which the trial is concerned, the guilt or innocence of the accused."

With the introduction of the exclusionary rule, the public lost its right to find out the truth in a criminal procedure. At the beginning, probably no one really imagined to what an extreme this principle would be carried and how vanishingly insignificant the "Constitutional violations" would eventually become. But the law works on precedent, and precedents can rapidly develop an enormous weight of inertia.

Once the door was opened, criminal defendants and criminal attorneys were given an enormous opportunity to turn the tables on the police and prosecution and start demanding that the state be judged by more and more perfectionistic standards.

It wasn't long before they began taking advantage of it.

In 1964, a man named Edward Coolidge put up a sign in a laundromat in Manchester, New Hampshire, asking for a babysitter. Fourteen-year-old Pamela Mason answered the ad and agreed to babysit for Coolidge the following Friday. That night there was a huge snowstorm. Pamela heard a horn blowing outside her house and told her father she was going babysitting. She was never seen alive again.

Eight days later, Pamela's body was found in a melting snowdrift along an interstate highway just outside Manchester. She had been sexually molested, her throat had been slit, and she had been shot in the head.

The killing shocked the small New England city. Police canvassed the entire community, literally going door-to-door asking if anyone knew any person who had done anything unusual the night of the snowstorm.

When they reached Coolidge's house, they did hear an interesting story. Neighbors said that Coolidge had been out most of the evening, not getting home until after midnight. Coolidge was not home, but his wife told the same story. She allowed police to enter and search the house. She also gave them the clothes that Coolidge had worn the night of the storm and a gun he kept in the house. Ballistics tests showed it was the murder weapon.

With a strong case building, the police obtained a search warrant for Coolidge's car. They vacuumed it and found dirt and other particles that eventually proved identical to dirt and particles found on the girl's body.

Faced with a strong case, Coolidge responded with a strong alibi. He said he had been out late but had been stuck on the side of the interstate highway for several hours, far from the murder scene. Several people had stopped to ask if he needed help. He appealed for them to come forth and confirm his story.

One young man did indeed come forth. He said he had seen Coolidge's car stopped on the highway and had asked if he needed help. As it happened, he made regular deliveries to a house right next to Coolidge's and had recognized the car from its old-fashioned sun visor over the windshield.

There was only one problem. Instead of placing Coolidge miles from the scene, the young man said he had encountered Coolidge *right across from the place where Pamela's body was discovered.*

With an overwhelming preponderance of evidence against him, Coolidge was convicted of first-degree murder and sentenced to death.

Seven years later, the appeal wound up before the Supreme Court. By this time, the following key issue was at stake:

When police obtained the warrant to vacuum the car, it was issued by the state attorney general, serving in a dual capacity as a justice of the peace, as permitted under New Hampshire law. Because the warrant had not been signed by a "neutral" magistrate, it was argued, the warrant was invalid. Without a valid warrant, the search of Coolidge's car became "illegal," and Coolidge was entitled to a new trial without mention of the dust particles.

Incredibly, when the Supreme Court reviewed the Coolidge case, it didn't even stick to the issue of the warrant. Instead, seven years after the fact, the nine justices became embroiled in a debate over whether Coolidge's wife had been "coerced" by police into giving up the incriminating evidence. The key point became whether the police had been able to "coerce or dominate her, or, for that matter, to direct her actions by the more subtle techniques of suggestion that are available to officials in circumstances like these."[2]

None of the justices had ever met any of the principals in the case. They had no idea what had happened between the police and Mrs. Coolidge, except for the sketchy record in the transcript. Yet the Court still decided that there had probably been enough "coercion" of Coolidge's wife to grant him a new trial. (Mrs. Coolidge's "Constitutional right" to *cooperate* with the police counted for nothing, of course, when compared to her husband's Constitutional right to try to get away with murder.)

On this ground, Coolidge's conviction was overturned, and he was awarded a second trial. He was convicted again, but avoided the death penalty, and recently became eligible for parole.

In the twenty-five years since its adoption, the exclusionary rule has become one of the most extraordinary exercises in intellectual sophistry ever imposed on a democratic people. Medieval scholars debating how many angels can stand on the head of a pin would feel right at home amid contemporary judges and lawyers arguing what constitutes "probable cause" or what serves as an adequate "description of persons or things to be seized."

The target of all this pointless casuistry is the broad language of the Constitution itself. As Richard Morgan, professor of Constitutional law at Bowdoin College, writes:

> The original six articles [of the Constitution] and the . . . Bill of Rights and Fourteenth Amendment are written in a majestic and general idiom—not the language of a corporate charter or a municipal bond issue. And everyone across the spectrum of Constitutional politics agrees that this choice of idiom was meant to afford flexibility to future generations in applying the language to ever changing circumstances. The general language was meant, in other words, to allow for a "living Constitution."[3]

Unfortunately, this majestic idiom is also flexible enough so that if judges and attorneys try hard enough, they can work this "living Constitution" into something that would make a municipal bond issue read like the Declaration of Independence.

The Fourth Amendment is so vague and broad that it doesn't even say specifically that every search requires a warrant. It simply states in two separate phrases that the people shall be "secure" from "unreasonable searches" and that "no warrants shall be issued, but upon probable cause . . . and particularly describing the places to be searched, and the persons or things to be seized."

There are many instances when a search and seizure does not require a search warrant. The police may always search premises if they have the owner/occupant's permission. If the police stop a suspect in flight, or if they believe evidence is about to be destroyed, they may act without going to the trouble of asking a judge's permission. Likewise, if the police stop a car on the highway, they do not have to seek a search warrant since there is a chance the car may escape.

Even here, though, the situation has tended to turn into a Chinese puzzle. If the police search a car they may look in the trunk. But if they find a bag in the trunk, the courts have ruled, they may not search the bag. There, the person has a "reasonable right to privacy." This right holds, however, as long as it is a *cloth* bag. If it is a *paper* bag, then the police may search. But what if the police find a cloth bag within the paper bag? The courts have not yet ruled on that one.

That's a relatively simple situation. Where the Fourth Amendment becomes even slightly specific, however, the language has been literally tortured into meaninglessness—like a familiar word repeated over and over so many times that it becomes a nonsense syllable.

Searches are not to be conducted, or warrants issued, without "probable cause." But what is probable cause? Do the police have to be 100 percent sure that a crime is taking place? Eighty percent sure? Sixty percent? And how is this certainty to be measured? No one ever really knows until an appeals court makes a ruling one or two years later. If the judge decides there was not probable cause for the *initial* investigation, then no matter what kind of incriminating evidence eventually turns up, all of it must be excluded from court.

As an analogy, imagine that a newspaper reporter gets an anonymous phone call one day from a person who tells him that if he looks at the financial records of the city sewer commission he will find something interesting. The reporter decides to investigate and soon finds that the books don't add up. He launches a six-month investigation that reveals that the city treasurer has embezzled half-a-million dollars in city funds. The newspaper prints the story, which quickly leads to indictments for grand larceny. The city treasurer is forced to resign in disgrace. The newspaper reporter receives a promotion and is awarded a state journalism prize.

Now, six months later, on an appeal from the treasurer, a federal district judge orders the story retracted. The treasurer must be reinstated to his job, the newspaper must print an apology, and the reporter must give back his prize money. The reason? Even though the story panned out, the reporter did not have "probable cause" for beginning the initial investigation. The original information was too sketchy and unreliable to justify his pursuing it any further.

Absurd as this may sound, this is *exactly* the way things are being done in American courtrooms today. The key to getting crucial incriminating evidence thrown out of a trial is to invalidate the method in which it was gathered. The quickest and easiest way to do this is to argue that the initial information that set off the investigation lacked "probable cause."

Most decimated by all this has been the normal seat-of-the-pants type investigations that experienced police officers often undertake on nothing more than a "hunch" or a "feeling that something is wrong."

In Cleveland in 1963, for example, a plainclothes police detective named McFadden with thirty-five years experience in patrolling the downtown area saw something he regarded as suspect. He first spotted two men "he had never seen before" conferring on a streetcorner. Stopping to watch them for a few moments, he observed them performing a strange ritual. In turn, each of them would stroll casually down the street, look into a jewelry store window, and then walk back again. Together they repeated this routine almost two-dozen times. They were joined on the corner for a moment by a third man, who then disappeared.

Finally, they both strolled down the street and were joined in front of the store by the third man. As they were about to enter, the detective stopped them and asked them what they were doing. They "mumbled a few words," so he spun them around and patted them down. He found guns on two of them. He took them into the store, had the owner call the station-house, and arrested them. Two of them were tried and convicted for possession of guns.

Five years later, their appeal reached the Supreme Court, on the grounds that Detective McFadden did not have sufficient "probable cause" in searching them for guns. The American Civil Liberties Union and the NAACP Legal Defense Fund, which argued the case, claimed that such tactics would allow police to go around randomly patting down people on the streets.

The Warren Court, under tremendous pressure by this time, finally upheld the conviction and carved out a "stop and frisk" procedure that allowed police to make minimal searches for their own protection. In countless other cases, however, similar evidence has not survived.

The main casualty in all this has been good police work—particularly the kind of "street smarts" and "sixth sense" that good patrolmen are supposed to develop. Like most other professions, police work is basically a matter of refined sensibilities. After a few years on the job, a good patrolman can spot things that other people might overlook. To the average person, three men standing on a streetcorner may not seem unusual. But to a patrolman who has walked the same beat for many years, there can be something very suspect about it.

The problem, of course, is that such suspicions are very difficult to explain in court—particularly since many policemen aren't very articulate. Defense attorneys, on the other hand, are usually articulate to the point of being glib and easily run circles around the average patrolman in court.

None of these restrictions, of course, ever protects the average citizen. Had the three men in *Terry vs. Ohio* been picking out jewelry for their wives, the incident would have had the significance of a tree falling in the forest. It was only because a crime was about to be committed that the whole thing became a question of "Constitutional rights."

Thus, every criminal proceeding in the United States now begins with an "evidentiary hearing," at which the judge and attorneys decide among themselves what evidence the jury is going to hear. The art of contemporary defense work is to get as much evidence as possible excluded from the trial on the grounds that it was seized "unconstitutionally." One of the quickest ways to do this is to argue that a warrant or search was undertaken without "probable cause."

As a result, some of the following results have occurred:

—In Denver in 1982, a woman looked out her window and saw a man peering into a neighbor's house. A half-hour later she saw him again standing at a bus stop with a television set under his arm. She called the police. The patrol car arrived, questioned the man, and arrested him. The television turned out to be stolen from another house down the block. The Colorado Supreme Court threw out the conviction on the grounds that police did not have "probable cause" in making the arrest.

—In an Illinois case that reached the U.S. Supreme Court in 1983, an anonymous tipster had given police the name and address of a couple who, he claimed, were dealing in marijuana. The tipster said the couple were leaving for Florida shortly to bring back a large shipment. The police checked all this out and found it to be true. They met the couple when they returned home and found $35,000 worth of marijuana in their car. Lower courts overturned the conviction on the grounds that an anonymous tip could not constitute "probable cause." The Supreme Court, however, eventually upheld the search.

—In a Michigan case in 1976, the owner of a rented trailer became suspicious because he hadn't seen for some time the married couple who occupied the trailer. He went to the trailer and found a large box from which emanated a strange odor. He removed the box from the trailer, opened it, and found the husband's body. He called the police, who reopened the box and then charged the wife with murder. The woman was convicted and sentenced to life in prison. A Michigan appeals court overturned her conviction on the grounds that the search was conducted without a warrant. The woman was free on bail for two years before the Michigan Supreme Court reversed the decision.

—In California in the early 1970s, police closed in on two suspected heroin dealers, a husband and wife, while they were walking their baby in the park. The police searched the couple and found nothing. Then one officer got a bright idea and searched the baby's diaper. There he discovered the heroin. The case was dismissed, however, when a California appeals court ruled that the baby had been too young to consent to the search, and therefore a warrant was required.

—In a 1981 Texas case, the Texas Court of Criminal Appeals voided a drug seizure by narcotics agents who had entered and searched a room after being told by an informant that people inside were selling a white powder they referred to as "speed." The court said that police did not have "probable cause" because they failed to consider that "speed" might be the name of a new brand of laundry detergent.

For all this, "probable cause" is only one ground for invalidating warrants and throwing out evidence. An even more fertile ground for defense attorneys has been the innocuous phrase of the Fourth Amendment that says that warrants must "describe the place to be searched or the persons or things to be seized."

Just what constitutes adequate "description" of a person or an object? Philosophers have spent millennia debating the issue. All things considered, it is probably safe to say that the Founding Fathers were not concerned over whether the house had brown shutters or green shutters, or whether a man named Leon Czolgosz spells it with one or two "z's." Yet these are exactly the sorts of minutiae that the judges and lawyers have turned into "Constitutional issues."

Search warrants have been routinely invalidated in American courts over the past fifteen years because a pair of digits was inverted on a license plate number, or because a dark green car with a white top was described as blue with a beige top, or because somebody's name was spelled wrong on a search warrant. Even typing errors have been sufficient to make a warrant "invalid." Without the warrant, of course, the search is illegal, and the evidence must be dismissed. In addition, any subsequent evidence that turns up from information gathered in the original search must also be excluded as "fruit of the poisoned tree."

It was under these circumstances that the Boston murder case of Osborne Sheppard and the Burbank, California, drug stake-out and cocaine seizure finally reached the Supreme Court in 1984.

After more than twenty years of this, the Court finally decided it had had enough. Ruling on the Sheppard murder and the Burbank case, the Court decided to attach a "good faith exemption" to the exclusionary rule. This says that if the police act in "good faith" in obtaining a warrant, the warrant cannot be voided later on minute technical grounds. The evidence in both cases was reinstated.

The problem is that no one knows exactly what a "good faith" amendment is going to mean. It suggests that warrants probably will not be thrown out of court on technicalities such as spelling mistakes or typographical errors. But it may not go much further than that. The exclusionary rule offers defense attorneys a tremendous opportunity to blow holes in otherwise almost irrefutable cases. Defense attorneys are not going to give up without a fight. A quick poll the day after the Burbank decision was announced showed that 40 percent of all attorneys opposed any change in the exclusionary rule.[4] Civil libertarians are already calling the Court's action "the repeal of the Fourth Amendment."

Beyond that, the Burger Court has been trying to roll back the exclusionary rule inch by inch. In a recent decision, for example, the Supreme Court decided that house trailers are *cars* not houses and therefore do not require search warrants. The house trailer in question was a headquarters for selling drugs, and the police seized the drugs and arrested the inhabitants without a search warrant. The Court ruled that, because the trailer could be moved and could have made an escape, it should be classified a "car" under the Constitution.

At this rate, we may be back to a sensible system of law enforcement in this country sometime around the twenty-first century.

In truth, the problem goes far beyond the problem of the exclusionary rule and the hair-splitting sophistries surrounding the few general phrases of the Fourth Amendment. The fundamental problem is that the Supreme Court has completely misunderstood the whole nature of criminal investigations.

In mounting its attack on searches and seizures and on interrogation of suspects (to be discussed in the next chapter), the Warren Court always added a comment saying that crimes should be solved through "good police work." Yet somehow the Court never got around to defining exactly what "good police work" was supposed to be.

Unfortunately, it is easy to surmise from the Court's decisions just what the justices had in mind. Somehow, somewhere, the judges seem to have gotten the idea that good police investigators solve crimes the way Hercule Poirot does in the Agatha Christie novels. The detective sits in his chair, thinks very hard about the facts, and then comes up with the solution to "whodunit."

In fact, when you get right down to it, the Court's conception of "good police work" seems to be very close to the work of Supreme Court justices in their own deliberations. The police should begin with a set of first principles and follow them through to their logical conclusion—just the way the justices do in deciding the Constitutionality of certain laws. The reasoning is *a priori*—logical deduction—rather than the more practical method of *empirical* reasoning through "trial and error."

In reality, police work is not much like judicial reasoning. It has much more in common with scientific investigation. Both detectives and scientists begin by formulating a theory. This theory then leads to them to frame certain questions. Could something have happened in this specific way? What would happen if we looked there? What would happen if we did such-and-such? Once these questions are *asked* it is possible to go out and look for the answers.

The purpose of formulating questions is twofold. First, it suggests what facts to look for. Second and equally important, it suggests *where to look for the facts.*

In the Pamela Mason murder, for example, police had no theories other than that the person who did it probably lived in Manchester and that the unusual weather might cause people to remember what they or their friends and neighbors were doing. This led them to a broad, house-to-house canvassing that eventually proved successful.

In most cases, however, the possibilities are much narrower. When the police obtain a warrant to search a specific place, they already have a pretty good reason for looking there—which is just what the Constitution intended.

When these places are searched, however, the results are unpredictable. The police may find evidence that their theory led them to expect. They may find evidence that contradicts the theory. Or they may find something that confirms and expands the theory in a way they did not anticipate. There is never any way to know in advance. Or, to put it another way, if they already knew exactly what they were going to find, there wouldn't be any real reason to have to go and look.

For several decades, however, the Supreme Court has lost track of this simple idea. The justices have gotten the idea into their heads that the police go out to look for evidence they already know is there, simply for the purpose of bringing it into court. They do this, in the Court's version of police work, only after they have figured out everything they are going to find. Criminal investigation, the judges seem to believe, goes on in the detective's mind. Evidence is not something a detective discovers by figuring out the right place to *look.* Evidence is something he gathers only for trial purposes after he has already decided it is there.

But that is not the way any investigation can work. As the saying goes, you never know what you are going to find until you go look for it.

All scientific investigation works in this way. In the seventeenth century, for example, Anton van Leeuwenhoek, a Dutch lens grinder, started making lenses that enabled him to see things invisible to the naked eye. He didn't know exactly what to look for, but he guessed that a drop of water might be interesting. There he found a whole universe of what he called "little animalcules"—the microscopic world.

Likewise, when Darwin went around the world in *The Beagle*, he didn't know exactly what he was looking for. He was investigating species, however, and when he reached the Galapagos he found the famous finches that had diversified into about a dozen different species. The unusual evidence nudged along an idea that had already been forming in his mind—that similar species descended from a common ancestor and that all living forms had resulted from the process of this gradual "evolution."

Police investigators, of course, do not have the broad mandate of scientists. They do not have a license to go anywhere looking for evidence of any crime. But they do have society's mandate to look in *specific* places, investigating *specific* crimes. Once a crime has been committed, society has a right to find out what happened.

Unfortunately, under the rules of investigation that have evolved from the Supreme Court, *neither van Leeuwenhoek's microscopic world nor Darwin's finches would be legally admissible as evidence in court.* The reason is that neither researcher could adequately describe what he found *before* he found it.

Under the Supreme Court's vanishingly narrow interpretation of the Fourth Amendment, the police can no longer simply state *where* they expect to find evidence of a crime. They also have to describe in meticulous detail *what* they expect to find *before* they find it. If they find something different from what they expected, even though that evidence incriminates the *same* person in the *same* crime, that evidence is not admissible in court. The reason is that the police have not properly "described" the evidence as "required" by the Fourth Amendment.

Let us look at how this works in practice. Say that the police discover a body that has been killed with a puncture wound. They hypothesize that the person has been shot, although they are unable to find the bullet. They have a firm suspect, so they obtain a warrant to search his house. Instead of finding a gun, they find a bloodstained stiletto, plus other materials tying the suspect to the crime. Suspecting now that the stiletto may be the actual murder weapon, doctors reexamine the body and discover—as sometimes happens—that a knife wound has been mistaken for a bullet wound.

The knife is inadmissible as evidence, and the other evidence probably will be thrown out of court as well. Because the police did not correctly describe what they expected to find, the warrant is invalid and the evidence inadmissible.

In fact, the easiest way to understand the Supreme Court's logic would be to think of Christopher Columbus's discovery of America. When Columbus sailed west from Spain, he knew *something* had to be out there. He expected to find India. Instead, he found the New World. Under the Supreme Court's rules of evidence, however, North and South America would have been inadmissable as evidence in the court of Ferdinand and Isabella when Columbus made the report of his discoveries.

The Supreme Court actually got on this tack well before the Warren era. As far back as the 1940s, the Court developed the principle of "mere evidence." This rather peculiar doctrine went roughly as follows: Just because the police suspect that a person has committed a crime, and just because they have obtained a search warrant to enter his home, that *still* doesn't mean they can go looking around his house for "mere evidence." The police have to say specifically what they are looking for. If they don't find what they described, then they can't use anything else they find in court.

What is under attack here is not just "unreasonable searches." What is under attack is the whole process of scientific investigation as applied to police work. The police are not allowed to use the same trial-and-error method that is used in almost every other form of human endeavor. In other words, the police are not allowed to *think* the same as everyone else while investigating crimes.

The failure to make any distinction between legitimate investigation into one particular crime and a *random* search for evidence of *any kind of crime* lay at the heart of the Court's misapprehension of the *Mapp* case. Obviously, there was *something* grossly unfair about the way evidence was seized from Dolree Mapp's home and used to convict her. But the Court never quite managed to put its finger on it.

Certainly, the police had acted in a roughshod manner in gaining entrance to Mapp's home, but that was not the *fundamental* unfairness of her conviction. The police had acted on a tip, but that was customary at the time, and tips from a reliable source are still sufficient grounds to issue a search warrant. In entering Miss Mapp's home, the police may not have had a valid warrant, but that was still not the crux of the issue. If the police had taken the trouble, they almost certainly could have obtained a warrant.

Mapp did not know whether the warrant was valid or not, but she resisted anyway. At that point the police actions would have been perfectly justified. Forced entries are made all the time when people refuse to admit the police, and they are considered Constitutional.

No, the real crux of the unfairness in Dolree Mapp's conviction had nothing to do with the way in which police forced their way into her home. Where the obvious violation of her Fourth Amendment rights occurred is when she was *tried and convicted on a charge that the police weren't even contemplating when they entered her home in the first place.* It was at this point that the search ceased to be pursuant of the particular crime of harboring a fugitive or running a numbers operation and became nothing but a random ransacking of her home in search of evidence *of any kind of criminal activity.* It was here that the search became patently unreasonable and the police unquestionably violated the Fourth Amendment.

Having failed to make this distinction at the outset, however, the Supreme Court has gone on to compound this oversight into a continually evolving logical absurdity. Under the "mere evidence" doctrine, the courts now not only prevent the police from seizing evidence for a *different* crime from the one they are investigating. They now prohibit the police from seizing evidence for the *same* crime they are investigating if the police have not already described the evidence in the most specific detail in the original warrant. Criminal investigation is now a guessing game in which the police get one guess.

The courts have turned the investigation of crime into a guessing game in which the police get only one guess. Anything the police have not sufficiently described *before* they find it is not evidence. It is only "mere evidence."

In the Sheppard murder case in Boston, for example, the warrant used to search Sheppard's home directed police to look for "a fifth bottle of amaretto liquor, 2 nickel bags of marijuana, a woman's jacket that has been described as black-gray (charcoal), any possessions of Sandra D. Boulware, similar type wire and rope that match those on the body of Sandra D. Boulware, or in the above Thunderbird. A blunt instrument that might have been used on the victim, men's or women's clothing that may have blood, gasoline burns on them. Items that may have fingerprints of the victim."

What the police actually found was "a pair of bloodstained boots, bloodstains on the concrete floor, a woman's earring with bloodstains on it, a bloodstained envelope, a pair of men's jockey shorts and women's leotards with blood on them, three types of wire, and a woman's hairpiece, subsequently identified as the victim's."

The judge ruled at a pretrial hearing that the evidence was inadmissible. The warrant "failed to conform to the commands of the Fourth Amendment because it did not particularly describe the items to be seized."[5] (The decision was later reversed on another "good faith" ruling.) It would appear that, in order to conform with the courts' bizarre interpretations of the Fourth Amendment, the police have to be either prescient or psychic.

Unfortunately, the problem does not even stop there. These absurd subtleties and hairsplitting interpretations of the Fourth Amendment have eventually left so much power in the hands of judges—and particularly appeals court judges—that they now have broad latitude to substitute their own predilections for any decision reached in a fair and open trial procedure.

In California in 1978, for example, Dr. Theodore Frank, a convicted sex offender with a long record of child molestation, was released from a state mental hospital on the ground that he was "cured" of his condition. Six weeks later, 2-year-old Amy Sue Seltz disappeared from her front yard while being watched by a baby-sitter. A man answering Frank's description was later seen leading a small child into a wooded ravine. Amy Sue's body was found in the ravine a few days later. She had been raped and tortured. Foreign objects had been shoved into her anus and vagina, and her nipples had been crushed by a plierlike instrument.

A report quickly surfaced that a man answering Frank's description had been involved in another attempted abduction of a child on the same morning. Acting on this information, police obtained a warrant to search Frank's home. In the warrant the police specified they were looking for a plierlike instrument, articles of clothing, plus any "writings which could relate to the death of Amy and would indicate either participation and/or an interest in that death by Theodore Frank."

They discovered a pair of locking pliers that easily could have been the torture instrument. They also found diaries that Frank had kept while he was in the mental hospital. In them he had written, "Children, made to order outlet for my anger and sex. Innocent, trusting, scared, vulnerable and submissive . . . I want to give pain to these little children. I want to molest them. I want to be sadistic. I want to harm them."

Frank was tried, convicted, and sentenced to death by the gas chamber.

In 1985, the California Supreme Court—which is widely regarded as opposed to California's law on capital punishment—overturned Frank's death sentence (but not the conviction) on the grounds that the diaries, which had been read to the jury both during the trial and subsequent death-penalty hearing, were illegally seized.

Why were they illegally seized? The answer is a perfect illustration of Ambrose Bierce's dictum that a lawyer is "a person skilled in circumventing the law."

Had the police *failed* to offer a description of the evidence they eventually found—"writings which could relate to the death of Amy"—the California Supreme Court could have easily excluded the diaries on the grounds that they had not been sufficiently "described" in the warrant.

But in this case, the police had furnished an almost exact description of what eventually turned up. So the California Supreme Court simply turned the issue around and argued it the other way. The warrant, the majority ruled, had been "overbroad" and based on mere "speculation." The meticulous description was only "boilerplate" material, written as a pretext to allow police to "rummage" through Frank's belongings.[6]

One way or another, after all these years, the police still just can't seem to get it right.

The exclusionary rule has become a kind of unilateral disarmament of American law enforcement. The police are not allowed to use the normal tools of human reasoning that have been employed by human beings since time began and are applied to every other human pursuit, from scientific investigation to learning to play the saxophone.

All this has nothing to do with "police brutality" or breaking down people's doors, or even—as the Court commonly phrases it—"invading the defendant's reasonable right to privacy." What the police are being prevented from doing here is *thinking.*

Civil libertarians continually argue that we need the exclusionary rule because it is all that stands between us and a police state. That claim seems a bit exaggerated. Every European country, Canada, Australia, Israel, the whole "Free World," in fact, all function without the exclusionary rule. None of these countries is a police state. On the other hand, the only other country that has adopted the exclusionary rule is the Philippines. That country is, arguably, a police state.

The Fourth Amendment—in a reasonable interpretation—needs some kind of enforcement mechanism. I will suggest one possible solution after I have discussed the expanded use of habeas corpus proceedings. But it must be pointed out that the whole premise that we have to prevent the police from investigating crime in order to avoid a "police state" is a dangerous misunderstanding. If we ever have a police state in this country, it isn't going to be imposed by the *police*. It would only come after the vast majority of people has given up hope that the current system can ever "establish justice" or "ensure domestic tranquility." In a small way, the exclusionary rule continually pushes us in that direction.

The exclusionary rule has been a failed experiment, an ill-thought-out idea, hastily imposed by the Supreme Court in the unrealistic expectation that turning dangerous people loose on society would somehow "improve respect for law enforcement." At one time there may have been some general deterrent effect that trickled down to the average citizen. But these protections have long since been institutionalized through other means. Their effects have now been completely overwhelmed by the relentless pressure from criminals and their attorneys to exploit the flaws of the exclusionary rule to their own advantage.

The exclusionary rule obviously trifles with the rights and fears of the majority. In a way, it is hard to understand why it isn't unconstitutional, since its benefits are bestowed almost exclusively on guilty criminals. This seems to clearly violate the principle of "equal protection under the law."

In attaching the exclusionary rule to the Fourth Amendment, the Warren Court was trying to prevent the police from "acting as judge and jury" in making unwarranted searches and trumping up charges against unsuspecting people. After many years, however, the result has gone much further. The *judge and jury* are now frequently prevented from acting as judge and jury. The public's representation in the courtroom—the jury— often doesn't get to hear the real facts of a case because so much of the evidence has been excluded from court. In countless American courtrooms today, *no one* has the right to try a defendant with evidence that clearly suggested that that person has committed a crime.

Is it any wonder in such a situation that people start to think about "taking the law into their own hands?"

CONFESSIONS 6

PERHAPS NO CASE has symbolized the controversy generated by the Supreme Court under Chief Justice Earl Warren as much as *Miranda v. Arizona,* the case that required police to read suspects their "Miranda rights."

That the case caused mayhem in the justice system there can be no doubt. Right from the initial day of June 16, 1966, when the Supreme Court overturned the conviction of four obviously guilty criminals, one of the most visceral spectacles in American justice has become the confessed criminal getting off because police "didn't properly inform him of his rights."

That there was need of some kind of reform, there can also be little doubt. One of the factors that influenced Earl Warren in the decision was the "dragnet" arrests of dozens of blacks in the District of Columbia "on suspicion" of some crime committed by one or two people of similar description.

Miranda also served as the high-water mark of the Warren era. Only two years later, Senator Sam Ervin, soon to be called one of the nation's greatest Constitutional scholars, was leading the fight against the confirmation of Justice Abe Fortas on the basis of broad-scale opposition to the Court's decisions on "the rights of defendants." Although the Warren majority never assembled itself for another major decision, the *Miranda* was the capstone of their efforts.

More than anything, though, the *Miranda* decision is high drama. It pits the well-meaning and vaguely plausible liberalism of the Warren majority against two opposing viewpoints—the logically impeccable Constitutional scholarship of Justice John Harlan and the devastatingly hard-nosed realism of Justice Byron White.

Justice White's dissent, in particular, is a monumentally prophetic document. The whole flavor of his criticism can be summarized in one bitterly reproachful passage:

> I have no desire whatsoever to share the responsibility for any such impact [this decision will have] on the present criminal process.
>
> In some unknown number of cases the Court's rule will return a killer, a rapist or other criminal to the streets and to the environment which produced him, to repeat his crime whenever it pleases him. As a consequence, there will not be a gain, but a loss of human dignity. The real concern is not the unfortunate consequences of this new decision on the criminal law as an abstract, disembodied series of authoritative proscriptions, but the impact on those who rely on the public authority for protection and who without it can only engage in violent self-help with guns, knives and the help of their neighbors similarly inclined. There is, of course, a saving factor: the next victims are uncertain, unnamed, and unrepresented in this case.

In March 1963, a mildly retarded 18-year-old girl in Phoenix, Arizona, reported that she was raped by a small, light-skinned Mexican man. Several days later, after an investigation, police went to the home of a man named Ernesto Miranda who had a history of similar offenses. Police took him to the station house, where the young woman observed him in a line-up. She identified him as the offender.

Police then took Miranda into an adjoining interrogation room and confronted him with the victim's testimony. At first he denied any involvement in the case, but after two hours of questioning he signed a written confession. He was tried, convicted, and sentenced to twenty years in jail.

Civil-liberties attorneys seized the case as an example of a "forced confession" and appealed it all the way to the Supreme Court. There, on June 13, 1966, the Court overturned the conviction, along with three others based on confessions, and announced its new "Miranda rule" for informing suspects of their rights, prior to police interrogations.

In the most specific terms, the Court stated:

> In the absence of other effective measures the following procedures to safeguard the Fifth Amendment privilege must be observed: The person in custody must, prior to interrogation, be clearly informed that he has the right to remain silent, and that anything he says will be used

against him in court; he must be clearly informed that he has the right to consult with a lawyer, and to have a lawyer with him during interrogation, and that, if he is indigent, a lawyer will be appointed to represent him.

The confession issue had been brewing for many years. It involves, as often happens, a conflict of two Constitutional principles. It brings to the fore several ambiguities at the heart of our legal system.

The criminal justice system in America and England is "accusatory," rather than the "inquisitional" system of continental Europe and most other parts of the world. In the European system, the judge is an investigator. He can examine witnesses and direct the efforts of the prosecution. The judge embodies society's right to get to the truth of any situation.

Our system, on the other hand, is adversarial, originally derived— strangely enough—from trial by combat. The prosecution and defense are the opposing contestants, and the judge is the referee. The presumption is that if both parties vigorously present their side of the question under neutral rules, the truth will eventually emerge. (We do occasionally depart from this format. Judge John Sirica, a federal trial court judge, for example, went considerably beyond his neutral role to get to the bottom of the Watergate situation.)

The British system itself, even apart from the embellishments we have added, is far more lenient toward the defendant than most other countries. There is a "presumption of innocence," and the burden of proof rests on the prosecution to prove guilt "beyond a reasonable doubt."

In Japan, by contrast, there is a strong ethic that favors confession. Admitting guilt is regarded as a step toward rehabilitation. Defendants are subject to extensive pretrial examinations, and there is little defense mounted. Conviction rates are about 95 percent, as opposed to about 60 percent here. (Interestingly enough, American defense attorneys themselves usually estimate that 90–95 percent of their clients are guilty.) Japan also has crime rates about ten times lower than ours.

The presumption of innocence in our system is emphasized by several provisions outlined in the Bill of Rights. Among them is the Fifth Amendment's guarantee that "no person . . . shall be compelled in any criminal case to be a witness against himself."

Traditionally, in both England and the United States, this phrase has meant that no accused person could be compelled to take the witness stand *at his own trial.* This refusal to offer a defense, however, carries a strong implication of guilt. Indeed, in the British system today, judges and prosecutors are allowed to make this point to the jury.

We have refined the system even further by saying that the defendant's refusal to testify cannot be taken as a presumption of guilt. Judges regularly instruct juries "not to hold the defendant's failure to testify on his own behalf against him"—although it seems likely that occasional jurors fail to heed this instruction.

The question that has always nagged the system, however, is this: If a person can't be forced to testify against himself at trial, why should he be forced to cooperate with the police at any point? Answering questions at the station house is, after all, just as potentially self-incriminating as answering them in court, especially when "anything you say may be held against you."

Of course a defendant can always repudiate his confession later—and in fact this has happened in a great number of instances, both before and after the *Miranda* decision. Still, if a defendant's self-incriminating testimony can be read in court, what difference does it make at that point if he has the "right to remain silent" before the judge and jury?

Balanced against this are the compelling realities of police work. Like it or not, there is little the police can do to solve numerous crimes without interrogating suspects. With many murders, rapes, and robberies, there is little physical evidence. Eyewitness identifications, although they usually impress juries, are actually regarded as the most unreliable form of evidence by police and prosecutors. There are very few instances where an airtight case can be made from circumstantial evidence.

This does not mean that the only recourse of the police is to beat confessions out of people. Usually it is just the opposite. Guilty people often confess readily. In other cases, they offer alibis and excuses that turn out to be demonstrably false. Only when faced with these inconsistencies and obvious falsehoods do they break down and admit their guilt.

The importance of interrogation can be seen from the work of one of America's most famous detectives, Ellis H. Parker, often called the "American Sherlock Holmes." Parker, who served as chief of detectives in Burlington County, New Jersey, during the early 1900s, personally solved 226 of the 236 murders he investigated during his career.

Parker had a unique theory of investigations. He believed that the person who had the *best alibi* was usually the guilty party. "The average person doesn't know precisely where he was every minute of the day," he often said. "He has no reason to. It is only someone who has carefully rehearsed his whereabouts who is likely to have a good story."

Parker once solved the murder of a Fort Dix soldier by concentrating on the one suspect among over a hundred interviewed who had a precise accounting of his whereabouts at the time of the murder. He was eventually able to punch holes in the story, and the suspect finally confessed.[1]

While popular interpretations of *Miranda* concentrated on the image of innocent men being beaten into confessing, even the five Supreme Court Justices who made up the Warren majority on *Miranda* were willing to admit that beatings and police brutality were not their major concern. Rather it was *confessions themselves* and the whole "coercive" atmosphere of police interrogation that was the subject of their concerns. Wrote Chief Justice Warren for the majority:

> To maintain a "fair state–individual balance," to require the govern-
> ment "to shoulder the entire load," to respect the inviolability of the
> human personality, our accusatory system of criminal justice demands
> that the government seeking to punish an individual produce the
> evidence against him by its own independent labors, rather than by the
> cruel, simple expedient of compelling it from his own mouth.

Thus, it was not simple admissions of "I did it" that the Warren majority wanted to head off. The court also wanted to shield defendants from statements and alibis that might later prove false. In fact, the Warren majority was striking at what had long been regarded as the heart of the "detective" process.

Perhaps the easiest way to summarize the Warren majority's decision is to say that the justices decided to look at things from the criminal's point of view. Would a rational person ever confess to a crime? Would an individual ever open himself to certain punishment if he or she were surrounded by "the proper influences," as the majority wrote? "The entire thrust of police interrogation . . . in all the cases today, was to put the defendant in such an emotional state as to impair his capacity for rational judgment . . . [T]he compelling atmosphere of the in-custody interrogation, and not an independent decision on his part, caused the defendant to speak."

As Justice White replied in his dissent, "The obvious underpinning of the Court's decision is a deep-seated distrust of all confessions . . . [T]he result adds up to a judicial judgment that evidence from the accused should not be used against him in any way, whether compelled or not, [and] that it is inherently wrong for the police to gather evidence from the accused himself."

The *Miranda* ruling addressed four cases. In each instance, there was not the slightest doubt about the individual's guilt. Each conviction had ample corroborating evidence. In only one case was there any extended detainment, and that was a murder where there was a question of which one of a number of individuals had committed the crime. In the other cases, the confession was only a kind of "finishing touch" to an investigation in which guilt had basically been established.

Michael Vignera was a small-time New York City crook with a history of armed robberies. On October 11, 1960, a man answering his description robbed a Brooklyn dress shop. Three days later Vigera was brought in for questioning. He was identified by the store owner and a saleslady. He admitted to a detective that he had committed the robbery.

Eight hours later, he made the same confession to an assistant district attorney in the presence of a court stenographer. He was tried and convicted. As a three-time loser, he was sentenced to 30-to-60 years.

On appeal, it was argued that he hadn't been formally informed of his rights either by detectives or the assistant district attorney. The Warren majority overturned the conviction.

Carl Calvin Westover was a career criminal with a warrant outstanding against him in California. On March 20, 1963, he was picked up in Kansas City as a suspect in two robberies. He was booked and held overnight. The next morning he was questioned for a few hours by local police, but he denied any involvement in the crimes.

Around noon, the FBI entered the case and began questioning him on the California charges. Ironically, the FBI already had a system for warning suspects of their rights. One of the keystones of the Warren majority's opinion, in fact, was a long letter from the U.S. solicitor general testifying that the FBI had long told suspects of their "right to remain silent," and that this had not disrupted law enforcement. The Warren majority offered this as proof that such an elaborate set of rules could work.

In this instance, though, the majority said the FBI did not show enough consideration for the rights of the accused:

> Although the two law enforcement authorities are legally distinct and the crimes for which they interrogated Westover were different, *the impact on him* was that of a continuous period of questioning. There is

no evidence of any warning given prior to the FBI interrogation nor is there any evidence of an articulated waiver of rights after the FBI commenced its interrogation. The record simply shows that the defendant did in fact confess a short time after being turned over to the FBI following interrogation by local police. Despite the fact that the FBI agents gave warnings at the outset of their interview, *from Westover's point of view* the warnings came at the end of the interrogation process. In these circumstances an intelligent waiver of constitutional rights cannot be assumed. [my emphasis]

In the last case, Roy Allen Stewart, "an indigent Los Angeles Negro who had dropped out of school in sixth grade," came under suspicion for a series of purse-snatchings in which one victim had resisted and was beaten to death. Police went to Stewart's house, where they encountered Stewart, his wife, and three other visitors. They asked and received Stewart's permission to search the house. Police quickly discovered items taken from five other robbery victims.

Anticipating—as often happens—that Stewart might blame the robberies on one of his companions, police arrested the whole group. They were all held in jail for five days during which Stewart was identified by several robbery victims. He was interrogated nine times before he eventually confessed, saying he "hadn't meant to hurt the woman." He was sentenced to death. The conviction had already been overturned by the California Supreme Court on the basis of a coerced confession, and the Warren majority upheld this decision.

As Chief Justice Warren wrote:

> Again we stress that the modern practice of in-custody interrogation is psychologically rather than physically oriented. As we have stated before, . . . "coercion can be mental as well as physical, and that the blood of the accused is not the only hallmark of an unconstitutional inquisition." (*Blackburn v. Alabama,* 1960)

One of the chief concerns of the Warren majority was that police questioning went on out of the hearing of the Court:

> Interrogation still takes place in privacy. Privacy results in secrecy and this in turn results in a gap in our knowledge as to what in fact goes on in the interrogation rooms.

As Justice White pointed out, this was demonstrably false. Most interrogation sessions were recorded, sometimes by the detective's notes, often by a professional court stenographer. "Insofar as appears from the Court's opinion," he wrote, "it has not examined a single transcript of any police interrogation, let alone the interrogation that took place in any one of these cases which it decides today."

It was here that the Warren majority made its most controversial decision. Instead of trying to investigate real interrogations, it referred instead to several police manuals and commercial textbooks on interrogation that were in wide circulation at the time.

> [T]he setting prescribed by the manuals and observed in practice becomes clear. In essence, it is this: To be alone with the subject is essential to prevent distraction and to deprive him of any outside support. The aura of confidence in his guilt undermines his will to resist. He merely confirms the preconceived story the police seek to have him describe. *Patience and persistence,* at times relentless questioning, are employed. To obtain a confession, the interrogator must "patiently maneuver himself or his quarry into a position from which the desired objective may be attained."
>
> Even without employing brutality, the "third degree" or the specific strategems described above, the very fact of custodial interrogation exacts a heavy toll on individual liberty and trades on the weakness of individuals . . . [emphasis added]

Some of the tactics described in the interrogation manuals were admittedly manipulative and would easily be acknowledged as illegal. *Fundamentals of Criminal Investigation,* for example, written by a former federal investigator, described the following tactic:

> The accused is placed in a line-up, but this time he is identified by several fictitious witnesses or victims who associated him with different offenses. It is expected that the subject will become desperate and confess to the offense under investigation in order to escape from the false accusations.

But for the most part, the manuals recommend only what the Warren majority referred to—critically—as "patience and persistence." The books outline the "good cop, bad cop" routine, where one officer tries to win the defendant's confidence while the other questions him harshly. One manual even recommends that, if the suspect exercises his right to remain silent, the request should be readily granted. "This usually has a very undermining effect. First of all, he is disappointed in his expectation of an unfavorable reaction on the part of the interrogator. Secondly, a concession of this right to remain silent impresses the subject with the apparent fairness of the interrogator."

Most important to the Warren Court's scenario for a proper interrogation was the presence of a defense attorney. In dealing with the defendant's right to counsel, the Warren majority tried to paint a picture where the attorney would somehow *assist* the police by "guarantee[ing] that the accused gives a fully accurate statement to the police and that the statement is rightly reported by the prosecution at trial." Justice Harlan quickly saw the hypocrisy of this pious hope:

> The Court's vision of a lawyer "mitigat[ing] the dangers of untrustworthiness" by witnessing coercion and assisting accuracy in the confession is largely a fancy; for if counsel arrives there is rarely going to be a police station confession. [Quoting Justice Jackson:] "Any lawyer worth his salt will tell the suspect in no uncertain terms to make no statement to the police under any circumstances."

Indeed, many defendants have since been able to have their confessions thrown out of court on the grounds that their lawyers were "incompetent" for allowing them to make statements to the police.

It is nearly impossible to read the decision of the Warren majority, then, without coming to one simple conclusion. The Court was feeling a little sorry for criminals. It was beginning to "look at things from the criminal's point of view"—as the majority specifically stated in considering the case of Webster and the FBI.

There is nothing wrong with this. The continuing evolution of our culture demands that we constantly renew our perspective and consider different viewpoints. Of course it is a lot safer when this enterprise is undertaken by novelists and movie directors than by a majority of the Supreme Court.

Nevertheless, that is what happened. Now, twenty years after *Miranda*, it should be possible to get a pretty good picture of the effects that the decision has had on confessions, on law enforcement, and on the whole society.

First, and probably most important, the justice system has largely absorbed *Miranda*. There are very few cases on confessions that reach the Supreme Court anymore. Confessions are still disputed, but they are usually argued at the state level—especially in states like New York and California, where the state judiciary has tried to extend these protections far beyond even what the Supreme Court has required.

Second, there have been real improvements. Few police officers I have talked to have said they would want to undo *Miranda*. Almost all argue that awareness of the defendant's Constitutional rights against self-incrimination have increased "professionalism" among the police. Indeed, the beat officers I have met can often give you a full dissertation on the subtleties of the law, including citations of key cases.

Third, there seems to be a strong feeling among minority communities that the worst police practices have been eliminated by *Miranda*. Claude Brown still calls the passing of the Warren Court "the biggest loss for black people in the last twenty years."

What have the effects been on crime, however? It is almost incontestable that Miranda weakened law enforcement during the late 1960s and early 1970s. It probably contributed to the surge in crime rates during that era and continues to slow the process of justice today.

Critics of this perspective always parade out the statistics showing that only a small percentage of cases are lost entirely due to disallowed confessions. However, these bottom-line numbers once again do not begin to measure the actual results. Once again, the real action has been in plea-bargaining.

Miranda had two basic results. First, it gave the defense more leverage, allowing defendants to drive a harder bargain in plea-bargaining, which clogs the courts and gives the defense even *more* leverage. Second, in a number of highly visible cases, confessed criminals go free on "improper warnings." This severely demoralizes the public.

There is nothing more horrifying to the average person than the sense that the state cannot even deal with *confessed* criminals. People depend on the government to be stronger than themselves in dealing with crime. When the picture emerges that criminals are stronger than the government, a huge demoralization takes place. People become afraid to stand up to crime because they fear the government is weak or not on their side. This paralyzing fear that "the criminals are winning" then becomes itself a major impediment to law enforcement.

Once again, almost all of this was anticipated by Justice White in his remarkable dissent:

> The rule announced today will measurably weaken the ability of the criminal law to [protect the public.] It is a deliberate calculus to prevent interrogations, to reduce the incidence of confessions and pleas of guilty, and to increase the number of trials.

Justice White's prediction was right on target. An extensive study of the California superior courts over the 1960s and '70s shows a dramatic change in the way criminal charges were resolved after 1966, the year *Miranda* was announced. In 1966, over 60 percent of accused persons pleaded guilty to the *original* charges, while 27 percent of the cases were resolved by guilty pleas to *reduced* charges.

One year later the entire pattern had changed significantly. In 1967 alone, pleas on the original charges dropped to 42 percent, while reduced pleas rose to 39 percent. The change was never as dramatic after 1967, but an inexorable drift toward reduced charges set in, so that by 1973, 47 percent of all cases were settled on *reduced* charges (up from 29 percent) while only 39 percent were pleaded at the original top charge (down from 60 percent).

Throughout this period, the percentage of convictions won through full-dress trials remained stable at 10–12 percent. Looking for the results in the area of trial convictions might lead to the belief that *Miranda* had changed nothing. The real action, however, was among the 90 percent of cases that are settled by plea-bargaining. There *Miranda* changed everything.[2]

The new rule allowed defense attorneys to "clog the courts" with motions challenging confessions. (The almost identical situation in searches and seizures also helped, of course.) When police had reached a stage where they were fairly certain they had solved a crime, they usually sought a confession. Now it was not so easy. Even if a confession was obtained, it might be thrown out of court as "coerced." As a result of dealing with the new rules, prosecutors gradually gave ground. No longer were "career criminals" sent away for thirty years at a stretch. By 1973, out of 31,000 felony *arrests* made in Manhattan, only 4,100 resulted in *felony* convictions. The vast majority were plea-bargained down to misdemeanors.[3]

In addition, of course, there is the usual catalogue of atrocities in individual cases. In some states it now seems as if it is almost *illegal* to confess to a crime. Consider some of the following:

—In Philadelphia in 1970, a man murdered his grandmother and elderly aunt with a hatchet. He was read his rights and readily confessed. Philadelphia police, however, had made up a "Miranda" card that read, "anything that you say may be held *for or* against you," instead of simply "against you," as the original Supreme Court decision specified. The courts held that the wrong wording had "created a false sense of security" in the suspect. The conviction was dismissed and the man went free.

—In 1977, in upstate New York, Linda Jill Velzy, an 18-year-old student at the State University College at Oneonta, was abducted during a snowstorm while hitchhiking back to campus. Suspicion immediately fell on Ricky Knapp, a 27-year-old convicted sex offender with a long series of similar crimes.

A friend of Knapp's, who was facing a minor charge himself, agreed to help police. He talked to Knapp, who confessed to him. On the advice of police, the friend persuaded Knapp to try to move the body to a safer burial ground. Police caught the pair red-handed. "I'm sick. Kill me," Knapp blurted out, and readily confessed.

Knapp was convicted on second-degree murder and sentenced to twenty-five years in prison. In 1982, however, the New York State Court of Appeals threw out the confession. They said that because Knapp's friend had in effect become a "police agent," when talking to him he should have warned Knapp of his "right to remain silent."

At the second trial, Knapp changed his story considerably. He now argued that Velzy had demanded to have sex with him and had started attacking him when he refused to pay her. He killed her only "accidentally" and in "self-defense." Hearing nothing of the original circumstances or confession, the jury convicted Knapp only on the charge of failing to get Velzy medical attention after beating her to death. He is appealing again.

—In 1968, Pamela Powers, a nine-year-old girl, went to the YMCA in Des Moines, Iowa, to watch her brother participate in a wrestling match. While going for candy, she was abducted by 23-year-old Robert Anthony Williams, a convicted child molestor and escapee from a Missouri mental institution, who was staying in a hotel room on the eighth floor. Williams took Pamela to his room and raped her. She died, apparently from choking on his semen.

Williams attempted to dispose of her body by carrying it through the lobby, wrapped in a blanket. A twelve-year-old boy saw him and reported it to the police. Two days later, with warrants out for his arrest, Williams surrendered in Davenport, Iowa. He was advised of his rights and spoke to a lawyer in Davenport over the phone. The police captain who was scheduled to pick up Williams heard the lawyer tell Williams over the phone, "You're going to have to lead them to the body."

The murder had occurred on Christmas Eve, and on the ride back from Davenport the captain casually remarked, "The Powerses want to give their daughter a good Christian burial." Over an hour later, without any prompting, Williams suddenly told the police that he would take them to the body.

Williams was tried and convicted of murder. In 1977, however, the Supreme Court ruled 5-to-4 that the police captain's statement about the "Christian burial" had been "psychologically coercive." The Court ordered a retrial. The body was admitted as evidence, since its discovery was ruled as "inevitable" (search parties were within 1/8th of a mile at the time), but the method of its discovery was inadmissible.

Williams was convicted a second time, and appealed again. In 1983— fifteen years after the murder—the Eighth Circuit Court of Appeals once again overturned the conviction and ordered Iowa to either retry Williams in thirty days *without* the body or let him go free. Only a hasty ruling from the Supreme Court reversed this decision and once again reinstated the conviction.

It could be argued, I suppose, that these cases are simply important legal exercises carried on by judges and attorneys for the benefit of defining and redefining the law for future reference. But before I ever heard of the case, I met a 26-year-old congressional staff member who had grown up with the Pamela Powers story in Des Moines. She said the Williams case had cast a pall over her entire childhood. For years she was unable to overcome the quiet terror that a man who had killed a little girl was going to be allowed to go free and no one could do anything about it. As an adult she had joined a national victims organization precisely because of the residue of fear that remained from that childhood experience.

—In 1980, Stephen Zwickert, a high-school honor student in Queens, New York, was robbed on his way home from a school dance. When he resisted giving up his class ring, he was killed with a .38-caliber revolver. The story made the front page of the New York papers.

Three days later, Angel Claudio, one of the two attackers, was stricken with remorse. He picked a lawyer out of the yellow pages and told him he wanted to confess. The lawyer accompanied him to the Queens district attorney's office where Claudio made a statement. He was charged with second-degree murder.

Less than two months later, a trial judge threw out the confession on the grounds that Claudio's lawyer had been "incompetent" for allowing his client to confess. It was only after several months of public outrage that a New York appellate division reversed the trial judge and reinstated the confession.

Meanwhile, Claudio had changed his mind. On the advice of his new attorney, he repudiated his confession. His new lawyer appealed to the New York State Court of Appeals, which again upheld the confession. It wasn't until five years after his voluntary confession that Claudio was finally convicted of murder and sentenced to 35-years-to-life in jail.

—In Las Vegas in 1983, a man walked into the police station and confessed to murdering a patron during a hotel robbery a year before. He said he wanted to get the matter off his conscience. After hiring a lawyer, the man agreed to make a videotaped confession with the understanding that the state would not seek the death penalty.

The state accepted the bargain. However, after spending several months in jail awaiting sentencing, the man changed his mind about wanting to go to prison. He now said he wanted to withdraw the confession. A Nevada appeals court ruled that, since the original confession had been made voluntarily, it could also be withdrawn voluntarily—*even though the state had done everything to hold up its end of the bargain.* The killer walked out of jail a free man.

The Warren Court's efforts to "see things from the criminal's perspective," then, has had a profound impact on American life. Perhaps the strangest outcome of all, however, is that, despite all the procedural safeguards that the Warren Court put in place, *criminals regularly continue to confess to crimes.*

The Warren majority recognized this possibility from the beginning. Several parties who argued the case charged that what the court really wanted was a "station-house attorney" permanently on hand to represent all accused criminals. The majority specifically rejected this possibility. But it did perceive the dilemma that—short of a Constitutional "interpretation" that all suspects *must* have the aid of an attorney while being questioned by police—there was no guarantee that accused criminals weren't going to go ahead and talk to the police anyway.

Chief Justice Warren agonized over this possibility in his majority opinion. He wrote "The defendant who does not ask for counsel is the very defendant who most needs counsel." Still, the Warren majority had to admit that if the defendant waived his rights, "voluntarily, knowingly, and intelligently," there was nothing the Court could do about it.

Confoundedly, accused criminals continue to do just that. In Washington, D.C., in the late 1960s, a team of legal activists set up a 24-hour hotline offering free legal counsel to anyone brought in for questioning throughout the district. A year later, the project quietly closed down. Less than 15 percent of all arrestees were using it.

To be sure, many confessed criminals decide *afterward* that maybe they would have been smarter to keep their mouths shut. But that is a different story altogether.

Every police detective I have interviewed has always made the same observation. In one way or another, they say, most criminals *want to confess.*

"They want to get it off their chests," said Mike Sheehan, a New York City police detective who has heard hundreds of confessions. "Or they may want to rationalize it. Very often they don't think they've done anything wrong. They often have a strange kind of value system. Or else they have their own interpretation of events that they want you to know. But the idea of police giving suspects the third degree in order to force confessions out of them is silly. All you have to do is find the right framework to make them feel comfortable, and they'll usually tell you the whole story."

And so, all over the country, accused criminals continue to sign the police forms and waive their rights to silence and counsel with remarkable regularity. As one assistant district attorney told me "God bless these people who still make statements to the police. Without them we probably couldn't prosecute 85 percent of our cases."

There seem to be many reasons for this. Some criminals obviously feel challenged by taking on the police. They relish the idea that they can match wits with detectives. Criminals often have a very exaggerated idea of their own intelligence and regard calling a lawyer as a cop-out.

Other criminals plainly distrust their legal counsel—especially when it is supplied by the public defenders' offices. One recent study showed that 50 percent of all convicted criminals felt their state-supplied attorney had been worthless. This is plainly not true and most public defenders seem to be doing a very worthy job. But to the guilty criminal, a state-supplied attorney is likely to seem just another part of "the system."

One experienced California detective has still another theory. He has found that guilty people are usually the *most eager* to waive their rights and get on with the interrogation. "They're usually dying to find out what the police already know," he said.

Finally, many accused people tend to see invoking their rights to silence and legal counsel as an admission of guilt, which despite everything the courts have done to dispel this notion, it plainly is. Only the most experienced, prison-wise defendants know enough to invoke their right to legal counsel. As Earl Warren said, they are the ones who need it least anyway.

That is one side of the story. But there is another element to all this—one that Justice White once again anticipated in his remarkable dissent. "Moreover," he wrote, "it is by no means certain that the process of confessing is injurious to the accused. To the contrary it may provide psychological relief and enhance the prospects for rehabilitation."

Despite all their efforts to "put themselves in the criminals' place," the Warren majority never seems to have realized that, at bottom, most people who commit crimes know somewhere in their minds that they have done something wrong. As Dostoyevsky showed in *Crime and Punishment,* criminal acts separate people out from normal society in a way that most people eventually find too difficult to bear. At bottom, there is a great psychological relief in finally admitting guilt—even if it means opening the way to punishment.

Even Karl Menninger puts confession at the center of his psychological approach to curing crime. Quoting one doctor's description of a successful pre-release program, Menninger said:

> The thing that impressed me most was the need to confess, not only about previous misdeeds but about current temptations. The similarity between this meeting and that of an Alcoholics Anonymous group came readily to mind as member after member recited his success in painfully turning his back on an open cash register, or forcibly taking himself in hand to pass up a parked car with a key still in the ignition. . . . Listening to these troubled accounts of convicts grappling with

inner urges they don't understand, one could become convinced of the "addictive" nature of crime.[4]

It is remarkable that for all the psychological studies we have about death and dying, the loss of loved ones, marriage breakups, and the effects of divorce on children, etc., there is almost no contemporary literature on the psychology of guilt and confessions. A search of the periodical indexes over the last fifteen years reveals that although there are about seventy-five law articles written each year on the various subtleties of *Miranda*, not a single article has been written in this country over the last ten years on the psychology of why people confess to crimes.

The only article in the entire literature is a piece written in 1979 by two British sociologists. They noted that confession is "inherently contradictory." Although it is "part of the apparatus of state control," it also "offers the individual offender an opportunity for moral regeneration in the sense that having violated one of society's most sacred norms, he is provided with a means of reconciliation." For the society as a whole, it is "a confirmatory indication of the validity of the set of social relations within which the offender is enmeshed" and "an important means of indicating the shared humanity upon which the justification of a whole way of life is based."[5]

My own impression is that there seem to be four basic responses to having committed a crime: denial, defiance, rationalization, and confession.

Unapprehended criminals often show defiance, even if they felt guilty about the crime in the first place. Many criminals start to feel "invincible," especially if they have gotten away with things a few times.

On the other hand, criminals often have the ability to deny the reality of their crimes, even to themselves. Defense attorneys I have talked with have often expressed amazement at their clients' abilities to deny guilt in the face of overwhelming evidence. "I think these guys could probably pass lie-detector tests," one attorney told me. "They seem to be able to fool themselves in a way that most ordinary people find impossible."

Rationalization often accompanies confession. In fact, many confessions are in fact rationalizations. As Baldwin and McConville note, many confessions are "ways of alleviating the burden of guilt and placing part or whole of the responsibility on others or on the force of circumstances."[6]

Complete confession, with the full accompaniment of guilt and responsibility, only comes with some social prodding.

Newspaper reporters often get a very good lesson in the psychology of confession when they cover politics. One of the most common occurrences during a political scandal or debate is to have one of the principals call you into his office and spend the better part of an hour-and-a-half pouring out his heart and relieving his conscience on an issue. Then he will look at you and say, "Of course, all this is off the record."

Criminals want to confess, but they want their confessions to be "off the record." They want the psychological relief and purging that comes with admitting their role in something, but they don't necessarily want to live with the consequences.

It is at this moment that the defense attorney enters. Faced with an admission of guilt, he immediately argues the confession was made "involuntarily, unknowingly, and unwillingly given." Why, he asks incredulously, would anyone make statements that are so obviously self-incriminating?

Six months later, the trial judge encounters a neatly dressed, polite, composed defendant who tells him sincerely that his incriminating statements were coerced from him by the police. Three years later, five appellate-court judges will look at the written record of the trial and say to each other "Why would anyone ever admit to all this stuff? The police must have coerced him. He never would have said these things on his own."

And so, the prosecution will be forced to go back and retry the defendant "without the confession"—*and without any other evidence that was produced as a result of the confession.* The *Miranda* case, it must be remembered, has added its own "exclusionary rule"—with more arbitrary rights bestowed on *guilty* people—to the Constitution. Nor can anything gathered as the *result* of a confession be admissible at a trial once the confession is ruled unconstitutional.

What this all means in practice can be illustrated by the case of Emmanuel Torres, a 22-year-old New York gang member eventually convicted of killing aspiring actress Caroline Isenberg after trying to rape her on a rooftop in 1984.

Torres came under suspicion because he frequented the building where his father was the janitor. He resembled the man described by Isenberg (she lived seven hours before succumbing to knife wounds). He also had a reputation for violence—and was in fact originally mentioned to police by a member of his own family.

When brought in for questioning, Torres was advised of his rights, but he refused counsel. After seven hours of questioning, he admitted to the attempted rape and murder. He argued that he had met Isenberg on the elevator, that she had responded to his advances and agreed to go to the rooftop, but that she had then changed her mind and started hitting him—at which point he was forced to knife her in "self-defense." (This explanation was cast in doubt by an override button on the elevator that could send the car directly to the roof bypassing all other stops, which would have made it possible for Torres to take Caroline to the roof against her will.)

Torres made a videotaped confession and then wrote out his own two-page version of the story in longhand. "He was very articulate," said Mike Sheehan, who handled the interrogation. "His spelling and grammar were perfect."

When television and newspaper cameras caught Torres on the way to his arraignment a few hours later, he shouted at them, "She deserved it! She was a slut!" His sneering face was on the front page of the newspapers.

Five weeks later, Torres's defense attorney, Louis Levner, filed a motion to have the confession ruled inadmissible. He argued that it was only "bragging" by "a poor guy who wanted to prove his manhood."

Torres's trial was preceded by an extensive preliminary hearing in which half-a-dozen New York City detectives testified for almost a week about the exact circumstances under which Torres confessed.

At the proceedings, Torres was now a changed man. No longer sneering and defiant, he sat composed at the defense table, dressed in matching sports clothes, avidly following the testimony.

The 23-year-old defendant took the witness stand, saying he had never been read his rights and had been held incommunicado for hours by police detectives. He said that police had beaten him severely, and that he wrote his confession only after detectives threatened to cut off his hands.

In the end, Judge Stephen Crane ruled the confession admissible, saying he found the police detectives' account "totally believable." When the ruling was announced, Torres burst into tears, sobbing, "Why don't you just put the rope around my neck and hang me now." (New York does not have a death penalty.)

Torres was later convicted on the basis of his confession, including those made before television cameras. He is now appealing his case.

Even few *confessed* criminals, then, are willing to stand by their confession very long. Once they have purged themselves of guilt feelings, or rationalized their crimes, reality sets in. At the very least, their lawyers will coach them to come up with a different story, and will routinely challenge the constitutionality of their confession.

All this, however, does not mean that people are not guilty or that they don't confess to crimes. All it means is that after they have confessed, they now have a body of law to help them repudiate their confession. *Miranda*'s largest impact, in the end, has not been on defendants but on defense lawyers. They routinely arrive on the scene and charge that the police have already coerced their new clients into confessing.

But beneath these legal manipulations lies the truth. Trials were once forums in which society tried to find out what really happened. If they no longer function that way, then we must live without knowing the truth. But somehow the truth has a way of emerging anyway.

Even Ernesto Miranda eventually found this out. Although his first conviction was overturned, Miranda later confessed to a friend, who testified against him, leading to a second trial and a second conviction. He received a much shorter sentence and was back on the streets in 1973.

For a while he was making a small living selling personally autographed copies of the police department's "Miranda" cards. Then, one night in 1976, he got into a fight at a poker game. Somebody pulled out a knife and stabbed him in the chest. He died immediately.

The police arrived and read everybody their "Miranda rights." No one felt like talking. Since there had been a fight, and nobody was willing to testify against the killer, the matter was soon dropped.

No one was ever prosecuted for the murder of Ernesto Miranda.

HABEAS CORPUS 7

NOT ALL THE reforms of the Warren Court have had the same effect as the *Miranda* case and the exclusionary rule. Some of them have worked out very well.

Probably the most successful reform of the Warren era was the 1963 decision of *Gideon v. Wainwright,* which held that indigent defendants are entitled to legal representation at state expense. The 9-to-0 verdict is a reflection of the decision's obvious fairness.

Clarence Gideon was a small-time Florida criminal who was convicted of burglary in 1959. At his trial, he asked the state to provide him with legal counsel. He was refused, under *Betts v. Brady* (1942), which said that the state need only provide legal representation in capital cases where the death penalty was a possibility. Although many states then supplied indigents with attorneys in most cases, Florida was one that still did not.

Gideon appealed, filing the habeas corpus petition on his own behalf. He based his case on the Sixth Amendment, which states, in part:

> In all criminal prosecutions, the accused shall enjoy the right . . . to have compulsory process of obtaining witnesses in his favor, and to have the assistance of counsel for his defense.

Prior to the *Gideon* decision, the courts had interpreted this as meaning that a criminal defendant could not be prevented from hiring an attorney of his choice. Gideon was asking for a positive interpretation—counsel had to be provided even if he couldn't afford it.

The Florida State Supreme Court rejected the argument. So Gideon appealed to the U.S. Supreme Court where the case was joined by civil liberties groups. Abe Fortas, soon to be a justice himself, presented the oral arguments. The Court ruled that indigent defendants must be given free counsel in all felony cases. In 1971, the Court extended the ruling to any case where there was a possibility of imprisonment.

The decision marked the birth of the public defender's office. Attorneys in many large cities were already providing legal counsel to indigent defendants on a voluntary basis. Now it is done at public expense. Chicago, for example, spends $15 million each year on legal aid to the poor. In some rural areas, the entire legal communities may rotate in serving as public defenders. New York's Legal Aid Society—originally a volunteer group founded by German immigrants—now has sixty full-time attorneys.

The 5,000 full-time public defenders around the country now just about match the 8,000 attorneys working for the prosecutors' offices. An additional 150,000 private attorneys spend at least part of their time defending criminals.

All these new rules, involving protection against illegal searches and coerced confessions, plus the right to "competent" legal representation, have been packaged together in a new procedure that has made the appeal of criminal convictions infinitely easier. This package is based on the greatly expanded concept of habeas corpus.

Originally a judicial order to deal with people being jailed *without charges,* the writ of habeas corpus was turned, during the Warren era, into a sweeping mandate for federal oversight of the state courts. Even though the Constitution specifically states that criminal trials must take place at the state level, the expanded concept of habeas corpus has given the federal courts blanket permission to review all criminal cases. The rationale is that, although criminal prosecutions are a state matter, the convicted individual has "Constitutional rights" that are ultimately the responsibility of the federal government.

As a result, a single federal district judge can now overturn a criminal conviction that has been tried before a jury, appealed through the higher state courts, and ultimately approved by the state's entire judicial apparatus.

In practical terms, this means that criminal cases never really end— unless, of course, the defendant is acquitted. The prosecution never really wins a case, and the defense never really loses. Instead, after once convicting a person, the state must continually retry the case in state and federal appeals courts—often in the face of changing Constitutional interpretations. If the prosecution can be shown to have made any "significant error" in procedure (and often these errors seem rather insignificant), the defendant must be granted a new trial. The state must try to reassemble witnesses, persuade people to testify, gather evidence, and once again go through a full-blown trial, usually at great expense. If the defendant is reconvicted, he can simply start the appeals process all over again.

Habeas corpus petitions have no "statute of limitations." Nor is there any limit to the *number* of times a convicted person can go back into the courts to try to raise new issues. Thousands of convicted felons serving long-term sentences have become jailhouse lawyers, combing the statute books in search of some technicality or new ruling that may overturn their convictions. For convicted murderers facing the death penalty, habeas corpus has become an indefinite postponement of sentence.

Often called "The Great Writ," habeas corpus goes back to the Magna Carta. It was one of the major concessions that the nobility forced upon King John in 1215 at Runnymede.

The words mean, literally, "you have the body." It was intended to prevent people from being thrown in jail and detained indefinitely without formal charges. Kings and tyrants had the habit of dealing with political opposition by throwing people in jail and forgetting about them. Habeas corpus was meant to prevent this. A writ of habeas corpus, issued by a judge, told the sovereign to "fish or cut bait"—either bring the prisoner to trial on formal charges, or let him go.

The founding fathers considered habeas corpus such an essential part of the law that they wrote it into the main body of the Constitution. Article I, section 9, paragraph 2 reads as follows:

> The privilege of the writ of habeas corpus shall not be suspended, unless when in cases of rebellion or invasion the public safety may require it.

Like the rest of the Constitution, habeas corpus was originally interpreted as only applying to the federal government. During Reconstruction, however, the writ of habeas corpus was extended to state prisons. Then, in 1915, the Supreme Court agreed to hear a petition from a state convict who claimed that his trial had been a sham, overly influenced by hostile mobs. It was the first time the principle of habeas corpus had been extended to a prisoner *already* tried and convicted, and not simply being detained without any charges being brought against him.

For the next forty years, this extension of habeas corpus was used sparingly but effectively. It was a tool whereby the federal courts could intervene in state decisions where an injustice was obviously being done. To keep a measure of things, the Court developed the concept of "fundamental fairness." Not concentrating on technicalities, but looking at the entire question, the Court asked "Did the defendant really get a fair trial?" Many cases involved blacks who were being railroaded or punished unduly by Southern juries. The execution of the nine Scottsboro Boys for the rape of two white women, for example, was forestalled by a Federal writ of habeas corpus.

Still, intervention was rare and judicious. In accepting a habeas corpus petition in 1944, the Court wrote:

> Where the state courts have considered and adjudicated the merits of [a state prisoner's petition], a federal court will not ordinarily reexamine upon writ of habeas corpus the questions thus adjudicated. . . . But where resort to state court remedies has failed to afford a full and fair adjudication . . . a federal court should entertain his petition for habeas corpus, else he would be remediless.[1]

In *Brown v. Allen* (1953) the Court again expanded the scope of habeas corpus, saying that petitions could be "routine." But the floodgates didn't really open until 1963, when Earl Warren scrapped the fundamental fairness doctrine and wrote in *Townsend v. Sain*:

> If [a Federal district judge] concludes that the habeas applicant was afforded a full and fair hearing by the state court resulting in reliable findings, he may, and ordinarily should accept the facts as found in the hearing. *But he need not.* In every case he has the power, constrained only by his sound discretion, to receive evidence bearing upon the applicant's constitutional claim. [my emphasis][2]

As Macklin Fleming, former Justice of California Court of Appeals, wrote in 1974, "Thus was given to every federal district court a roving commission to intervene in any state criminal case that caught its fancy, either as to law or as to fact."[3]

Justice Tom Clark, who wrote the majority opinion in the *Mapp v. Ohio* decision on searches and seizures, but never joined the Warren majority on another important criminal case, said in his dissent:

[T]he effective administration of criminal justice in state courts receives a staggering blow. . . . Essential to the administration of justice is the prompt enforcement of judicial decrees. After today state judgments will be relegated to a judicial limbo, subject to federal collateral attack—as here—a score of years later.

This federal oversight has turned state criminal proceedings—and, above all, jury verdicts—into relatively unimportant events. A jury's "guilty" verdict is now often the *start* of a criminal proceeding. Once guilt and innocence are out of the way, then the real questions—the "Constitutional issues"—can begin.

This ballooning of the appeals process has created a whole new type of defense attorney. Once, defense attorneys were silver-tongued orators like Clarence Darrow, F. Lee Bailey, or William Kunstler, who waxed eloquent in the courtroom, playing on the sympathies of the jury.

Today the defense attorneys are likely to be Constitutional nitpickers who don't even bother to appear before the jury. They do all their work at the appellate level, dealing only with judges. Here is how Alan Dershowitz, perhaps the most successful of the new breed, describes his own vocation:

I am primarily, though not exclusively, an appellate lawyer—a lawyer of last resort. Defendants (and their lawyers) generally turn to me after the jury has rendered a verdict of guilty—and often after the appeal has been lost as well. They want me to try to obtain review in the United States Supreme Court or have them freed on a writ of habeas corpus. They are desperate.[4]

Nor does Dershowitz have any illusions about the nature of his profession:

Several of my clients have gone free because their constitutional rights were violated by agents of the government. In representing criminal defendants—especially guilty ones—it is often necessary to take the offensive against the government: to put the government on trial for *its* misconduct . . .

I am not unique in representing guilty defendants. That is what most defense attorneys do most of the time. . . . Any criminal lawyer who tells you that most of his clients are not guilty is either bluffing or deliberately limiting his practice to a few innocent defendants . . .

I do not apologize for (or feel guilty about) helping to let a murderer go free—even though I realize that someday one of my clients may go out and kill again. Since nothing like this has ever happened, I cannot know for sure how I would react. I know that I would feel terrible for the victim. But I hope I would not regret what I had done—any more than a surgeon should regret saving the life of a patient who recovers and later kills an innocent victim.[5]

The analogy is a little weak (a doctor who saves a dangerous patient expects someone else to isolate that patient from society, while the judges and lawyers *are* that someone else). But the point is clear. Jury verdicts, public participation—"the truth"—are no longer the important factors. Everything is done in shadowy appeals courts that not one citizen in 1000 ever sets foot in.

All this is in flagrant violation of the Seventh Amendment of the Constitution, which says:

... no fact tried by a jury shall be otherwise reexamined in any court of the United States, than according to the rules of the common law.

But no one pays the slightest attention. Judges regularly circumvent the amendment by arguing that they are retrying cases on "the law," not on "the facts." In overturning Claus von Bulow's first conviction, for example (for which Dershowitz argued the case), the Rhode Island Supreme Court took pains to say that the jury verdict was correct but technicalities were more important.

Very often, however, appeals courts plainly retry the cases on the facts, simply substituting their own verdict for that of the jury.

In 1940, eighty-nine state prisoners were in federal court seeking to overturn their convictions on writs of habeas corpus. Today there are over 12,000. Moreover, petitions for retrial have become merely the tip of the iceberg of prisoner litigation.

In the early 1970s, civil liberties groups unearthed U.S. Code Title 42, Section 1983, a post-Civil War statute that allows state prisoners to petition the federal courts about their conditions of incarceration. At first, "1983" suits were put to good use. One petition ended the practice in Arkansas's prison farm of administering electric shocks to inmates by hooking them up to telephone wires.

But these suits have quickly gotten out of hand. The federal courts have turned themselves into a "complaint bureau" for state prisons. Where there were 2,000 civil rights suits filed in U.S. district courts in 1970, there were over 17,000 in 1985. Federal district judges spend huge amounts of time dealing with prisoner petitions that are frivolous, deceitful, and sometimes downright hilarious.

Cases can involve any issue imaginable. Prisoners have brought suits on anything from demanding that wardens call them by a different name to asking Congress to change the wording of the Declaration of Independence. Some petitions have been nothing more than cartoons of the wardens or prosecutors. Several have been written on toilet paper.

In 1972, Milan Radunovich, an imate at New York State's Attica prison, came to breakfast and found there was no orange at his place. He complained to the kitchen about it. He ended up in an argument and wound up in a detention cell for five days.

Radunovich brought his complaint about the missing orange, and his subsequent argument and detention, to court. He made it through the state courts, and all the way to the Second Circuit Court of Appeals, before his appeal was ultimately rejected.[6]

Since nearly all state and federal prisoners can plead indigence, their access to the courts is unlimited. Some prisoners accept assigned counsel, but in this playpen atmosphere many act as their own attorneys. The Supreme Court has ruled that inmates must have access to statute books, and some prisons now have better libraries than the law schools. Many inmates regularly browse through them for new material. Even the wardens sometimes encourage the suits as a kind of "occupational therapy."

The current record for 1983 cases seems to be held by Harry Franklin, an Oregon burglar who once had 120 petitions pending in federal court. He sued everybody at his own trial, including the judge, the prosecutor, the jurors, and his own attorney. He sued the prison for $50 million for trying to starve him to death because they put him on a diet for his diabetes. He sued the Muscular Distrophy Association and several college fraternities for $100 million for rolling beer kegs down Interstate 5 during a fundraising. (He claimed they were misusing his tax dollars.) And he sued the Union Pacific Railroad for $2 billion for blowing a train whistle every afternoon that woke him up from his nap. He claimed the railroad had begun blowing the whistle in the 1920s to spite a prisoner who had killed a Union Pacific employee in a train robbery. "It all sounds funny, but we

have to respond to every one of these suits," said Scott McAlister, of the
Oregon State Attorney General's Office. "It wastes a tremendous amount
of time in this office and in the courts."

The numbers may also sound funny (Franklin's later suits were for
trillions of dollars), but the chance of shaking some money out of the
system is not impossible. In 1983, a convicted kidnapper in New York's
Green Haven prison won $35,501 on a civil-rights verdict from a federal
jury. The inmate sought damages on the grounds that: 1) the prison doctor
had failed to fit him with reading glasses; 2) guards had handcuffed him to
cigarette-smoking prisoners against his will; and 3) a jail guard had failed
to deliver his copy of *Newsweek* on time. Fifty other civil-rights suits he had
filed at the same time were rejected.

In short, the Supreme Court has turned the federal judiciary into a slot
machine in which inmates can continually insert pieces of paper called
"habeas corpus petitions," with the reasonable hope that they may one day
hit the jackpot. They may get a retrial, they may get out of jail free, or they
may get a financial settlement for thousands of dollars. The only cost is
time. Inmates have plenty of time.

Habeas corpus petitions first mushroomed after the *Gideon* decision on
the right to state-supplied counsel. Unfortunately, the Supreme Court
made this ruling retroactive. Any indigent convict who claimed he was
tried without legal assistance could petition for a retrial *even though the
states had been adhering to the Supreme Court decision of 1942, which said
that indigent defendants were not entitled to free counsel except in capital
cases.* In Florida alone, 4,000 defendants petitioned to overturn their
convictions.

A typical case involved a man named Walker, who had raped a female
child in 1937. He was caught in the act by a group of neighbors, who
turned him over to the police. On the recommendation of his lawyer, he
pleaded guilty to avoid the death penalty and was sentenced to life
imprisonment.

In 1968, while out on parole, he committed another crime and was
reincarcerated. He then challenged the Constitutionality of his 1937 conviction on the grounds that he hadn't had a lawyer, and had been coerced
into confessing. Despite a clear record of the attorney's participation, a
federal judge granted an evidentiary hearing. The Florida attorney general's office was forced to locate the retired sheriff who, thirty years before, had made the arrest. The sheriff testified that the whole thing was

absurd—Walker had been caught in the act by neighbors and had pleaded guilty on the advice of his attorney. The federal judge dismissed the petition, finding Walker not credible.

One year later, Walker was back in federal district court. This time he argued that his attorney—who on the last petition didn't even exist—had been "incompetent" for allowing him to plead guilty. The attorney had since died, and none of the original witnesses could be located. (Walker, in fact, was the only principal in the case still living.)

The state was unable to present any witnesses to countervene Walker's testimony that he had been "incompetently" represented. The federal judge granted the writ of habeas corpus, and Walker went free.

Another typical case occurred recently in Arizona. In 1973, James Burgoyne, 18, and Cathy Koger, 17, were picnicking in the desert outside Phoenix when they were accosted and shot to death by Shawn Jensen, a 23-year-old Vietnam veteran, who may have robbed them of a few dollars. He left their bodies at the picnic site.

Jensen took his wife into the desert three days later and "discovered" the bodies. He reported it to the police. After a monthlong investigation turned up no leads, detectives started becoming suspicious of Jensen's story. He said he had "smelled" the bodies, but they had not yet begun to decay. Police checked Jensen's background and found that he had a previous conviction for check forgery under another name. His war record turned out to be exaggerated. He had not received four Purple Hearts, as he claimed, and had been discharged from the Marines under less-than-honorable conditions.

Looking for both .22- and .38-caliber weapons, sheriff's detectives noticed that Jensen carried a .22 rifle in the back of his truck. They asked to examine it, and Jensen consented. It turned out to be the murder weapon. On the same day, a friend of Jensen's called the police and said Jensen had asked him to hide a .38-caliber pistol and had confessed to killing the two young people. Jensen was charged with murder.

At first Jensen pleaded innocent but then changed the plea to innocent by insanity. At the trial, he argued he had had a "flashback to Vietnam." He was convicted and sentenced to life in prison.

Twelve years later, after several long appeals through the state and federal courts, Jensen won a reversal from an Arizona Superior Court judge on the grounds that new medical evidence about post-traumatic stress syndrome in Vietnam veterans strengthened his insanity defense. County prosecutors were forced to try him again.

By this time, the guns and bullets had been misplaced. The psychiatrist who had interviewed Jensen in 1973 had died in a scuba-diving accident. The state had no other witness to testify about Jensen's sanity at the time of the killings, and the judge would not admit the dead psychiatrist's testimony from the first trial. The mothers of both victims had to testify again about their children's murders. Nonetheless, the jury once again convicted him after only a short deliberation. Jensen is appealing again.

As Justice Sandra Day O'Connor observed in a recent decision:

> We must also acknowledge that writs of habeas corpus frequently cost society the right to punish admitted offenders. Passage of time, erosion of memory, and dispersion of witnesses may render retrial difficult, even impossible. While a habeas writ may, in theory, entitle the defendant only to retrial, in practice it may reward the accused with complete freedom from prosecution.[7]

Of course, not every one of the 12,000 prisoners now petitioning in federal court is going to get a retrial. But that is not the point. What is far more significant is the effect that habeas corpus petitions have on the average trial.

The important thing to remember is that the whole appeals process is a one-way ratchet. It can be tightened in only one direction—in favor of the defendant. Only the defense is allowed to appeal verdicts, and only the defense can pursue these appeals for years and decades after the original trial.

No trial judge likes to be overruled on appeals. It is a frustrating experience, a plain accusation of incompetence, and a blot on any judge's record. As a result of the hugely inflated appeals process, enormous pressure is brought to bear on every trial judge to make decisions in favor of the *defendant.* A questionable call made in favor of the defense can only lead to an acquittal, and acquittals cannot be appealed. But a questionable call in favor of the prosecution can lead to endless appeals and ultimate overturning of the case. (The prosecution can appeal during a trial in an interlocutory procedure, but once the trial is over, the game belongs to the defense.)

As a result, all trial judges in this country now know one thing—*you can't go too far wrong leaning in favor of the defendant.* Ruling in favor of the prosecution carries the risk of being overturned in a post-conviction appeal, whereas ruling in favor of the defense carries no risk of subsequent reversal.

In addition, there are very different rules for prosecuting and defense attorneys. Once again, it is a one-way ratchet. In order to give defendants "the benefit of the doubt," the two sides are usually held to very different standards.

During pretrial discovery proceedings, for example, the prosecution is required to turn all exculpating evidence over to the defense. But the defense is not required to turn any *incriminating* evidence over to the prosecutor. There is always the chance, long after the trial, that an appeals court will decide that a certain piece of evidence *might have been* exculpatory.

A guilty verdict can also be overturned because a mistake was made in admitting evidence from the prosecution, or failing to admit evidence from the defense. But once again the situation cannot be turned around. The prosecution has no post-trial recourse.

So it is, for a whole raft of potential "errors." Prosecutors can make faulty closing arguments, but defense attorneys cannot. Judges can give instructions that unfairly favor the prosecution, but not the defense. Jurors can be "tainted" by reading newspapers or making their own inquiries outside the courtroom, but these mistakes can work only for the benefit of the *defense*, not the prosecution.

It is not entirely true, however, to say that defense attorneys "cannot make mistakes." They can. But these mistakes *also* benefit the defendant in post-trial procedures.

One of the favorite arguments in habeas corpus appeals has become "incompetent counsel." Here, the convicted criminal—or, more likely, his new attorney—will argue that the defense attorney at the original trial *didn't make the right decisions* in presenting a defense. Therefore, the convict deserves a new trial.

In practice, all this means is that the convict and his new attorney go through the trial record and second-guess each decision that the original defense attorney made. Did the attorney let the defendant take the witness stand? If he didn't, maybe he should have. If he did, maybe he shouldn't. Did the attorney advise an insanity plea? Maybe that was wrong. Did he spurn the insanity plea and try to prove innocence? Maybe he should have ignored the evidence and pleaded the defendant insane.

Any decision made by a defense attorney in a trial leading to a conviction can later be second-guessed by a new attorney—or by the inmate himself—and then argued as proof of "incompetent" or "ineffective" counsel. In fact the courts have already overturned so many convictions on "ineffective counsel" that it is hard to figure out how all these people ever passed the bar exam.

The "incompetent counsel" argument is particularly effective when attorney and client have disagreed—which often happens. Say a defense attorney feels that the only real chance of acquittal lies in an insanity defense. But the defendant refuses to see the psychiatrists—as truly disturbed people often do. How can he avoid being "ineffective?" If he consents to his client's wishes, he is not offering effective counsel. But if he insists on defying his client, he risks violating the client's "Constitutional right" to counsel of his choice. Such tensions, which always exist, become very exploitable by other attorneys on appeal.

Another favorite trick of a veteran convict is to insist on acting as his own attorney. If the judge consents, the convict always has an appeal for "incompetent counsel" on the grounds that he didn't know enough to defend himself. If the judge refuses and assigns an attorney, then his right to choose his own counsel has been violated.

There are even rumors of a new kind of defense attorney who is "willing to take a dive" and present an intentionally poor case in order to create a case for "incompetent counsel" at the appeals level. This tactic is useful in death-penalty cases where there seems to be very little chance of avoiding conviction. "We've seen attorneys who will freely admit to incompetence at a post-trial hearing just to get their guy off," said Ed McMurray, deputy attorney general of California.

All this may seem like an unseemly sideshow to the main current of American jurisprudence. But let me assure you it is not. Every state attorney general's office now spends hundreds of man-hours and hundreds of thousands of dollars responding to these claims. California has three full-time attorneys *coordinating* the efforts of other attorneys in "defending the prisons." Keeping people in jail *after* conviction is now a full-time job.

The California Supreme Court has rejected thirty-four out of thirty-seven death penalties that it has reviewed since 1979—every one of them on the type of minutia described above. The other 120 death sentences are still before the court. California has not had a single execution since 70 percent of the state's voters approved the death penalty in 1978.

"In one case we had two convicted felons who had strangled another inmate," said McMurray. "They were both being represented by the same attorney. We knew there were eventually going to be arguments that the attorney had had a conflict of interest, so we went all the way to the California Supreme Court asking that they accept different counsel. But the Court said they had the right to have the same attorney.

"So we go to trial and both of them get convicted. They immediately appeal on the grounds that there was a conflict because they both had the same attorney. We went back to the [California] Supreme Court, and the court overturned *both* convictions. I know right now we don't have a chance of winning on any of these death-penalty cases. It's like Alice in Wonderland to go into that court."

What does all this amount to? In effect, the prosecution of criminal cases is being held to a standard of perfection that no human institution could ever achieve. Even the space shuttle couldn't operate under these conditions. The post office would close in a matter of hours. Yet appeals courts are constantly forcing state and local prosecutors to go back and retry people over and over—at a cost of millions and millions of dollars—all on the grounds that their trials have not yet reached constitutional perfection.

As Supreme Court Chief Justice Warren Burger—a dissenter in all this—has argued himself:

> I have seen cases . . . where three, four, and five trials are accorded to the accused, with an appeal following each trial and reversal of conviction on purely technical grounds. . . . In some of these multiple trial and appeal cases the accused continued his warfare with society for eight, nine, and ten years and more. In one case, more than sixty jurors and alternates were involved in five trials, more than thirty different lawyers participated either as court-appointed counsels or prosecutors, and more than fifty appellate judges reviewed the case on appeals. The best estimates [of the cost] added up to a quarter of a million dollars. The tragic aspect was the waste and futility, since every lawyer, every judge, and every juror was fully convinced of the defendant's guilt from beginning to end.[7]

Even Edward Bennett Williams, the famous Washington, D.C., defense attorney and owner of the Baltimore Orioles, has long felt that things are getting out of hand. In 1970, he said:

When [criminals] do get into court, a very bad thing takes place. The average lawyer today—if he *exploits* all the rights of his client—can keep his client at liberty on the street for from eighteen months to two years after he commits an armed robbery. . . . [T]he whole system stalls because, even after the defendant is brought to trial—which may be several months after he's arrested and indicted—and even after he's convicted by a jury, it takes from six to eight to ten months before an opinion comes out of the appellate court affirming or reversing his conviction.

And then there is an equal amount of time to be used up while the Supreme Court avenue is *exploited.* [my emphasis][8]

It may seen odd to hear about Constitutional rights as something to be "exploited." But the choice of words here is very exact.

It would be wrong to give the impression that all 12,000 inmates filing habeas corpus petitions are going to get retrials, or that all 17,000 prisoners' rights suits are going to end up in $35,000 judgments. For the most part, these suits are simply clogging the courts and wasting judicial time.

Every public defender does not argue his 16-year-old mugger's case all the way to federal district court. Sure, some jailhouse lawyers have also figured out the game. But, as Edward Bennett Williams suggests, the system is really set up so that *when the time is right,* a skillful defense attorney can "exploit" all the options available.

This seems to happen in two instances: 1) when a strong principle, such as the death penalty, is at stake; 2) when there is a lot of money involved.

Particularly since the acquittal of Claus von Bulow, it has become evident that a wealthy defendant and a skillful attorney can buy their way out of some very difficult situations in the American justice system.

What is not always clear, though, is just how the money is being spent. People tend to imagine that the defendant must be bribing the judge, or persuading the prosecutor to throw the case, or slipping $500 bills into the pockets of the jury.

That is not how it is done. Justice is bought these days through the skillful appeal of minor technicalities that force retrial after retrial until the verdict comes out "innocent"—at which point the case is over.

All this might make sense if guilt and innocence were at issue. But it is never the issue. As Judge J. Edward Lumbard, of the federal court of appeals in New York's Southern District, put it:

For all our work on thousands of state prisoner cases I have yet to hear of one where an innocent man had been convicted. The net result of our fruitless meddling in search of the non-existent needle in the ever-larger haystack has been a serious detriment to the administration of criminal justice by the states.[9]

The "presumption of innocence" has essentially become a "Constitutional right" that says the defendant must be afforded every conceivable opportunity to escape society's judgment.

As Justice John Harlan, said in one of the Supreme Court's earliest habeas corpus cases:

Both the individual criminal defendant and society have an interest in insuring that there will at some point be the certainty that comes with an end to litigation, and that attention will ultimately be focused not on whether a conviction was free from error but rather on whether the prisoner can be restored to a useful place in the community . . .

No one, not criminal defendants, not the judicial system, not society as a whole is benefited by a judgment providing a man shall tentatively go to jail today, but tomorrow and every day thereafter his continued incarceration shall be subject to fresh litigation on issues already resolved.[10]

THE BILL OF RIGHTS AND THE CONSTITUTION

8

THE CURRENT conundrum of Constitutional interpretation goes like this. There is nothing in the Constitution that says you can't murder anyone. However, the Bill of Rights does say a person has a right to legal counsel. If the police look in a cloth shopping bag, then that is a violation of the Constitution. But if you murder someone, then you are only committing a crime. Therefore the greater violation—the "Constitutional" one—must take precedent.

How did we get ourselves into this convoluted situation, and how do we get out? Was it a mere oversight that caused the Founding Fathers to forget to mention murder, robbery, rape, and arson as serious violations worthy of society's attention?

Perhaps the best way to approach the Constitution and the Bill of Rights is to realize that when the Founding Fathers wrote the First Ten Amendments, they didn't mean them to stand in place of the Ten Commandments.

The Constitution was not written to be a prescription for a whole civilization. It was simply written as a framework around which we were to form our government and go about resolving our own differences. The Constitution did not sanctify "individual rights" any more than it did group rights, or public rights, or states' rights, or religious rights.

To quote Richard Morgan once more, the Constitution and the Bill of Rights are written in a "majestic idiom," meant to afford "flexibility to future generations in applying the language to ever changing circumstances—'a living Constitution.'"[1]

The basic idea of American government was to diversify the centers of power, spreading authority and *impeding* decision-making in many ways,

so that no group could gain tyrannical control. As Madison wrote in
"Federalist X":

> The federal Constitution forms a happy combination in this respect;
> the great and aggregate interests being referred to the national, the local
> and particular to the state legislatures.[2]

Like the Bible and other great documents, the Constitution is at some
times pointlessly specific, at others necessarily vague. There are parts of it
that are so familiar that the average American can quote them by heart.
There are others that have been completely forgotten.

The task that faced the Founding Fathers when they met during the
Summer of 1787 in Philadelphia was delicate. Americans, as always, were
suspicious of centralized power. The Thirteen States had long been governed by legislatures that were immensely popular institutions. In a
country where it took some of the delegates almost a month to make their
way to Philadelphia, there was little perceived need for a strong national
framework.

Nearly all the Founding Fathers, however, were men of vision. As
Madison wrote in *The Federalist*:

> [T]he intercourse throughout the Union will be facilitated by new
> improvements. Roads will everywhere be shortened and kept in better
> order; . . . an interior navigation on our eastern side will be opened
> throughout . . . the whole extent of the Thirteen States. The conjunc-
> tion between the Eastern and Atlantic districts . . . will be rendered
> more and more easy by those numerous canals which art finds it so
> little difficult to connect and complete . . .
>
> Hearken not to the unnatural voice which tells you that the people of
> America, knit together as they are by so many cords of affection, can
> no longer live together as members of the same family; can no longer
> continue the mutual guardians of their mutual happiness; can no longer
> be fellow-citizens of one great, respectable, and flourishing empire.[3]

The greatest problem the Constitutional Convention faced—anachron-
istically—was reconciling the big and small states. Rhode Island, the most
obstreperous opponent of a national government, didn't even bother to
send delegates.

Looming over this immediate interest, however, was the growing economic divergence between the North and South. Tariffs were already a point of conflict, and slavery was an ever-present dilemma. In addition, the eternal clash between the "propertied" and "unpropertied" classes was never far from anyone's mind.

Even after all these problems were finally ironed out in the course of that sweltering summer, there remained, however, a residual distrust of centralized authority.

Much of this was rooted in the colonial experience. The colonial legislatures had been extremely clamorous and independent institutions. They were generally regarded as "the people's" government, while the executive and judiciary belonged to the British administration.

Although nearly all the delegates who attended the Constitutional Convention ultimately accepted the need for a national government, there was a handful of delegates who rejected it. These delegates were the ones who also felt most strongly about adding a Bill of Rights.

George Mason, commonly referred to as the "Father of the Bill of Rights," is the best example. Like Jefferson and Washington, he was a slaveholder who opposed slavery and who wanted to use the money from selling western lands to recolonize the slaves in Africa. He wrote the Virginia Bill of Rights, generally regarded as the forerunner to the Constitution's Bill of Rights. He was one of three delegates—all Southerners—who refused to support the Constitution. He lamented the lack of a Bill of Rights and the Constitution's tacit acceptance of slavery.

In arguing against the need for a Bill of Rights, on the other hand, Federalist leaders like Hamilton and Jay argued that the Constitution had only *delegated* powers to the federal government. If something wasn't specifically permitted in the Constitution, they said, then it couldn't be done. Why worry about a federal government restricting freedom of speech or of the press when nothing in the Constitution would permit it?

Still, people were suspicious. During the ratification debates in the state conventions there was a hue and cry for more specific prohibitions. Many of the states made their ratification of the Constitution contingent upon the adoption of a Bill of Rights.

In the end, James Madison seems to have been the only person who successfully bridged the gap between the two sides. The most eloquent and reflective supporter of the Constitution, he became convinced during the ratification debates that a Bill of Rights would also be necessary. As Representative from Virginia, he introduced the proposed amendments on the floor of the First Congress.

All thirteen states except New Jersey already had their own bills of rights. The question that arose immediately was whether the Constitutional Bill of Rights would also apply to the states. Madison told the states they should accept the Federal Bill of Rights or possibly face something worse. As it turned out, this was prophetic. But strong state chauvinism, plus the inherent suspicion of the federal government, prevailed. The provision to extend the Bill of Rights to the states—which Madison called "the most valuable amendment in the whole list"—failed.

Thus, the first words of the Bill of Rights are, "*Congress shall* make no law..." Whether or not the first ten amendments should apply to the states was left unsettled. It has still not been entirely resolved today.

The basic points to be included in the Bill of Rights were not a serious matter of contention. There was general agreement on most issues. The real contention arose between those who, like Madison, wanted to "confine ourselves to the enumeration of simple, acknowledged principles," and those who wanted to add amendments almost to the point of rewriting the Constitution itself.

Freedom of speech, freedom of assembly, and the right to practice religion were foremost in everyone's mind. Taking a negative example from England, Congress also declared that "Congress shall make no law respecting the establishment of religion."

The amendments guaranteeing the "right to bear arms," and forbidding the "quartering of soldiers" were historical grievances that produced little debate and have had little use. (Despite its constant invocation, the "right to bear arms" has never been used to overturn a gun-control ordinance.)

Specific attention was given to criminal procedures since that is where state tyranny could assert itself most swiftly. Most of the principles were well accepted in British jurisprudence, with some dating from the Magna Carta.

I have already quoted the full text of the Fourth Amendment to the Constitution on searches and seizures. Here are the Fifth, Sixth, Seventh, and Eighth Amendments:

Amendment V

No person shall be held to answer for a capital, or otherwise infamous crime, unless on a presentment or indictment of a grand jury, except in cases arising in the land or naval forces, or in the militia, when in actual service in time of war or public danger; nor shall any person be subject for the same offense to be twice put in jeopardy of life or limb; nor shall be compelled in any criminal case to be a witness against himself, nor be deprived of life, liberty, or property, without due process of law; nor shall private property be taken for public use without just compensation.

Amendment VI

In all criminal prosecutions, the accused shall enjoy the right to a speedy and public trial, but an impartial jury of the State and district wherein the crime shall have been committed, which district shall have been previously ascertained by law, and to be informed of the nature and cause of the accusations; to be confronted with the witnesses against him; to have compulsory process for obtaining witnesses in his favor, and to have the assistance of counsel for his defense.

Amendment VII

In suits at common law, where the value in controversy shall exceed twenty dollars, the right of trial by jury shall be preserved, and no fact tried by a jury shall be otherwise reexamined in any court of the United States, than according to the rules of the common law.

Amendment VIII

Excessive bail shall not be required, nor excessive fines imposed, nor cruel and unusual punishments inflicted.

The picture of the criminal justice system outlined in the Bill of Rights, then, is one where *local juries* are in control. The right to "trial by jury" can be read as a right of the accused, but it can also be read as the right of a jury. The thing that the Founding Fathers were trying to forestall was a meddlesome interference of the *federal* government in *local* criminal procedure.

This is particularly clear in the long forgotten and totally ignored Seventh Amendment. "No fact tried by a jury shall be otherwised reexamined in any court of the United States" is an unmistakable attempt to give *juries* power.

As Raoul Berger, professor emeritus of Constitutional history at Harvard, states: "The Founding Fathers saw the jury as the buffer between the individual and the power of the state. The common law tradition was that both juries and grand juries were the organs best suited for making the decisions in important criminal matters. It was the arbitrary power of *judges* that was being curtailed in the Bill of Rights."

In particular, many members of the Constitutional Convention had worried about the vague, undefined powers of the federal courts. They were concerned that these courts would proliferate and eventually become meddlesome, intervening organs of federal power. One proposed amendment would have prohibited the creation of any federal courts below the Supreme Court.

As Broadus and Louise Mitchell stated in *A Biography of the Constitution,* "The judicial power as it stood in the Constitution gave special dissatisfaction in the states, where many believed the federal courts would intrude, or, in appealed cases, would override determinations of local juries."[4]

This fear was not limited to "overzealous prosecution" as people tend to assume today. The colonials had had their own painful experiences with lenient courts. British soldiers and other officials who committed crimes against American colonials often had their convictions forestalled or overturned by royal intervention. Jefferson wrote this grievance into the Declaration of Independence when he condemned King George III:

> For quartering large Bodies of Armed Troops among us;
> For protecting them, by a mock Trial, from Punishment for any
> Murders which they should commit on the Inhabitants of these States.

Thus, the amendments relating to criminal procedure were not written just to protect criminals. They were written to protect the public as well.

Once the commonly accepted principles were settled, the First Congress still faced several problems.

First, there were many proposals to tamper with the main body of the Constitution. Representatives wanted to enlarge the House, limit the term of senators to one year, and the president to two years. Southern delegates wanted to give states the right to lay tariffs. Madison saw the danger of all this, however, and argued successfully against cluttering the Constitution.

Then another question arose. If the Bill of Rights purported to enumerate "basic rights," might not some individual come along and say these are the *only* rights allowed under the Constitution? One delegate facetiously suggested that Congress had better add amendments saying that people could "wear hats, go to bed, and get up when they please." Otherwise, someone was likely to come along and say they couldn't do them.

It was a crucial question—the kind of problem often faced by computer programmers or parents trying to instruct small children. "Don't forget to wear your rubbers," a parent will say, and the child will soon emerge wearing rubbers and nothing else. "But you didn't tell me to put on my socks, shoes, pants, shirt," comes the response.

Congress solved the problem with a brilliant stroke, the Ninth Amendment. It states simply:

> The enumeration in the Constitution, of certain rights, shall not be construed to deny or disparage others retained by the people.

This *proscriptive*—rather than *prescriptive*—reading of the Bill of Rights was also reinforced by the Tenth Amendment, which reads:

> The powers not delegated to the United States by the Constitution, nor prohibited by it to the States, are reserved for the States respectively, or to the people.

We still encounter the failure to understand these principles all the time. Civil libertarians and defense lawyers, for example, are constantly arguing that "crime victims have no rights" because nothing is enumerated in the Constitution. "The Bill of Rights only protects the accused," they say. "There is nothing in the Constitution that says anything about the rights of victims."

This is literally, precisely, and completely wrong. The Ninth Amendment speaks to the rights of crime victims. It doesn't say so in so many words, but the intent is clear. Nothing is more traditional than the right of crime victims to be treated fairly by the justice system.

Thus we have the paradox of current Constitutional law. "The rights of the accused" were enumerated at length, largely because they were something of an historic exception. The rights of victims, on the other hand, were so traditional that no one thought to mention them specifically. But with the inertia of time and precedent, the exception becomes the rule, while the rule is completely forgotten.

It is only through long years of unfortunate misreadings and ever-more-literalistic interpretations that the Bill of Rights has come to mean that no one *except* criminals has any "rights" in the Constitution. It is only through the willful neglect of the clear intent of the Bill of Rights that the public now needs protection from its own judiciary.

The question that arises out of all this, of course, is: How did so many of these amendments get lost while others have been magnified out of all proportion?

At least part of the answer lies in a judicial concept called the "selective incorporation" of the Bill of Rights.

Once again, Madison originally perceived the problem when he told the states that not accepting the Bill of Rights could lead to something much worse.

Almost since the document was written, the question has persisted: Should the Bill of Rights also apply to the states? John Marshall upheld the First Congress by ruling that it didn't. This view remained in place until after the Civil War. During Reconstruction, however, Congress became worried that southern states might abridge the rights of southern blacks. It initiated the Fourteenth Amendment, which reads in part:

> No State shall make or enforce any law which shall abridge the privileges or immunities of citizens of the United States; nor shall any State deprive any person of life, liberty, or property, without due process of law; nor deny to any person within its jurisdiction the equal protection of the laws.

Almost immediately the question arose: Did the "privileges and immunities" that the states could not abridge include the Bill of Rights? And did this mean that the Bill of Rights now applied to the states?

In 1873, the Supreme Court ruled that the Fourteenth Amendment had *not* incorporated the Bill of Rights into state procedures. The doctrine of "total incorporation" was once more rejected.

Since a great deal of the activity of the late nineteenth century Supreme Court was concerned, once again, with striking down *state* legislation, certain portions of the Bill of Rights did tend to creep into the Court's decisions. One phrase that particularly caught the interest of the nineteenth century Justices was the last phrase of the Fifth Amendment, which states: "nor shall private property be taken without just compensation."

Gradually, as the Supreme Court began to delve into state laws on the matters of freedom of speech and religion, the concept grew that, while the entire Bill of Rights did not apply to the states, the Supreme Court could "selectively incorporate" certain portions into state procedures. The obvious ones—freedom of speech, assembly, and religion—were soon incorporated as what Justice Benjamin Cardozo once called the "preferred freedoms."

As a result, a great deal of twentieth-century Constitutional history revolves around the "selective incorporation" of certain amendments— and certain portions of certain amendments—into state procedures. The principle work of the Warren Court was to incorporate portions of the Fourth, Fifth, Sixth, and Eighth Amendments, plus the "exclusionary rule" that had been attached to the Fourth Amendment, into state procedures. Since nearly all criminal trials take place at the state level, this has had an enormous impact.

On the whole, however, the results of "selective incorporation" have been rather unexpected. Although it certainly wasn't planned this way, selective incorporation has meant that *the federal judiciary can choose which portions of the Bill of Rights to enforce and which to ignore.* In general, the Supreme Court has chosen to incorporate those portions that *strengthen* the power of the judiciary and *ignore* those amendments that were directed against the judiciary itself.

The case of grand juries is an interesting example. The Bill of Rights forbids anyone from being "held for a capital, or otherwise infamous crime, unless on a presentment or indictment of a Grand Jury." This is the first—and presumably most important—portion of the Fifth Amendment.

The grand jury had its origins in twelfth-century England as a prosecu- torial arm to help the Crown ferret out criminals. In a landmark case of the seventeenth century, however, a grand jury withstood enormous royal pressures and refused to indict two prominent critics of the king. As a result, grand juries won enormous respect for protecting citizens from arbitrary authority, as well as for protecting people accused of crimes.

In the American colonies, grand juries again won respect during the 1735 case of John Peter Zenger. Two grand juries refused to indict the New York newspaper publisher for libel under pressure from the British Crown. He was finally indicted in a rare "prosecutor's information" charge but was acquitted by a jury, despite a specific instruction from the judge demanding conviction. Needless to say, the enormous respect for juries and grand juries led to their prominent mention in the Bill of Rights.

In recent years, however, grand juries have come under criticism from the legal profession. Among law school faculties and federal and state judges, the grand jury has come under cricitism as a mere "rubber stamp" for the prosecution. "Under the grand jury system, the prosecutor could indict a ham sandwich," Sol Wachter, Chief Justice of the New York Court of Appeals, told the newspapers after a second grand jury had indicted Bernhard Goetz. Law professors are particularly concerned because the defense cannot make a presentation to the grand jury. They regard this as an "abridgment of the defendant's rights."

Thus, there has never been much pressure to incorporate the grand jury provisions of the Fifth Amendment into the state criminal process. In fact, it has been just the opposite. The bar associations of many states are attempting to *abolish* grand juries and turn the power to make indictments over to judges. "The only reason we still have grand juries is because they're so popular," one law-school professor told me.

In light of all this, it probably doesn't even have to be said that the Seventh Amendment, with its restrictions on the abilities of appeals courts to overrule juries, has never been seriously considered for enforcement or selective incorporation into state procedures.

In fairness, it must be noted that, even if the Seventh Amendment were remembered, appeals courts would regularly overturn jury verdicts anyway. They would argue that the jury was being overturned on "the law" rather than on "the facts." Thus, the provisions of the Amendment would be circumvented. Judges have also reserved the right to overturn decisions if they are not what a "reasonable" jury would have concluded.

Thus, in practice, both state and federal appeals court judges substituted their own judgment for the jury's—exactly as the Seventh Amendment was meant to prevent. Two years ago, in overturning a civil jury award of $500,000 to a Kansas City newscaster, a federal district judge said he was "firmly convinced" the verdict was "the result of passion, prejudice, confusion, or mistake on the part of the jury."

What can be done about any of this?

One of the most useful ideas coined by the "deviance" sociologists is the concept of "moral entrepreneurs." Every society, say the sociologists, has a lot of rules. Some of them are observed without much thought while others are ignored and forgotten. Still others become the subject of vigorous and passionate enforcement campaigns.

The activist portions of the community that direct these law-enforcement energies are labeled "moral entrepreneurs." The prohibition of alcohol, a concern about pesticides, a campaign against illegal gambling, a crackdown on drunk drivers—all are the result of "moral entrepreneurship" by groups trying to enforce their vision on society.

A useful way to classify the role of Supreme Court justices and other members of the judiciary would be to think of them as "Constitutional entrepreneurs."

There are a lot of things said in the Constitution and the Bill of Rights. Some of them have been routinely accepted. Others have been completely forgotten. Some have been enlarged and enforced so vigorously that they have essentially been carried beyond their original purpose.

All this, of course, is "Constitutional." "We live under the Constitution, but the Constitution is what the Supreme Court says it is," was an offhand remark of Chief Justice Charles Evans Hughes that is widely remembered and often repeated in legal circles.

The Constitution, as interpreted by Chief Justice Roger Taney, protected slavery—and it took the Thirteenth Amendment to undo that interpretation. It wasn't until 1941 that the Supreme Court finally approved the Constitutionality of federal child labor laws. On many occasions, the Supreme Court has declared something unconstitutional one year and then turned around and made it Constitutional the next.

Judge Robert Jackson, in dissenting from one of the earliest habeas corpus cases, wrote:

> Whenever decisions of one court are reviewed by another, a percentage of them are reversed . . . However, reversals by a higher court is not proof that justice is thereby better done. There is no doubt that if there were a super-Supreme court, a substantial proportion of our reversals of state courts would also be reversed. We are not final because we are infallible, but infallible because we are final.[5]

There are the "great dissenters" like Oliver Wendell Holmes, who want to exercise restraint and let legislatures do most of the lawmaking. But these voices are usually raised in dissent. The Supreme Court's power of review gives the Justices an enormous opportunity to "make law." Whatever faction finds itself in the majority almost inevitably takes advantage of this opportunity.

What we need, I think, is some new Constitutional entrepreneurship. It is not going to be necessary to "repeal the Bill of Rights"—as some people morbidly predict—in order to tip the balance of our system more against crime and in favor of the law-abiding public. It is only necessary to interpret the Constitution as it was originally written.

The "establish justice" and "insure domestic tranquility" clauses are, to my mind, a clear mandate for reestablishing the *public's* interest in the judicial system. They invite more vigorous interpretation. At the same time, the criminal portions of the Bill of Rights, if interpreted correctly, give power to juries. Distortions like the exclusionary rule, on the other hand, which bestow rights only on *guilty* people, are clear violations of the "equal protection" clause of the Fourteenth Amendment. Anything as broad and sweeping as a "Constitutional right" should be available to anyone at any time—*not* just after they have committed a crime.

We have had such areas of broad Constitutional reinterpretation before. The Warren era was certainly one. Another was the New Deal, when Congress and hordes of legal scholars gave new meaning to the "general welfare" clause of the Preamble. It was argued that the "general welfare" clause was proper Constitutional grounding for social legislation—and that it was the Nine Old Men themselves who were misinterpreting the Constitution. This is why we have social legislation today and why these laws are called "welfare" programs.

Justice Sandra Day O'Connor has been leading the way toward more accurate and sensible interpretations of the Constitution since her appointment in 1981. With daring and refreshing simplicity, Justice O'Connor has reaffirmed that long forgotten truth—that the public has just as many rights in the outcome of a criminal proceeding as does the criminal, and that law enforcement is not just a confrontation between "the individual and the state."

In a recent case in Covington, Kentucky, a man was convicted on a federal firearms charge when, after being detained on the basis of a "wanted-for-questioning" flyer issued by a nearby police department, firearms turned up in his car. The man challenged his arrest and conviction all the way to the Supreme Court on the grounds that the "wanted-for-questioning" flyer was not a valid warrant.

Instead of opening up new Fourth Amendment grounds about whether "flyers" are "warrants" and whether these new "flyer-warrants" should be subject to standards of "probable cause," Justice O'Connor, writing for the majority, stated, "It is in the public interest that a crime be solved and a suspect be detained as promptly as possible."

"It may sound like plain old common sense," said Frank Carrington of Americans for Effective Law Enforcement. "But it's been a long time since anyone on the Supreme Court has been willing to state such an obvious truth."

The broad expansion of the concept of habeas corpus also offers an opportunity to put teeth into the Fourth Amendment without disrupting law enforcement in the process.

Instead of overturning convictions in order to keep the police from breaking into people's homes, why not let the federal district courts accept direct "habeas corpus" petitions from citizens who feel they have been "unconstitutionally detained" in their own homes by illegal police searches? If convicted criminals can appeal directly to federal court for "violation of their Constitutional rights," why can't everybody? That, after all, is "equal protection." Such a procedure would give the federal courts strong supervisory behavior over local police departments, without making a mockery of criminal trials in the process.

We can no longer afford to trifle with law enforcement and turn criminal trials into forums for trying everyone but the criminal. Our ability to control crime and create a peaceful society suffers too much damage in the process. We can't simply go on interpreting the Constitution to death— or worse, twisting small phrases in order to fit our own contorted purposes. At some point, we have to rely on common sense.

As I write this, the day's newspaper brings the latest accounts of quotidian American violence. A Yemenite grocer in Brooklyn, harassed by young black children since he opened his store six months ago, finally pulls a gun and kills three of them after an argument over whether they paid for a bottle of soda. A Vietnamese immigrant, working in a Long Island furniture factory, had had his welding tools broken by two Ecuadorian illegal aliens who say he is working too fast. He returned to the factory with a rifle and killed them.

None of these people are "real criminals." They simply are people who are saying to themselves, "What the hell, everybody else is getting away with these things. I'm going to do it myself."

We have a responsibility to establish and enforce law and order in this country. What else can the Constitutional prescriptions to "establish justice" and "insure domestic tranquility" possibly mean? Time is short. If we don't improve, we are soon going to find ourselves living in a country filled with people who don't care a whit about the Constitution, except where they think it gives them the "right" to grab guns and start shooting at each other.

As James Madison said in urging his fellow Americans not to believe there would be more "freedom" in remaining a squabbling collection of disorganized individuals:

Is it not the glory of the people of America, that, while they have paid a decent respect to the opinion of former and other nations, they have not suffered a blind veneration for antiquity, for custom, or for names to overrule the suggestions of their own good sense, the knowledge of their own situation, and the lessons of their own experience? . . .

And if novelties are to be shunned, believe me, the most alarming of all novelties, the most wild of all projects, the most rash of all attempts, is that of rending us in pieces in order to preserve our liberties . . .[6]

Part II

How the System
Should Work

"People are capable of anything."

—an assistant district attorney

COOPERATION 9

WHEN I WAS in college, I took a course in ethics. After a few uneventful months in which it seemed no one was getting anywhere, one student posed a brilliant question.

"A tree in the forest frequently drops a seed right next to it, and that seed grows into another tree," he said. "That young tree may eventually grow up so it shades the parent and may eventually kill the other tree. This disturbs no one.

"Yet if a parent gives birth to a child, and after growing up the child eventually turns on the parent and kills it, we call that one of the most horrible crimes known to humanity. Why is there a difference?"

I don't recall that we ever answered the question in my ethics course. But I think I have realized since that the answer has something to do with human cooperation.

Aristotle called humans "the political animal." It would not be changing the meaning at all to paraphrase this as "the cooperating animal."

Like many scientific truths, this statement is profound in its simplicity. "How could it be any other way?" We want to ask. "Of course humans cooperate." It is not until we recognize how little other animals do cooperate that we recognize how unique the human species really is.

In Werner Herzog's movie, *Aguirre, Wrath of God,* there is an eerie scene right at the end. Aguirre, having lost his whole party in a failed expedition to find the El Dorado, ends up alone on a raft floating down the Amazon. Finally, the raft is invaded by strange and menacing monkeys. They are soon everywhere, getting into food, climbing all over everything.

You wait for something to happen. Aguirre is alone and defenseless. The monkeys—although not more than two feet tall—are numerous enough to overwhelm him. Yet they remain strangely unaware of him.

Finally you realize what is going on. *These creatures have no organization.* They act in a loose congregation but more or less independently of each other. They are no more responsive to each other than they are to Aguirre.

What differentiates us from all other creatures is the way our smallest actions—our whole psychic makeup—is governed by our intensely entwined interaction with each other. Other animals demonstrate rudimentary forms of cooperation, but no creature is as completely reliant on the efforts of other members of the species as we are. We are the "cooperating animal."

Our ability to cooperate has been the key element in our evolution. We would not have become human beings without it. We probably would have remained loosely congregated and relatively less specialized creatures like our primate cousins, the gorillas and chimpanzees.

But what is cooperation? How did it arise? And most important, how do we persuade/cajole/threaten/convert our fellow human beings into acting in a cooperative fashion? These are important questions. Understanding cooperation is the first step to understanding how crime occurs.

Most books on criminology begin with a short chapter on cooperation. They note that humans live together in mutually dependent communities. Frequently cooperation is presented as a vague "caring and sharing" for each other. Or else it is described as the *absence* of individual desires and competitive behavior. Here is one example from a recent text:

> [H]umans *evolved* as communal creatures. For over a million years before the evolution of biologically modern humans some 40,000 to 50,000 years ago, ancient hominids [ancestors of modern humans] were living in small economically cooperative groups . . .
> Humans evolved not as individual, egoistic creatures but as members of cooperative social groups.[1]

So far, so good. But this acknowledgment of cooperation is almost inevitably followed by the argument that, because we already have cooperation, selfish behavior shouldn't exist, or can somehow be wished away, in human societies:

> If we assume . . . that human communities emerged as uneasy associations of individuals seeking to maximize their own egotistic

gains, we will tend to believe that the problem of crime arises from the inherent or inevitable desire of humans to use others, in whatever ways possible, as means to their own selfish ends . . .

According to this view of human nature, the primary (and perhaps only) method available for reducing crime is to *restrain* the inherently bestial instincts that lie just below the thin surface layer of socialization.

If on the other hand we recognize that collective organization and cooperative action were of elemental importance in human evolution, other alternatives begin to appear. Specifically, we can begin to ask not how do we restrain wrongdoers, but how can we create societies which foster social and cooperative, rather than self-seeking and competitive, forms of behavior.[2]

At this point it is almost inevitably suggested that what we need is "a society based, not on competition, but on cooperation." As this author says: "There is little evidence that humans are self-seeking and competitive *by nature* or that they have an instinctive drive to acquire more material possessions than other people around them."

Thus, criminal behavior is somehow "taught" by our "competitive" society. All we have to do is "eliminate competition" and crime will disappear. Whatever little behavior quirks remain can be handled by "shaming" and "collective rejection," the mechanisms employed by primitive societies. Remarkably, these "shaming" devices are virtually indistinguishable from the "labeling" process that criminologists criticize so much in other contexts.

In any case, the point is clear. Punishment and imprisonment shouldn't be necessary. "The criminal justice system is likely to work best when it is used least," concludes another recent text in a comment that occurs over and over again. "It should not be used routinely, but exceptionally."[3]

The trouble with all these exhortations about "cooperating" societies is that no one ever takes the trouble to explain exactly how cooperation works. It is usually pictured only as an amorphous "caring and sharing." People get along because they get along.

There is little recognition that cooperation always carries with it the possibility of betrayal. If you are going to spend your time helping other people, what guarantee do you ever have that they are going to help you in return? And if they don't reciprocate, what are you going to do about it?

Moreover, the more we cooperate with each other, the more the possibilities for betrayal open up. The hugely efficient and highly coordinated system of world travel we have developed, for example, has only made it much easier to hijack airplanes and set off bombs at airports, randomly sacrificing hundreds of innocent people to highly idiosyncratic motives and desires.

Recently, a game has been invented that serves as a model for simple cooperation. Ironically, it is called "The Prisoner's Dilemma." Here is how it goes:

Two accomplices are brought into the station house and questioned separately by police for a crime they have committed together. Each is told that if he confesses and implicates the other, he will get a lighter sentence. (This is all pre-*Miranda,* of course.) But if the other confesses and implicates him, he will get a heavier sentence for not confessing.

Each prisoner knows that if they *both* cooperate with each other and refuse to confess, they will both go free (there is no other evidence against them). But neither has any guarantee that the other will hold up his end of the bargain. Playing the good guy and not confessing carries the risk that the other person will betray you. Then he will make out better, and you will make out worse. If, on the other hand, you both betray each other, neither of you does very well.

In order to give the game a quantitative aspect, the sociologists have given the game the following scoring: Both cooperate and don't confess, 3 points each. You cooperate, your partner betrays, you get 0 (the "sucker's payoff"), he gets 5. He cooperates, you betray, he gets 0, you get 5. Both betray each other, 1 point each.

When the game is played over an extended series of encounters, interesting patterns begin to emerge. Some players try to cooperate all the time. Others will play the game by consistently trying to betray the other player. How trustworthy is your partner? How trustworthy are you? These are questions that quickly begin to emerge when two people try to cooperate.

Sociologists have been fooling around with the game for almost two decades, using it as a model to study cooperation in various situations. Playing the game is surprisingly flustering. "There ought to be a law against this," is the comment one professor said his students always make after only a few rounds. It is extremely frustrating to have to keep guessing what your "partner-opponent" is going to do.

Then in 1982, Robert Axelrod, a political scientist at University of Michigan, took the game one step further. He invited mathematicians and and game theorists around the country to enter a computer tournament.

Each of them was asked to submit a strategy for playing the game. Axelrod then played all the strategies off against each other in a massive round-robin.

The results were rather astonishing. *The simplest strategy won.* This strategy, submitted by Anatol Rapoport, a Canadian mathematician, was called "Tit for Tat." Here is the way it works:

1) on the first round, Tit for Tat always cooperates.

2) on each succeeding round, it does what the *other* player did on the *previous* move.

That's it. This simple strategy accumulated the highest score in a long series of encounters with over sixty other strategies, some of them designed to act in the most subtle and devious ways.

In his book, *The Evolution of Cooperation,*[4] Axelrod gave a detailed description of the outcome and drew a variety of interesting conclusions.

First, he said, cooperation evolves *spontaneously.* It does not need to be directed from the outside—and probably *cannot* be directed from outside. Thus, people who say "we should design a society in which people cooperate" aren't talking sense. People have to learn to cooperate among themselves.

Second, cooperation and competition are essentially the same thing. All the players were competing *against* each other for the highest score. Successfully betraying the other player offered the highest score. Yet the players that did best were those who cooperated and who evoked cooperation from others.

Thus, to use "cooperation" and "competition" as opposites is to misunderstand the terms. Cooperation *is* a form of competition where both players learn how to work together.

The key to cooperation is to realize that it is not a "zero-sum game." In a zero-sum game, one person's gain must be another person's loss. In a "positive-sum game," one person's success can be another person's success as well. This is what cooperation is all about—and in fact what all social progress is about. People who learn to work in a positive-sum situation do best. People who insist on seeing life as a zero-sum game do worst.

The characteristics that made Tit for Tat the most successful strategy were particularly revealing. Axelrod noted that it had four major qualities.

First, he said, Tit for Tat is "nice." *It always begins by cooperating.* (I would use the word "optimistic.") Many strategies were based on deception—either refusing to cooperate at first, or trying to set the other player up to betray him. *These strategies inevitably ended up losing.* Over the long haul, all the "nice" strategies clustered at the top, and all the "betraying" strategies clustered at the bottom.

Second, Tit for Tat *retaliated.* It did not let defections by the other player go unpunished. Whenever the other player failed to cooperate on a turn, Tit for Tat retaliated on the next turn. The strategy did not "play the sucker."

Third, Tit for Tat was *not vindictive.* It did not "overpunish," or try to teach the other player a lesson "once and for all" by imposing a penalty greater than the original infraction. It "let the punishment fit the crime."

Fourth, Tit for Tat was *understandable.* It was easy for the other player to figure out what it was doing. Many strategies were too complicated for their own good. Whatever message they were trying to convey was lost on the other player. (The exclusionary rule, which attempts to improve respect for law enforcement by letting guilty criminals go, is a good example of a strategy too complicated for its own good.)

What was perhaps most remarkable about the success of Tit for Tat was the self-effacing nature of its victory. Although it ran up the highest long-range score among sixty-three other competing strategies, it *never won an individual encounter with another player.* The best it could ever do was tie, which happened when both players cooperated all the time. As Axelrod noted: "Tit for Tat's success came, not from successfully out-competing other players, but in *eliciting cooperative behavior from them.*"

The key, said Axelrod, is in learning to play a positive-sum game. Many players often betray, even after a long series of mutual cooperation, *simply because they see the other person winning as well.* They assume because the other person is doing well, they themselves must be losing. "Don't be envious," concluded Axelrod. "Envy is self-destructive."

In addition, it is important to make a distinction between cooperation and *sharing.* Cooperation is not sharing, and sharing is not cooperation. Sharing does not ask for reciprocity, and is unlikely to get it in return. Sharing requires altruism, while cooperation does not. As Axelrod concluded: "Altruism is not needed; successful strategies can elicit cooperation even from an egotist."[5]

One other inference that can be drawn from the tournament: People are not "naturally" cooperative. Of the sixty participants in the tournament—all of them eminently successful game theorists and academics—about half submitted strategies built around the idea of *betraying* other players.

Without any exaggeration then, it is possible to say that Axelrod and Rapoport seem to have discovered a mathematical model for our justice system. In fact, Tit for Tat *is* the justice system. The reason we have a justice system is to moderate people's behavior in favor of cooperation. Punishing infractions in a fair and comprehensible manner is the way to do this.

Moreover, there is *no better way to do it.* Trying to win people over by being nice to them or giving them chance after chance doesn't work. They only learn that they can get away with things, which makes them less cooperative.

Nor does "individualizing" punishment help. Another fallacy of the 1960s was that we could "treat the criminal, not punish the crime." But, as Thomas Sowell points out in *Knowledge and Decisions,* information is one of the most costly and limiting factors in any society.[6] It is impossible, even on a small scale, for the criminal justice system to have enough information to tailor punishment to individual criminals. All individualization does is make punishment more *unpredictable,* which in turn makes it more difficult for people to learn to cooperate.

To understand how the justice system plays Tit for Tat, it is also necessary to understand that *the victim is not the only person hurt by a crime. Society* is also victimized. Everyone is hurt because there is a breach of trust, and because everyone is a potential victim. That is why punishment must include more than "restitution."

"Restitutionists" often argue that making the criminal pay the victim back is sufficient to deter crime. "If I'm burglarized, all I want is my possessions back," Karl Menninger argues. "Anything else is needless punishment inflicted on the criminal."

However, it is easy to see why such a system wouldn't work. If the only penalty for burglary is giving back what you have already stolen, then there is no risk. Every time you get away with it, you get a free ride. If the chances of getting away with a single burglary are about nine out of ten, then the punishment must essentially be *ten times* the haul of a single burglary—or its rough equivalent in jail time—in order to provide a disincentive.

Punishment must take into account the potential harm created by a successful burglary as well as the actual injury to the victim. This punishment will always exceed the "restitution price." But this does not mean that punishment need be sadistic, or that we inflict ten times the punishment on one apprehended burglar in order to vent our wrath for the nine unapprehended ones, as Menninger, for one, implies. Each burglary sentence must carry enough punishment to make *all* burglaries uneconomical. If these costs are not paid by the burglar at sentencing, then they are pushed back onto society in the form of an incentive to burglarize.

"The Prisoner's Dilemma" also serves as a handy tool for predicting the consequences of all forms of criminal justice "reform."

Say we decide, as many states have done, that juveniles shouldn't be "labeled" criminals and that they should automatically be given a "second chance" when they commit their first crime. What we quickly breed—as has already happened—is a generation of juveniles who know that they are entitled to "one free crime."

Or say we decide that criminals are really mentally ill and that they should be "treated" instead of "punished." If the treatment becomes less rigorous than the punishment—which it inevitably is—then we will get hundreds of criminals ready to admit that they are "insane."

It is only through swift, sure, and judicious punishment, as represented by "tit for tat," that we can elicit the best cooperative behavior out of the broadest range of individuals.

To be sure, punishment will not work in *every* instance. There are always going to be some people who constantly try to get away with things. But trying to make the system more lenient in order to try to win them over only elicits *less* cooperation out of everyone else. Making justice extremely indulgent may eventually win concessions out of a hardened criminal somewhere. But whatever gain is made is going to be more than lost in diminished cooperation elicited from other citizens.

The system must pitch itself to the broadest possible constituency and the most general case. The best way to do that is to play tit for tat.

Thus, when Karl Menninger tells us, "Crime problems have been dealt with too long with only the aid of common sense. Catch criminals and lock them up; if they hit you, hit them back. This is common sense, but it does not work," we know that he is entirely wrong. Punishing people, tit for tat, is the *only* way to elicit long-term cooperation from the broadest range of individuals.

The wisdom of this principle appears in most cultures. When asked to describe justice, people almost inevitably think of Hammurabi's ancient phrase, "An eye for an eye, and a tooth for a tooth." Nowadays, this system is likely to be viewed as harsh. What is interesting is that it was originally a form of *moderation.*

When "an eye for an eye" was instituted, people were taking *more than* an eye for an eye. Punishment was always likely to be "cruel and unusual." But, as the "prisoners' dilemma" indicates, excessive punishment produces the same counterproductive results as excessive leniency. When people insist on extracting their "pound of flesh," it promotes further retaliation and mutual recrimination.

This has been the great insight of historical criminology. For centuries, punishment was far too excessive. Torture and disembowelment were practiced regularly, and the death penalty was invoked for adultery, blasphemy, pickpocketing, and horse thievery.

The mistake society made was in believing that the more harrowing the punishment, the more people could be deterred from crime. In fact, there is a clear point of diminishing returns, where greater punishment stops doing any good. A whole series of great criminologists—Cesare di Beccaria, Jeremy Bentham, John Stuart Mill—perceived that *swift and certain punishment* of a moderate nature is far more effective than severe torture-punishments wreaked on individuals for relatively minor crimes.

The trouble with most modern criminologists is that they have decided to take things to the other extreme. If reducing punishment to moderate levels is good, then reducing it even further must be better. The less punishing we do, the more "civilized" we will become. If eliminating the death penalty for rape and burglary is good, then eliminating it for serial- and mass-murders must be even better.

All this takes no account of the original function of punishment—to deter crime and elicit cooperative behavior. At some point on the scale (we probably passed it around 1968) punishment becomes so lenient and easily avoided that people feel they can get away with anything. Like Ken Auletta's 21-year-old ex-convict, they begin to feel "invincible."

Dispensing justice, then, should be a fairly easy task. We simply play tit for tat. If someone breaks the rules, we punish them—not harshly, unless the crime itself is harsh, but in accordance with the offense.

The trouble is that it is too simple. People get bored with it. As one New York judge once said, "When you see one murder, you've seen them all."

Judges, lawyers, social workers, and psychologists—all are intelligent people. They get tired of playing the same old game, day after day. Nor are they likely to be satisfied with the *passivity* that comes with meting out tit-for-tat punishment. The strategy, it should be noted, is entirely responsive. There is no opportunity to initiate anything.

And so, the temptation grows to be "creative," to think up novelties— "crime as a social sickness," "crime as a product of the environment"—and to develop "alternate approaches" to "solving the problem of crime."

There is every indication that this is what happened in the late 1960s and early '70s. The literature of the period is filled with judges complaining,

"All we see day after day in our courtrooms are criminals, and all we ever do is punish them. There must be a better way."

Unfortunately, the better way is almost always *not* to punish or to start doling out shorter sentences. That is what happened during the late 1960s. It is another reason why prison populations were lower in 1972 than in 1962 and why crime soared.

One of the favorite games of criminologists and psychologists is to look for the "root causes" of crimes. History has been filled with "root causes" of crime. In the nineteenth century, lack of education was a root cause of crime. Educate people and crime would end. In the 1930s, poor housing was a root cause of crime. Build public housing and crime would end. Today poverty and racism are the most commonly mentioned root causes.

Public education was instituted widely in this country in the nineteenth century, and is undoubtedly a foundation of our social system. But it did not necessarily reduce crime. A survey in 1940 found the major discipline problems in the nation's high schools were "talking," "chewing gum," and "running in the halls." A survey taken in 1982 found them to be "assaults on students," "assaults on teachers," and "bringing weapons to school." Education, or lack of it, does not "cause" crime.[7]

Beginning in the 1930s, public housing was built, partly in the hope that the elimination of slums would reduce crime. In some cases these efforts have worked, but in others "the projects" have turned out to be crime-infested slums worse than the housing they replaced. Housing, good or bad, does not "cause crime."

America has undergone a remarkable change in racial attitudes over the last twenty-five years. When I started college in the 1960s, it was still customary for many respectable institutions to ask for a photograph with your application "so they could tell whether you were a Negro." Institutional racism has essentially been eliminated. Everyone, black and white, has made enormous psychic efforts to adjust to the idea of a biracial society. Even the most militant black activists will rarely argue that things are *worse* today than they were twenty-five years ago in terms of racism.

Yet crime among blacks—both as criminals and as *victims*—has literally exploded during the period. In 1972, murder was the leading cause of death among young black men, and blacks are now less likely to be murdered in prison than on the streets. Racism may have been a cause of lynchings in the South, but it can hardly be argued as a cause of the violent street crime of today.

For a long time during the 1960s and '70s, it was argued that drugs caused crime. Give the junkie free heroin instead of making him rob and burglarize to feed his habit, it was argued, and crime would disappear.

Yet a recent article in *New York* magazine indicated that, while heroin is now going out of fashion in some neighborhoods, it is not taking crime with it. "The new robber is not the lone, tattered junkie of the past," writes Michael Daly. "He is a fit young man who shuns narcotics and who stalks his victim with all the skill and deliberation of a woodsman hunting wild game ... Mark does 150 pushups at a time, and says, 'I hit hard for my size.' He tells of a dedicated thug named Drac who does not drink or smoke." Many young criminals are realizing that drugs and alcohol only detract from their abilities as muggers and yoke artists (who quickly incapacitate their victims by grabbing them around the neck).[8]

"Crime amidst plenty," says James Q. Wilson, was "the paradox of the Sixties."[9] Unemployment fell, income rose, prosperity abounded, yet crime rates exploded. (Strangely enough, the graph of national crime rates from 1968 to 1980 looks exactly like the price of oil.) Poverty does not "cause" crime. More poor people may commit violent crimes, but the rate at which they commit them cannot be matched to their changing economic circumstances.

Crime is an independent variable, not caused by anything except itself. It is a *style* of life—a persistent neglect of the rights of other individuals. The continual attempt of criminals to cheat others, and to cheat society, is based on *pessimistic* motives. Criminals always insist that "everybody is doing it too," and that "only they got caught." This cynical attitude becomes a justification to betray others.

Thus, it doesn't make sense to deal with crime outside the framework of punishment. Psychoanalyzing criminals usually just produces criminals who can use psychoanalytic terms to justify their own behavior. Educating prisoners—teaching them basket weaving or the great books—may produce wonderful basket weavers or classic scholars, but it doesn't have anything to do with curbing crime.

Willie Bosket, Sr., the father of New York's thrill-killing Willie Bosket, Jr., was probably a genius. He studied classical mathematics and could casually quote Dante's *Inferno*. He was the first person ever to make Phi Beta Kappa while earning a college degree in prison. While out on parole from a murder charge, he taught computer science at the University of Wisconsin and did programming for a Milwaukee firm.

Yet he also committed hundreds of armed robberies during his lifetime and was convicted for murder and attempted murder. As a University of

Wisconsin student who befriended him in prison said, "He had the social skills of a rhinoceros. He said there were three kinds of people—the sheep, the jackals who feed on the sheep, and the lions who take anything they want. He was a lion."[10]

After being paroled at age 45, he was soon back in jail for raping his girlfriend's 6-year-old daughter. Six months later, the same girlfriend smuggled him a gun and helped him make an escape. When the couple was cornered by police a short time later, Bosket shot himself to death—but not before turning the gun on his girlfriend and killing her first.

It was as cruel a way as anyone ever devised for playing "The Prisoner's Dilemma."

The criminologist and sociologists are right, then, when they tell us that man is a "cooperating animal." But what they rarely realize is that cooperation only works if someone is willing to punish infractions. It must be done as a purely neutral phenomenon, with the punishment fitting the *crime,* not the *criminal.* Ideally, every individual should carry with him the remorseless sense that *somewhere someone* cares whether they break the law.

The terrible thing is that if the officials appointed to the task no longer want to do it—or get distracted by other things—people will start doing it themselves.

After all these years, then, I think I have realized the answer to that philosophy student's problem about the tree killing its parent.

What makes a human child killing its parent—or any other human being—so terrible is that it is such a betrayal of cooperation.

A parent tree may produce the seed for the next generation, but it does nothing more. With human beings, however, it is different. Fertilizing the seed is only the beginning. No one who has ever raised children can forget the enormous sacrifices involved—and the number of times the most casual inattentiveness could lead to disaster.

It is that way with all human relationships. The horrifying thing that people always realize when someone near to them is robbed, raped, or murdered is that the whole thing is really so *easy.* It can happen at any time. The web of cooperation and mutual forbearance we live in is extremely fragile. The justice system is the only thing we have to hold it in place.

WHAT IS CRIME? 10

I F SOCIETY IS BASED on cooperation, then what is crime? Crime is the refusal, or inability, to cooperate. Criminals are people who don't cooperate. They are people who break the rules, who don't abide by the generally accepted conventions upon which society is based.

Now, of course, this is probably too simple. There are many rules to a society, and no one could possibly obey them all. If everyone even tried, society would be impossibly stultifying. As the deviance theorists suggest, "There are rules, and there are rules." If all the rules were ruthlessly enforced, everyone would be a criminal.

Deviance theorists have been basically correct in pointing out that there are certain marginal areas—often called "victimless crimes"—where the rules are necessarily arbitrary. Prohibition is one of the best examples of a counterproductive effort to make a crime out of a commonly accepted social activity.

What the deviance theorists missed, however, was the two-way interaction between the rules and the people who break them. Every human interaction involves some standards of behavior. You can't play poker with someone unless you both agree on the rules of the game. Yet once these ground rules are established, people will differ individually in how they respond to them. Some people always play by the rules. Others will always try to cheat. Most people will probably play the game honestly unless the opportunity to cheat becomes too easy to ignore.

Take the matter of driving on the right-hand side of the road, one of our simplest conventions. The rationale is purely arbitrary. The British drive on the left-hand side and suffer no ill effects. Yet once the standard is established, it is necessary that society enforce rules against deviance from the norm. Everyone can't set his own standard.

Why do people occasionally disobey the rules? It might be ignorance or poor education—fitting the sociological model of people who stumble into crime because they don't know any better. Or it might be a question of belonging to a different "subculture." A person from Britain, for example, might accidentally drive on the left in America and end up in trouble with the law. But most people who find themselves in such situations will not persist in rule-breaking for very long.

On the other hand, some people like to break the rules just for fun. Anyone who has ever been a teenager remembers how much fun it is to defy social convention. Thus, teenagers often like to joyride in the wrong lane, not out of any malicious motive, but just for the excitement of doing something wrong.

There can be other reasons as well. I once saw a woman swerve into the opposite lane and scatter cars for half a block. It turned out she was a depressive and had blacked out at the wheel. This behavior earned her a "label" as mentally ill and led to further deviant treatment as a mental patient. But there was not much punishment inflicted in this. She was a danger to other people, but also to herself.

Deviance theorists originally tried to categorize all criminals as relative innocents who "stumbled" into crime in one of these ways. Psychologists added their contribution that crime was a sign of being mentally ill. Yet this obviously doesn't cover all cases.

The one case that we condemn more than others and that carries the broadest social implications is when people deliberately drive on the wrong side of the road to gain some advantage—to beat a traffic jam, for example. This is the instance that is likely to bring punishment, and the "label" of having committed a crime.

Almost any mutually-agreed-upon social convention will bring some advantage to an individual who breaks it as long as everybody else agrees to obey it. It is this kind of activity that the law is most concerned about. There is only one way to deal with this sort of infraction, and that is to punish it as an infraction.

Historically, America had a reputation as a society that didn't tolerate much deviance. Even though we have always had higher crime rates than Europe, we also had a "puritan tradition," and Europeans often laughed at our prudishness on matters of alcohol and sex.

The vague suggestion that came during the 1960s was that if we stopped being so "uptight" about small things, maybe we wouldn't have so much crime. It was our intolerance of small infractions, it was argued, that pushed so many people into larger ones. Unfortunately, as plausible as this academic theory sounded, it did not work in practice.

In an apparent attempt to shed our puritanical and conformist heritage, we became an almost obsessively *tolerant* society during the 1960s. For a long while, it seemed as if there was almost nothing that Americans wouldn't convince themselves to tolerate.

Marijuana smoking, formerly limited to small subcultures, such as jazz musicians and urban blacks, became a widespread phenomenon. Nudity and pornography became commonplace. Public profanity became almost the mark of an educated individual. Running naked through public places became an initiation rite. (I once knew a woman whose streaking episode had been almost a religious experience. It had changed her personality completely, "liberating" her from her strict upbringing.)

As always, the avant-garde—not to be outdone by all this bourgeois recklessness—kept pushing the limits further and further. If simulated sex scenes became routine on Broadway (and real sex scenes just off Broadway), then the true artists would move on to something else. During the early 1970s, there was always some theater director around (usually French) announcing that he would not be fulfilled as an artist until he could murder someone on stage. One avant-garde artist actually had himself shot in the arm, causing composer Laurie Anderson to write a song observing sensibly, "It's Not The Bullet That Kills You, It's The Hole."

Whether all this experimentation was a form of decadence, or cultural adaptability—or just extreme self-indulgence that only affluence makes possible—is still an open question.

But the one lesson we did learn is that easing the rules on marginal deviance does not necessarily reduce crime. In fact, the reverse seems to be true. Ignoring infractions and allowing people to get away with small things only seems to encourage them to get away with larger things. Unfortunately, there are people out there who tend to see greatly increased tolerance for deviance as a sign that violent crime may be tolerated too.

Deviance theory works best at the margins of some of these "victimless" crimes, where no one is immediately hurt in the process—except perhaps the "criminal" himself. True, smoking marijuana is probably not as dangerous as originally feared. Although it may incapacitate people for short periods, it is surely not worth the 20-year jail sentences that were once handed out.

Heroin is different. Its effects make people nearly nonfunctional. They become dependent on illegitimate activities, or the good will of others, for their survival. Cocaine seems to fall somewhere in between—certainly not something we want to license broadly by decriminalizing, but perhaps not worth long jail sentences for possessing in small amounts.

Prostitution, public drunkenness, gambling, or other "vice" crimes, all fall into the same nebulous categories. They can be tolerated in small amounts, even legalized or licensed. But there is a clear danger in letting them get out of hand.

One thing to remember about such "victimless" crimes, however, is that there are certain people who will gravitate toward them precisely because that is where society draws the line. Once they become illegal, they also become more profitable.

It is in these areas that "organized crime" functions best. Organized criminals are people who cooperate with each other even more intensely than normal people for the purpose of preying on the rest of society. The rules among organized criminals are much harsher and more strictly enforced than in the rest of society. The death penalty is alive and well among organized criminals.

It is sometimes suggested that we could outflank organized crime by legalizing the forbidden activities in which it engages. Although superficially appealing, this argument basically misses the point. True, many rum-runners settled down after Prohibition to become the liquor companies of today. But legalizing questionable activities quickly hits a point of diminishing returns. Many people pursue these certain activities precisely *because* they are illegal. The profits are higher—and the risks greater—on the social margins.

Thus, if adult pornography is legalized, then criminals will move into child pornography. If the state operates numbers games, organized criminals will mimic the state lottery but offer a bigger payoff. Renegade marijuana growers in the mountains of Oregon and California are the last people who want marijuana legalized. They could never compete against the farmers of the San Joaquin Valley.

While there is a certain amount of cultural leeway among these "victimless" activities, however, there is a hard core of crimes that no society can tolerate. These are the actions that create *victims.*

A recent cross-cultural study of mores in India, Indonesia, Iran, Italy, the United States, and Yugoslavia found that, while there was wide difference of opinions on questions like abortion and homosexuality, there is also "a high—indeed, virtually universal—agreement that certain behaviors were wrong and should be prohibited by law." These "universal crimes" include murder, robbery, rape, burglary, and incest.[1]

Thus, when deviance theorists argue that "certain things are only wrong because certain people say they are wrong," they are only half-right. Certain things are wrong because *everybody* thinks they are wrong.

The common characteristic of these crimes is that they deprive others of life, liberty, or property. Sometimes they are achieved through cunning or deception, sometimes through physical force.

The most feared crimes are those where people are placed in immediate physical danger. Although all forms of crime should be punished, there is no question that people fear assaults and armed robberies more than they fear pickpockets or mail fraud, even though they may end up losing less money. A burglary is not quite as frightening as an armed robbery—and does not usually carry as severe a penalty.

One of the things that criminologists tried to do in the 1960s was to argue that people should be more concerned about organized crime than about street crime. Some of the literature that came out of the President's commission now has a remarkable anti-Italian flavor.[2] It has always been my impression that the "Godfather" craze of the early 1970s was the public's way of rejecting these suggestions. People were telling the crime experts that, when it came right down to it, they would much prefer *crime* and order to law and *disorder.* One couple I know moved into a reputed Mafia neighborhood in Brooklyn precisely because the streets were so safe.

It is true that more money is lost each year through fraud, tax evasion, and white-collar crime than through burglaries and street robberies. Yet it is obviously violent crimes that are feared most. People are not triple-locking their doors and carrying cans of mace these days in order to protect themselves from bank embezzlers.

What makes these "universal crimes" wrong? Let us turn the question around for a moment and ask instead, Why *shouldn't* people who are stronger or more violent or cunning have the right to take whatever they want from people who are unable to defend themselves?

It is a question worth pondering. Nietzsche was one of the earliest of modern philosophers to argue that society's laws are really lilliputian devices whereby the weak are able to tie down and strangle the abilities of the strong.

Articulated or unarticulated, many criminals hold to this view themselves. Conservative philosopher Russell Kirk has described the experience of his grandfather, a bank manager named Frank Pierce, who was once held-up by a pair of robbers, one of whom he later learned was Machine-gun Kelly:

> They took my grandfather to his bank long before any customers would appear and ordered him at gunpoint to open the safe. He would not do so. The two robbers sat down to converse with Mr. Pierce; there was plenty of time yet. The voluble robber, in rather friendly fashion, recounted the story of his own life. He had been a victim of circumstances, he said; but he had transcended them by taking up the robbing of banks. He held a theory of law and society rather like that of Thrasymachus, it seemed to my historically minded grandfather: that is, the robber maintained that might is right, and that he was by nature one of the strong, which truth he was presently demonstrating. He then requested Mr. Pierce, once more, to open the safe. My grandfather still refused.
>
> "Then, Mr. Pierce, though I've come to like you, I'm going to have to kill you."
>
> Convinced of his companions' sincerity, my grandfather opened the safe.[3]

The truth is that, during certain portions of history, might *has* made right. The nineteenth century philosopher Herbert Spencer had a very compelling theory that there have been two stages of history—the military and the commercial.[4] Throughout most of history, military force and physical strength have ruled. History at that time was, as Mark Twain said, "one damned battle after another."

Gradually, however, the commercial phase has gained the upper hand. People still compete, but they compete in a cooperative fashion. Force and violence, after all, is a zero-sum game, while commercial transactions are positive-sum. That is why commercial nations have gradually—if tenuously—come to dominate history.

In "civilized" societies, contests of sheer physical prowess are likely to be confined to recreational activities or sports—where they are often, in turn, commercialized. But sheer physical violence is never far removed from everyday life. Occasionally, it explodes, as in atavistic behavior. When it does, we call it "crime."

I remember once sitting at a municipal town-board meeting watching an elderly councilman berate a police sergeant. The village elder must have been about sixty years old, small, wizened, with a bald head. The police sergeant probably weighed about 230 pounds. I remember thinking that, if the police sergeant had wanted to, he probably could have wrung the councilman's neck with one hand. Yet the sergeant sat there taking it all in a very chastened manner. How strange it is, I remember thinking, that we live in a society where the weak so frequently dominate the strong.

Another time, I saw a group of black teenagers sitting on a park bench in a Hudson River village where I lived. One of the boys suddenly jumped up and started shadowboxing with the people—mostly white—who were passing by. Race relations were fairly good, and no one particularly panicked although a few were clearly frightened.

I remember thinking, once again, how strange and unfair the world must seem to this young individual. Here he was, at age seventeen, easily a match for any of the "respectable" and "successful" people around him. He could easily overpower any one of them individually. How peculiar it is, then, that such an obvious, natural talent is disallowed by a web of invisible restrictions that thwart such clear physical superiority. (It is not like this everywhere, of course. Most of the "guerrilla armies" roaming the world today are these forces set loose.)

There is not getting around it. One of the things that generally characterizes criminals is that they are *physically stronger* than most people.

To begin with, nearly all criminals are men. In an age of "equal opportunity," this should catch our attention right away. Certainly, women do a lot of shoplifting, and prostitution is basically a female profession. But *violent* crime is clearly a male province.

Ninety-five percent of prison inmates are male. Men commit nearly all the assaults, burglaries, car thefts, robberies, and murders. Rape, of course, is almost by definition a male crime. (Women can be accomplices to a rape, and in some states adult women can be charged with statutory rape of underage boys.)

Even at the domestic level, these imbalances persist. Forty percent of all women who are murdered die at the hands of their partner. The figure is only 10 percent for men. Battery by men is the leading cause of injury to women, more significant than auto accidents, rapes, or muggings.[5]

Even the most casual observer of jail inmates could tell anyone that convicted criminals are generally stronger and tougher than the citizen-at-large. There are many exceptions, and some criminals are remarkably unprepossessing. But most jail inmates are tough, vigorous males between 20 and 30 years of age.

What we call "crime," then, is in many ways a reversion to a more physical form of interrelationship that the rules of civilization have generally led us to forego.

The overwhelmingly *physical* quality of violent crimes is something that is often hard to keep in mind. One of the first things that always strikes one in seeing an accused murderer or armed robber in the courtroom is how harmless he looks. It is difficult to imagine him doing the violent deeds of which he is accused.

Only people who are continuously exposed to criminal activities become respectful of this underside of human nature. I once asked a young district attorney what he had learned in his few years on the job. He thought for a moment, shrugged, and said, "People are capable of anything."

Thus, a refusal to take criminal acts seriously, or to think they can be forgotten or excused, is not really an act of generosity or higher wisdom. It is a failure of imagination.

The "earlier biological" quality of violent criminal activities can be illustrated in the surprising observation that, even though the average criminal is far younger, stronger, and more agile than the average citizen, most criminals take special pains to pick out the *weakest possible victims.*

In nature, this kind of behavior is called "predatory." It is always surprising to realize that, no matter how swift the cheetah, or powerful the polar bear, these animals usually prey upon the youngest and weakest of their prey animals. There is nothing in nature that says predation has to be a fair fight.

So too, one of the most horrifying realizations about the crime waves sweeping American cities is that it is often the weakest people who are preyed upon first. Fifteen-year-old muggers in housing projects do not go after plumbers and construction workers. They do "push-in" robberies against 75-year-old widows, who are always believed to have thousands of dollars under their mattresses. (Overall statistics do show the elderly are less victimized by crime in urban areas, but that may be because they restrict their movements so much in order to avoid crime.)

Willie Bosket, Jr., New York's "thrill killer," is not a particularly prepossessing individual. He weighs only about 160 pounds and doesn't look much different than thousands of other 21-year-olds in New York City. But he has been careful to pick his victims. When he went to jail again in 1984 (after serving only short "juvenile-justice" sentences for two murders), it was for beating up a 70-year-old diabetic man in his Harlem apartment building.

In 1977, I moved to New York City, somewhat apprehensive about crime. After a year, I was wondering what the fuss was all about. I never had the slightest incident where I felt preyed upon or threatened. Then my wife moved to New York, and I realized what was going on. She was constantly being harassed and grabbed on the street by men, shadowed in the subways. (After a few months, however, she developed that "invisible shield" that all New Yorkers learn to carry, however, and hasn't had much trouble since.)

Who are criminals, then? They are basically people who don't cooperate and play by the rules. Why do we have rules in the first place? In order to protect the weak from the strong.

But is this fair? Wouldn't it be better—as Nietzsche vaguely suggested— to "breed a better population" by letting the strong take what they want?

Such ideas have been proposed more than once in history. The reason they don't work is this. Crime produces a negative-sum game. The criminal wins, but he does so by taking from someone else. In the process, he creates distrust in everyone. The result is a net loss for society. Crime creates two victims—the individual who is robbed or injured and the society, which suffers a loss of trust and security.

Transactions in which two people participate voluntarily, however, benefit society. They create a positive-sum game, in which both people gain, and the society benefits from their example (as long as they aren't scheming together against everybody else). A voluntary, positive-sum transaction creates a whole that is bigger than the parts. It is the way social progress has come about.

To use the language of "Tit for Tat," crime doesn't pay because it is not "nice." It doesn't enhance cooperation. The criminal may benefit, but everyone else loses more. Crime is a negative-sum game, creating distrust and causing people to cooperate *less*. It injures the whole society.

Criminals do not follow Kant's categorical imperative to "choose for yourself as if you were choosing for everyone." Criminals want to rob and kill others, but they don't want to be robbed and murdered themselves. They want to isolate themselves from society—which is often just how they end up. By failing to consider themselves as one of many, they strike against everyone. That is why crime is detrimental to all of society, and not just to the individual victim.

The rules, then, are biased against certain people. They are biased against those who are conniving and untrustworthy—against those who use their strength to dominate the weak. The aim of all these restrictions is to promote broad social cooperation.

The payoff for this renunciation of violence and the build-up of trust in society is that cooperation benefits everyone. Even though some may not do as well as others, creating a positive-sum game is the only way that the great mass of people can ever hope to improve their situation in a society. Cooperation requires rules, but when these rules are drawn up with the approval of the majority it is only fair that they should be obeyed by all.

What can we do about people who refuse to cooperate or who take advantage of everyone else's cooperation in order to defect? The only thing we can do with these people is punish them, tit for tat. There is no other way to "educate" people into playing the game of civilization.

Realizing that reciprocal behavior is behind humanity's successes also explains why it doesn't make sense to say that "poverty causes crime."

The truth is just the opposite. *Crime causes poverty.* Poverty is the historical rule, the place where all societies began. The real question is how some societies ever overcame their original poverty. The answer is, through cooperation.

Crime is the unwillingness or inability to engage in cooperative behavior. It turns society into a zero- or negative-sum game. When the strong continually prey upon the weak, when rules are continually broken, when people cannot feel any security or trust in their lives, it is difficult, if not impossible, to overcome poverty.

This is the reason why the worst black ghettos in America have proved so impervious to prosperity, in good times or in bad. These sub-societies are so overridden with distrust and predatory behavior that mutual effort is difficult, if not impossible.

These high crime rates come from several historical factors. Probably the most prominent is a long history of *lax* law enforcement for black-on-black crimes by the larger white society. But these historical tendencies were also extraordinarily exaggerated by the general leniency that was introduced into the justice system during the 1960s and '70s.

All this, however, is not "caused" by poverty. Other American ethnic groups—the Japanese on the West Coast, for example—have had similar histories of poverty and discrimination. Yet they never let their communities become dominated by mutual exploitation and criminal behavior. As a result, they have emerged from poverty and are now, on the average, more prosperous than the society at large. The Jews have also had a long history of isolation and discrimination, but they have never let random violent crime dominate their communities.

As long as black neighborhoods in America are unsafe—even for black people themselves—there is little hope that they will ever prosper. Too much energy must be spent on self-protection, and too little time is left for the trust that can lead to beneficial enterprise. You don't know what crime really feels like until you walk into a friendly neighborhood hamburger store in Detroit or Bedford-Stuyvesant and find yourself staring at a four-inch-thick wall of bulletproof glass.

Poverty does not automatically turn people to crime. Poor people all react differently to their situation. Many of the black poor are the hardest working people in society, often working two and three jobs at once.

What defeats these efforts is the continual cycle of insecurity and violence that pervades these neighborhoods. When hardworking black people cannot be protected by the larger society, there is little hope that their decent, law-abiding efforts can lead their communities to much economic progress.

Poverty does not cause crime. It is just the opposite. Crime causes and perpetuates poverty.

CRIMINALS

11

ALTHOUGH Freudian psychology has had a far greater impact on the public, the psychologist who really understood criminals best was Alfred Adler.

Whereas Freud concentrated on the depths of the unconscious, Adler simply posited that success in life means "cooperating with other people." People who learn to cooperate with others are successful while those who don't become failures. That failure can take several forms—including neurosis, alcoholism, or lonely isolation. One form of failure is criminality.

> The criminal's striving for significance is limited and distorted. He lacks the ability to cooperate; he lacks interest in other people. Wherever he finds a problem which demands this *interest in others* for its solution, he throws himself into a great tension. He feels incapable of solving it, since he has never been trained to solve such problems.[1]

While most people are able to achieve feelings of superiority and accomplishment through successes that benefit other people, said Adler, the criminal feels he must achieve success *at the expense* of other people. In other words, he is playing a zero- or negative-sum game, where one person's gain must be another's loss:

> All his striving for significance . . . is in the direction of an imagined personal superiority: to outwit the police and prove himself more cunning than they are; to deprive others of their property; to have command of life and death; to prove his own importance at the expense of others . . . To deprive others—this is his idea of superiority.[2]

All this may seem perilously close to homily. But it is grounded in the fundamental insight that non-cooperative behavior is *self-defeating* while cooperation is the cause of its own success.

Despite the ease with which criminal behavior can be described, Adler did not have any illusions that criminals can be easily won over:

> The task is not quite as simple as it looks. We cannot win [the criminal] by making things easy for him, any more than by making them hard for him. We cannot win him by pointing out that he is wrong and arguing with him. His mind is made up. He has been seeing the world in this way for years.[3]

Nor did he necessarily believe that punishment—especially corporal punishments—could make much difference:

> Corporal punishment is ineffective.... Many criminals are not very fond of their lives. Some of them at certain moments ... are very near suicide. Corporal punishment does not terrify them. They can be so intoxicated by their desire to outdo the police that it does not even hurt them.... If they can be so intoxicated by their desire to outdo the police that it does not even hurt them.... If attendants are harsh, or if they are severely treated, they are put on their mettle to resist.... They see their contact with society as a sort of continuous warfare, in which they are trying to gain victory; and if we take it the same way ourselves, we are only playing into their hands. Even the electric chair can act as a challenge in this sense. The criminal conceives himself as playing against odds; and the higher the penalty, the greater is his desire to show his superior cunning.[4]

Adler's approach contrasts sharply with the Freudian approach, which often suggests that criminals are "sick" and that counseling and treatment can wean people away from criminal behavior.

Karl Menninger has been one of the foremost apostles of the idea that criminals are sick and therefore should be given special consideration:

> Remember, we are talking about a human being, a handicapped one at that, one who needs all the things that the rest of us do and a little bit more! You and I can get along without committing crimes (most of the time); but obviously the criminal cannot ...[5]

Sometimes this perspective is taken to the point where crimes are seen as nothing more than blundering efforts to obtain professional counseling by people who are otherwise too embarrassed to ask. There is always a "cry for help" behind each violent deed. "The Holocaust was Hitler's cry for help," is the way a friend of mine deals with this argument.

The underlying logic of this school seems to be that if, after committing a crime, a person can be "cured" and "restored to being a useful citizen," then all can simply be forgotten. Such an approach treats life as if it were nothing more than a series of appointments with "professional counselors." As long as a person is getting better, it doesn't matter how many people he hurts along the way.

Recently, Ann Landers received a letter decrying a situation where a Texas youth had killed his parents, was now being treated in a mental hospital, and would soon be eligible to inherit their estate. Landers, who is a trustee of the Menninger Foundation, told readers, "Obviously, the boy had serious behavioral problems. He should be monitored closely from hospital life to private citizen. I hope some caring relative will be on the scene to make sure David gets emotional support as well as professional counseling."[6]

Such an approach completely ignores the underlying logic that impels the justice system. ("Our old friend justice," as Menninger derisively called it.) Suppose a man suffering from severe depression and hostility kills his wife. He is judged "insane," as frequently happens, and receives intensive psychiatric treatment. Three years later he is cured—legitimately—and is leading a happy and healthy life.

Is such a situation a triumph for society? I don't think so. It sounds as if killing his wife was the best decision the man ever made. Nor is this example far-fetched. New York City police say there are young muggers everywhere in New York who regularly commit crimes in order to take advantage of the dental services at Riker's Island.

The non-Freudian approach to crime has been expanded in recent years by Drs. Samuel Yochelson and Stanton Samenow of St. Elizabeth's Hospital, a federal psychiatric facility for the criminally insane in Washington, D.C.

Both Yochelson and Samenow had become independently disillusioned with the ability of depth analysis to "cure" criminals. "All we were doing was producing criminals who knew psychiatry," said Yochelson.

Instead, they began to concentrate on the way most adult criminals seem to have become set in a pattern of antisocial behavior from very early childhood.

Samenow and Yochelson have noted that there seem to be several personality traits that almost all criminals have in common. Prominent among them is a consistent pattern of lying, even about petty and inconsequestial things. After a while, they said, it becomes very difficult for the criminal himself to separate the falsehood from the truth.

In addition, criminals are extremely self-centered. "To the criminal, the world is a chessboard, with other people serving as pawns to gratify his desires,"[7] writes Samenow in one memorable phrase. As Adler noted fifty years ago, criminals seem to lack the normal empathetic feelings that lead to cooperation with others.

Samenow notes that these antisocial attitudes can often be present when a child is only two years old. Children with criminal dispositions are often beating up brothers and sisters and tyrannizing their families before they are five. "It is truly amazing to see how some extremely disturbed families are instantly at peace once the criminal member leaves home."[8]

Far from the picture of the innocent bumbler that the deviance sociologists painted, criminals, says Samenow, are likely to be overconfident and have a very inflated image of their abilities.

This is a particular handicap in dealing with the world of work. "The criminal believes that because he is inherently more capable than others, previous experience and training requirements should be waived in his case. He is positive that his expertise and unique talents distinguish him from the common herd. . . When the doors do not open immediately to a criminal, he complains about lack of opportunity or discrimination."[9]

These observations have been echoed by Richard Cloward, author of *Delinquency and Opportunity,* who helped found New York City's Mobilization for Youth. After years of working with crime-prone youth, Cloward lamented candidly:

> We are plagued, in work with these youth, by what appears to be a low tolerance for frustration. They are not able to absorb setbacks. Minor irritants and rebuffs are magnified out of all proportion to reality. Perhaps they react as they do because they are not equal to the world that confronts them, and they know it. And it is the knowing that is devastating.[10]

Unfortunately, such people always tend to blame others for their predicament. Says Samenow:

> If the criminal is held accountable he blames the victim for the violence because [the victim] interfered in the successful execution of the crime. Exclaimed one man who shot his victim during a robbery: "That man must have been nuts! It wasn't my fault that he was crazy enough to risk his life for fifty bucks in his wallet."[11]

The frustrations and deferred gratification of the "square's world," then, are usually too much for a criminal. He can't stand "the square life, with all its loneliness and no fun," as one criminal put it. The high-risk, high-excitement life of crime—with its obvious payoffs for sheer prowess and cunning—offers an almost irresistible alternative.

The thing that much of contemporary criminology seems to miss is that *crime can be fun.* There seem to be few criminals who will not admit in their candid moments that they enjoy what they are doing.

In Michigan in 1985, I did a long interview with a 38-year-old career shoplifter who was doing another long stretch in prison. Although divorced from his wife, he said his last shoplifting binge had been to put one of his daughters through college. "I just give the money to my wife," he told me. "She doesn't ask where it came from."

As it turned out, his contribution had only been $3,000 while his wife—he said—was one of the highest paid social workers in the state, making close to $40,000. On the whole, it was hard to see how making $3,000 in a few months compensated for a few years in jail. He claimed, however, that in good years he had made over $100,000 tax-free, spending most of it on heroin.

As the conversation progressed, it became obvious that he enjoyed his work. "It's fun to be doing things that are wrong," he said candidly. "One time the county chief of detectives caught me in a store. He knew what was going on. He walked up and down the aisles with me telling me how I ought to straighten out and get a steady job. While we were walking, I was slipping things into my pocket." He demonstrated with a smile. "It's exciting to do that sort of thing and get away with it."

John Allen, the Washington, D.C., street robber who eventually ended up in a wheelchair, admitted that excitement was one of his main payoffs:

Even though my whores were making a lot of money, I just didn't like pimping that much. It ain't my style, even though a lot of dudes said I had the coldness for it as far as heart went. I missed stickup quite a bit. I always kept my eyes open for different things—casing joints. I would watch places and watch different people. Watch dudes going to night deposit boxes. It was a habit that I couldn't break. In fact, I do it even now. What I really missed was the excitement of sticking-up.[12]

At the annual meeting of the Academy of Criminal Justice Sciences in Las Vegas in 1985, I ended up sitting in a panel about prisons. The speakers talked mostly about how "overmanaged" the prisons were, and how guards were dangerous and incompetent people in whose hands the inmates were at great risk.

After a while a man stood up and identified himself as Leland Leak, corrections specialist at the Colorado State Prisons.

"I don't see how you can say we've overmanaged," he began. "Most of the time I'm on duty there are two of us supervising 120 prisoners. We don't even carry guns. What good would they be against 120 inmates? In that kind of situation you can't survive unless you learn to get along with people.

"I've been talking with inmates for thirty-two years now," he continued, "and I think somebody's pulling the wool over your eyes. I've made a collection of the things I hear most often from inmates. Here is what they usually say:

'Crime is easy and full of excitement. I get caught maybe one out of ten times.'

'I am what I want to be, and I enjoy it.'

'Being in jail like this just gives me a rest. Nothing changes when I get out again.'

'I chose what I want to be, just like you. There's no difference between us.'

'Nobody is the victim of my crimes except myself. I'm the one who has to do time in jail.'"

Several of the speakers were red-faced. There was a general murmur of disapproval in the audience. But a few people were vigorously nodding their heads.

I caught up with Leak in the hall afterward. "I go to these meetings because I finally realized it's academics who decide what happens in the prisons," he said genially. "I've got to give them an idea of what things are really like in there. Most of these sheepskin criminologists never met a real criminal in their lives."

One of the most popular root-cause arguments—that "drugs cause crime"—is probably an inversion. It would be more accurate to say that "criminals often do drugs."

The satisfactions offered by drugs, once again, fall into the kind of hit-or-miss, shoot-the-works pattern favored by people predisposed toward criminal behavior.

Although heroin addicts are commonly pictured as "dope-fiends," desperately seeking their next "fix," what people tend to forget is that heroin addicts—when they are on heroin—are experiencing a world of self-enclosed pleasure that apparently few of us ever experience.

I once had a friend who had experimented briefly with heroin. She said it was such pure bliss that she knew right away she probably would give up her job, stop eating, and maybe even sell her children in order to feel that way again. She was able to recognize the consequences, however, and never went back to it.

For criminals seeking escape from the frustration of the real world, however, heroin is the natural focal point of a whole lifestyle.

Bruce Jackson found this out during his prison interviews in one remarkable session with three women—Margie, Big Sal, and Judy—all addicted to heroin and in and out of prison most of their lives.

"In the AA meeting the other day," said Margie, "the question was raised about what made us return to the penitentiary, and I told them, 'Because I love dope.'"

Jackson noted that only a few minutes before one of them had said that being on heroin is the only way they ever feel "normal."

"You know, this reality bit, facing reality," said Big Sal, "I don't know, but it seems like most junkies, it seems like we see reality in its harshest... [T]here's all that responsibility on us that none of us were mature enough to accept to begin with."

Isn't it a little ironic, though, Jackson asks. "You've told me you don't like to face reality, and here you are dealing with a reality that is so much harder than the one you're getting away from."

"I don't know," says Sal. "I just know that if I'm on stuff I make more money. I'm more on my feet, I'm myself more. I like myself when I'm on a natural."

"You mean natural when you're on a fix?" Jackson says.

Margie tries to explain, "I don't really know. It's a heck of a thing. I guess you love all that goes with it. All the excitement. Maybe we're even a little geared. And maybe we're masochists and love to be punished."

The conversation then turned to whether heroin should be legalized. Big Sal, who was doing a life sentence as a habitual criminal, thought it should. Jackson mentioned the efforts of Marie Nyswander, founder of a methadone clinic in New York City. The three women began to discuss whether methadone or legalized heroin is a better solution.

"It's a big waste," said Sal. "That's all it is, you know. Because really and truly, like if we were out and got with this woman that's got this thing going in New York, that's our out. If we could go and get this legally. We could work even."

"You know what?" says Judy. "Let's just get down to the nitty-gritty."

"What?" says Sal.

Judy says, "If we make this woman and she's willing to do this for us, we could figure some way to fuck her out of her stuff."[13] And so it goes.

Criminals are criminals because they think like criminals. It is a habit of mind. They are always looking for the shortest route possible. They find it hard to believe it can be done any other way. When George Gilder was interviewing inmates in an Albany prison, he discovered a common rumor that John D. Rockefeller had really made his money as a secret member of the Jesse James gang.

In the light of all this, Freudian analysis, with its explorations of the psychological depths, does not seem to shed much light. It seems to be of absolutely no use in *treating* criminals. In fact, a few experiments in psychoanalysis have actually produced an *increase* in recidivism.[14]

It is easy to see why. Psychoanalysis offers a kind of allegorical reality—a world in which people are really "acting out" some "unconscious fantasy." The implication becomes that what actually happens in reality isn't very important.

Writing on crime recently, Roger Starr, author of *The Decline of New York,* recalled:

As a temporary "prisoner chaser" during World War II, I carried a loaded rifle through an army camp in Georgia behind two fellow G.I.'s convicted of holding up a cab driver with a knife. They explained to me that one of them was afflicted by a disastrous father image, activated by the driver's resemblance to that father. The other announced that by attacking the driver he was acting out *his* desire to clear the way to make love to his mother. These explanations of all future misdeeds had been vouchsafed years before by a social worker in Cook County where, I took it, they first ran into the law.[15]

After reviewing two centuries of literature on criminal psychology, David Kelly, former professor of philosophy at Vassar, has concluded that the best analysis of criminals may have been by nineteenth-century psychologists, who saw criminality as a *moral* failing:

> Psychologists in the nineteenth century noticed a disorder which seemed to involve no cognitive impairment—those who had it were often quite intelligent and clearheaded—but a gross deficit in what used to be called the *moral* faculties: the capacities for feeling, valuing, acting for goals, living by standards, in cooperation with others. Such people seemed profoundly amoral. Despite their intelligence, they were unable to detach themselves from the impulse of the moment. They seemed constitutionally incapable of empathy, or concern for others, or even the most elementary sense of fairness and reciprocity... The psychologists called them "moral imbeciles."[16]

Kelly also cites the work of Hervey Cleckley, whose book, *The Mask of Sanity*, published in 1941, is still used in diagnosing criminal personalities:

> [Cleckley's] subjects exhibited a normal range of intelligence; many were very well-informed, many were talented. . . They were not victims of delusions and were remarkably free of anxiety. Yet they seemed incapable of learning from experience, making the same mistakes over and over . . . Cleckley came to believe that the intelligence they showed was merely verbal; he was struck by a . . . complete absence of long-range planning in their lives.
>
> Most of his patients, especially those with criminal records, were able to size people up quickly; they were good at manipulating others and *mimicking* conventional feelings when it suited them. Yet on other occasions their actions revealed a complete incapacity to anticipate how others would react. One woman, in applying for jobs, routinely gave as references people whose trust she had violated repeatedly. His patients were chronic liars and thieves, even when no clear gain was

involved. . . Their egocentricity was so profound as to differ in kind from ordinary self-centeredness.[17]

These observations appear over and over in the literature of criminality. Stanton Samenow writes:

> Although criminals differ in the crimes they find acceptable, they are carbon copies of one another in their view of themselves and the world. All are liars and hide behind a mask of secrecy. They have an inflated self-image in which they regard themselves as special and superior and assume that people will do their bidding. Contemptuous of the world of law-abiding people, they share the view that the responsible world is a barren wasteland.[18]

St. Clair McKelway, who wrote "Annals of Crime" for the *New Yorker* in the 1930s and 1940s described this encounter with a young hoodlum named "Joseph," whom he called the "Times Square Kid":

> I told Joseph I wanted to cash a check at my bank, on Fifth Avenue, before we went to lunch . . .
> While I cashed my check, Joseph sat down just inside the entrance of the bank, and I noticed that his eyes swept the place in a studiously casual way. We continued up Fifth Avenue to a Schrafft's, and he said, "You know, that would be something big—really big—taking a bank like that. It would be a big score."
> In Schrafft's, Joseph seemed quite at ease. His manner with the waitress was gentle. "I don't agree with a lot of guys about some things. . . When I have money, I like to spend it. One time, I made a nice, big score—about eight hundred bucks. I moved into a fancy hotel and stayed there for almost a month. I hung around the bar, and I got to be known. The bartender introduced me to people a couple of times. . .
> Sometimes, hanging around a nice bar, you meet an older man and get talking, and he invites you up to his room for a drink when the bar closes. You can hustle a buck that way. You tell him you'll accuse him of being queer unless he comes across with some dough. They always come across and there's no beef. Some of them really are queers. It burns me up—all the people that have dough and don't spend it. Like those old dames you read about, living in some old house or in a hotel, with thousands of dollars tucked away in their mattresses or hidden in

an old tin can. What the hell? Why should they have all that dough? They can't do anything with it. They're too old to enjoy it. It burns me up.[19]

It is sometimes suggested that extreme intelligence is the mark of criminality—the "criminal genius." Criminals often appear intelligent because many get away with things. Some criminals are geniuses. It is said that Meyer Lansky or Bugsy Siegel could have run General Motors. But intelligence does not seem to be the guiding principle of criminality. Their only basic insight is that if everybody else obeys the rules, they can win temporary advantages by breaking them.

At the same time, one of the most common things is an attraction among intellectuals for certain criminals. Intellectuals often harbor many resentments against ordinary middle-class society, but express them only through satires or social criticisms that ordinary people do not understand anyway. When such an intellectual encounters a real criminal, the intellectual is likely to regard the criminal as "heroic" because he dares do things the intellectual acts out only in fantasy. Political rhetoric can also bridge the gap between intellectuals and criminals, particularly when criminals are clever enough to ape it.

Thus, while solving a crime can be a fascinating intellectual exercise, most intellectuals usually become involved in the exercise of trying to prove a certain person *didn't* commit a crime or should be absolved of it. Often these campaigns to free a person are carried on without the slightest knowledge of the facts of the case but only with the certainty that whatever the police and prosecutors do must be wrong.

Thus, crime is a very stable phenomenon. Although criminals in the past two decades have definitely become more violent, the parameters differ little from generation to generation. The task of learning cooperation must always be undertaken anew. There will always be people who seek shortcuts or decide not to participate.

The rewards of "life's fast lane" are enticing but generally superficial. After awhile even the most hardened criminals seem to find them exhausting. "You get tired. You get tired of trying to be a tough guy all the time," said John Allen, the Washington, D.C., mugger who ended up in a wheelchair. "There were a couple of times in my life when I tried being square. But something always seems to happen to mess it up."[20]

After living steadily among criminals for more than a year, Bruce Jackson summed it up this way:

> I remember sometimes hearing stories about good bars and pneumatic women, being told how we could go to these places and drink the good booze and groove on the groovy music and ball the pneumatic ladies. Sometimes I went with some people when they were on the streets and found the attractions depressingly grubby. It *is* a grubby existence, as a rule. . .
>
> In this world everybody seems to sleep a lot, sex is too often completely lacking in affect, and the kicks found the rest of the time never seem to satisfy very long. . .
>
> For most successful criminals, life is terribly lonely.[20]

A few of the old-timers in my Brooklyn neighborhood still remember Willie Sutton, the famous bank robber, who grew up in Park Slope in the 1920s and '30s. In his later years, they say, he used to spend a lot of time in a little coffee shop right across from Greenwood Cemetery.

He always sat in the same booth near the back of the store. He never talked to anybody, and nobody ever talked to him. If you watched closely though, they say, you could see him darting little glances out of the corners of his eyes, quietly sizing up his surroundings.

VICTIMS 12

WHENEVER A group of reporters gets together for late-night shoptalk, the conversation inevitably turns to the time when each had to interview the family of someone who had just died. Deep in his brain, every reporter carries the memory of walking up to a door somewhere and saying, "Hi, I'm from the newspaper. Would you tell me how you feel about your son/daughter/father/mother getting killed?"

I once had to interview a large family whose youngest son had been killed by a bus. The family was donating his heart to a transplant patient. When I arrived, the shock had pretty much worn off, and the room was filled with edgy, nervous conversation. I sat down at a table, opened up my notebook, and asked what the son had been like. Before I had finished speaking, the room had fallen silent. I looked up to find a dozen silent faces waiting to see what I was going to put on paper. I felt like St. Peter making an entry into the Book of the Fates.

Another reporter I knew found, when she got to the home of the victim, that no one knew he was dead yet. She became the bearer of the bad news.

Imagine what it's like, then, to walk into a room full of people, each one of whom is there because someone very close to them has been the victim of a tragic crime.

The National Organization of Victims' Assistance (NOVA) holds its national convention at different places around the country every year. We are, it turns out, a society in which crime is so common that victims themselves have started their own organizations. I attended the 1983 conference in Jacksonville, Florida, with about 400 other people.

From all appearances, it was just another gathering of boat dealers or television repairmen that occurs every day around the country. There were cocktail hours, information booths, and the usual straining to read name tags. One whole evening was dedicated to a talent show while another afternoon featured the "water olympics" in the Jacksonville Sheraton's outdoor pool.

"We try to keep everybody's spirits up," said Dorothy Morefield, who was serving as director of NOVA at the time. "We don't want things to get too gloomy. But nobody ever forgets entirely why they're here."

Morefield was typical. Her son Rick, a 19-year-old college freshman, was killed execution-style along with four other people by a 39-year-old career criminal in the freezer of a Roy Rogers Restaurant where Rick was working at a summer job. She and her husband, Dick—who later became an Iranian hostage—founded the Washington, D.C., chapter of Parents for Murdered Children, an organization that now has chapters in thirty-five states.

Dick Morefield still thinks of his Iranian experience as only his "second-greatest trauma." "At one point the Iranians lined us up against a wall and said they were going to shoot us," he said. "The only thing I thought was, 'So this is how my son felt.'"

Although everyone held up pretty well, composure was often strained when the meeting settled down to its workshop sessions. There, people were forced to face their common experiences.

"My daughter was kidnapped and murdered by a neighbor of ours in 1975," said a mother from Portland, Oregon, gripping the lectern, her face gray and haggard from years of pain. "We know who did it—everybody knows who did it. But the police can't prove it. The man has already had another child murder conviction overturned twice on technicalities. The second time he got off because he hadn't been allowed to argue that he was drunk when he did it. Sometimes you get the feeling there's nothing the law can do to touch these people."

The participants all seemed to have two things in common—their pain at suffering from a crime and their mutual frustrations with the justice system.

"People who are victims of a crime just don't know what they're getting into," said Marlene Young, now executive director of NOVA. "They go into court expecting to find something called 'justice.' They feel they're owed some debt, some restitution, some *explanation* from society.

"Instead, they find themselves in a procedural maze where they keep going back over and over, and nothing ever seems to happen. They take a day off from their job to go and testify, and they find a continuance has been granted at the request of the defense. They go back a month later, and the same thing has happened. Of course, the defense attorneys are just trying to wear them down. The best way to win a case is to get the complainant to give up."

In New York City, for example, the average victim who follows the procedure to completion now makes an appearance at the courthouse seventeen times.

Over and over, the victims of serious crimes report the same frustrations. Diana Montenegro, a high-school senior, was stabbed to death by another girl at a concert in a neighborhood park in Queens, N.Y. Her mother, also Diana, soon found the case was going to be plea-bargained. "It was going to be a wrist-tap sentence. I wanted to know why she killed my daughter, and why 200 people stood around and did nothing," she said.

Mrs. Montenegro took her story to the newspapers and finally forced a trial. "I wasn't even informed of the court dates," she said. "When the prosecutor saw me, he told me to go home, I wasn't needed. Right on the other side of the courtroom I could hear the defense attorney leading her family step-by-step through the process. I feel the girl who murdered my daughter was treated better by the system than I was."[1]

"People demand an explanation when this kind of thing happens," said Linda Barker, of Families and Friends of Missing Persons and Violent Crime Victims, in Seattle. "When the justice system can't come up with an answer, people begin providing their own."

So it went, day after day. Paul Garland is a Westchester County attorney whose daughter Bonnie was killed in his own house by her Yale boyfriend, Richard Herrin. They had gone together for three years when she tried to break it off. On the night he was supposed to leave her house for the last time, he went to the basement to get a hammer and then clubbed her to death—or so he thought—as she slept in her own bed. Herrin then fled for upstate New York, thought about suicide but decided against it, and finally turned himself in at a police station the next morning. When police notified Bonnie's family, they didn't even know she had been hurt.

Herrin talked to a priest and showed absolutely no emotion or remorse until word came back from Westchester that Bonnie wasn't dead, but in a coma. Herrin became hysterical. "She has to be dead," he shouted. "Her head split open like a watermelon. The hammer stuck in her head and I had to pull it out." Then he broke down crying. A few hours later, Bonnie died.[2]

By the time of the trial, of course, Herrin was composed and well rehearsed. A nun from a Catholic order at Yale had "adopted" Richard and came to court each day, sitting silently saying the rosary. After each session, she rushed up to Richard, and hugged and kissed him in front of the jury. Yale University even supported Herrin, sending letters testifying to his good character. "It was like he was filing a job application, not on trial for murder," Paul Garland said. Meanwhile, Herrin's attorney argued strenuously against having Bonnie's mother testify how she went upstairs and found her daughter's head bashed in because it would be "too emotional." He later tried to have both of Bonnie's parents barred from the courtroom.

In the end, Herrin was convicted only of manslaughter, on the grounds that he had been emotionally upset over losing Bonnie. Willard Gaylin, a Westchester County psychiatrist who followed the trial, later wrote:

> When one person kills another, there is immediate revulsion at the nature of the crime. But in a time so short as to seem indecent to the members of the personal family, the dead person ceases to exist as an identifiable figure. To those individuals in the community of good will and empathy, warmth and compassion, only one of the key actors in the drama remains with whom to commiserate—and that is always the criminal. . . He usurps the compassion that is justly his victim's due.[3]

But despite all these personal tragedies, there was a strong feeling at the convention that the "day of the victim" has arrived.

"The courts are rapidly beginning to realize that the victim of a crime has just as much right to a fair trial as does the accused," said Lois Haight Herrington, U.S. deputy attorney general, who headed President Reagan's Task Force on the Victims of Crime. "For too long, the victim has been the forgotten person in the criminal justice system."

Especially encouraging, she said, were two recent Supreme Court decisions on habeas corpus. In both instances, criminals who had been convicted of rape had won appellate court decisions for retrials on minor technicalities. In both instances, the Supreme Court—coming under the increasing influence of Justice Sandra Day O'Connor, an outspoken advocate of victims' interests—rejected a retrial. "The decision was based on the grounds that in each case a second trial would be traumatic for the *victim,*" Herrington told a cheering audience.

The Victims' Rights movement appears to be bringing together a very broad coalition of generally liberal-minded people. A great many of them have come right out of the women's-rights movement and other activist organizations.

"To be frank, a lot of us were working on the other side of this issue five years ago," said Veronica Zecchini, of the victims' assistance program in the Sacramento district attorney's office. "I was involved with juvenile justice, trying to get more lenient treatment for young offenders. But after spending time at the courtroom and seeing what's going on there, a lot of us started asking ourselves which side we really wanted to be on. Times have changed."

"We still have a court of appeals in Oregon that is very, very pro-defendant," said Marilyn Culp, another former women's activist and now head of a victims' assistance program in Portland, Oregon. She was addressing a workshop called "The Trauma of Going to Court," packed with an audience that was 90 percent women. "There is a new group called 'United Victims of Crime,' working to elect two new judges. We're only six months old, but we've already had an enormous impact."

The specter of vigilantism often stalked the halls. "We've got one vigilante group in Mobile that is going off in all directions," said Anita Armstrong, founder of Victims of Crime and Leniency (VOCAL) in Alabama in 1982, which has been lobbying the state legislature for stricter law enforcement. "We feel we've got to head these people off before something happens. We've got to offer people a better alternative."

What stuns most victims in court these days is the brazen qualities of some defense strategists. "I've seen a case where a man caught a burglar red-handed in his living room at twelve o'clock at night," said Justice Charles Weltner, a justice of the Georgia Supreme Court. "The victim gets on the stand and the defense attorney says to him, 'Now sir, isn't it true that you approached this young man over here on the street and offered to pay him to engage in homosexual relations with you; that you invited him into your house and he changed his mind and then you called the police?' When the witness becomes upset, the defense lawyer pounces on this as proof that the charge of homosexuality is true."[4]

The best way to forestall complainants and witnesses is simply to wear them down. Going to court is always traumatic, and the more things drag on, the more difficult it becomes. First there are grand jury hearings, then preliminary trial hearings, then evidentiary hearings, and finally the trial testimony.

Sprinkled throughout are the endless continuances and postponements that judges grant almost automatically. There is no way of punishing a defense attorney who can't make it to court because of a schedule conflict. One of the simplest tactics the defense lawyers use is to take dozens of cases so that they can rarely meet all their court appearances. William Kunstler has frequently had so many cases pending around the country that prosecutors' offices are often fighting over him.[5]

Once the trial begins, the victim—or the victim's family—is in for another ordeal. This is particularly true at murder trials where the victim cannot be present.

Dominique Dunne, the 22-year-old actress who had starred in *Poltergeist,* was strangled to death by her jealous boyfriend, John Sweeney, who had become obsessed with her and had a history of violence. Only five weeks before her death, Sweeney had beaten her so badly that she was able to appear as a battered teenager in an episode of "Hill Street Blues," without wearing make-up.

As the murder trial progressed, a former girlfriend of Sweeney's came forth to say that he had severely beaten her on ten separate occasions, putting her in the hospital twice, breaking her nose, puncturing her eardrum, and collapsing a lung. He had even thrown rocks at her once as she was trying to escape. She said she still feared Sweeney and was extremely frightened about testifying.

The woman first gave her testimony out of the hearing of the jury, so that the judge could decide whether it was "relevant." As the woman told her story, Sweeney became so upset that he actually tried to bolt from the courtroom. Yet the judge eventually decided the evidence was "prejudicial" and refused to allow the jury to hear it.

Meanwhile, Sweeney took the stand in his own defense, and argued that Dominique had deceived him, baited him, and in various ways had been responsible herself for the crime.

The jury convicted him of only voluntary manslaughter, carrying an effective jail term of three and a half years—although the jury foreman said later if they had heard all the evidence, they would have given him first-degree murder.

"It is part of the defense premise that the victim is responsible for the crime," wrote Dominique's father, veteran film producer Dominick Dunne:

> It is always the murder victim who is placed on trial. John Sweeney, who claimed to love Dominique, and whose defense was that this was

a crime of passion, slandered her in court as viciously and cruelly as he had strangled her. . . . His violent past remained sacrosanct and inviolate, but her name was allowed to be trampled upon and kicked, with unsubstantiated charges, by the man who killed her.[6]

More and more, defense attorneys have begun to argue that victims—and the families of murder victims—simply don't belong at trials. The defense attorney in the Dominique Dunne case asked that her mother, Lennie Dunne, not be allowed in the courtroom because she is confined to a wheelchair with multiple sclerosis. He argued it would generate undue sympathy. The judge himself instructed at one point that, "If any member of the Dunne family cries, cries out, rolls his eyes, exclaims in any way, he will be asked to leave the courtroom." At one point, the defense attorney actually complained to the judge that one of Dominique's brothers "had tears in his eyes."

In legal terms, the victim is a non-person. Instead, we use the legal fiction that the state is the victim of all crimes. This puts the powers of the state on the side of defending the victims of crime. Unfortunately, it has also tended to make people forget that there are real flesh-and-blood victims.

In 1981, the Reagan administration assigned a task force to tour the country holding hearings on the conditions of crime victims. They were rather horrified at the findings.

Courts and prosecutors, for example, have almost routinely ignored the basic concerns of victims. The experience of Theresa Maybury, of Falls Church, Virginia, is typical. When she went to the trial of the man who had murdered her 18-year-old son, the first thing court officials did was put her into a waiting room with the murderer's relatives and character witnesses. "It was absolutely devastating to have to sit in there with all those people," she said later.

The President's commission also discovered that defense attorneys commonly initiate contacts with complainants and witnesses, often badgering them to change their stories or drop charges. Many victims and witnesses are constantly fearful that the person they are complaining against will threaten them, even try to kill them.

These fears are not unfounded. In Harlem in 1982, Nathaniel Sweeper, one of seven brothers in an alleged drug ring, got into an argument with a Newark man over a parking space. The other man was shot dead. Bobby Evans, a 38-year-old drug addict who witnessed the shooting, became the prosecution's chief witness.

The district attorney tried to keep Evans's identity a secret, but at a preliminary hearing Judge Miriam Altman suddenly decided the prosecution had to reveal Evans's name and address so that Sweeper's attorney could "confront the witness." The prosecution warned it was dangerous, but the judge insisted. When police arrived at Evans's apartment a few hours later to protect him, he had already been shot dead. With no eyewitness testimony against him, Sweeper won an acquittal.[7]

On the witness stand, victims and witnesses are often subject to ruthless cross-examination by defense attorneys. This has become particularly apparent with weak, poor, elderly, or inarticulate victims of crime.

"It's particularly galling to watch a defense attorney go after an elderly victim," says one New York City detective. "They'll start them off with, 'Are you wearing your glasses today?' 'Do you have more than one pair of glasses?' 'Do you happen to remember which pair of glasses you were wearing the day this alleged attack took place?' It's easy to confuse old people—they tend to forget small details. Pretty soon the young legal-aid lawyer has the victim nearly in tears."

Defense attorneys do not generally dispute the charge. "Our business is to make people doubt they have two arms and two legs," one New York City Legal Aid Society attorney told *New York Magazine.*[9]

More than anything else, though, the thing that all crime victims dread is a retrial.

"It's absolutely devastating," said Linda Barker, who has handled several painful experiences in Oregon. "For a murder victim's family, it's like digging up the dead body. They've gone through their grief, they've tried to put their lives back together, and then there it is staring them in the face again.

"For a rape victim, it's almost impossible. Facing the defendant once in court is bad enough. Then you find three years later that you have to go through the whole thing over again. By this time, the victim has already begun to lose faith in the justice system. Most victims just won't bother a second time."

Indeed, *Mallory v. United States* (1957), one of the Supreme Court's first significant expansions of habeas corpus, involved a rape. After the Supreme Court overturned the conviction on a technicality, the victim refused to testify at another trial, and the defendant went free.

Victims' organizations have generally been pursuing a three-part strategy. First, they want better treatment of victims in the judicial process. Second, they want some financial compensation for victims. And third, they want the justice system itself reformed so that trial outcomes more closely conform to the truth.

On the first score, they are already achieving considerable success. Responding to pressure from victims groups, prosecutors' offices are now scrambling to offer better services to victims and witnesses to crimes. Most district attorneys' offices now have "victim/witness assistance" units that provide a wide range of services. They keep victims and witnesses notified of court appearances and postponements and keep them protected in the courthouse. Former victims—like Theresa Maybury—often work in these programs.

Oddly enough, one of the biggest complaints—and one of the most difficult things for prosecutors to provide—is clothing and other articles that have been left by murder victims. They are usually required as evidence.

"Sometimes it's just a shirt or a cheap piece of jewelry, but it's the only memento a family has of the day the person died," said Marlene Young. "Often prosecutor's offices lost these things, or simply discarded them. But they're getting better now."

Twenty-three-year-old Jerome Pitchie, Jr., had just mustered out of the Navy in San Diego and was driving home to Lincoln, Nebraska, when he picked up two brothers hitchhiking near Phoenix. The brothers killed him, dumped his body in the desert, and drove the van all the way to North Carolina before they were finally apprehended. They were prosecuted for murder in Phoenix where they received long sentences.

When Pitchie's mother, Betty Daharsh, of Lincoln, tried to recover Jerome's van—which contained the only mementos she had from the day of his death—she was first told the police had to hold it for evidence. "They made me wait for months," said Mrs. Dahrash. "Finally, the people in North Carolina called and said I could come pick it up—as soon as I payed them $1,200 in storage charges."

Sometimes it is even the body itself that the police must keep for interminable amounts of time. "We didn't get our daughter's body back for four months," said Mary Miller, of Seattle. "We think we have the right to bury our children."

For the most part, however, both victims groups and prosecutors feel they are making rapid progress. "The victim is no longer the forgotten person in the justice system," says Jack Yelverton, executive director of the National Association of District Attorneys. "They are having tremendous impact on the way things are done in court."

Financial compensation for victims, on the other hand, remains more problematic. "Victims need compensation," said Marlene Young, of NOVA. "The criminal is getting free housing, free medical care, and probably the opportunity for an education as well, when he goes to jail. But victims get nothing. We think the state should bear some responsibility for compensation."

Other people worry, however, that victims' compensation will become another government subsidy that will quickly mushroom out of proportion. "It's basically open-ended," said one critic. "The main problem is that there are too many victims. We can't handle them all. Trying to compensate a few is likely to raise more bad feelings."

The Omnibus Crime Control Bill, adopted by Congress in 1984, seemed to take a good middle ground. It created a victims' compensation fund of $2 million. The money will be entirely taken out of fines collected on federal offenses. Many states are requiring convicts to contribute to restitution funds through money they earn in prison.

The third effort—changing trial procedure itself—has been fraught with the kind of snares and loopholes that only the legal system can generate.

California victims' groups have made the most concerted effort. In 1984, state voters passed Proposition 8, a "Victims' Bill of Rights" that contained several state constitutional amendments about trial procedure.

Most notable was the Proposition's "Truth in Evidence" section, which stated that "relevant evidence shall not be excluded in any criminal proceeding." The section was meant to try to override the various exclusionary rules.

But the effort has backfired. Prosecutors are still hesitant about introducing doubtful evidence, for fear that the "Truth in Evidence" rule will eventually be declared unconstitutional. This could mean retrying thousands of cases.

Meanwhile, defense attorneys—with nothing to lose and no chance of having acquittals overturned—have used the law to introduce all kinds of marginal evidence on behalf of defendants. In particular, they have used Proposition 8 to overturn changes that had been made in exploring the sexual history of rape victims. They have also used the law to introduce favorable lie-detector results (previously inadmissible) and have also started to force victims and witnesses to undergo psychiatric exams to determine their emotional stability.

"We believe the judges are simply taking the law and misusing it to teach the public a lesson," said George Nicholson, a former candidate for attorney general who wrote much of Proposition 8. "They're telling us, 'Don't meddle with our system.'"9

Sadly, a great many victims are abandoning the criminal courts altogether. Having grown disillusioned with the ability of the justice system to provide justice, they are turning to the civil courts for the satisfaction of large—if often unpayable—financial judgments.

Henry Howard is the father-in-law of the late Michael Alden, the 23-year-old waiter and aspiring-actor who was knifed to death by Jack Abbott, the long-time prison inmate who had recently been freed from a murder sentence, partially through the efforts of author Norman Mailer.

At the trial, Abbott first denied the murder altogether. Then when the prosecution produced a witness who had seen the slaying from only a few yards away, Abbott changed his plea and said that years of prison life had made him unstable. He got off on a charge of manslaughter.

"The next thing we knew, he was collecting all kinds of royalties for a book he had written," said Howard. "Murdering my son-in-law had given him a lot of publicity. So we went to civil court and sued him for all the money he'll ever make. He'll be out of jail again in a few years, but at least we'll own him for the rest of his life."

None of the exclusionary rules apply to civil proceedings. Because of the far more lenient rules of evidence in civil court, the jury gets to hear the whole story. Many victims' groups feel that civil cases may eventually become the real centerpiece of the justice system. "If we had it to do over again, we wouldn't even bother with the criminal trial," said Paul Garland, Bonnie Garland's father. "We'd just go ahead and concentrate on the civil litigation."

Why, then, do most victims still pursue justice so doggedly? It's a difficult question. Many critics openly accuse victims or their families of simply "seeking revenge." There is often a tacit suggestion that says, "The person is already dead, why bother?"

Yet there is every indication that there is a profoundly deep-seated need in all of us to see justice done.

Ann Rule, the Seattle crime reporter who writes under the name "Andy Stack," has described the experience of Beth Wilmot, a 20-year-old girl who was raped and shot in the head by Randy Woodfield, the "I-5 Killer" who raped two-dozen women and murdered at least four in a brief rampage up and down Central Oregon's Interstate Route 5 between 1980 and 1982.

Beth and a friend, Shari Hull, had been finishing a nighttime office-cleaning job when Woodfield accosted them in the parking lot. He forced them back into the building at gunpoint, sodomized both of them, and then shot each twice in the head. Shari died, but Beth miraculously survived.

When the police found her, Beth was barely conscious. She could not even remember being sexually molested. Yet she was able to give the police an extremely accurate description of the killer. Only when a police detective tried to help her describe the killer's gun by showing her his own did she become hysterical. The sodomization was not revealed until lab tests.

Beth began following the case avidly. She had been a very close friend of Shari and felt guilty for having lived when Shari hadn't. She eventually became close with the prosecutor's office, which got her a job working in the courthouse cafeteria.

She was working there two years later when police arrested Woodfield on a parole violation from a previous rape conviction. Numerous pieces of evidence—including eyewitness identification from several victims—led police to charge him as the I-5 killer. Rule writes:

> Only one victim witness was called to testify at this pretrial hearing: Beth Wilmot.
>
> Beth described the events of January 18, and then [district attorney] Chris Van Dyke asked her: "Is that man in the courtroom?"
>
> Beth rose from the witness chair and walked stiffly toward the table where Randy Woodfield sat. She stood directly in front of him, her hands clenched into fists.
>
> Screaming, she cried, "I hate you! I hate you! I hate you!"
>
> And then Beth walked back to the witness chair, sobbing.[10]

Six months later, when Woodfield was pronounced guilty of murdering Shari, "Beth Wilmot and Shari Hull's mother were in the gallery . . . They both broke into tears.

"But later as she reached the second-floor elevator, Beth Wilmot was, at last, smiling.

"'This is the happiest day of my life,' she said."[11]

It would probably be easy to dismiss this all as a silly, girlish reaction. Why should a victim feel it is the "happiest day of her life" to see someone else sent to jail? Does it bring back the victim? Obviously not. Does it protect her from future harm? Her risk was probably infinitesmal anyway.

Does she feel some bloodlust seeing the criminal finally suffer? I doubt it. Yet there is obviously something very fundamental at work here.

What we call "justice" is really our way of putting the world together. A sense of justice may be the most fundamental *rational* faculty we possess.

Justice is a purely human invention. It does not exist in the paths of the stars or the orbits of the planets, although plenty of astronomers and astrologers have often tried to read it there. It does not exist among animals, either. Animals retaliate and play tit-for-tat on a very primitive level. But they do not carry a sense of justice around in their heads.

People who have been victims of crimes often report that for long periods they are unable to function in the simplest ways. "It was as if there were no order in the world, no rules to be depended on," said Barbara Kaplan, a Boston social worker who was shot in the head by a former mental patient at the same time two other psychiatric workers were killed. "I didn't count on other cars to stop at red lights, or yield, or follow directional signs. I never trusted what anyone might do."

"You're in a fog most of the time," said Mary Miller, who lost her daughter in Oregon. "You find you can't add numbers. You can't spell the simplest words. You don't realize how fragile your mind really is."

Remarkably, judges have found that when victims are allowed more say at sentencing hearings only rarely do they ask for more punishment than the court is prepared to impose, and often they ask for less. They are *not* vengeful. They only want to regain a sense of control over their situation and see justice done.

Trials and criminal procedures are the dramas by which we put the world back together. Justice heals us after something horrible has happened. Of course, the world is never *exactly* the way it was before the crime occurred. But we try.

THE POLICE 13

I T IS LINE-UP TIME IN a Cincinnati police station. For about half-an-hour, the ten o'clock shift has been assembling. About a dozen officers sit around the long locker-room table, engaging in the endless wisecracking that seems to be a part of police work.

"Hey Charley, heard you were out partying Friday night." A smallish lieutenant with a bushy mustache sits at the end of the table acting as master of ceremonies.

Charley is at his locker and looks over indifferently. About a half-dozen heads are chuckling around the table.

"Heard you were doing a little drinking."

No response.

"You know, just because that Lite beer from Miller has less calories, it doesn't mean you're supposed to drink a whole case-and-a-half."

The table chuckles. People are checking notes, doing paper work, waiting for something to happen.

"Charley's telling us he's going to go on a diet next week," the lieutenant addresses the table. More chuckles. "Hey Charley, weren't you telling us you're going on a diet next week?"

Charley's girth is pretty wide. He doesn't reply.

A black officer in plainclothes wanders in. He has the homely look of an orphan, his face almost entirely hidden beneath a large woolen cap.

"Hey, what's this I hear, you guys aren't giving me a party? I'm going over to Investigations after three years, and you guys ain't going to give me a going away party?"

"Lester, you're only going over there three months. We're not even going to miss you," says the lieutenant.

"Well, the last guy that left got a party. I think I've been a victim of racial discrimination."

"You're not a victim of racial discrimination, Lester. We just don't like you."

Everyone laughs and line-up begins. Things are already pretty unruly. The pushing and shoving and laughing continues as they try to stand at attention. They look like a motley troop of boy scouts.

The lieutenant paces slowly down the line, trying to keep a straight face. Several officers turn their heads to avoid grinning at him. One woman officer, no more than five feet tall, cannot stop laughing. She puts her head down, tries to put on a serious face, then giggles uncontrollably.

"All right, everybody, nightsticks," says the lieutenant. Twelve different nightsticks slap out in twelve different positions. Everyone is checking out of the corner of his eyes, trying to achieve some kind of uniformity.

"Flashlights." Back go the nightsticks, out come the flashlights. Same thing.

"Guns." Standing across the room, I suddenly find myself staring down the barrels of a dozen .357 Magnums. I hope they know what they are doing.

"All right, boys and girls, let's get out there and do it to them before they do it to us."

In visiting police stations around the country, I have somehow always ended up asking the same question. Which television show most resembles what police work is really like?

The answer has always come back the same. "Barney Miller." "I don't know how they do it, but they've got somebody in there who must have spent an awful lot of time in a police station," one cop once told me.

There seems to be an inevitable boyishness among the men—and women—who do police work. It is, after all, the job that all boys grow up wanting to have.

On television, "Hill Street Blues" seems gritty and realistic, while Barney Miller seems like "I Love Lucy" set in a detective bureau. Yet strangely, after seeing the real thing, "Hill Street Blues" seems like real life run on fast-forward. Where do you ever see that many people at one time in a police station?

Instead, time and time again, sitting in a police station, I have had the feeling I am watching a situation comedy. There are always the stock characters—the gray-haired veteran who pushes brooms and runs the elevator, the athletic patrolman who hurt his leg last year and is now confined to desk work, the terse desk sergeant who would barely blink an eye if the world blew up behind him.

Sometimes this comedy also turns into tragedy. The morning after I visited the police station there was a story in the papers that a Cincinnati police officer had killed a friend by shooting him right between the eyes while horsing around in another station house the night before.

"Police work is hours and days of incredible boredom interrupted by moments of sheer terror" is a comment you hear over and over again. "You're a social worker with a nightstick" is another favorite. "You're the guy who gets to carry the gun—that symbol of authority," a third.

The average cop is still male, still likely to be white, but with much more education than twenty years ago. Police departments have "professionalized" all over the country, and the results show.

Public attitudes have changed as well. Recent polls have shown that 80 percent of the public now views the police favorably—one of the highest rankings for any profession.

The police have loosened up extraordinarily. One of the most common pieces of advice lawyers used to give their clients was, "Never walk into a police station alone at night." Nowadays ordinary people feel much more welcome in a police station. Departments have instituted "ridealongs," where they actively encourage citizens to spend a few hours in the police car to see what it's like "behind the badge."

I have found that it isn't always entirely comfortable. Riding in a Dallas police car, answering a routine call about a traffic tie-up, I suddenly found myself crawling through throngs of rowdy Southern Methodist University students celebrating St. Patrick's Day. The patrol consisted of the veteran sergeant at the wheel, and me sitting next to him, who everybody naturally assumed was a plainclothes detective.

The usual jeering and cop-baiting wasn't really unfriendly. But with more than a thousand T-shirted students swigging beer and milling in the streets, it was easy to see how things could get quickly out of hand. A couple of weeks later, a ridealong in San Diego got caught in the middle of a shootout with armed robbers, and was slightly wounded.

The thing that most people who study the police always seem to want to ignore or forget is that the cop is one of the only people in society who is continually confronted with the dark underside of human nature.

Professor George Kirkham is one of the few people to have seen the situation from both sides. In 1973, he became a full-time member of the

Jacksonville Sheriff's Department while teaching criminology at Florida State University. After six months, he wrote, "I will never again be either the same man or the same scientist who stood in front of the station on that first day."

> As a college professor, I had grown accustomed to being treated with uniform respect and deference by those I encountered. I somehow naively assumed that this same quality of respect would carry over into my new role . . . I quickly found that my badge and uniform, rather than serving to shield me from such things as disrespect and violence, only acted as a magnet which drew me toward many individuals who hated what I represented.[1]

On his first night out, Kirkham and his partner were called to quell a disturbance in a bar. Confronting the loudest troublemaker, Kirkham smiled and said, "Excuse me, sir, but I wonder if you could step outside and talk with me for just a moment." The man promptly slugged him.

> "Something is very wrong," I remember thinking to myself as we headed for the jail. I had used the same kind of gentle, rapport-building approach with countless offenders in prison and probation settings. It had always worked so well. . . For the first time in my life, I encountered individuals who interpreted kindness as weakness, as an invitation to disrespect or violence.

A few weeks later, Kirkham asked a man to move his double-parked car, which was blocking traffic in front of a bar. Instead of complying, the man started shouting that he was being harassed. A crowd gathered. When the two officers arrested the man, the crowd attempted to free him. A woman tried to strip Kirkham of his gun. "I remember the sickening sensation of cold terror which filled my insides as I struggled to reach our car radio." In another moment, he was facing a hostile mob, armed with a shotgun.

> The memory flashed through my mind that I had always argued that policemen should not be allowed to carry shotguns because of their "offensive" character and the potential damage to community relations . . . How readily as a criminology professor I would have

condemned the officer who was now myself, trembling with fear and anxiety and menacing an "unarmed" assembly with an "offensive" weapon.

Kirkham found himself infuriated when the man who started the riot was on the street the next day, laughing at him, and when the "resisting arrest" was finally dismissed to "breach of peace."

> When I put the uniform of a police officer on, I lost the luxury of sitting in an air-conditioned office with my pipe and books calmly discussing with a rapist or armed robber the past problems which had led him into trouble with the law. Such offenders seemed so innocent, so harmless, in the sterile setting of prison . . .
>
> From all the human misery and suffering which police officers must witness in their work, I found myself amazed at the incredible humanity and compassion which seems to characterize most of them.

In one evening on a ride-along in Omaha, I felt I got a good look at two different sides of law enforcement.

One call came from a burglary in progress. It was in a black neighborhood. As several officers investigated a broken window, a black man, about 30, wandered up and tried to offer some information. He said he had made the call. "You know, there's always break-ins around here. I just like to help the people so they don't have to put up with so much crime."

After a minute, though, the officer I was with asked him for his ID. The man backed away and tried to leave. "Oh no, I didn't do nothing. I'm just here trying to help." But the officer insisted, at which point the man started to reach into his back pocket. Another officer grabbed him from behind. "He might have had a gun," someone said.

As it turned out, he was only reaching for his wallet. A check on the radio, however, revealed that there was an outstanding warrant against him. He was soon in cuffs and heading for police headquarters. "Oh my God," he said as we rode downtown. "Now I'm going to miss work tomorrow and probably lose my job. It seems like every time I get started on the right track something goes wrong." Labeling theorists are not wrong when they say that some people are caught in the web of the system.

An hour later, we were called to a burglary at a construction site, a small, medical office wrapped in plastic tarpaulins. What happened inside was almost like a dream.

A scuffling noise came from one small, dark room. A soft-looking man in his thirties came out, his eyes wide with fear. Inside, a husky construction worker lay on the floor. Beneath him, barely even visible, was a wiry black man, about 23. As the officers untangled the pile, the black man started screaming, kicking, raging: "Get off me, motherfuckers. Get off me. I'll kill you motherfuckers. I'll kill all you."

Two officers held him down. When another, female, officer arrived to put handcuffs on him, he became even more enraged. "Get that bitch off me! I'll kill all of you. I'll kill your whole family."

It emerged that the two construction workers had caught the man stealing tools out of their truck, which had already been burglarized several times while they worked all night. The man had come inside quietly, but when they called the police, he flew into a rage.

For ten solid minutes, the husky construction worker and the wiry black had wrestled up and down the halls. There were scuff marks everywhere and the wall was kicked in in several places. The construction worker had bite marks all over his chest. "I'm going to go get a rabies shot," he said, still infuriated.

After the handcuffs were finally on him, the burglar stood like someone from another planet. (He may have been high on something.) He responded to no ordinary human signals but stared into his own private universe. Then he baited the cops. "You ready?" he said enigmatically. "You ready?"

When it came time to take him to the police car, he went into a rage once again. He fought, kicked, screamed, and tried to bite. It is easy to see how people end up getting killed in such situations. Four people couldn't force him into the car, and it was finally necessary to lay him on the ground and sit on him until a van arrived. A small crowd of blacks started gathering and it was easy to see "police brutality" charges taking shape.

Police work, then, is all they say it is. You are the "social worker with the nightstick." You must also be the "pig" occasionally. I have no doubt that policemen occasionally abuse their power. But it is also easy to forget that life on the edges of civilization does not always fall into comfortable patterns. There is something irreducible about that physical confrontation that exists in no other profession.

Why do people stay in it? Many burn out, of course. They move up, out of uniform, and into special investigative units or desk jobs, where life is more predictable and safe.

What makes the average policeman feel good about his job, though—

when he does—is that he is protecting the public. As George Kirkham wrote:

> Night after night, I came home and took off the badge and blue uniform with a sense of satisfaction and contribution to society that I have never known in any other job. Somehow that feeling seemed to make everything—the disrespect, the danger, the boredom—worthwhile.[2]

Despite the timeless qualities of police work, we are actually facing one of the biggest revolutions in police behavior in the past twenty-five years. The reason is that, despite the growing respect for the law enforcement officials, the recognition is growing among the police themselves that, to a large degree, they are no longer doing a big part of their job.

The thing that police reformers and civil libertarians never seemed to have realized during the 1960s is that, when you get right down to it, there isn't really any reason that police *have to* pursue criminals. Most police officers do it out of common human decency and a dedication to their job. But when you tie down officers with all kinds of regulations and quasi-Constitutional proscriptions, the officers may conclude that, in the end, there isn't any reason why they shouldn't just say the hell with it and sit in the patrol car all day.

And that is just what has happened. It hasn't entirely been laziness or indifference on the part of individual officers. Technological changes geared to rapid response have taken policemen off the sidewalks and put them in patrol cars, restlessly cruising up and down the streets waiting to respond to radio calls.

Response time has been cut dramatically. In most cities there are now few complaints about the police responding to emergencies. On the contrary, people are often amazed at how quickly the police can respond to an emergency call. In many cities, the smallest fender-bender can produce three or four patrol cars in a matter of minutes.

The problem is this. By gearing the average patrol officer to quick response—the "911" calls—the police may have lost touch with the community. As one woman in a Brooklyn precinct council meeting asked recently, "I remember when I was a little girl, we used to have our police officer standing right on the corner. Everybody knew all about him, and he knew all about them. We used to feel safe. Why can't we have it that way again?"

The same question has been raised by James Q. Wilson and George Kelling, two Harvard political scientists who have turned the world of police work upside down over the past three years.

Wilson is an airy and confident political scientist, perhaps the outstanding mind working in criminology today. "I was dragooned into the field when I was the low man on the totem pole at the University at Chicago and a grant came through to do a study of the police," he says. "When I saw how many bad things were being written in the field, I decided I'd better stay in it."

Kelling, on the other hand, is a former seminarian and social worker with a big heart and a tough mind. "I'm a liberal who finally decided that we can't ignore reality," he said, sitting in his small office just off Harvard Square. Kelling has done most of the legwork on the ground-breaking studies that have come out of the Program in Criminal Justice Policy and Management at the John F. Kennedy School of Government.

In the 1970s, Kelling masterminded an exhaustive study of police patrols in Kansas City. The conclusion that came out of it was "patrol cars don't deter crime."

"We found that the patrol cars have very little contact with the community. They get places quickly, but then they leave quickly. The criminals learn to avoid them. Basically, it doesn't matter if you double the number of cars in an area. Crime stays about the same."

Then in 1983, Wilson and Kelling formulated the "Broken Windows" hypothesis. Writing in *Atlantic Monthly,* they pointed out that the *appearance* of public order and police presence seems to be as important in restoring public confidence as actual reductions in crime.

"If a window in a building is broken *and is left unrepaired,* all the rest of the windows will soon be broken," wrote Wilson and Kelling. "One unrepaired broken window is a signal that no one cares, and so breaking more windows costs nothing."

Similarly, they said, one of the greatest inducements to crime in a neighborhood is when disorderly behavior is allowed to get out of hand. "Much of the anxiety now endemic in big-city neighborhoods stems [not] from a sense of 'real' crime [but] from a sense that the street is disorderly, a source of distasteful, worrisome encounters... The prospect of a confrontation with an obstreperous teenager, or a drunken panhandler, can be as fear-inducing to defenseless persons as the prospect of meeting an actual armed robber; indeed, to a defenseless person, the two kinds of confrontations are often indistinguishable."[3]

Researching early American history, Wilson and Kelling found that most police work originally concentrated on *order maintenance*. "Solving crime" was often done by private detectives. The policeman on the corner was there to patrol the beat, not solve murders. It was only when many of these private detectives were hired by the police department that "crime-solving" became more important—and the cop-on-the-corner started bucking for detective.

In his lectures to police groups, Wilson frequently uses sidewalk three-card-monte games as an example of one of those "harmless" street activities that quickly become the basis for more street crime. As one woman recently wrote the New York *Daily News*: "I was walking past one of those card games when somebody pushed against me. I looked, and saw my wallet was gone."

Since such games are known to be illegal, their presence gives rise to the presumption that the police aren't watching. Once this presumption is established, then people are tempted to try other things. "As one Japanese visitor remarked to me," said Wilson, "'Whenever I see those card games going on, it makes me wonder what else people are getting away with.'"

What Wilson and Kelling have posited is that *little things do matter*. Maintenance of public order is the *first step* in controlling crime. As they wrote in the *Atlantic*: "The citizen who fears the ill-smelling drunk, the rowdy teenager, or the importunate beggar is not merely expressing his distaste for unseemly behavior; he is also giving voice to a bit of folk wisdom that happens to be a correct generalization—namely, that serious crime flourishes in areas in which disorderly behavior goes unchecked. The unchecked panhandler is, in effect, the first broken window."[4]

This is one thing that the Warren Court never seems to have appreciated when it was striking down public drunkenness and vagrancy rules, and questioning the routine habits of the police in checking out suspicious behavior.

"What harm do public drunks really do?" was a question widely asked by criminal reformers in the 1960s. "The police just waste all their time locking people up in 'drunk tanks' for what are really victimless crimes." The same thing held true for bizarre public behavior. Whereas obviously disturbed people were once institutionalized, the courts began awarding them "civil rights" to refuse treatment. David Bazelon, former Chief Judge of the U.S. Court of Appeals for the District of Columbia (often dubbed the "mini-Supreme Court") and a leading judicial psychiatric reformer, once suggested in an opinion that an obviously disturbed woman who was being granted a habeas corpus release from a Washington, D.C., mental hospital could have her name and address sewn in her clothes so that the police could return her home if they found her wandering the streets. It is only a short step to the hundreds of homeless people who now spend the winter in Grand Central Station.

What these policies never calculated was the effect on *public morale.* Although they seem like "little things" that the public ought to "tolerate," these activities quickly add up in terms of the general community confidence that public order can be maintained.

Once the police "lose control of the streets," then a vicious downward spiral takes place. People stop trying to uphold community standards, and retreat into an every-man-for-himself isolationism. Nobody feels he can trust anyone else, or expect people to act in predictable ways. In this kind of atmosphere, crime thrives.

As Wilson and Kelling put it:

> This wish to "decriminalize" disreputable behavior that "harms no one"—and thus remove the ultimate sanction the police can employ to maintain neighborhood order—is, we think, a mistake. Arresting a single drunk or a single vagrant who has harmed no identifiable person may seem unjust, and in a sense it is. But failing to do anything about a score of drunks or a hundred vagrants may destroy an entire community.[5]

Since 1982, the "broken windows" hypothesis has had an enormous impact on law-enforcement agencies. When I talked with Robert Wadman, Omaha Chief of Police, he had a copy of the *Atlantic* article on his desk. The conviction is growing everywhere that a mistake was made when the police went for high-tech, high-mobility radio cars, and lost touch with the community. "Quality-of-life" crimes have become a buzzword in police departments. Law-enforcement officials now believe that in order to reduce crime they must first "win back the streets."

Just how this is going to be done without running afoul of the courts and civil libertarians—and without bringing out some of the worse aspects in police behavior—is still a very big question.

At 27, Michelle Marshke has a wiry look. With her brown hair tucked under her cap, there is still a bit of the tomboy about her. She doesn't look entirely out of place in a policeman's uniform.

One gusty March afternoon in 1985, Marshke walked me through "The Hollow"—a run-down neighborhood in Flint, Michigan, that has been her beat for over a year. The Hollow looked just like a Hollow should—sad, wooden houses with sagging porches, tarpaper roofs, and broken dishwashers on the front lawns.

"One of the first things I did when I came down here was make a list of all the abandoned cars that were sitting in people's yards and down in the creek bed. We traced all the owners and then persuaded people to remove them. I thought it would give everybody a little more pride. We got rid of most of them, but then as soon as we relaxed, they started piling up again."

Flint, the home of Buick Motors, is a rapidly shrinking Rust Bowl community. Almost 100,000 people have departed in the past five years, leaving about 150,000. The downtown area is half-abandoned, with a huge redevelopment project still nothing more than gaping holes. Stores and people have fled to the suburbs. The city working-class population is nearly half black. The Hollow, near the outskirts, is a little self-enclosed community of poor whites from Appalachia.

"I can't think of more than a couple of families in here that are still intact," Marshke said as we trudged the windy streets. "These kids are primed for delinquency."

Marshke is doing something that anywhere else would be known as "community organizing." She knows nearly everyone, is known in turn by most. Tucked in a small equipment room at the junior high school she has a desk that serves as her home base. In her files are the names and addresses of every kid under 21 in her mile-square beat. Most of her information is benign. But she did use her files recently to solve a murder.

"When I first came down here, there were a lot of burglaries going on," she said as we sat in her office. "People knew who was doing it, but they were afraid to say. Everyone feared retaliation. Once they got to know me, though, a few people stuck their necks out and we made some arrests."

Only a small part of Marshke's job, however, is cops and robbers. Foot patrol officers in Flint organize block-watch groups, put out newsletters, counsel dropouts to stay in school, run errands for shut-ins, and take kids on outings to Detroit Tiger baseball games. The object is to make police once again an integral part of the community—the social worker with a sidearm.

I ask Marshke why she became a cop. "I was selling real estate. I wanted something more exciting."

Which television show most resembles real police work? "Barney Miller."

Has she ever been the victim of a crime? "My parents were," she said quietly. "Two guys with guns caught them in a motel room. They forced them into the bathroom and then ransacked the room. My parents were afraid to come out until an hour after they left. They said they felt like two scared little puppy dogs."

Is that one reason she became a cop? "I don't think so."

Back on tour again, we stopped by a few stores, trudged through the snow to the perimeters of her beat, then visited a woman's house for coffee. They sat so long discussing the news of the neighborhood that I finally had to wonder if the taxpayers of Flint were really getting their money's worth.

"Oh no, we love having her around," the woman told me as she served another round of coffee. "We feel so much safer now."

Flint started its foot patrols in 1979 with a $1.2 million grant from the Stewart Mott Foundation, the old Buick family that once lived there. In June, 1985, Flint taxpayers approved a special millage assessment that will support the foot patrols entirely out of property taxes.

The Flint experiment has also given scholars the chance to study its effects. "They've generally been pretty positive," said Rudy Trojanowicz, head of the Criminal Justice department at Michigan State. "People feel better about getting involved with the police. We had one instance where a woman came forward right away and said she knew who had been setting fires in the neighborhood. The patrol officers said to her, 'Why didn't you tell anyone before?' She said, 'If I had called you three months ago, the patrol car would have come over and parked right in my driveway, and then everybody in the neighborhood would have known who told the police.'"[6]

Even in the most crime-ridden areas, police are discovering there is almost always a frightened majority that knows exactly what is going on but is afraid to do anything about it.

Hubert Williams, chief of police of Newark and now president of the Police Foundation, recounts the following experience:

> In 1979, people organized "crime marches" on our police headquar-
> ters. One group from a housing project, said, "Look, Mr. Director, we

know you have a manpower problem. But we cannot live under these conditions. We are scared to death and you've got to help."

My response was, "Well, if you look at the statistics, you don't *have* any crime in your area." People in the projects don't report crime even though a lot occurs there. I told them that they had to tell the police what was going on. "We're afraid to," they said.

We finally persuaded them to meet with us outside police headquarters and tell us what was going on. Later we slipped a police officer into a vacant apartment in the project to gather evidence. After we compiled a book on the criminals, we met the group again and said, "Look, we know who is committing the crimes. We are going to arrest these people, many of them for relatively minor offenses. You will not have to go to court or testify publicly, but you must tell the judges privately what is going on in your neighborhood.

Well, we arrested those guys. We arrested one for possession of a knife. But the judge, who had been told what was going on, sentenced him to six months in jail. The people in the projects were ecstatic. That's the kind of cooperation we were able to encourage.[7]

Unfortunately, foot patrols and extensive community participation are luxuries that many municipalities really cannot afford. It is expensive to put large numbers of officers on the street, while still maintaining radio response.

The effort to reinvolve the police in basic order maintenance also raises very serious difficulties. Many police departments have begun trying to crack down on "quality-of-life" crimes—playing loud radios in public, selling drugs on street corners, prostitution, numbers rackets, and the like.

But the police and courts are already swamped with serious crime and will be hard-pressed to add petty offenses to their lists.

In addition, many police departments left off policing petty street rackets because they are "corruption-prone"—meaning that beat officers can easily end up taking small payments to leave them alone.

When I was riding with a patrol car in East Harlem, the two veteran officers took me to a new illegal gambling parlor that had just opened on their beat. "Grand opening" pennants still hung outside, and it was the only store still open at eleven o'clock at night. They suggested I go in and make a bet.

The young woman at the counter was terrified, certain that I was a police officer. She finally made me swear on the health of my child that I wasn't going to arrest her. Even then, her hands were shaking so badly that she tore two policy slips before finally writing out my number.

Outside again, the two officers were disgusted. "Ten years ago we could have closed down a place like that in one day. Now we have to buck it up to the vice squad, where it takes months. Only the neighborhoods that know how to scream get them closed down."

Then it suddenly occurred to them that somebody might have seen the police car parked outside with me going inside, and there might be a charge of police corruption. We rode in glum silence for a minute. Finally I told them, "I don't know about you guys, but I'm pleading freedom of the press."

Unfortunately, policing petty street crime can also bring out the worst in cops. They know that nobody is going to jail and that their arrestees will be back on the street the next day.

The temptation builds to "hold court" in the station house, or in a back lot somewhere, and forget about formal charges. ("The rule is, if you mark 'em up, you have to arrest them," one former New York City cop told me.) In 1985, a special "quality-of-life" squad in a Queens precinct was charged with torturing suspects with stun guns over $5 marijuana sales.

Do we need a "vigilantism of the majority"—a vast public willingness to cooperate with the police in reporting and prosecuting crime?

Sociologists and criminologists like to remind everyone that "the police can't really control crime," and that only a public effort to help *prevent* crime can really make a difference. But they rarely want to acknowledge what that means. It means rediscovering a certain unwillingness to tolerate bizarre, dangerous, or irresponsible behavior, and redeveloping a taste for public order.

Historian Peter Shaw has used the example of John Hinckley's shooting of President Reagan to illustrate how *informal* mechanisms for preventing crime have broken down in the country. He notes that Hinckley "repeatedly evidenced disturbed or suspicious behavior in public. In Lakewood, Colorado, he attracted the attention of a policeman who found him deeply suspicious, but let him go. In Nashville, Hinckley was arrested for carrying firearms and cartridges onto an airplane, but was only briefly detained. Outside the Hilton the morning he shot the President, Hinckley was observed by several people who noted he was acting strangely. In the closed press-section, one reporter even overheard Hinckley muttering to himself and realized that he was seriously disturbed and did not belong in the restricted area. Yet none of these people ever dared to broach anything or tell anyone to do something about him.

"The pendulum has swung so far from a rigid conception of propriety in public that for the crowd gathered outside the Hilton, bad manners would have consisted in objecting to behavior like Hinckley's," Shaw concluded.[8]

It is sometimes shocking to realize how frequently people still fail to participate in crime prevention. When 6-year-old Etan Patz was kidnapped in New York, the man who took him immediately got in a cab and promised to take him to school. The cab driver overheard their conversation and realized that Etan was being kidnapped. Yet he did nothing to prevent it—and didn't even tell the police until a year later.

When 21-year-old Penny Serra was stabbed in a parking garage in New Haven in 1973, the murderer paid his parking ticket as he made his escape. The attendant thought the man was acting nervously and saw his arm covered with blood. Yet he didn't note the license plate and couldn't even give police an adequate description of the man or his car. An arrest was not made until ten years later.[9]

Cutting crime and restoring public order is going to mean coming back from the extremes of public apathy on the one hand and occasional outbursts of vigilante violence on the other. We need a public that is willing to undertake an everyday working cooperation with law-enforcement authorities. The police can help, but they can't do it all. The real revolution is going to have to take place in the hearts and minds of the people.

PROSECUTION 14
VERSUS
DEFENSE

I T IS OFTEN PUZZLING to step into a courtroom and watch a trial going on.

The proceedings seem excruciatingly slow. Lawyers shuffle papers and haggle over objections. "Your Honor, may I approach the bench on this?" The attorneys and judge huddle a minute. "All right, I'm going to call a five minute recess while we discuss this in chambers," announces the judge. About forty-five minutes later, court resumes.

Now it's back to testimony. The state is trying a sidewalk drug dealer who allegedly sold $25 worth of cocaine to an undercover police agent. Testimony has been going for two days, and all the jury has seen are two back-up police officers who say they were sitting in a car two blocks away and didn't see anything happen.

Finally the lab technician arrives. She has traveled all the way across town to give three minutes of testimony. She says she is indeed a lab technician and did indeed receive the package that has been placed into evidence, and that it is indeed cocaine. The defense does not try to refute her statements.

When the undercover officer finally appears, he has a crisp manner, answering yes-or-no questions, "Negative" and "positive." During cross-examination, the defense attorney asks if he has been in the military, apparently looking for a sympathetic jury reaction. The policeman says he has.

The defense attorney probes, and the undercover officer's prose becomes more and more stilted as he tries to avoid getting tripped up.

"You went to the doorway with the defendant and then what happened?"

"He motioned for the other dealer."

"Motioned to him to do what?"

"He motioned to him to come forth."

"Come forth?"

"Come forth."

Forsooth.

And so it goes. The defense attorney makes a halfhearted attempt to argue that the officer couldn't make a proper identification through his dark aviator glasses, but the officer scoffs. Finally the prosecution rests. Throughout the entire testimony, the defendant has been sitting at the table shaking his head as if to say, "No man, no—it couldn't have possibly happened."

Now it is the defense's turn. The first (and only) witness is the defendant's brother. First question: Were you on the same streetcorner the day the sale took place? He refuses to answer on the grounds of self-incrimination. The jury is immediately dismissed for half-an-hour. When the jury returns, he is asked the same question. Again he refuses to answer. Now the judge and attorneys huddle in chambers for a full forty-five minutes. When the jury returns, the brother is gone. That's the defense's case. "Every case I've ever sat on, they always try to get the brother to say he was the one who did it," one jury veteran told me later.

Testimony to describe this simple drug sale, which took place in the space of four minutes, has taken a week. The jury comes back with a guilty verdict in five hours. When they file back into the courtroom to read the verdict, the defendant's identical twin brother is sitting in the back of the courtroom. "Why didn't they put him on the stand to try to take the rap?" one juror says aloud. The defendant gets a two-year prison sentence.

This is a case in which I sat as a alternate juror in 1984. None of the jurors collapsed under the strain, so I didn't get to deliberate on the verdict. I would have voted guilty. I suspect one reason the deliberation took so long is that after spending so much time in court, the jurors would have felt cheated coming to a decision too quickly.

No defense attorney I have ever talked to has ever estimated that *less* than 90 percent of his clients are guilty. They usually put the figure around 90–95 percent. Prosecutors place the number somewhere between 99 and 99.9 percent. "If they're not guilty, we don't prosecute them," they say. In fact, the whole premise that more than an occasional defendant is actually innocent seems to be something manufactured for public consumption.

Defense attorneys in particular have a macabre private humor about the notion that more than a handful of their clients may be innocent. At a criminal attorneys' seminar I attended in New York City in 1984, one speaker finished by saying, "Of course, I'm just talking here about the usual instance where your client is guilty. I'm sure you've seen enough of those. But the ones that are really going to keep you awake at night—and I'm sure you're going to run into one of these once in a while—is when you actually believe your client may be innocent."

Thus, the criminal courtroom is basically a place for lawyer to play in, testing wits, battling wills. It is not this way everywhere in the world. In Japan, which has one-tenth the crime rate we have, about 95 percent of defendants are found guilty.

Here, however, the game works differently. Despite the estimates of both sides, only 60 percent of American jury trials lead to conviction. Even by the defense attorneys' own estimates, this means that one-third of all defendants are guilty people who are acquitted. All this comes *before* the appeals process, which makes conviction an entirely new ballgame.

What is the reason for this? The biggest, of course, is that we don't like the idea of punishing innocent people. Oliver Wendell Holmes is often quoted: "It is a lesser evil that some criminals should escape than that the government should play an ignoble role." Judge Louis Brandeis once said it with a flourish: "Better a hundred guilty criminals go free than one innocent man should be punished."

This figure should not be taken as an exaggeration. If the prosecutors' estimates are true and only one in a hundred defendants is actually innocent, that means we are regularly acquitting forty guilty people in the hope that the one innocent man will be among them.

The major premise of our system, of course, is the presumption of innocence. A defendant never has to *prove* he isn't guilty. He only has to show that the state hasn't proved its case "beyond a reasonable doubt." Just what constitutes reasonable doubt, of course, is open to reasonable doubt. "Some defense attorneys believe that if the public really understood reasonable doubt, there wouldn't be any convictions at all," a lawyer once told me.

The presumption of innocence, however, has become merely a *starting point* for protecting the rights of defendants in the American justice system. The procedures are now arranged so that the defendant must get every conceivable benefit of every doubt up and down the line.

I have already suggested some of the ways in which the prosecution is deliberately handicapped on the grounds that the Constitution is set up to protect only individual defendants. Let me now list them categorically so that their full import will be clear.

Basic responsibilities. The adversary system suggests that both prosecution and defense battle things out while the judge sits as an umpire, calling balls and strikes. But this is not entirely true. The prosecution is also responsible for the "integrity of the system," which means that the prosecutor must also assure that the defendant gets a fair trial. But the defense attorney does not have a similar responsibility. He is only responsible to his client—"getting his guy off." Prosecutors must reveal everything they know, defense attorneys need not.

Discovery. The prosecution is required to hand all its evidence over to the defense. However, the defense is not required to hand over any evidence to the prosecution. Failure by the prosecution to hand over any potentially exculpatory evidence is grounds for overturning a conviction. But the defense is not required to give incriminating evidence to the prosecutor.

Self-incrimination. In neither the English nor the American system can the defendant be forced to testify against himself. In Great Britain, however, the prosecutor and the judge are allowed to note that this failure to testify is in fact somewhat suggestive of guilt. In America, this tradition has been abandoned.

Verdicts. Only the defense can appeal a jury verdict. An acquittal cannot be appealed, even if the prosecution feels there were flagrant errors in rulings by the judge or flagrantly unfair tactics by the defense. Prosecutors can interrupt a trial to take an interlocutory motion to an appeals court, but this is done only rarely and in great haste. Once the verdict is in, only the defense gets a second chance.

In addition—although it doesn't happen often—the judge himself can immediately overturn a jury conviction and acquit the defendant. However, he cannot reverse a jury acquittal and turn it into a conviction.

Legal counsel. A victim, of course, cannot fire the prosecutor or change attorneys (although in a long case, the victim is likely to be bounced from one deputy prosecutor to another). The defendant can hire his own attorney. If he changes attorneys on appeal, one of the first things the new attorney will probably argue is that the first attorney was "incompetent."

Appeals. Only the defense has access to the federal courts on Constitutional grounds. Thus, if a convicted defendant loses all his appeals in the state court system, he can always appeal into the federal courts. But if the prosecution loses in the state courts on *state* constitutional grounds, it cannot appeal into the federal courts. "The people" do not have the same "Constitutional rights" as the defendant in this respect.

Defendant-oriented state appeals courts, like the California Supreme Court, have used this very skillfully. They are careful to overturn convictions or death sentences on *state* constitutional grounds, so that the prosecution cannot appeal into the federal court system.

State constitutions v. U.S. Constitution. The Warren Court continually struck down criminal procedures outlined in the state constitutions on the grounds that the federal Constitution had overriding authority. However, since the Supreme Court has become more conservative, it is now being argued that state constitutional procedures can override the federal Constitution *if they give more rights to the defendant.*

In other words, the states can be more *lenient* with criminal defendants, but they cannot be more *strict.* Because of this new, one-way ratchet, civil libertarians are now turning much of their efforts to the state courts in trying to expand the rights of defendants.

The result of all these one-way ratchets has been a huge institutional momentum that has not been stemmed by recent Supreme Court decisions. Although the more conservative Court is continuously rearranging the furniture and occasionally changing the paint on a wall, the house that we live in is still the one built by Earl Warren.

To get an idea of how these effects work in concert, let us look for a moment at the two trials of Claus von Bulow. Let me begin by saying—just to avoid any possibility of libel—that von Bulow is beyond a shadow of a doubt *innocent* in the eyes of the justice system. The verdict is in, and he has been acquitted. All I am going to explore here is how the many tactics available to defense attorneys made it possible to hold two trials in which the second verdict turned out differently than the first.

Perhaps the best thing to keep in mind thoughout this review would be the words of Alan Dershowitz himself, who headed a defense team that was reportedly paid something between $500,000 and $1 million (by different estimates) for its effort in overturning the first conviction and winning acquittal on the second. As Dershowitz says in the introduction to *The Best Defense*:

In representing criminal defendants—especially guilty ones—it is often necessary to take the offensive against the government: to put the government on trial for *its* misconduct. In law, as in sports, the best defense is often a good offense . . .

It is the job of the defense attorney—especially when representing the guilty—to prevent, by all lawful means, the "whole truth" from coming out.[1]

During the first trial, von Bulow was defended by Herald Price Fahringer, a silver-haired, silver-tongued Buffalo attorney who has been generally regarded—next to F. Lee Bailey, perhaps—as the best defense attorney on the East Coast. His last case had been Jean Harris's appeal in the "Scarsdale Diet Doctor" murder.

Sunny von Bulow had mysteriously fallen into a brief coma in 1979 and then an irreversible coma in 1980. Her two children by a first marriage became suspicious of their stepfather, Claus, when Sunny's maid told them she had seen vials of insulin in a little black bag that Claus kept in his closet.

The two children hired a private investigator. The son, the detective, and a locksmith went through the von Bulows' Newport mansion until they discovered the little black bag in his closet. It contained three hypodermic needles, drugs, but no insulin. They turned the material over to a private laboratory, which discovered traces of insulin on the needle. The drugs were not tested.

The children turned all the material over to the Rhode Island police, who sent the needle to a state laboratory for more testing. The drugs were also analyzed and turned out to be barbiturates of a very unusual variety—a type that can be put into food, while most barbiturates cannot. The needle once again turned up traces of insulin.

The prosecution also investigated stories that von Bulow had been having an affair with soap-opera actress Alexandra Isles. This turned out to be true. At the trial, Isles testified that she had given von Bulow an ultimatum to leave his wife or break off the affair.

The jury also heard evidence that Claus had little money of his own and had never made more that $30,000 a year. He had lived almost entirely off Sunny's fortune from 1973 to 1980. The manager of Sunny's estate testified that Claus stood to inherit $14 million on her death.

Fahringer presented a defense that tried to raise "reasonable doubt" about all this. At von Bulow's specific request, he did not cross-examine Isles. Neither did von Bulow take the stand in his own behalf, although he said later he wished he had. The defense did present testimony that Sunny drank a lot and had tried to commit suicide. However, this was sharply disputed by testimony from several of Sunny's friends. After their testimony, it became apparent that while there had been rumors of Sunny's dissolute habits, the source of almost all these stories appeared to be Claus himself.

The jury returned a verdict of guilty on two counts of attempted murder. Von Bulow was sentenced to thirty years in prison. He would become eligible for parole in ten years.

Now the *real* trial began. Von Bulow dismissed Fahringer and hired Dershowitz. An appeals process was begun. Von Bulow was out on bail the entire time, living in Sunny's Fifth Avenue apartment.

More than two years later, the Rhode Island Supreme Court overturned the conviction on the grounds that von Bulow's constitutional rights had been violated.

What were those rights? Here is the explanation.

First of all, the court argued, while the police did not violate the Constitution by accepting the black bag from the private detective, they did violate it when they "expanded" the search by sending the hypodermic to the laboratory. This constituted a violation of Claus's Fourth Amendment rights against illegal searches and seizures.

Second, Claus's Constitutional rights were violated because the trial court judge had refused to require the private detective to turn over his notes from the investigation to the defense during discovery proceedings.

The case is interesting because it reflects strongly on why people feel more and more compelled to take the law into their own hands. One of the problems the courts have created by putting so many arcane restrictions on the police and prosecution is that it encourages people to forget about the police and do things for themselves. This proved to be the case with the von Bulow affair. The police probably could have never gotten into Claus's home and made an extensive search without making some "technical" error. The locksmith and the detective hired by Sunny's children, however, could do it without the slightest concern for the Constitution. None of these issues arise when you do things yourself.

However, Dershowitz was able to persuade the court that while there was no "search" involved when the police received the bag, they had "expanded" the search by sending the needle and the drugs to the laboratory. Thus, the fruits of this "illegal search" were not admissible in court. The needle, of course, had already been tested at the private laboratory and those tests were still admissible. But the identification of the barbiturates was not. Therefore, there had to be a new trial without the barbiturates.

Had Sunny's children had both the needle and the barbiturates tested in the private laboratory there would have been no "violation of the Constitution." Their mistake was *not going far enough* outside the channels of normal law enforcement in trying to make their case.

The detective's notes also revolved around the same problems of private law enforcement. The supreme court ruled that they should have been made available to the defense for possible exculpatory evidence, the same way police notes would be. Dershowitz hailed the court's decision, saying it presented an "end run around the Constitution," but it was a run that was stopped only after a 12-yard gain. The fact remains that if you want to investigate a possible attempted murder, you have a lot less chance of "violating the Constitution" if you hire your own detective than if you rely on the police. The lessons for private law enforcement and vigilantism are obvious.

Whether or not these bizarre minutiae were sufficient reason to allow von Bulow a second bite of the apple is, of course, a question of "justice" that no longer attracts much discussion in American appellate courts. The four-member majority took pains to say that they thought the evidence proved von Bulow guilty anyway—just for readers of detective fiction, one must suppose.

The lone dissenting judge—apparently an old-fashioned kind of fellow—took the opportunity to throw a brick at von Bulow from the bench. The "reasonable inference," he said, was that "in December 1979, the defendant, mindful of the ultimatum of his intended bride [Alexandra], decided to take matters into his own hands, one of which contained a syringe containing a copious quantity of insulin." One of the enjoyable things about writing dissenting opinions is that you get to say just about anything you want.

And so, Claus von Bulow got a second bite of the apple. In theory, of course, it was only to see what the jury might say if they *didn't* know that Claus's black bag also contained barbiturates. (The implication, which ran loud and clear at the first trial, was that he could have sedated her before injecting her with the near-fatal dose.)

But of course the practical effect of the second trail was that the defense got to do the whole thing over again, knowing what went wrong at the first trial.

To begin with, there was the realization that there had not been much sympathy for von Bulow in Newport. Out there where everybody was a millionaire, Claus was just another rich person. The defense felt Claus's aristocratic bearing might make a better impression in a more scruffy environment. Therefore, a change of venue was obtained to Providence.

Second, the first jury had said that Isles's testimony was the deciding factor. During the second trial, Isles mysteriously disappeared. Claus's new attorney, Thomas Puccio, had promised to cross-examine her, and she told friends she feared it would be brutal. In addition, she complained that she had been "ostracized" by friends for testifying at the first trial while Claus had been easily accepted back into the same social circles. Isles eventually did show up at the last minute, though, and her testimony was effective.

Third, the defense had made a poor showing in trying to challenge the medical evidence on insulin. Its only expert proved to be relatively unqualified. For the second trail, the defense produced a whole battery of medical experts who argued that insulin was not necessarily the cause of Sunny's condition.

The new defense team was also extraordinarily aggressive at playing the new game of "put everyone but the defendant on trial." When Sunny's personal doctor said he had never said positively that her coma had to be the result of insulin, Puccio asked for a mistrial. The proceedings were halted while the prosecutor from the first round was put on the witness stand to explain why he had bothered to bring von Bulow to trial in the first place. (He told the court he had always felt the doctor favored Claus's side of the story.) All this was done out of the hearing of the jury and did not affect the verdict. But groundwork was being laid for another appeal.

In addition, the defense again "put the victim on trial," arguing that Sunny had abused drugs and alcohol and probably drank herself into the coma. But this time—incredibly—the judge did not allow any of Sunny's friends or relatives to rebut the testimony as they had, effectively, at the first trial.

Finally, the judge did not allow the prosecution to present the evidence about Claus's finances on the grounds that the prosecutor had not "produced the proper framework for the evidence." Without this information, the financial motive for the alleged crime basically disappeared.

Thus, in effect, the jury heard an entirely different case than it did the first time. It is not surprising that the jurors came back with a different verdict—"not guilty."

The judge in the case was widely viewed as favoring the defense in these rulings (although her instructions to the jury reportedly leaned toward the prosecution). *New York Post* columnist Ray Kerrison, who covered the trial, reported a rumor that she might be "bucking for higher office."

Yet to argue that the judge might have favored the defense for some *personal* motive entirely misses the point of contemporary American justice. Up and down the line, judges have been told one thing over the past twenty-five years. *You can't go wrong ruling for the defense.* If the jury acquits, there is no appellate review. The case is over. But if there is a conviction, any decision the judge makes may end up being reviewed by as many as forty or fifty appeals-court justices. Every small decision will be put under a microscope, and *any* error, no matter how small, will be grounds for overturning the case. As former Justice Macklin Fleming says, "A defendant hasn't had a 'fair trail' until he has F. Lee Bailey for an attorney and Oliver Wendell Holmes as the presiding magistrate."

Judges are now under such enormous pressures that they sometimes end up blaming the whole thing on the jury. After Dominique Dunne's murder trial, the judge, who had refused to admit the testimony of John Sweeney's former girlfriend that he had twice put her in the hospital, turned around and berated the jury for not coming back with a murder verdict. "I will state on the record that I believe this is a murderer," the judge stated at sentencing. "I believe that Sweeney is a murderer and not a manslaughterer ... This is a killing with malice ... The jury came back—I don't understand it for the life of me—with [the wrong verdict.]"[2]

Trial court judges are often forced into this sleight-of-hand by the enormous conflicting pressures they are under. The public generally wants verdicts that reflect the facts of the case. But the appeals courts are lost in the minutiae of the law and won't be satisfied until the defendant has had every conceivable opportunity to escape detection. In the end, the easiest thing for a judge may be to make all the decisions in favor of the defendant, and then blame someone else for the verdict.

Yogi Berra is justly famous for saying, "It's not over 'til it's over." This is still true for baseball and real life, but no longer true in American criminal justice. The rule that presides in American courtrooms is now: "It's never over until there's an acquittal."

And so, the von Bulow trial is "over" in the sense that the jury has finally returned the only verdict that the justice system accepts as final: "not guilty." In actuality, a second conviction would have been no more of a "verdict" than the first. The defense team was already preparing an appeal on "malicious prosecution" by putting the first state prosecutor on the witness stand. There would have been appeals on prosecutor's statements, judge's rulings, and instructions to the jury, with the same scholastic standards of technical perfection ruling the day.

It is likely that all we missed because of the jury's "not guilty" verdict is the third trial of Claus von Bulow.

How did the system get in such an extraordinary mess?

One possible answer is the enormous gap in experience that has opened up between the prosecution and defense offices.

People who become victims of crime are often surprised at the youth of today's prosecutors. "We went down to the courthouse after we were burglarized, and the prosecutor was about the same age as my paperboy," one Texas crime victim told me. "The defense attorney, on the other hand, was a gray-haired veteran."

There is a very good reason for all this. The vast number of law-school graduates who take jobs in prosecutors' offices are essentially *training* to become defense attorneys. As Seymour Wishman writes in *Confessions of a Criminal Attorney*:

> I knew I wanted to be a defense lawyer, but I also knew that the best way to become a good one was to spend a few years prosecuting first . . . [Although] some of my friends . . . said I was on the verge of joining the enemy . . . I finally decided to take the job, largely because I knew it would be for only a short time, a few years at most before I could move on to the defense work I had always intended to do.[3]

The unavoidable economics of the situation is that a good criminal attorney with five years experience in a prosecutor's office can often *triple* his or her salary by jumping over to private defense. "About 15 percent of our defense attorneys are former prosecutors," said Marilyn Culp, director of the Victims' Assistance Program in Portland, Oregon. "And believe me, they are the best. They know every little loophole of the law."

Before the Warren Court began revamping the justice system, criminal attorneys were sometimes a rather seedy breed. Charles Silberman writes about the "plead-em-out" courthouse lawyers in Southern counties who would charge $5 to take a defendant inside and plead him guilty.

In general, there have usually been two ways to start off as a defense attorney—either work for the prosecutor or starve while defending indigent criminals. Even today, one of the major concern of most defense attorneys is *getting paid by their clients*. "Ninety percent of the people who come in here really can't afford a lawyer," said a partner in one fairly prominent New York City defense firm with offices only a few blocks from the courthouse.

It is generally known that one of the main reasons defense attorneys ask for endless continuances of cases—and why judges grant them—is because the attorneys *haven't yet been paid by their clients*. Once a guilty verdict is returned, the lawyer's chances of getting paid rapidly diminish to zero. Thus, lawyers try to string out their cases in the hope that their clients will somehow come up with the money.

The public defenders' offices have changed the situation somewhat. It is no longer necessary to train in the prosecutor's office—and consequently, the district attorney can no longer even be assured of having the best young minds from the law schools, if only for a couple of years. Despite the complaints of convicted criminals, the public defenders generally do a good job. "There were times back in the early 1970s when my wife and I [both working in the public defender's office] used to come home and say, 'I think it's getting too *easy* to get people off,'" said Burt Neuborne, legal director of the American Civil Liberties Union. "For a while there, the prosecution seemed very weak."

But this fairly even match-up between the prosecutor and public defender is all but completely overshadowed by the 150,000 *private* attorneys who are working at least part-time in criminal defense (approximately one-quarter of all the nation's attorneys). This vast pool of defense attorneys is what gives the entire legal community—from the law schools to the bar associations—its "defense-oriented" posture.

In order to check what happens to young prosecutors who have made a name for themselves, I decided to see what happened to Richard Ben-Veniste and Jill Volner, the two federal attorneys who became famous in the early 1970s for their dogged prosecution of John Mitchell, Robert Haldemann, and John Ehrlichman in the Watergate scandal. Sure enough, both of them are now working in criminal defense.

"I felt I had run the course with prosecution work," said Ben-Veniste, who now has his own Washington firm and defended one of the principals in the Abscam case. "I find my present practice much more invigorating and challenging."

Volner, on the other hand—now Jill Wine-Banks—was one of the few former prosecutors I have met who had some misgivings. "I still feel a little bad about switching over to the other side," she said. Volner now defends white-collar criminals with Jenner and Block, a blue-chip firm in Chicago. "There is a part of me that will always be a prosecutor. But the economic rewards are pretty hard to withstand. The rule of thumb is that you triple your income when you switch from prosecution to defense work."

Thus, in highly visible trials, the legal talents on the two sides are often a remarkable mismatch. In the second von Bulow trial, for example, Puccio was a former federal prosecutor who had won a very high reputation trying Abscam and several important drug cases. On the other hand, Mark De Sisto, the Rhode Island prosecutor, was still in law school when Claus was being tried the first time. *Time* magazine said he was "visibly nervous and shaken" by his responsibilities.[4]

The same situation recurs in hundreds of important cases around the country. The sad fact is that, among lawyers, prosecution work is not regarded as either very appealing or rewarding.

As a result, prosecutors' offices now have an embattled air about them. In fact, I found them to be almost exactly like the police were fifteen years ago—defensive, suspicious, and certain that they have been driven into a corner by the system. I attended two prosecutors' conventions over the last three years, and both times I was regarded suspiciously and eventually asked to leave—the only times I was kicked out of any meeting during the preparation of this book.

"We're the bad guys," one defensive 28-year-old prosecutor told me at a seminar in Philadelphia. Said another, "My old law-school professor keeps saying, 'You're the best student I ever had, and you ended up a prosecutor. Where did I go wrong?'"

One North Carolina University Law School professor told me, "The liberal students now think of going into criminal defense, while the conservative students think of business. Nobody really thinks of making a career out of the prosecution." Another commented, "Being a prosecutor is like being a lineman in football. It's unglamorous and unrewarding. If you do your job right, nobody tends to notice you. It's only when you make a mistake that you call attention to yourself."

This imbalance tends to carry up right into the bar associations and state legislatures. The President's Task Force on Victims of Crime reported:

> In many parts of the country, prosecutors simply do not fulfill their responsibility to be active members of bar associations on behalf of crime victims. As a result, rules of court, legislation, jury instruction, sentencing, and the like are composed primarily or even exclusively of defense practitioners.[5]

The imbalance carries right up to the state legislatures, where defense attorneys are everywhere, but prosecutors cannot even serve. In many states, legislative committees on criminal justice are completely dominated by defense attorneys.

"We tried to have our 'victims bill' introduced in the Alabama legislature and found that both judicial committees were chaired by defense attorneys," said Anita Armstrong of Victims of Crime and Leniency (VOCAL), an Alabama organization. "They didn't want to have anything to do with us. We had to do an end run around them just to get our prosposals onto the floor of the legislature."

"The justice committees in the California Legislature have long been a graveyard for crime legislation," said Ed McMurray, deputy attorney general of California.

What can be done about all this? There seem to be two possibilities.

The English system offers one alternative. Instead of practicing either prosecution *or* defense, attorneys practice "at the bar." They are randomly assigned to either side. Thus, because attorneys regularly argue both sides, they tend to shy away from the extremes.

A more American solution to the problem, however, would be to allow *private prosecutions*. Under this system, a victim of crime would have the *option* of hiring his or her own attorney to *prepare the case* for the district attorney or even argue the case in court. This way, private criminal lawyers could work on both sides of the issue, and the extremes might be avoided.

Private prosecutions were actually common in the nineteenth century. Their Constitutionality has been approved many times. Only one state—Massachusetts—has specifically outlawed them. In many Southern states—North Carolina in particular—they are still fairly common. In all parts of the country, every defense attorney I talked to said that at least once or twice a year a crime victim wants to hire them to prosecute the crime.

Privatizing the prosecution would have several beneficial effects. First, it would put more legal minds to work on behalf of prosecuting crimes as well as defending accused criminals. As Alan Dershowitz writes: "I also take on cases that raise novel issues suitable for class discussion [at Harvard. In one] murder case ... my students helped me win by providing the solution to a perplexing legal dilemma."[6] Private prosecutions would help put the prosecution back into the mainstream at the law schools as well as the legal community.

Second, private prosecutions would provide some of the "trickle-down economics" that now works so well for accused criminals of every economic stripe.

As I suggested in an earlier chapter, violent criminals are "disorganized" in their random illegal activities, but organized in the courtroom by their attorneys. This becomes particularly important in the matter of setting precedents. Once a precedent is established in the legal system it can be used anywhere else.

Once again, the defense has an enormous advantage. Because only the defense can appeal, defense organizations such as the American Civil Liberties Union can plan "national strategies." They pick up diverse cases from different jurisdictions—like the four cases that made up the *Miranda* decision—and tie them into a package for the federal courts. Prosecutors, who do not have the same options, are essentially on the defensive in the appeals process. "We have no national strategy," admitted Jim Smith, Florida's attorney general, who writes on appeal work for the National Association of State Attorneys General.

The result for the defense is that there is also a certain cross-subsidization between the wealthy and the indigent. An impoverished rape-murderer in Arizona may supply the legal precedent that will overturn the conviction of a wealthy oil millionaire in Palm Beach. Meanwhile, the money that the oil millionaire spends for his defense subsidizes the indigent defendant, whose case will be handled by a high-priced attorney for free.

As Alan Dershowitz writes:

> I select my cases without regard to whether the defendant is guilty or what I think of him personally. Nor do I consider the likelihood of winning . . .
>
> I try to pick the most challenging, the most difficult, and the most *precedent-setting* cases.[7] [my emphasis]

On a more personal level, many defense attorneys also "advertise" their services by deliberately taking hopeless cases of indigent defendants as a way of proving their abilities. Gerry Spence, the famous Wyoming civil and criminal attorney, has written a book about his success in getting a poor Mexican defendant acquitted of murdering his Anglo-American wife.[8] Richard Hawk, a flamboyant California attorney who defended mass-murderer Juan Corona in 1972, told author Tracy Kidder, "If I win this one, It'll propel me past F. Lee Bailey."[9] Typically, although Kidder thought Hawk did a credible job against overwhelming evidence, Corona's second defense team overturned the conviction on the grounds that Hawk had been "incompetent" for not arguing "diminished capacity." At the second trial, ten years after the murders, the new team decided not to argue diminished capacity either. Corona was once again convicted in a new trial that cost the State of California $5 million.

Privatizing the prosecution would put all these economic mechanisms to work on behalf of *victims* as well as criminals. In effect, wealthy victims would subsidize poor victims. Certainly the wealthy might get a little better legal representation, but they would also draw skillful attorneys into the field of prosecuting crime and would create an institutional momentum that would work on behalf of *all* victims.

Having created a system where so much depends on the skills of the individual attorney, criminal lawyers now like to argue that the justice system is "unfair" because every indigent defendant can't afford the most expensive legal counsel.

Almost every defense attorney and judicial offical I interviewed believes the major injustice in the justice system is that "the poor don't get good enough legal representation." Says Barry Slotnick, the high-priced attorney who represents both the Colombo organized-crime family and Bernhard Goetz, "The system is unfair because the poor can't afford me."

Yet no one ever mentions that victims—both rich and poor—have no option except the state-assigned counselors of the prosecutor's office, who are often low-paid, inexperienced, and essentially training to work for the other side. Although most prosecutors I have talked to are totally dedicated to the job they are doing—and many are immensely skilled—the whole prosecution effect is simply overwhelmed by the economic imbalances of the system.

The prosecution of criminals is a state monopoly. The defense of criminals is a free enterprise. It doesn't take much knowledge to guess who is going to get the upper hand. It is like pitting the computer industry against the post office.

Defense work is where the economic opportunity lies. As a result, the entire legal profession—particularly the law schools—has become noticably "defense-oriented." It is time we evened up the scales for the other side.

POWER TO THE JURY

15

STOPPING IN LAS Vegas for three days to attend the convention of the Academy of Criminal Justice Sciences, I am struck by a small newspaper item in the evening edition:

Judge Nixes Testimony in Trial of Ex-Athlete

A District Court judge refused Monday to allow jurors in the murder trial of Oscar Williams Jr. to hear testimony from a woman who said she took drugs and slept with Williams within days after his wife's shooting death.

"Aren't you in mourning?" Linda Sue Isaacs said she asked Williams at the time. "He just got this cheesy grin and took off his clothes."

Williams is accused of fatally shooting his wife, Toy . . . to collect $220,000 in insurance.[1]

An interesting bit of testimony in an interesting case. I have no idea whether the man was guilty or innocent, nor how the trial turned out.

What amazes me, though, is that I, a casual observer passing through Las Vegas for three days and reading the newspaper, now have *more knowledge* about the circumstances surrounding the murder than the jury of twelve individuals who have been asked to decide on the case.

This, however, is the way the American justice system is currently working.

Juries are a very old institution. Every small African or Polynesian tribe has a "council of elders" that decides important matters and resolves disputes that arise between individuals. The full membership of the tribe often sits in on these decisions and lets its feelings be known.

In *Out of Africa,* Isak Dinesen tells of a situation where one young man killed another in a shooting accident. The feud festered for over a year until the tribal chief came to resolve the dispute. The chief awarded the family of the victim a cow in compensation. The offender's family naturally offered its worst cow. A huge commotion ensued, which lasted five minutes. The chief sat there until "the people stopped shrieking and began to talk in an everyday manner." Thus the matter was settled to public satisfaction.

As an outsider, Dinesen was often asked to arbitrate personal disputes among the Kikuyu tribesmen who lived on her property. "It is likely that the Kikuyu of the farm saw my greatness as a judge in the fact that I knew nothing whatever of the laws according to which I judged," she wrote.[2] That is exactly right. As Raoul Berger, of Harvard, says, "A jury is chosen precisely for its ignorance of the law."

The Greeks seem to be the first civilization to institute formal jury deliberations. In Athens, trials were held in the public square, and anyone who wanted could act as a juror. As many as 500 would gather to listen to testimony and cast their votes, with only a majority needed to decide the case.

This pattern of public comment as a backdrop to the questionable actions of individuals serves as a model for the chorus in Greek tragedy. The chorus is the voice of "public opinion," constantly offering commentary and serving as a backdrop for the action of heroes.

The chorus's offerings are usually banal—the "conventional wisdom." It scolds, warns, praises, worries, and says "I told you so." It is often perceived as a dead weight of social convention.

Yet it was the genius of Greek tragedy to recognize that individual actions—no matter how bizarre or heroic—must always be played out against a backdrop of public opinion. The Greek chorus—like a jury—serves as ballast to offset the temperamental, dangerous, or heroic actions of individuals. Its verdicts often seem harsh, routine, and unimaginative. But it is the chorus's counterbalancing wisdom that prevents the actions of heroic characters from degenerating into individual tyranny.

The reduction of the power of juries in American life has led to just that—a tyranny of individualism.

The jury as we know it was carved out of English legal history. As recounted earlier, the jury and the grand jury were once the same body.

Appointed by the king, the grand jury roamed the countryside, ferreting out crime, trying it, and returning verdicts.

As time passed, however, the "petit" jury was split off. Instead of representing the king, the petit jury was drawn from the local population. This limited the prosecuting power of the central government and created a "jury of peers" that served as a buffer between the state and the individual. All this was done with the presumption that centralized authorities might be either too harsh or too lenient. The jury was given the power to stand firm in either case.

The rights of the jury were, as previously stated, one of the common-law traditions that the Founding Fathers insisted on carrying over into the newly constituted American republic. The Sixth and Seventh Amendments are efforts to make juries the final arbiters in both criminal and civil matters.

In England, where our jury system was invented, it still works well. Juries are chosen by lot. The jury is essentially the first twelve people to walk into the courtroom. No time is wasted on jury selection, and as a result trials are swift and certain. The longest trial in English history—the Great Train Robbery, lasting forty-eight days—is now surpassed almost routinely in American courts.

Juries also function well in parts of the world that don't have the British system. We are not, after all, the only country in the world that worries about civil liberties.

In continental Europe, judges join the jurors in their deliberations and have a vote in the decision. This may seem constraining and patronizing, but the system also gives more authority to the jury. Jurors can ask questions during a trial and make suggestions to the judge. Both judge and jury have a general mandate to get to the bottom of things, rather than serving as passive umpires between adversaries.

Thus, juries and community participation are by no means the invention of our system. Strange as it may seem, the American public has lately become more circumscribed in its influence over the outcome of criminal trials than is the public in many other parts of the world.

How did this happen? As you might expect, the jury has been gradually squeezed out of the decision-making process under the rubric of "reform" and "protecting the rights of the defendant."

Throughout the twentieth century, juries have come increasingly under criticism from lawyers and academics for their "majority passions." Juries are subject to "prejudice" and "hysteria." If the public is "inflamed" over a particularly heinous crime, then none of this should be reflected on the jury.

In rare instances, these objections have obviously been justified. The example of white juries hanging black rapists in the South always presents itself. But even though "hard cases make bad law," the defense community has quickly learned that the exception can be made the rule. Safeguards in jury selection set up for the worst case can soon be applied in every case. With no "fundamental fairness" principle guiding decisions anymore, the results can often become ludicrous.

Recently, for example, in New Hampshire Clarence Albert, a convicted murderer, successfully challenged his conviction on the grounds that New Hampshire's ancient system of picking pools of jurors violated his Constitutional rights. Under the old system, town selectmen nominated jurors from their district, who were then chosen randomly by the court clerk. Albert charged that the system excluded blacks from the jury—even though he is not black. The federal court didn't accept this argument, but it did reverse Albert's conviction because young people were underrepresented on his jury—even though he wasn't particularly young, either.

Once the shadow of Constitutionality had been cast on New Hampshire's venerable jury-selection system, other petitions began to pour in. Carl Smith killed a man in a barroom brawl in Portsmouth. He is black, but since the federal court hadn't ruled favorably on the issue of excluding blacks he challenged on the basis of the exclusion of young people as well. Strangely, the jury-selection system had been changed in the middle of his proceeding, so that while he was indicted by a grand jury chosen in the old, discredited method, he was *convicted* by a jury chosen in an acceptable manner. Nevertheless, the federal court overturned his conviction on the grounds that he had been improperly indicted.

As almost everyone knows, it is hard to get young people on juries, and easy to get older people. Young people have plenty to do while retired people often volunteer for jury duty. Nor is there any clear evidence that in a rural area like Vermont old people and young people think very differently. Nevertheless, picking a jury is becoming almost as complicated as picking the delegates to the Democratic National Convention.

The public once again is the loser. Essentially, people have lost the right to sit on juries simply by being who they are. Instead, jurors are subject to quotalike systems to insure they are not "biased." As anyone who has been on jury duty knows, jury selection in most states is now a long, tedious process, dominated completely by the lawyers.

Jury selection begins with a process called *voir dire,* which means, somewhat paradoxically, "to see speak." *Voir dire* is supposed to be a process in which the attorneys and judge watch the jurors expressing themselves, in order to see if the jurors are of sound mind and body.

In practice, however, *voir dire* extends far beyond this. Attorneys use the procedure for two purposes: first, to try to select "a jury that is impartial in my favor," and second, to "seed" their case in the jurors' minds. This process, it should be noted, is by no means limited to the defense. The prosecution does it just as well.

Seeding works like this. In purporting to "probe for some kind of bias" in a juror, the attorney will present many of the main features of his argument, first to get the jury thinking about things, and second, to see how they react.

A prosecutor will start off something like this: "Now, suppose you were faced with a situation where a man came home and found his wife in bed with another man, and the man in bed happened to be a business associate with whom he had just had an argument over money the previous day. Do you, as a juror, think you could differentiate between the justifiable anger this man might feel in finding this man in bed with his wife and the unjustifiable revenge in shooting his partner over a business dispute?"

What the juror replies, of course, is immaterial. Already, the prosecutor has been able to outline the main features of his case—the defendant may have killed the man who seduced his wife, but it was not done in the "heat of passion." Instead of just probing for "sound moral character," the attorney also has a chance to see how the juror will react to the meat of his argument. The other potential jurors sitting in the courtroom, of course, also have the chance to mull over the prosecutor's case in their minds.

Beyond this "seeding," however, the main purpose of *voir dire* is so the attorneys can "get a jury that is impartial and unbiased in my favor."

The different tricks for determining predisposition, of course, are legendary. Men are supposed to be more conviction-oriented than women. Self-employed people are conviction-oriented while employees of government institutions are not. Rape cases have always been tricky. For many decades, attorneys believed that women tended to acquit, blaming the victim, while men tended to be much more offended by the crime. Now they are not quite so sure.

Burt Neuborne, director of legal services for the American Civil Liberties Union, has the classic *voir dire* story. He says that, before the Dodgers and Giants left town, the question every criminal attorney in New York used to ask was "Which baseball team do you root for?" Yankee fans were considered "pro-establishment," and therefore with the prosecutor. Dodger fans were for the underdog and therefore with the defense. "The only people both sides could ever agree on were people who rooted for the Giants," he said.

Although many attorneys believe that jury selection is "80 percent of the ballgame," the best attorneys also say that the standard formulas don't always work.

One former Los Angeles federal public defender told me he routinely followed the formulas for his first two years and got nowhere. "Finally, I decided to rely on my instincts. If I liked someone I would choose them, regardless of their age, sex, or occupation. In my last year, I won eight straight cases."

Another Manhattan assistant district attorney recounted a similar experience.

"I was just a country boy when I came down here, and the first case they gave me involved two black teenagers who had viciously mugged a white woman. I said, 'Oh boy, this is easy. I'll just use my peremptory challenges to get all the black people off and get an all-white jury.'

"After about an hour, the defense attorney said to the judge, 'Your honor, I think the prosecution is simply using his challenges to eliminate all blacks.' I must admit I was a little embarrassed. I didn't realize it would be so obvious. So I took a couple of blacks on the jury, and they came back with a conviction.

"After that, I forgot all about the racial stuff. I kept blacks on the jury all the time and even had several black foremen. The hard-working black people actually seemed to be the toughest on crime. I finally decided it was the upper-income white people in Manhattan who were most likely to be lenient toward criminals."

Unfortunately, the only thing that both prosecution and defense seem to be able to agree upon in practice is the lowest common denominator. In particular, lawyers seem to prefer people who are less intelligent than they are.

In *Juries on Trial,* Paula DiPerna described jury selections at the second trial of Ricky Knapp, the killer of Linda Jill Velzy, whose first conviction was overturned because his barroom companion hadn't advised him of his rights. After two days of *voir dire,* DiPerna reported, the attorneys had only been able to agree on two jurors, a postmaster who "voiced few opinions," and a railroad engineer:

The railroad engineer smiled a lot; he did not seem to register exactly what he was being asked to do, except that it would be a break from work. Having established that the juror would not lose salary during his jury service, the DA asked if his mind would wander to his employment should he be selected. "Oh, no," the man replied with a laugh. He told the attorneys his wife might be a cousin of the local sheriff, but he was not sure. He had had previous jury service a few years prior—"they" found him guilty, he said. When asked what the case had been about, he replied, "I don't know. I just sat on the jury."[3]

On the other hand, another juror who showed signs of intelligence and civil responsibility was vigorously rejected by both sides:

T. W. MacDowell looked like a typical liberal—bearded, young, wearing jeans and plaid shirt. A self-employed carpenter and sheep farmer, he was building a cabin in the woods. On sizing him up, the DA went immediately for a cause challenge, trying to get MacDowell to say he would suffer financial hardship during the trial because of being self-employed. But MacDowell would not say it: "It won't break me. I could have easily gotten out of it but I thought I would do my civic duty." When hardship appeals didn't work, the DA moved on reasonable doubt. MacDowell was one of the few who remembered the judge's prescreening allusion to reasonable doubt. The district attorney tried then to make him say he would require removal of all doubt but MacDowell said, "Not all doubts are reasonable doubts." When the district attorney tried again to confuse him—often the DA would rephrase the juror's answer so it sounded like an answer the DA did not want—MacDowell said simply, "I think we are into a semantic problem here." People who can tell a semantic problem from any other kind are not usually welcome on juries.

The DA eventually used a peremptory challenge to remove Mac-Dowell, but the defense had also intended to challenge him, because [the defense attorney] interpreted MacDowell's willingness to serve as wanting to be on the case—that is, to "get Knapp." The idea that anyone might simply want to do his civic duty seemed lost on both attorneys.[4]

Anyone who has ever been on jury duty will recognize this pattern. I knew one college English teacher who said he quickly figured out a winning formula. If he told the attorneys he taught "English," they would usually pick him. If he said he taught "rhetoric," he would be excused. Generally, attorneys do not like to deal with people on juries who may know more than they do.

But the problem goes way beyond that. Most people see jury duty as a burden—mainly because of the long hours spent waiting around. The vastly expanded "dismissals for cause" generally allow people to select themselves out.

When I was on jury duty, the first pool of jurors consisted of about eighty people. The case, as I said, involved a single drug sale and promised to be short.

"Is there anybody who believes they cannot sit for one week because of health reasons?" the judge began. A few people raised their hands and were excused. "Is there anybody who would find it inconvenient to be sequestered overnight?" More hands went up, and off they went. "Is there anybody who would not be able to serve over the next week because of a religious holiday?" There were about fifteen Orthodox Jews on the panel, and all immediately left. (Orthodox Jews celebrate a lot of holidays.) "Is there anybody who has any relative in law enforcement?" Off they went. "Is there anybody here who has ever been the victim of a crime so that they think they might be unable to deliberate without bias in this case?" More departures. "Since this case involves drugs, is there anybody here who works in pharmacology, or in a laboratory, or is connected in any way with drugs in a way in which they think might prejudice their deliberations in this case?"

And on and on it went. Nobody ever tried to verify any of these excuses. In fact, a few people made up their own excuses, which were also readily accepted by the judge.

After a while, it became obvious what was going on. Anyone who could possibly come up with a reason for not serving was going to be allowed to go. Thus, as seems to happen with most juries the only people left were: 1) those who sincerely wanted to do their civic duty; and 2) the bored, the retired, and the unemployed.

The power of a jury lies in its very randomness. If juries are chosen randomly from the community, without the constant winnowing and self-selection, then public opinion will be represented. This works exactly the way that pollsters are able to measure "public opinion" by randomly making about 200 phone calls. It is only when this increasingly arbitrary and detailed selection process takes place that the public begins to *lose* its power of representation.

Unfortunately, as bad as the system has become, it is quickly getting worse. Both criminal and civil attorneys are now starting to practice "jury investigation"—a process of doing prior opinion surveys and extensive background checks to try to select a favorable jury.

The process was begun in the early 1970s by Dr. Jay Schulman, a sociologist at New York University, who used it in the trial of anti-war activists Daniel and Philip Berrigan. The practice has since exploded— much to the disgust of Dr. Schulman, who only wanted to use it in cases of which he approved. "I did not start out to create a profession, but to help my friends," he said.[5]

Extensive jury investigations are now purchased by both sides in important civil trials, where millions of dollars are at stake, and by the defense at well-financed criminal trials. (Claus von Bulow's defense teams did extensive investigations of potential jurors around Providence, R.I.) The best jury-investigation companies now promise prediction rates for individual jurors of around 80–90 percent.

What is most remarkable is that, in the criminal area, this extensive investigation into people's backgrounds and opinions has been spearheaded by civil libertarians who are constantly warning of a "police state." The civil libertarians assuage their consciences by arguing that "the public is already prosecution-oriented" and that these techniques are necessary to "balance the situation." [A]lthough it is morally regressive to emulate the enemy, a people's lawyer has no political alternative, given the state's enormous advantages, to seeking and using third-party information," said Dr. Schulman, who continues to practice it himself.[6]

In criminal trials, jury investigation is done almost exclusively by the defense. Typically, attorneys will commission samplings of public opinion and do background checks on people in the jury pool. In some jurisdictions the jury clerk's office collects some basic information from potential jurors. This information must be made available to the defense for further investigation. One Georgia lawyer regularly takes pictures of jurors' homes. "It's amazing how much you can tell about a person just by looking at where they live," he said.[7]

Although backgrounds are scrutinized, jury investigation isn't always a matter of getting jurors who are pro-defense. One technique is to try to pair up people on a jury who seem naturally incompatible in the hope that they will oppose each other on a verdict. "I sometimes recommend people with obnoxious characteristics," said one jury investigator. "The other jurors may not like the person, and that can hang the jury."

The results of all this are predictable. In addition to putting the state and the victim on trial, defense attorneys are now starting to put the *jury* on trial. "I felt that the defendant was allowed to learn more about me as a potential juror than I was allowed to learn about him as an accused murderer," one woman told me in describing her jury experience.

The whole premise, once again, is that *juries have no rights*. If there is a right to a jury, it lies only with the defendant. Yet that is not the way the Constitution was written. The Sixth and Seventh Amendments were intended to guarantee the rights of the jury as well. But because of these one-sided interpretations of the Constitution, a jury is not judged as "impartial" until the lawyer has had every conceivable opportunity to tamper with it.

Beyond this, the most critical problem in the courtroom is the elaborate rules of evidence that often prevent the jury from hearing crucial parts of the case.

The adversary system creates many peculiarities in the way the jury is allowed to reach its decision. Books or passages from books, for example, cannot be introduced as evidence. If you have a civil case revolving around a problem in electrical engineering, you may have a relevant passage in the world's most respected electrical engineering textbook, but it cannot be presented to the jury. Instead, the individual who wrote the book must appear in the courtroom to give testimony.

But what if that person is dead, or in Australia? Then another expert can be called in to "interpret" the book. But then the other side can hire its own expert to interpret the book another way, and so it goes. The court itself—the judge, that is—can never call in its own expert for a neutral opinion.

The result of this adversary approach is that both sides push to the extremes, and the middle gets washed out. Almost every field of expertise, for either criminal or civil suits, now has its "hired guns." There are psychiatrists who go around the country saying every criminal is insane, and psychiatrists who go around saying every criminal is sane. In medical malpractice, there are now doctors who make a profession of criticizing other doctors in malpractice suits.

In addition, jurors are generally required to sit mum during trials. There are even court rulings saying that jurors are not allowed to take notes because it might confuse them or prove they aren't paying attention. In 1983, a Maryland judge overturned a $750,000 liability verdict because the jury had used a dictionary to check the meaning of the word "legal."[8]

One of the strangest practices in criminal cases is that the jury is never allowed to learn of the defendant's previous criminal record. This is done to preserve the defendant's "presumption of innocence." But in terms of getting at the truth, there seem to be few better ways of judging a case against a person than whether he has been convicted of similar offenses.

"It's always the first question jurors ask us after the trial—'Did he ever do it before?'" is a common remark of district attorneys. Without this knowledge, the jury never has any way of telling whether the defendant has been in and out of jail ten times for the same thing or is just an unfortunate individual picked off the street.

The defendant's previous record can only be brought up if he takes the stand to testify on his own behalf. Then, his record may be introduced as a way of "impugning his character and testimony." If a defendant testifies in his own behalf in a burglary trial, he will have to admit any previous convictions for burglary. (This is one reason few defendants take the stand.) The judge will then instruct the jury: "You are not to consider these prior convictions in the light of the present burglary charge, but only as a way of evaluating the credibility of defendant's testimony that he was vacationing in the Caribbean on the night of the burglary." The jurors promise to keep the distinction in mind, but few judges or lawyers seriously believe they do.

Even this procedure got to be too much for the defendant-oriented New York State judiciary. Recently the Court of Appeals adopted the "Sandoval" ruling—an ingenious device that only lawyers could imagine. When defendants take the stand in New York cases, juries may be told of the defendant's previous record to impugn his testimony—*but only in terms that an attorney can understand.* Instead of being asked, "Isn't it true that you were convicted of a burglary in 1983?" the defendant is now asked, "Isn't it true that you were convicted of a class E felony in 1983?" Thus the jury receives the information, but in an incomprehensible manner.

The California Supreme Court didn't even stop there. It ruled that impeaching a defendant's testimony with prior convictions for similar or identical crimes was prejudicial. This practice was only overturned by a statewide voter referendum.

All this would make some sense if it were not for another rule that sometimes allows the prosecution to introduce evidence of other crimes of which the defendant has *not* been convicted. This has been allowed when there is a "pattern of crime" or "mode of operation" that is recognizable. In California, this is called the "rattlesnake rule," after a famous case where the prosecution was allowed to introduce evidence suggesting that the defendant had made a habit of trying to kill people with rattlesnakes.

Thus, for example, when Wayne Williams was tried for the murder of two Atlanta boys, the prosecution was allowed to introduce evidence of over a dozen other killings of which Williams was *not* being accused in order to show there had been a pattern of similar crimes.

Strangely, if Williams had already been convicted of these crimes, they would have been *inadmissible* if he had chosen not to take the stand in his own defense.

What can be done to straighten out this mare's nest?

First and foremost, the thing that is lacking in the entire criminal justice system is public participation. The public has to be brought back in order to restore some common sense to the system.

Specifically, the following suggestions seem in order:

1) Juries should be chosen at random. Ideally, the jury should be the first twelve people who walk into the courtroom. That is the only way to ensure *true* public representation. (Most judges I have interviewed say that in 80–90 percent of all trials this practice would not make one bit of difference in the texture of the trial.)

In particular, personal opinions should have no bearing. This works both ways. The Supreme Court, for example, has just ruled that jurors can be excluded from trials where the death penalty is in oked if they are opposed to capital punishment. Why should this be? If opposition to capital punishment represents a segment of public opinion, why should it be excluded any more than any other opinion?

2) *Voir dire* should be performed by judges, as it is in the Federal system. In Federal courts, it often takes less than an hour to impanel a jury. There are few peremptory challenges, and the judge asks most of the questions. The system works very efficiently. Complaining about a case in which a Federal jury was picked in 32 minutes, Jay Schulman, the father of jury screening, observed that "we learned almost nothing about those people." That's exactly the way it should be.[9]

3) Shortening jury selection, and eliminating the humiliating ordeal of being "put on trial" by the opposing attorneys, should broaden public enthusiasm for participating on juries. States like Colorado and Massachusetts have adopted a "one day/one trial" procedure in order to ease the

burdens of jury duty. If jurors aren't picked for a trial the first day, they go home. People are called more often, but they are more willing to participate.

4) Jurors should be allowed to keep notes and ask questions. This doesn't mean the courtroom has to be turned into a free-for-all. Questions can be submitted at discreet intervals, in written form, through the foreman to the judge. But jurors shouldn't have to act as if they are deaf and dumb, or—as Paula DiPerna puts it—"empty receptacles into which attorneys pour the evidence."

5) The jury should hear *all the evidence.* With the various exclusionary rules knocking out confessions and hard evidence, and with other important testimony being ruled "prejudical" or "irrelevant" by judges, the jury often ends up being the least informed body in the courtroom.

Of course, there have to be some limitations. A group accused of burning draft cards can't present a five-week pageant on the history of warfare in order to dramatize its case. But particularly in criminal trials, the jury should be able to hear al the evidence *that is relevant* to the matter it is supposed to be deliberating.

The whole notion of "prejudicial evidence," in fact, seems rather absurd. If evidence is "prejudicial"—meaning formulated of incomplete notions, or without all the facts—then the other side should be able to fill in the gaps.

Quite often, however, evidence is called "prejudicial" precisely because it is so relevant to the case. For example, it is often ruled "prejudicial" to show pictures of murder victims, particularly when the crime has involved viciousness or torture. What could be more relevant to the matter at hand?

The difficulty in enforcing the Constitutional protections provided for juries is that, unfortunately, nobody thinks of himself as a full-time juror. Being a member of a jury is like being a member of the public. It is something we keep in our peripheral vision.

Being an accused criminal, or a person who defends accused criminals, focuses one's interest. Naturally, these people have put more energy and initiative into shaping the system.

As Raoul Berger says: "The Founding Fathers were very suspicious of judges and attorneys. They knew how lawyers tend to get entangled in their musty precedent, and lost in their own subtleties. The purpose of the jury is to bring a fresh breath of public wisdom into the courtroom. The jury's contribution is common sense."

Common sense has become a rare commodity in American courtrooms. The more juries are circumscribed, the rarer it gets.

PUNISHMENT AND PRISON 16

HERE ARE THREE generally acknowledged purposes for punishing criminals. They are: 1) to restrain and separate the individual to keep him from committing any more crimes; 2) to "do justice" by inflicting society's retribution on the individual; and 3) to deter others from committing crimes as well. In practice, it is probably hard to separate the three.

These interlocking purposes are easily recognizable in the justice systems in all human societies. There is no known human society that does not punish criminals by exacting some kind of compensation from them for committing crimes. In fact, there has probably been an evolutionary selection for vengeance and punishment—"justice"—in cultural practices. Societies that have been too punitive or too lenient have failed to produce cooperation. In the worst instances, they would slowly degenerate into unpredictable and chaotic behavior.

As stated before, restitution for the victim can be only a small part of this penalty. Society must also exact its price. The punishment for a burglary, for example, should probably be ten times the amount actually taken, since the burglar probably has only a 1-in-10 chance of being apprehended on each individual burglary. But probably few burglars can afford to pay such a large fine. The penalty must be even higher for armed robbery since there is physical danger to the victim. Just how "society's price" for crime is to be collected has been a matter long debated in history.

In earlier times, this "extra penalty" was often imposed through torture. These physical inflictions were sometimes administered in the most personalized and allegorical ways.

In *Discipline and Punish: The Birth of the Prison,* French philosopher Michel Foucault has described how medieval executions were often accompanied by little pageants that reenacted the crime. A woman who had stabbed her mother, for example, would be dressed as her mother and stabbed to death by another woman dressed as herself. When the assassin of William of Orange was executed in 1574, he first had his right arm (which had wielded the knife) immersed in boiling water, then cut off. All this was intended to give symbolic value to the execution, and to instill particular moral lessons.[1]

Branding criminals has been common, both to punish and to give permanent warning to the public that the individual is dangerous. Mutilation was also used to disable criminals. Thieves had their hands cut off. Heretics had their tongues cut out. Rapists and adulterers were castrated. Some radical women's groups have suggested that we return to this practice for incorrigible rapists.

Mutilations were also practiced in our own history. During the congressional debate over the Bill of Rights in 1789, one congressman worried that the Eighth Amendment forbidding "cruel and unusual punishment" might forbid hanging, whipping, and chopping off of ears. He was assured it wouldn't.

Even today, Cuba brands habitual criminals by putting a mark on the inside of their lower lips. Since Castro emptied his jails in the Mariel boatlift of 1979, law-enforcement officials in many American cities have become accustomed to "lipping" Cubans to see if they are veterans of Cuban prisons.

Most of this *physical* punishment (except the death penalty) was eventually superceded by the "birth of the prison." As Foucault points out, prisons were originally the "gentle" way to treat criminals. Until the eighteenth century, prisons were generally used to incarcerate people— often indefinitely—*before* any charges had been filed against them. Punishment, on the other hand, was handed out in executions, fines, branding, and torture.

Prison, then, was originally seen as a reform of the more "cruel and inhuman" practices it replaced. This fact is often lost on modern reformers, who argue that because prisons have become unpleasant places to live, and because they don't seem to rehabilitate many criminals, we should abolish them altogether.

For years, prisons were often used for questionable purposes. The English debtors' prisons are a commonly cited example. Whole families often lived in prison because they could not pay their debts. Yet incarceration itself made earning money to pay the debt almost impossible. Even today divorced husbands behind on their alimony are sometimes imprisoned.

With the birth of the prison came the birth of the prison reformer. Almost from the moment prison sentences were handed down, people have been suggesting that time in prison be used to turn criminals into useful citizens.

Every era has produced these efforts. When de Tocqueville came to America in 1831, he was studying a prison reform that had already attracted attention in other parts of the world. These efforts continued throughout the nineteenth century. In *The Blithedale Romance,* Nathaniel Hawthorne's gentle satire of nineteenth century American reform movements, one of the characters wastes his entire life dreaming of building a prison that will reform criminals.

One effort that was fully implemented was the Quaker idea of the "penitentiary." Modeled upon monasteries, the penitentiary was a place where inmates lived in solitary confinement, meditating on the errors of their ways. Inmates wore long cowls and could not talk to each other. Most of their days were spent doing handwork.

The results did not live up to expectations. When Charles Dickens visited a "Pennsylvania prison" he was horrified by the conditions. Men regularly went insane. He managed to show prison officials that one man they had presumed to be meditating was actually deaf. The system lasted until the early twentieth century, when it gave way to another reform movement.

The new idea of the twentieth century is the parole system. Inmates are sentenced indeterminately—"one year to life" was not uncommon— under the assumption that they will undergo rehabilitation. Their progress toward good citizenship is monitored by a "parole board." The indeterminate sentence, of course, encourages them in this effort. If they make progress in rehabilitating themselves, they will soon be returned to society.

The parole system has followed in the footsteps of many, many other prison reforms. Initially introduced with great enthusiasm, it seems to work in isolated instances. But soon it must be taken over by ordinary bureaucrats who must run it on a routine basis. Before long, the ideals are honored in only the most vague, perfunctory manner.

With parole, the results have at times been particularly distressing. The least harmful results have been in states where parole has become a routine way of taking time off sentences. This is usually bad enough, in that the public is perpetually deceived by "life" sentences that turn out to last only twelve years.

But the worst outrages have occurred in states where parole is actually honored as a valid concept. Parole boards have often become havens for activists who are able to find the gentlest of spirits in people who have committed the most heinous crimes.

In 1969, Earl Berendes, the 60-year-old police chief of Bellevue, Iowa, surprised two men and a woman while they were breaking into a garage. They beat Berendes to death with a shovel. Both men were sentenced to "seventy-five years in prison."

A scant two years and nine months later, the Iowa Parole Board announced that one of the men was now "rehabilitated," and could be released. "Our only excuse for keeping him incarcerated any longer would have been to punish him," said the parole board, quoting from a prison staff recommendation. "And to keep him only to punish him is not in keeping with the attitude of correction."[2]

For decades, every California prison inmate was under the supervision of the California Adult Authority, which supposedly monitored each prisoner's progress toward good citizenship. In 1976, the Adult Authority released Dr. Geza De Kaplany, a physician who had been sentenced to "life in prison" for the torture-murder of his wife only twelve years before. San Francisco City Supervisor Diane Feinstein (now mayor) described the situation in an angry letter to the *San Francisco Herald-Examiner*:

> De Kaplany, a physician, premeditated the murder of his wife. He assembled a lethal torture kit of three acids, strapped his beautiful 25-year-old wife to the bed, and for three hours mutilated and charred 60 percent of her body with acid.
>
> Her face was beyond recognition, ears and eyelids burned off, sight lost, breasts and genital areas mutilated.
>
> The prosecution asked for the death penalty because of the aggravated nature of the offense, which included torture and mayhem, and because of the intense suffering of the victim who lived for one month maimed and in terrible pain crying for the mercy of death.
>
> The jury sentenced De Kaplany to "life" after testimony that the case would be given a "special-interest" designation (by the Adult Authority).[3]

The "special-interest" category was supposed to mean that all nine members had to convene to grant parole. But twelve years later, the Adult Authority, not sitting in full, released De Kaplany anyway and made arrangements for him to leave the country. He is now practicing medicine in Taiwan.

It is with good reason, then, that state after state—including California—has decided on determinate sentencing, or has even abandoned parole altogether. The idea of "indeterminate sentencing" simply doesn't work. The system was perfunctory at best, licentious at worst. Releasing people who have committed heinous crimes—whether they are "rehabilitated" or not—clearly undermines the general deterrent effect of punishment.

Interestingly enough, inmates were also disgusted with the parole system. A poll in California prisons a few years ago showed that inmates would much prefer fixed sentences where they know how much time they have to do, rather than being forced to play "rehabilitation" games with the parole board. The California prisoners' union also opposed parole.[4]

In fact, the real purpose of parole in recent years may have had much more to do with deceiving the public. Charles Silberman neatly summed it up in *Criminal Violence, Criminal Justice*:

> Parole permits prosecutors and judges to have the best of both worlds: to satisfy public opinion by recommending and imposing long sentences without requiring inmates to serve them. . . . [F]or all the rhetoric about releasing inmates when they show evidence of having been rehabilitated, most parole boards in fact release most offenders when they have served the usual term for their offenses and prior record; in New York State, for example, the Parole Board releases seven inmates in ten at their first appearance before the Board . . .
>
> "In a system that seems addicted to barking louder than it really wants to bite," Franklin Zimring writes, parole "can help protect us from harsh sentences [sic] while allowing the legislature and judiciary the posture of law and order."[5]

So parole does not work. Penitence does not work. Indeterminate sentencing does not work. Determinate sentencing may not work either. Is there anything, then—from basketweaving to the Great Books—that can be said to reduce recidivism and turn criminals into useful citizens once they have finished their jail terms?

That was the question asked by Robert Martinson, a noted political scientist, in a justly famous and widely quoted article published in *The Public Interest* in 1974, entitled: "What Works?—Questions and Answers About Prison Reform."[6]

In 1966, Dr. Martinson had been hired by New York State to do a broad survey of penological literature to prepare—once again—to try to turn New York's prisons from "custodial" to "rehabilitative" institutions. Martinson made a complete survey of all studies ever written in English, and all experiments carried out everywhere in the world since 1945.

He reached some very unsettling conclusions. New York State officials found them so disturbing, in fact, that they refused to publish the results— and refused to allow even Dr. Martinson to have access to his own data. It took a court order before Martinson finally got his research back.

His conclusion was this: "[I]t is possible to give a rather bald summary of our findings: *With few and isolated exceptions, the rehabilitative efforts that have been reported so far have had no appreciable effect on recidivism.*"

"Nothing works," as the conclusions of the paper were soon summarized. Martinson looked into studies involving educational programs, job training, individual therapy, group therapy, parole, probation, medical efforts, and so forth. *Nothing* showed any effect in reducing the commonly expected rates of recidivism—which is about 65 percent. (In other words, about 65 percent of all criminals go back to crime, no matter how long they are incarcerated, or how harshly or solicitously they are treated in jail.) Interestingly, the only technique that seems to have had any significant impact on criminals was psychotherapy. As I mentioned before, a few experiments with psychotherapy actually *increased* recidivism.

Martinson's "Nothing Works" doctrine has had enormous impact on the criminal justice community over the last ten years. In 1984, I attended a retreat on prison sentencing sponsored by the New York City Bar Association. At one workshop, the moderator looked around the room of 25 individuals—district attorneys, judges, defense attorneys, civil liberties attorneys—and asked point-blank: "Does anybody here still believe in the rehabilitation of criminals?" Not a single hand was raised.

Without any reasonable hope of "reforming" criminals or weaning them away from crime, what choice do we have left? The only one is "deterrence." We must build and maintain prisons for their original and ongoing purpose—to punish wrongdoers, to deter others from committing crimes, and to separate criminals from the rest of society.

Prison reformers, of course, are still not satisfied. They have moved on to vague notions of "community-based corrections," which usually means letting people serve time in their living rooms, or in loosely supervised "halfway houses" that often end up becoming centers for more crime in the community.

One alternative already widely in effect is "probation," a supervised liberty in which the usual responsibilities only involve reporting to a probation officer once or twice a month.

Yet even probation is coming under fire. A recent study by the Rand Corporation noted that large numbers of serious felony offenders are now being diverted into probation programs. As columnist William Raspberry wrote, these hardened criminals "appear to have crowded out the traditional probation population—first offenders, petty thieves, drug offenders, and disrupters—many of whom evidently see the system's 'indifference' as encouragement to commit more serious crimes."[7]

Thus, we have proved once again that deterrence and imprisonment do work. Unfortunately, we keep proving it in the negative—"lack of deterrence encourages crime."

The only realistic alternative, then, is to build more prisons. This is difficult, however, for three reasons: 1) the federal courts have been carrying on their own campaign to shut down jails and prisons at the same time that more people are being sent to jail for longer terms; 2) prisons cost money; and 3) most communities do not want prisons.

There is little that can be done about the first problem, except for a change of heart—or makeup—in the federal courts. During the 1970s, federal courts closed down prison cells all over the country. They were hardest on city jails and county lockups, where accused criminals were traditionally detained before trial. But the effects have been felt everywhere.

In Cincinnati, I saw a dozen small—but not miserably uncomfortable—cells sitting empty in the back of a precinct house because they had been condemned by a federal court. The police now had to detain arrestees by handcuffing them to chairs. This required constant supervision and had led to several escape attempts.

In Flint, Michigan, I sat in on a conference among county prison officials while they decided which of the violent, convicted felons in their charge would be released from jail to make room for new prisoners who had just arrived from sentencing. The county prison—like so many others around the country—was under an ongoing federal court order to avoid crowding.

Even when the money is available to build jails, their location has become a severe problem. Few communities want prisons. Remote rural areas that once welcomed them as employment opportunities are now becoming reluctant. When the majority of a community does accept them, civil libertarians—who do not want *any* new jails—often help local opponents to tie them up in lawsuits.

I have a very simple solution for locating prisons—and other undesirable facilities, like toxic waste dumps, mental hospitals, and nuclear waste repositories. I think they should be "auctioned off" among municipalities.

Take the current efforts of Michigan to locate a maximum-security prison as an example. Currently, the state is making the usual rounds of "scientific studies" and other mechanisms designed to dragoon some community into taking the facility. Every announcement of a possible new site immediately sets off a wave of protest.

What the state should do instead is to have each county draw up a plan for where and how it would locate the facility within its borders. Then all the counties should be convened for an auction.

The bidding would start at, say, $50,000. This would be the amount that each county that does *not* take the jail would pay each year to the county that *does* take the jail. Since there are 116 counties in Michigan, each "losing" county would pay $50,000, while the "winning" county would receive $5.8 million. If no county found that offer attractive, the price would be raised to $75,000, with the winning county receiving $9.3 million. At some point, someone is going to bid for the facility.

Such a system would be eminently fair, since people would be setting the price themselves based on how much they valued accepting or rejecting the undesirable facility. If people did not want a prison in their neighborhood, they would pay a small price for sending it somewhere else. If they did accept the risks, they would be compensated for taking it at a price they set themselves.

Another alternative to reducing the costs of prisons has been to turn to private prisons. The idea started only a few years ago when the Immigration and Naturalization Service was having trouble handling hordes of illegal aliens. Entrepreneurs started to convert isolated motels and other facilities into temporary prisons. They proved to be cheap and efficient.

The idea has spread rapidly, so that there are now two dozen private prisons operating around the country, with dozens more on the drawing boards. Most of these are minimum-security facilities and "halfway houses." But Tennessee already has a maximum-security facility, and another is being constructed near Pittsburgh.

Private contractors' major advantage is that they are not bound by legislation that requires governments to employ the highest-paid construction union labor. In addition, they don't have to pay the large pension plans that go to state and federal employees.

Private facilities can also be more innovative. Many of the best companies are being run by former prison officials who were frustrated trying to make changes within the system. "I worked in corrections for 20 years, and saw everything they do wrong," said Ted Nissen, founder of Behavioral Systems Southwest, which has 12 facilities housing 500 people. "Now we're going to show them how to do it right." Nissen says his dream is to build prisons where inmates must work to pay their own expenses. "I want to run the first prison that accepts Mastercard and Visa," he said.

Turning prisons into workhouses or factories is an idea that continually presents itself. Since 1981, Chief Justice Warren Burger has been campaigning to turn prisons into "factories with fences" that would give inmates work experience, defer the costs of prisons, and provide funds for victims' restitution. At present, only 10 percent of American inmates work in prison.

The idea is a good one but faces perennial opposition. Labor unions and businesses resent having to compete with "forced labor." Almost every state has "state use" laws that prohibit prison workshops from making competitive products. As a result, these prison workshops inevitably become losing operations. Thus they must be subsidized and only become an additional cost in running the prison. Civil libertarians also worry about "slave" conditions, citing old Southern chain gangs.

In places where moneymaking prison businesses have surfaced, they have often upset the social structure and made prison authorities uneasy. In Maine State Prison in the 1970s, inmates were allowed to turn a small novelties program that sold handcrafts to tourists into a burgeoning enterprise. The novelties business soon dominated prison routine. Nearly two-thirds of the inmates were working in the program, which soon resembled a small, thriving corporation. Some of the most successful prison entrepreneurs were making over $50,000 a year.

Unfortunately, inmates soured the program by refusing to contribute a portion of their income to victim-restitution funds. State officials finally decided they had lost control of the prison and moved in the national guard for a ten-week lockup. The crafts program was scaled down to its original size.[8]

No matter what can be done to make inmates' time more productive, however, prisons will remain not very nice places to live. In the past, prisons have been criticized for their harsh routines and lack of consideration of prisoners' rights. Unfortunately, the ongoing experiment of the last twenty-five years has proved that there is an even worse aspect of being in prison: living with other inmates.

Thirty years ago, prisons in America were "total institutions." Inmates wore uniforms, kept a daily regimen, and had no basic rights. They were not allowed to communicate with the outside world and couldn't even say much to each other. Administrations ran a tight ship.

Charles Silberman cites Illinois's Statesville Prison during the 1950s, under the administration of state commissioner Joseph Ragen, as a model for the old system. The old wardens, writes Silberman, would "terrorize inmates . . . by sheer force of personality." Ragen himself used to walk alone among the inmates, accompanied only by two guard dogs. After hearing a man had threatened to kill him, another old-style warden once called the man into his office and allowed the inmate to shave him, in order to break his will. "If you stress the small things," Ragen would tell his staff, "you will never have to worry about the big things."[9]

Orderly behavior in the prisons was reinforced by policies that tacitly supported the informal hierarchy among prisoners themselves. Access to inside information and other special privileges were given to "old-timers"—relatively non-violent criminals serving long terms for safecracking or burglary. These senior inmates created a culture that emphasized "keeping things cool." Although inmates maintained a wall of solidarity against prison officials, they were also able to control violence among themselves. As Silberman writes: "By defining a 'real man' as someone who 'pulls his own time,' inmate culture turned the notion of manhood away from rebellion."

All this changed in the 1960s when a new breed of "reform wardens" entered the prisons. As Silberman writes:

> The "old" wardens generally came up through the ranks; any formal
> education they may have had was incidental to their sense of them-

selves or their conception of their role. The "new" wardens usually were college graduates with a background in social work, public administration, or some related field.[10]

When Ragen retired as Illinois state commissioner in 1965, every warden had started as a guard and none had a college degree. By 1974, no warden had started as a guard, and six of eight had master's degrees.

The new wardens had all kinds of new ideas. Prisoners were to be treated as "clients" while guards should consider themselves dispensers of social services. The product of the system was to be "rehabilitation." Oldtimers at Statesville still mark the changeover from the summer day in 1965 when Ross Randolph, the new liberal state prison commissioner, decreed that inmates did not have to wear their prison caps on hot days. As Silberman notes, old-time guards and prison officials believed that "capitulation" in even such a small matter "would only lead to further demands for 'privileges,' and to further capitulation by authorities. They were right."

Prison staffs were "professionalized," inadvertently eliminating many inmate jobs. The wardens opened up new channels of communication by talking with individual prisoners and allowing them more contact with the outside world. The unexpected result was to undermine the old inmate culture. Says Silberman: "Shorn of their privileges, inmate leaders lost their authority and, with it, their ability to resolve conflicts and settle disputes; the result was an immediate increase in violence and disorder."[11]

Faced with outbreaks of violence, the more liberal administrations quickly realized that they also had less means to control them. They had already granted all the small privileges that the old-style wardens used as disciplinary tools. "It is not surprising, therefore, that contemporary 'liberal' wardens often use punishment more freely than did the 'reactionary' officials whom they replaced," writes Silberman. "Nor is it surprising that prison reformers have had to invent new means of punishment."[12]

Quickly overshadowing much of this internal reform, however, was the "prisoners' rights" movement of the 1970s. The judges began intervening, giving prisoners whatever rights and privileges the wardens still withheld. Inmates secured almost unlimited access to the outside world. This completely broke down the old "grapevine" that had been the medium of inmate culture. Outside communication shifted loyalties to racial and ethnic gangs based both inside and outside the institutions. Divisiveness among inmates became the rule.

All this has resulted in a huge upsurge of violence. As Kathleen Engel and Stanley Rothman wrote: "Whereas at one time prisoners had to fear possible brutality by prison guards, today the chief perpetrators of violence against prisoners are other prisoners."[13] Guards—now severely restricted in their own authority—are often helpless to control it. Both murder and *suicide* rates have increased markedly over the past fifteen years.

Thus, the "individual rights" revolution within the prisons has had extraordinary consequences. On the other hand, prisoners have developed what one observer calls "an incredible legal sensitivity—a virtual obsession with 'the law' and with any real or potential violation of [their] rights."[14] On the other hand (it may actually be the same hand), they have become incredibly, ruthlessly violent.

Here is the account from a former inmate of what happened in the New Mexico State Penitentiary in 1980 when prisoners overpowered a few guards and took control of the prison:

> Down the corridor from Dormitory D, an angry mob had gathered outside the door of E-1, the semi-protection unit whose inmates had barricaded themselves in. Residents of E-1 were younger men who had problems being in the general population, problems like getting raped and harassed for money. They needed protection not because they were snitches but because they were not able to grow the teeth it takes to survive in the convict jungle. They didn't need to be caged in lone cells twenty-four hours a day because they were neither troublemakers nor informers, but whenever they ventured out into the main corridor they were escorted by guards. . . . These were men who just wanted to serve their time and get out without being touched by the bizarreness they'd experienced in the mainstream of prison life. In the eyes of most convicts, however, they were simply weak.[15]

Once the riot started, the main body of convicts went after this specially protected room. The E-1 group barricaded themselves in, breaking one rioter's arm when he tried to force his way through the door. Finally, the rioters got the bright idea of lighting a fire to smoke them out.

> Among this group of rioters was an inmate named Joe Madrid. He wasn't mad at anyone in E-1; in fact, he had a few friends in the unit. He'd been talking to one of those friends earlier, trying to convince him that it would be better all around for them to come out. Now he

understood his friend's reticence. While the rest of the group was off trying to find [something to burn], Joe called his buddy over the barricade.

"Listen I think the best thing for you guys to do is get outside the prison and give yourselves up to The Man."

"Yeah, that's a good idea, Joe, but how? We don't have anything in here we can get the windows out with."

"A pipe wrench will do it. I'll go find one in one of the shops downstairs. I'll be back."

In a few minutes, Joe returned with a three-foot wrench. As he was handing it to his friend through the opening in the barricade, the rioters were returning and saw the transaction.

"Hey, you sonofabitch," one of them called to him. "If they get out because of you, your ass is in trouble."

"Hey, man, some of those guys in there are my friends, and I don't think they should be hassled," Joe tried to explain to this group of mostly fellow Chicanos.

His explanation didn't hold. People began yelling, shouting curses at him; finally someone came from behind and hit him over the head with a riot stick. The mob began attacking him and knocked Joe to the ground, kicking and beating him mercilessly; beating the life out of him.

"Hey, man, I think he's dead."

When the rioters realized that indeed their victim had stopped breathing, they dragged his body the length of the corridor to the gymnasium, where others were busy tearing apart that facility. There they got a fifteen-foot length of rope. They would use it to demonstrate the proper treatment for the body of a traitor, for to them, homeboy or no, Joe Madrid was a traitor; he'd gone against them in favor of the weaklings. Tying the rope under his arms and around his chest, they strung him up on the basketball hoop for all to see. There he would hang for the rest of the riot: Joe Madrid, serving a one-to-five year sentence for possession of narcotics, dead at thirty-eight because he tried to be a nice guy in the penitentiary of the Land of Enchantment.[16]

Japanese prisons have gained some attention recently as a potential model for American prisons. Convicts follow a very strict regimen. They are not allowed to talk to other prisoners, and work eight hours a day in special shops or in their cells. (It isn't entirely different from the old "Philadelphia system.")

Japanese prisoners' mail is censored, they are not allowed writing materials, and they can read only books approved by the guards. Their cells are 9-by-5-feet and unheated. They are not even allowed to flush their cell toilets without permission. Their diet consists mainly of seaweed, fish, and rice.

In short, it is a civil libertarian's nightmare. Yet an American prisoner who has served time in both Japanese and American prisons says he preferred the Japanese "because it's fair."

"The Japanese never tried to trick me," said Ed Arnett, who did two years for possessing two kilograms of marijuana on Okinawa. "They were always trustworthy. . . . The guards at Fuchu were hard, but they never messed with you unless there was a reason. You didn't have to worry about the other inmates coming after you, either. And the laws of Japan are fair to everybody. That's the main thing. The laws in this country depend on how much you can pay. I'd rather live under a hard system that's fair."

Figures on prison violence reflect this. No prison guard has ever been killed in Japan, and only one inmate has died at the hands of another in the last ten years. Homosexual rape and other inmate violence are unknown. Interestingly, recidivism is not much lower than it is in America, however—50 percent as opposed to our 65 percent.

Could we institute such a regimen in America? When *Parade* magazine[17] asked Edward Koren, an attorney with the American Civil Liberties Union's National Prison Project, he responded:

"No heat in a prisoner's cell is outrageous. That would be a clear violation of the Constitution's prohibition against cruel and unusual punishment. The other living conditions are quite extreme. The denial of reading materials without clearly showing that they are a threat to prison order, the withholding of writing materials from inmates and the censorship of correspondence all violate the First Amendment. I think introducing Japanese prison methods into the American system would quickly lead to a flood of lawsuits."

INSANITY DEFENSE 17

THE ARGUMENT that law students are usually given to illustrate the insanity defense involves a horse. If a horse kicked a person in the head and killed him, it is postulated, you wouldn't put the horse on trial for murder, would you?

Thus, it is with insane defendants. They are bestial creatures, incapable of rational action. Punishing them is like trying to punish a dumb animal.

There are a few problems with this argument. Suppose you owned a horse and it kicked your neighbor in the head, killing him. Certainly no one would say the horse should be put on trial for murder. Only a lawyer would do that. (One New York attorney recently insisted on a "dog line-up" to see if the victim of a dog bite could identify his client's dog. The victim couldn't, and dog-and-client went free.)

First, what would *you* do? The most likely answer is, you would probably shoot the horse. Most people value human lives over horse's lives, and you would probably kill the horse as a symbolic affirmation of this. At the very least, you would take care to keep the horse confined so that it wouldn't happen again.

But that is only the start of the story. Suppose it was decided that the horse was dangerous and you didn't take enough care in making sure it didn't hurt someone? You might find yourself answering charges of criminally negligent homicide.

At this point, you might want to defend yourself and the horse. The neighbor, you may say, was careless himself. You had warned him about the horse and he didn't listen. Or he should have known enough to be careful around horses. Or perhaps you may argue that the neighbor provoked the horse. He only got what he deserved.

271

Even if there are no criminal charges, it's entirely likely that your neighbor's wife is going to feel aggrieved at losing her husband's companionship and income. She may seek compensation in a civil lawsuit. Even without criminal charges, you will probably end up in court.

The point is this: There are very few areas in life in which *someone* is not going to be held responsible for adverse effects on others. The point of the law has always been to fix *responsibility.* "Acts of God" is one of the ways insurance companies try to define an act where no one has responsibility, and even that doesn't always work very well.

Yet the whole thrust of "insanity" in the criminal law over the last twenty-five to thirty years has been to say that *no one* is responsible in a great variety of instances where real criminal acts produce real, suffering victims. People are "out of their minds," and so there is no one there to be punished. Or they are "temporarily insane," overcome by passions or irresistible impulses, and therefore it was "not really them" who committed the crime, but only some part of their unconscious.

The end result of this is that, more and more, each person's *private* perspective becomes a self-justifying rationalization for committing crimes. If carried far enough—which it often is—the logic is this: If you commit a crime, there must be a reason for it, and therefore that reason "diminishes" your "capacity" for rational judgment. On the other hand, if there doesn't seem to be any reason for the crime, then you must be "insane." More and more the definition of the insanity defense is being tailored to fit the individual criminal.

Even as I sit here writing this chapter, the newspaper brings another entirely predictable example. A 28-year-old bag lady, completely without provocation, has just stabbed a 31-year-old Ohio tourist nine times in Grand Central Station. The bag lady was well known to police. Only ten days before she had created another disturbance and was taken to Bellevue Hospital. The hospital refused to admit her because "she was not a danger to herself or to others."

These words are very carefully chosen. They speak volumes about how efforts to maintain public order have been shredded by the courts in the last twenty years.

Once upon a time, pleading insanity to a crime did not carry today's implication of getting off scot-free. Being judged "innocent by reason of insanity" didn't mean you were innocent. It meant you were insane. You had to go to a mental hospital, where you were likely to stay for a long, long time. In fact, one of the reasons the insanity defense came under fire in the 1960s was because people often ended up in asylums for *longer* terms than they would have spent in jail had they been found guilty of the crime.

Then came the movement to "liberate" mental patients. In the 1960s, somebody read the Constitution and decided that it said mental patients have a "right" to adequate treatment. It was also decided they had a right to *refuse* treatment—which is what they usually do. Habeas corpus petitions were accepted from patients in mental hospitals, and soon it required a court decision to keep anyone in a mental hospital against their will. The standard now is that they have to be "a danger to themselves or others."

And so the "insanity" defense took on a new light. No longer did it mean spending long years—possibly decades—in a mental institution. Escaping conviction by faking insanity meant you could suddenly experience a miraculous "recovery" and be out in a few months. This is exactly what has happened in thousands of cases. The average defendant judged innocent by reason of insanity is now out of the mental hospital in two years.[1]

The other side of the coin is that people who are obviously dangerous, but have not yet hurt anyone, cannot be restrained in any way. If they refuse treatment, there is nothing anyone can do about them. They first have to prove they are "dangerous to themselves or others." But the only way to prove that is to *hurt* someone.

But once you've hurt someone, of course, you are no longer going to be prosecuted. You are simply "insane." The Grand Central bag lady is certainly not going to be charged with knifing anyone. She has simply earned herself a ticket to a mental hospital.

The end result of all this is that *no one* is responsible for hundreds and hundreds of acts of violence. The crimes are all committed by people who are "out of control" and "incapable of rational planning." But somehow they all have an uncanny ability to hurt the people they want to hurt in exactly the way they might have intended.

In addition, the example of these people getting away with things acts as encouragement to thousands of others. It is true that only a small fraction of accused criminals successfully plead insanity. But there are countless others who are egged on to violence by the thought that they might be able to "put one over on the shrinks" and get away with it.

Once again, the people who bear the brunt of all this are those "unnamed, unknown, and unrepresented" members of the public—the next victims.

Roman law was the first system to deal successfully with the problem of insanity. The Romans realized certain people were irrational and couldn't be held accountable for their actions. So when a person was judged insane, he was appointed a lifetime guardian. His *guardian* was then *legally responsible* for his behavior.

Unfortunately, this provision didn't make it into English law. Most continental European countries still have it, and they do not have our bizarre problems of being unable to control irrational people.

English law regarding insanity, instead, has been shaped around several key common law concepts. All of them add up to the same thing. The state must prove that you were acting "responsibly" when you committed what invariably seems like an irresponsible act. If you were "irresponsible" when you *did* something irresponsible, then no one is responsible.

There are actually two kinds of "insanity" defenses, and it is important to keep them distinct in understanding how the system now functions.

First, a person can be declared "not guilty by reason of insanity." He is totally innocent because he is suffering from a "mental illness," or is "incapable of distinguishing right from wrong."

This defense is not used as commonly as supposed. Less than 1 percent of all defendants in serious crimes are now declared entirely *innocent* by reason of insanity—only about 1,500 cases per year, although they tend to be violent and highly visible crimes.

The real problem in the insanity law, however, is in the concept of "diminished capacity." This is not a plea for innocence. Rather it is a defense commonly used to *reduce* serious charges—sometimes right down to nothing. It is the concept of "diminished capacity" that defense attorneys have been able to tailor and expand so that it now seems that whatever emotion or circumstance led up to the crime constitutes a "diminished capacity."

The non-culpability of insane defendants had long been a principle of English law. It was not codified, however, until 1843, when a gunman named Daniel M'Naghtan tried to assassinate British Prime Minister Robert Peel. M'Naghtan missed, but hit Peel's secretary and killed him. The House of Lords, which also serves as Britain's highest criminal court, declared M'Naghtan innocent by reason of insanity—to great public furor.

The original M'Naghtan Rule was fairly straightforward. It read that

> every man is presumed to be sane, and . . . that to establish a defense on
> grounds of insanity, it must be clearly proved that, at the time of the

committing of the act, the party accused was laboring under such a defect of reason, from disease of the mind, as not to know the nature and quality of the act he was doing; or if he did know it, that he did not know what he was doing was wrong.

The original ruling was sensible in that it "presumed every man to be sane." This left the burden of proving insanity on the defense.

Unfortunately, the idea of "insanity" soon became entangled with "mens rea," a crucial legal concept that means literally "the mind for the thing."

In common law, the prosecution must always prove that the defendant did the *actus rea*—the actual deed itself—and that he also had the *mens rea*—meaning roughly the "intention" to do it.

The concept is a very ancient one in Western law. The original reference is supposed to stem from a sermon preached by St. Augustine, in which he said, "A crime cannot be committed without a guilty mind." In its simplest form, it is easy to understand. If you accidentally bump into someone and push them in front of a car, you are not guilty of murder. But if it is someone you have a grudge against, and you do it deliberately, you are.

But what if you were horsing around on the sidewalk and didn't act with "reasonable caution?" Then you are somewhere in between—involuntary manslaughter, perhaps. The consequence is the same, but the act in the eyes of the law is different. In fact, the concept of mens rea is not all that different from the insanity defense. It has been refined and argued in thousands of cases, but there is no commonly accepted legal definition.

Although the original M'Naghtan Rule "presumed everyone to be sane," this presumption was gradually washed out as insanity became attached to mens rea. The prosecution must always prove mens rea. Now, in most jurisdictions, this means proving the defendant *sane* as well. In effect, every man is now presumed to be *insane* unless otherwise proved by the prosecution. The same rule frequently applies to the various "temporary insanities," although there are wide differences from state to state.

I am not going to spend time trying to argue when people are insane and when they are not. Even the psychiatrists are undecided about that. As someone once said: "Mental illness is a disease that some people say other people have." What I want to show is how the concept has been expanded and redefined to become almost a definition of criminality itself.

The insanity defense has been through several metamorphoses. In the nineteenth century, it was generally defined as "not being able to distinguish between right and wrong." It succeeded in only a few instances. Charles Guiteau, who assassinated President Garfield, had his plea of insanity rejected by a jury, and was executed. For a long time the insanity defense was used most frequently at murder trials to avoid the death penalty.

In the nineteenth century, both the general public and the intellectual community were operating under commonly held conceptions of "free will." The German philosophers Immanuel Kant and, later, Arthur Schopenhauer had been particularly successful in establishing the concept that all people are generally responsible for their own actions.

In the early twentieth century, however, Sigmund Freud came along and blew them out of the water. He posited the unconscious mind and argued that human actions are largely under the influence of childhood traumas and forces that the conscious mind does not control.

Freudian psychology affected the concept of legal insanity in two distinct ways. First, it widely expanded the number of people who could be considered insane. Second, it suggested a form of diminished capacity—the "irresistible impulse"—that could occur even to ordinary individuals who were in all other respects reasonably sane.

Writing in the 1950s, Karl Menninger, a devout Freudian, was appalled at the execution of several people he said were obviously "sick." In one 1956 case, a 26-year-old married man became enraged because his mother was leaving him to fly to Alaska. He put a bomb in her suitcase, which exploded in flight, downing the plane and killing fifty-five people. Here is Menninger's diagnosis:

> My colleagues were asked to examine this man and did so very thoroughly. They found that in spite of his superficially acceptable social adjustment he had always been psychologically abnormal and socially maladjusted. He possessed a low tolerance for frustration and discipline, with egocentricity of a high degree, severely impaired judgment capacity, and a poor work record . . .
>
> My colleagues drew the obvious conclusion from these symptoms—that this man was suffering from a mental illness of severe degree at the time he blew up the airplane . . . He was undoubtedly irrational, illogical, psychopathic, sociopathic, disorganized, and schizophrenic.[2]

Note that the qualities that Menninger finds as evidence of a "sickness"—poor tolerance for frustration, egocentricity, a poor work record—are qualities that are frequently noted in nearly *all* criminals.

I do not mean to disparage the idea of feeling sympathy and empathy for criminals. Obviously, Menninger is a well-meaning individual with a great deal of insight into people's problems. But can the justice system simply function as a referral service, turning people over to the psychiatric authorities for treatment after they have committed inappropriate acts of violence? Or should we treat everyone as if they are real people doing real things that produce real consequences?

In many ways, psychiatric terminology simply substitutes large, Latinate words for concepts that are readily recognizable as common sense. To say that someone is "psychopathological" means there is something wrong in his head. To say he is "sociopathological" means he doesn't like other people. All this may sound fancy and forbidding in the textbooks, but does that mean that ordinary people are incapable of passing judgment?

In other ways, Freudian explanations are simple allegories. They substitute one reality for another. A man kills his wife, but he is "really" trying to kill his mother. Therefore the crime is somehow excusable. But the fact remains, he has *really killed his wife.* The purpose of the law is not only to punish. It is to bring people back to reality.

Apart from expanding the notion of complete insanity, Freudian psychology also provided the pretext for an earlier form of "temporary insanity," the "irresistible impulse."

During the 1920s, defense attorneys quickly absorbed Freud's suggestion that unconscious impulses could occasionally explode into violent acts, overcoming the conscious will. The term was first popularized at the Leopold and Loeb trial, when Clarence Darrow used psychiatric testimony to persuade the judge and jury to forego the death penalty for the two wealthy Chicago youths on the grounds that "irresistible impulses" had caused them to kill Bobby Franks.

That defense seemed to explain many crimes—too many perhaps. The suggestion was that it wasn't really *you* who committed the crime, it was "someone else"—your unconscious.

In truth, the terms are almost tautological. By psychiatric definition, all of us harbor these impulses. Some of us keep them under control, others don't. Those who keep them under control don't commit crimes. Those who don't, do. Why do they commit these crimes? Because the impulses were irresistible. How do we know they are irresistible? Because the person couldn't control them.

The "irresistible impulse" nevertheless remained fashionable for some time. The popular 1950s novel, *Anatomy of a Murder,* is about a defense attorney who gets his client acquitted for murdering his wife's lover on the grounds of "irresistible impulse."

The important thing to remember about both irresistible impulse and diminished capacity, however, is that they are only *"temporary"* forms of insanity. *They do not require any hospitalization.* If a person is acquitted on them, he goes free.

Irresistible impulse has now largely fallen out of use. It has been replaced by the broader concept of "diminished capacity." With diminished capacity, the individual supposedly suffers from a temporary condition that makes it difficult to understand or control what he is doing. But there is no suggestion of a permanent condition. It is simply a particular set of circumstances that drives him to a particular crime.

The original purpose of the defense may have been reasonable, applying to extreme emotional states. But once again the defense attorneys have been at work on it, pulling, kneading, and stretching until the defense now covers just about anything.

Diminished capacity now says, for example, that if a jealous boyfriend kills his girlfriend, his love for her may be a diminished capacity. If a person joins a satanic cult that performs ritual killings, being a member of the cult, and therefore under its influence, may be a diminished capacity.

As anyone will recognize, neither of these examples is far-fetched. In fact, they are just about the norm. In 1975, the head of a religious cult in New York City stabbed several of his followers on the grounds that his mystic powers made them invulnerable. He was charged with reckless homicide. The New York State Court of Appeals overturned the guilty verdict on the grounds that the jury should have been instructed to consider that *the man himself* really believed that his victims *were* invulnerable.

Where diminished capacity is taking us is obvious. *Each individual is allowed to become the judge of his own conditions.* If a jealous lover believes his jealousy warrants killing his girlfriend, well then—who knows?—maybe it was warranted. If a devil worshipper believes in sacrificing victims—well, you've got to give everybody his due.

The multiplication of pop ailments—"burnouts" and "stress syndromes"—has been another rich source of diminished-capacity defenses. Anyone who is frustrated, moody, lonely, or angry has diminished capacity. Practically anyone who ever went to Vietnam has a diminished capacity. One critic has caustically suggested "growing up in an urban ghetto" as a diminished capacity, since it obviously produces a propensity for crime. One day anyone who kills for money may be able to present a defense of "diminished *financial* capacity."

By far the most ominous development is the extension of diminished capacity to "being under the influence of drugs or alcohol." *Sixty percent of the violent crimes in this country are committed by people under the influence of drugs or alcohol.* What we may be witnessing is a broad-scale licensing of crime.

It is generally known that criminals frequently take drugs and alcohol to overcome their fears and inhibitions. "People underestimate the importance of alcohol," one professional burglar told Charles Silberman. "I never went out on even the simplest burglary without a drink under my belt. Make that a few drinks."[3]

Mass murderer Ted Bundy, who is suspected of killing more than thirty women, told authors Stephen Michaud and Hugh Aynesworth that "a person who would do the sort of thing he did" would undoubtedly calm his nerves and overcome his inhibitions by getting drunk before going out on his "hunting" expeditions. Many women who were attacked by Bundy said he reeked of alcohol. (Bundy did not actually admit his guilt to Michaud and Aynesworth, but gave them a long, third-person account of how "a person who did such things" would have committed the crimes.)[4]

In the 1984 "Palm Sunday Massacre" in Brooklyn, Christopher Thomas, a 35-year-old drug addict, was charged with killing ten people—a pregnant woman, her cousin, and eight children ranging from ages 3 to 14—because he thought the pregnant woman's husband was having an affair with his wife. In 1985, a jury found him guilty only of manslaughter on the grounds that his cocaine habit had left him "emotionally distressed" at the time of the killings.

All this may seem to argue against juries, which often come back with such bizarre verdicts. But it must be remembered that juries are usually given very little latitude in making these decisions. The law itself is the determinant.

Thus, the judge will instruct the jury, "If it appears to you that the defendant's capacity to judge right and wrong was in fact impaired by his addiction to cocaine, then you must find him guilty of manslaughter and not second-degree murder." Or "If you decide the defendant was in fact suffering from a mental impairment at the time of this act, then you must find him innocent by reason of insanity."

Juries do not make the law, but only try the facts as presented to them. If the law says being high on cocaine is a "diminished capacity," then there is nothing a jury can do about it. The judge's instructions to the jury are also crucial—which is one reason why so many convictions are overturned because of "improper instructions by the judge." The way the law is shaped and stretched over hundreds of judicial decisions—and, to a lesser extent, occasional legislative efforts—is the deciding factor.

Thus, as a result of this statutory drift, we end up with decisions like these:

—In 1978, Dan White quit his job as San Francisco City Councilman in a three-way dispute between himself, Mayor George Moscone, and City Councilman Harvey Milk, a homosexual. He soon changed his mind, however, and asked Moscone to reappoint him. Moscone at first agreed, but then changed his mind.

On the morning that Moscone was scheduled to appoint someone else to White's seat, White—an ex-cop—went to keep an appointment with Moscone carrying a .38-caliber pistol with him to City Hall. He avoided a metal-detector at the front door because it was being manned by a policeman who knew White was no longer licensed to carry a gun. After jumping through a basement window, White went to Moscone's office and shot the mayor. He left through a rear door, went to Milk's office, and shot him, too. He then escaped to a car he had left waiting, but turned himself in an hour later.

During the trial, White's attorneys argued that the stress of losing his councilman's job had forced White to "lose control." (The "Twinkies" defense, that he had been eating "junk food," was a small part of this argument.) The attorneys rehearsed his hard-working background, and suggested that the crush of events had pushed him over the edge.

Several psychiatrists testified that, on the morning of the killings, White was "incapable of premeditation or malice." It would seem more correct to say he was incapable of anything *except* premeditation and malice. Nevertheless, White was convicted only of voluntary manslaughter. He was released from jail in 1984, after serving only five years for the double killing.

—New York City Policeman Robert Torsney shot and killed a teenaged black for no apparent reason in a Brooklyn lot on Thanksgiving evening, 1976. He offered no explanation. His attorney, sensing the drift of psychiatric defenses, went out of his way to emphasize the senseless nature of the killing. "Of course this was a senseless killing," he told the jury. "That's why my client is insane." Torsney was acquitted and sent to a mental hospital. After nine months the hospital said they couldn't find anything wrong with him. He was released.

—In Northport, L.I., in 1984, a group of young men formed a Satan-worshipping cult, built around drugs, witchcraft, and violent rituals. Two of them, Richard Kasso, 17, and James Triano, 19, eventually took 17-year-old Gary Lauwers into the woods for an overnight ceremony. They bound him and forced him to repeat, "I love Satan." Then they gouged out his eyes and stabbed him 30 times.

Kasso committed suicide in his cell, but Triano's attorney presented a diminished capacity defense, arguing that his client had been under the influence of LSD. "There is a devil in this case, and the devil is LSD," he told the jury. "The devil has taken from them, and therefore from us, the ability to determine what is real and what is fantasy."

The argument seems to be that if a defendant is "unable to tell what is real and what is fantasy," then jurors shouldn't make these distinctions, either. Nevertheless, it worked. Triano was acquitted of all charges. When the verdict was announced, Lauwers's mother cried out, "Oh my God! I can't believe it! My son died for nothing!"

—In 1978, Lyman Bostock had just signed a $2 million contract with the California Angels. The previous year he had batted .336, the second-highest average in the American League. On September 23, Bostock was visiting a friend in his hometown of Gary, Indiana, after playing against the Chicago White Sox. His uncle invited him to visit the daughter of an old friend, and together they agreed to go out to dinner. The friend, in turn, invited her sister, Barbara Smith. Only a few blocks from the house, Barbara's estranged husband, Leonard Smith, pulled alongside the car and fired a shotgun into the back seat, killing Bostock. Smith thought Bostock was out on a date with his wife.

At the trial, extensive evidence was presented about Smith's broken home, his attempts to reconcile with his departed father, his troubled efforts to establish his own family, and his testimony that he "blacked out" the evening of the shooting. After one mistrial, he was acquitted as insane by a second jury. He spent seven months in a state mental hospital before being released. Less than two years after the killing, he was a free man.

Many states are now trying to change the rules by shifting the burden of proof to the defendant to show he *is* insane, by allowing verdicts of "guilty but insane" (which mean the defendant must go to jail if he recovers from insanity), or by eliminating the insanity defense altogether. But it is very likely that these efforts will soon be opposed by the courts. Legislative attempts to abolish the insanity defense were overturned long ago by the judiciary in Washington and Mississippi.

To its credit, the medical profession has rebelled against the insanity rule in recent years. A poll among doctors conducted by *MD* magazine in 1983 showed 65 percent opposed to the plea. Even a plurality of the psychiatric profession is now against it.[5] The American Medical Association wants the insanity defense abolished.

Yet both the American Bar Association and the American Psychiatric Association want to return to the simple formula that a person is innocent if he is "unable to appreciate the wrongfulness of his conduct at the time of the offense due to a mental disease or defect," which only opens up the same old can of worms.[6]

Lawyers who want to retain the insanity defense frequently argue that it is necessary to protect "someone who strangles a person but thinks he is squeezing a lemon."

Frankly, I doubt such people have ever existed. Anyone who has worked with insane or retarded people knows that they are almost never completely out of touch with reality and can often be remarkably crafty and clever in getting what they want. In any case, if there is an individual who can strangle others and think he is squeezing lemons, that is exactly the sort of person I want to see locked away.

One of the most simple and profound statements I have ever heard was an aphorism by Jean Cocteau. He said: "Everyone has his reasons."

That's just the trouble. Everyone does have his reasons. The insanity defense has become a way of letting each individual impose his own reasons on everyone else. If we are going to let people's own perceptions— or their alleged perceptions—be the measure of their actions, then naturally everyone is going to produce something that is self-justifying.

American law, with its peculiar indulgence for individual desires, is gradually losing its ability to impose sanctions for reasonable standards of behavior. Juries are constantly instructed to consider "whether the defendant, *in his own mind,* thought his actions were justified." This is not just limited to diminished capacity. In self-defense, the standard is whether "the defendant, in his own mind, thought he was threatened, and therefore justified in taking actions in self-defense"—even if any reasonable person in the same situation might not feel threatened.

The last thing the law wants to do anymore is to enforce objective standards—to say that, regardless of what any one individual might think in his or her own mind, normal and law-abiding people ought to be expected to act in certain ways.

Stanton Samenow and Samuel Yochelson reached the same conclusion after a decade of being asked to treat "criminally insane" people at St. Elizabeths Hospital. Wrote Samenow: "Criminals know right from wrong. In fact, some know the laws better than their lawyers. But they believe that whatever they want to do at any given time is right for them. . . . The criminal is rational, calculating, and deliberate in his actions."[7] Both Samenow and Yochelson—and many other psychiatrists who have dealt with criminals—eventually decided that Alfred Adler had by far the best perceptions of the situation when he wrote:[8]

> With criminals it is different; they have a private logic, a private intelligence. We can observe this in the way they explain their crimes. They are not stupid or feeble-minded. For the most part they conclude quite rightly, if we grant them their goal or a fictitious personal superiority. A criminal will say, "I saw a man who had nice trousers, and I hadn't; so I had to kill him." . . .
>
> The meaning they give to life is a private meaning: no one else is benefitted by the achievement of their aims, and their interest stops short at their own persons. . . . A private meaning is in fact no meaning at all.

DEATH PENALTY

18

T HERE ARE FEW public issues in this country on which as much as 65 percent of the American public agree. Yet a remarkable 75 percent now favor the death penalty. Sixty percent of all women are in favor of it, and for the first time in history a majority of blacks now wants a death penalty. Support has risen steadily since the low ebb in 1968, when only 45 percent of the public favored the death penalty.

These are not soft, opinion-poll figures. In California and Oregon, where death penalty referenda have been held in the last 10 years, both were approved by more than 70 percent of the vote.

Nowhere else has the shift on such an emotional public issue been so visible over the last two decades. Opinion on abortion, for example, has not moved for more than a decade. Over the past ten years a steady 60 percent of the public has opposed a Constitutional amendment that would ban all abortions. This is undoubtedly the reason why anti-abortion groups—despite their fervor and political maneuvering—have had so little success.

With the death penalty, unfortunately, it has been different. Although it has long been favored by the majority, capital punishment is opposed by a very powerful minority. These are the people who *run* the system—the judiciary, the law profession, and the college-educated intelligentsia.

The reason we do not have widespread implementation of the death penalty is not because the public has not made up its mind. It is because a minority has been so successful in frustrating the will of the majority.

Why should we have a death penalty? Foremost, I think we should have it because it is just. Tit for tat—an eye for an eye and a tooth for a tooth—is a fair and successful system. It is not vengeful. It says, quite simply, that "all men are created equal," and that one person's life is worth just as much as another's.

As with tit for tat, taking a life in return for another life is never entirely equal. The state only takes a life *in response* to the first act. It does not initiate the proceedings. There is no public guilt in this. The murderer still has first choice.

Likewise, the criminal receives the benefit of a trial and due process. The victim does not. Given all these advantages and privileges extended to the defendant, it seems strange to argue that a murderer who takes someone else's life without any pretense to fairness is unfairly treated when the state marshals large amounts of resources to insure that the murderer is judged fairly.

When a person willfully and ruthlessly takes the life of another and we say the only punishment we will inflict is life imprisonment, we are saying that the murderer's life is worth more than the victim's. We give tacit approval to violence and quietly say that perhaps the victim should have done better for himself. The person who is more aggressive, who takes the initiative in depriving other people of their lives, is given the advantage of knowing the state will not take his in return. This not only fails to afford a victim "equal protection," it is also extremely dangerous.

There was a time, of course, when the death penalty was imposed for lesser crimes. When the Supreme Court overturned the death penalty throughout the country in 1972, two of the four cases under review involved rape. Fifty years ago, some states were executing habitual criminals for crimes as minor as repeated burglaries.

All this has now changed. In over 35 states where the death penalty is now on the books, it is only applied for *aggravated* murder. This almost always means murders committed in the course of another crime (including arson), murdering someone for money (insurance awards or contracts), or murdering a police officer or prison guard. California has "special circumstances" that include murder by torture or multiple homicides. New Jersey asks for the death penalty if the person has previously been convicted of murder. But the basic pattern is uniform.

When the Supreme Court overturned the death penalty in 1972, in *Furman v. Georgia,* it argued that the death penalty in America was capricious—"like getting struck by lightning." In many Southern states, blacks were frequently executed for raping white women, while in other states mass murderers could not be executed.

Chief Justice Warren Burger was careful to point out in his dissent, however, this was not an argument against the death penalty itself, but only against the way it was being administered. It could just as easily be an argument for *more* executions.

Two Justices—William Brennan and Thurgood Marshall—have argued all along that the death penalty itself violates the Eighth Amendment as cruel and unusual punishment. Justice Marshall even argued that "the public" was opposed to it. When thirty-five states immediately adopted death penalties, he changed that to read an "informed" public *would be* opposed to it.

After the Furman Decision, the states immediately went about rewriting their death penalties to conform to the Supreme Court's standards for eliminating "capriciousness." Most states responded with statutes that *mandated* the death penalty for certain forms of murder. By 1976, there were eight hundred people on death row.

So death penalty opponents now began arguing the other way. They said that death penalties that *mandated* execution for certain crimes were *"too rigid"* because they didn't allow for individual circumstances. In 1976, the Supreme Court bought this argument. In a 6-3 decision, the Court overturned about half the existing death penalties on the grounds that they were too *uncapricious.* The states were required to go back and try once again. In the process, the sentences of nearly all eight hundred death row murderers were permanently commuted.

It is a tribute to the legislative genius of the American people that their representatives have once again been able to fashion thirty-five more death penalties in response to this damned-if-you-do, damned-if-you-don't approach of the judiciary.

New Jersey's law probably serves as a typical example. The death penalty is applied for aggravated murder. The jury first decides on guilt or innocence. Then, if the person is guilty, the jury goes back again and decides whether the death penalty should be invoked. This takes the decision away from the individual judge (and avoids disparities between judges) and puts it in the hands of the twelve jurors who are thoroughly familiar with the details of the case.

Many other states leave the decision to the judge, but almost all follow the "penalty-phase" principle where the decision over the death penalty is initiated only *after* a guilty verdict has been reached. This avoids the problem of having juries worry about punishment while deliberating over guilt or innocence.

The Supreme Court has now called a truce in its war against death penalties. Unfortunately, all this means is that the action has shifted to the lower federal judiciary and the state supreme courts.

The principal actors in this are again the American Civil Liberties Union and the NAACP Legal Defense Fund, very well-funded groups that litigate the appeal of more than half the scheduled executions in the country.

There are currently about 1,200 condemned murderers on death row. Few of them are likely to be executed soon. The most effective technique in blocking an execution is to appeal and reappeal through the state and federal courts on ever-shifting grounds. The latest issue has become "pro-portionality." The NAACP Legal Defense Fund is arguing that every execution must be *statistically* proven to be "proportional" to all verdicts in similar cases. The best way to avoid disproportionate sentences, of course, would be to make the death sentence mandatory. But then opponents would argue it is too inflexible.

A death penalty is crucial to the justice system for many reasons.

First it serves as an important deterrent to murder.

Criminologists generally talk about two kinds of deterrence—specific deterrence and general deterrence. Specific deterrence means that *this particular individual* will not commit a similar crime. General deterrence means that, by the example of punishment, others will be deterred from doing the same thing.

The death penalty assuredly provides specific deterrence. People do not commit more crimes once they are dead. As everyone knows, the "life sentences" imposed on murderers rarely turn out to last more than a decade. A study by the Twentieth Century Fund in 1976 found that the average sentence served for first-degree murder in the United States was ten years.

In 1981, ninety-one police officers were killed in the line of duty in this country. In 7 percent of those cases, the person arrested had a previous arrest for murder. In New York City in 1976 and 1977, eighty-five people arrested for homicide had a previous arrest for murder. Six had two previous arrests for murder, and one had four previous murder arrests. During those two years, New York City police made a murder arrest of someone previously arrested for murder about once a week.[1]

Even if people are kept in jail for life, they can still commit murders. Their victims are not likely to be average citizens, but they can be other convicts, or prison guards. When no further punishment can be meted out against them, there is very little to deter them from further murder.

New York State does not have a general death penalty. Although the majority favors it, and although the legislature passes one every year, two successive governors have refused to approve it, and the legislature has not been able to override their veto. The state did have a law on the books saying that if a prisoner serving a life sentence murdered a prison guard, he could be executed.

In 1983, just such a thing happened. A convicted murderer named Lemuel Smith, serving four life sentences for murder, lured a female guard into the prison chapel. He killed her and then dismembered her body. He was convicted and sentenced to be executed. The New York Court of Appeals quickly declared the law unconstitutional because it was "too rigid."

Thus, the only punishment available was to put him in solitary confinement for 15 years for "breach of prison rules." Shortly after being sentenced, Smith sued the state for "violating his Constitutional rights" by imposing an "excessive penalty." The Prisoners' Legal Services, which represented him, called the punishment an "overreaction."

While the specific deterrence of the death penalty is obvious, the general deterrence is much more in dispute. Intuitively, it would seem that most people fear death more than imprisonment. Some commentators have tried to argue that life in prison is a worse fate. Cesare di Beccaria, the first modern criminologist, used this argument to say the death penalty was less of a deterrent than life imprisonment. Jacques Barzun has used it in favor of the death penalty, saying life in prison is a worse fate.

It is extremely difficult to prove any of this statistically. The best effort was made in 1975 by Professor Isaac Ehrlich, of the University of Chicago, who did statistical regressions comparing murders in states where there were frequent executions to murders in states where there were not. He concluded that every execution probably saves about eight innocent lives.[2]

These figures were introduced during oral arguments before the Supreme Court over the death penalty in 1976. They may have saved those few death penalties that the Court approved, which have become the basis of all contemporary state laws.

Ehrlich's figures have since been hotly disputed by death-penalty opponents. Some people claim they are incomplete or wrong. Others have argued that Ehrlich's own figures do not support his conclusion. Ehrlich, however, has defended his work, and has since refined the figures, reaching essentially the same conclusions.

Probably the best argument for the general deterrence of the death penalty, however, has come from our own experience since capital punishment was effectively abolished in this country in the 1960s.

It was often argued that the death penalty couldn't deter murders because most murders occur in the "heat of passion." At the time, most murders did appear to fall into this category. The two people knew each other, and there were identifiable motives, about 90 percent of the time. "Why do we have a penalty for something that can't be prevented," asked opponents of the death penalty.

But it would be useful to remember the argument that Justice Byron White made in his *Miranda* dissent:

> That the criminal law is wholly or partly ineffective with a segment of the population or with many of those who have been apprehended and convicted is a very faulty basis for concluding that it is not effective with respect to the great bulk of our citizens or for thinking that without the criminal laws, or in the absence of their enforcement, there would be no increase in crime.

As it turned out, the death penalty *was* deterring many murders. The reason they weren't visible is precisely because they were being deterred. These were the "stranger murders," which have grown so rapidly over the last twenty years.

Stranger murders are usually "felony murders," that is, murders committed in the course of another crime. Armed robbery is the most common. Rape is another. They are murders in which the killer had some motive but still picked the victim at random.

The problem with not having a death penalty is this: Armed robbery and rape are serious crimes. For a habitual felon, an armed robbery arrest may mean a 20-year sentence. If the penalty for murder is only a 25-year sentence, then the risks incurred by committing an additional murder to try to escape punishment altogether are not that great.

George Agosto, for example, was a 24-year-old New York City criminal out on parole after a record of eight arrests and three convictions, including one 15-year sentence for manslaughter, for which he had only served 3½ years. On February 14, 1984, he stole a moped at gunpoint in the Bronx.

Riding in a patrol car, Officer Thomas Ruotolo heard a report of the robbery. A few minutes later, he saw Agosto pull his moped into a gas station. He got out of the patrol car to question him.

As Officer Ruotolo approached him, Agosto was probably looking at

10-15 years in jail. He already had the manslaughter sentence still hanging. He was a parole violator and had just pulled an armed robbery. The next few seconds were going to be his last moments of freedom.

So he grabbed his gun and shot Officer Ruotolo between the eyes, killing him. He was apprehended, convicted, and sentenced to 40-years-to-life. But the next 15 years of his life are not going to be much different than they would have been if he had simply given himself up. It was probably worth it for the chance it brought him to try to escape.

Things have been different, however, for Mary Beth Ruotolo, Tommy's widow. She once opposed the death penalty. Now she believes that capital punishment might have saved her husband's life.[3]

The situation with rape is even worse. Because of pressures from women activists, many states are now punishing rapists with 30-to-50-year sentences. What no one is paying attention to, however, is that some sentences for rape now exceed sentences being handed down for murder. Thus, a person who kills a woman after raping her is not incurring any great risk.

The horrifying outcome is this: From the criminal's point of view, in certain situations, *it now often pays to kill your victim.*

There are several factors involved. First, when you kill your victim, you eliminate the principal witness against you. Eyewitness testimony is generally the most effective in front of a jury—even though most crime experts regard it as more unreliable than physical evidence.

Second, a live victim can immediately go to the police and put them on your trail. Dead victims are often not discovered until days or weeks later. Killing your victim improves your chances for escaping immediate detection.

Third, a live victim can provide police with your physical description and other pertinent information. This is particularly true where the victim has gotten a good look at you or may know you casually from other situations. Killing your victim reduces the chances of long-range detection as well.

Of course there are arguments that mitigate against killing your victim. The police are likely to put more time into a murder investigation than an armed robbery. More murderers than robbers are eventually apprehended and many rape or robbery victims do not even report the crime.

But altogether—particularly if you are a long-time criminal and particularly where there is a chance your victim can identify you—killing your victim now has certain calculated advantages.

Testimony from murderers themselves indicates that this often happens.

In New York in 1985, a woman named Rosa Velez was home when a burglar entered her apartment. The man killed her. When apprehended by police, he said: "Yeah, I shot her. She knew me, and I knew I wouldn't go to the chair."[4]

On Long Island in 1985, a gang of youths who had committed a series of rapes picked up a teenage girl off the street and invited her to a party. It turned out she knew two of the men casually. They decided to rape her anyway. When she resisted, they knocked her unconscious. They dumped her in a cemetery, but she regained consciousness and threatened to tell police.

One of the youths later told police that the group became fearful because they realized that her identification would tie them to the other rapes. So they took a rope and strangled her.[5]

The difficulty with not having a death penalty is that, with the "top charge" lowered, the penalty for everything else has to be lowered accordingly. Otherwise we reach the point where two qualitatively dissimilar crimes—rape and murder, or armed robbery and murder—carry essentially the same penalty. To you and me it doesn't seem to make much difference. But to a habitual felon who knows the law backward and forward, it makes a tremendous difference.

Having a death penalty also promotes law enforcement far beyond the occasional execution of an aggravated murderer. It serves as a tremendous bargaining tool for the prosecution. Despite what some people argue, criminals will often do just about anything to "avoid the chair."

One of the most dramatic proofs of this comes from the history of habeas corpus petitions. In the early 1960s, when the Supreme Court was starting to encourage prisoner appeals, it soon discovered that many murderers who were serving life terms were unwilling to appeal their sentences. They feared they would receive the death penalty at a second trial. (Only the judges really believed they were innocent.) This actually happened a few times. So the Supreme Court quickly changed the rules to say that a person who escaped the death penalty on the first trial could not be executed after a second conviction. This helped open up the floodgates on habeas corpus petitions.

While there is ample evidence that the lack of a death penalty has increased the number of aggravated murders in rapes and armed robberies, the most remarkable development has been the recent emergence of the "serial murderer."

In 1971, the nation was shocked by the charge that Juan Corona, a

California labor contractor, had killed 25 migrant laborers, burying their bodies in mass graves. It was the largest mass murder in United States history. (Corona received two trials, and his lawyers are still appealing his 1981 conviction, even though he informed his lawyers at his second trial that he wanted to plead guilty.)

Corona's record for mass murder has now been broken far more often than has Ty Cobb's single-season mark for stolen bases. No one is sure exactly who holds the record now. John Wayne Gacy, Jr., was convicted of killing thirty-three young boys; Elmer Wayne Henley, Jr., was involved in the rape-torture-murder of twenty-seven teenage boys; Ted Bundy may have murdered over thirty-five women, and the yet uncaught "Green River Killer" in Seattle has been implicated in twenty-seven killings. Wayne Williams is believed to have killed as many as twenty-five young boys in Atlanta, Bruce Davis confessed to killing twenty-eight men and boys in Illinois, and Dean Corll is accused of killing at least twenty-four boys in Texas. George Eugene Stano, hardly a household word, has confessed to killing thirty-one young women in Florida.

Moreover, there is no doubt that some of these people are invigorated by the competition. Henry Lee Lucas, who confessed to two hundred murders, may have killed only a dozen, but was seeking notoriety and a chance to travel to other states while in custody. When Gacy was arrested for killing thirty-three boys in Chicago, Elmer Wayne Henley lamented to Texas prosecutor Doug Shaver that his name was no longer at the head of the list. "Why don't you release me for a while so I can find you some more bodies and get my record back," he suggested.[6]

In fact, most of history's famous "mass murderers" now have that quaint historical quality of Tinkers-to-Evers-to-Chance, baseball's early double-play combination that used to end the season with about twelve double plays. (Modern infields complete over one hundred.)

Jack the Ripper killed five London prostitutes in the 1890s. The "Boston Strangler, who terrorized that city in the 1960s, killed 13 women. Henry the Eighth only killed two of his wives.

In 1966, the total number of murders committed for no apparent reason—not including rape or robbery—totaled 644, or 6 percent of 11,000 murders. In 1982, the figure had risen to 4,118 or 18 percent of 23,000 murders. Moreover the figure of motiveless murders is rising at a rate of 6 percent a year, while total murders are declining by 3 percent.[7]

Once again the experts have tried to psychologize and sociologize the whole thing into oblivion. Searching for an explanation of the "serial murderers," *The New York Times* quoted one expert as saying: "All of them had real difficulties with their mothers early on."[8]

Has there ever been a time when a certain portion of the population didn't have difficulties with their mothers early on? And even if motherhood were the problem, how is it that this whole new breed of killers, ranging in age from their early twenties to their late fifties, should suddenly start expressing their hostilities right about 1972?

The only answer is this: These are the murderers who were *previously* deterred by the death penalty. We have probably always had such a collection of psychopaths in our population. But they were collectively deterred by the fear of their own death. Now that this fear has been removed, they have no outside impediment to help keep their impulses under control. They feel *more powerful* than society because they dare do things that the state itself won't do, take someone's else's life.

When Albert De Salvo sought F. Lee Bailey's help before making his confessions as the Boston Strangler, he told Bailey he would not confess to anything if the state wanted the death penalty. Ten years later, when John Wayne Gacy, Jr., was arrested for killing thirty-three boys and burying them in his cellar, he told police: "The only thing they can get me for is running a funeral parlor without a license." In a very real sense, he was right.[9]

All but one of these killers are adult, white males. (Wayne Williams is the only exception.) They inevitably prey upon boys and small-framed women. They live in a world of irresistible impulses and lurid, homicidal fantasies. The only thing that might conceivably break through all this is the fear of their own death. But that fear isn't there anymore. As Edmund Kemper, who has killed his grandparents, his mother, and six young women hitchhikers—and is now up for parole in California—told one reporter: "You can get away with it. There are no Kojaks out there!"[10]

What are the arguments against the death penalty? The most common is that we might make a mistake and execute an innocent person. The death penalty, of course, is irrevocable.

This may be true, but the chances of actually doing it are already known to be vanishingly small. Despite all the historical rumors that surround the situation, there has never been a time when justice was dominated by lynch mobs in American history.

Hugo Adam Bedau, professor of philosophy at Tufts and the country's leading spokesman against the death penalty, did an exhaustive review of nearly 7,000 executions performed in this country from 1892 to the present. Out of the total, he was able to find only seventy-four cases in which "the evidence suggested" an innocent person was *indicted* for a capital crime, and *eight* instances where a probably innocent person was put to death.

Even Bedau himself says that it is "false sentimentality to argue that the death penalty should be abolished because of the abstract possibility that an innocent person might be executed."[11] One person alone—Richard Biegenwald, of Asbury Park, New Jersey—killed half that number of innocent people in two years after being released from a previous life sentence for murder in the 1970s.

It is also argued that the death penalty is discriminatory in that it is more frequently applied to black people. This was true in the South 25 years ago—although in the North at that time there is very little evidence of any discrimination.[12] About half the people on death row are black, but nearly the same percentage of murders are committed by blacks.

The real discrimination occurs where the *victim* is black. One recent study showed that imposition of the death penalty is far more likely where the murder victim is white rather than black.[13] This probably goes a long way toward explaining why blacks are five times more likely to be murder victims. In light of all this, it is hard to see why the NAACP Legal Defense Fund spends huge resources fighting the death penalty. More executions— particularly for killing black people—would probably stem the cycle of violence within black communities.

There is only one basic reason why the judiciary continually thwarts the public will on the death penalty. This is because it does not want to feel responsible for taking human lives. Yet the judiciary is unwilling to acknowledge that its own stubbornness is probably accountable for the death of far greater numbers of *innocent* people—those unnamed, unknown, and unrepresented individuals who might not have been murdered had the courts not stood in the way of capital punishment.

Ernest Van Den Haag has suggested half-seriously that we test the deterrence of the death penalty by making it apply only for murders committed on Monday, Wednesday, and Friday. If murder rates go down on those days, and go up on the others, then we will have conclusive proof that the death penalty works. If nothing happens, then those who argue that life in prison deters homicide equally as well as the death penalty will have won the day.[14]

I have a suggestion that would offer the same test, but would also provide the American people the opportunity to exercise some individual choice on these matters. I think we should make the death penalty *voluntary.* Here is how it would work.

Everyone would be offered the option to sign up for death penalty "membership." This would mean, first, that if you are convicted of a capital crime you are subject to the death penalty. If the jury decides that you have killed someone under aggravating circumstances, it can impose capital punishment.

Second, if anyone kills *you,* they are also subject to the death penalty. People could even carry little cards to announce to muggers and rapists that they are members of the "death penalty club." (If a person who is not a member kills someone who is a member, then the victim's membership overrides.)

I think this would be an excellent way of settling all the arguments about the deterrence factor of the death penalty, and would also give people a chance to govern themselves without judicial interference. Those people who sincerely believe that the death penalty does not deter—or who sincerely feel it is "barbaric" or "wrong" to execute people—will have every opportunity to stand by their beliefs. But they will not be imposing the risks of those convictions on other people.

Judges and lawyers have always had a great deal of difficulty making the connections between their lofty and arcane proceedings and what happens in real life.

Justice Tom Clark, who wrote the Warren majority's decision in *Mapp v. Ohio,* once responded to a permissive decision on criminal matters by saying: "It is ridiculous to think that the criminals are reading our appeals-court decisions."

When asked once whether the Warren Court decisions were having an adverse impact on crime rates, defense attorney Edward Bennett Williams commented: "I think this is really not addressing . . . the real problem. Because I could take you tonight to the precinct stations in the inner city and we could sit there . . . for weeks. And of all the kids who are brought in off the street under arrest . . . you wouldn't find one kid who ever heard of the Mallory case or the Mapp case or the Escobedo case, or the Miranda case."[15]

True, most criminals may not know the names of those decisions or read them word-for-word (not until they are jailhouse lawyers, at least). *But that does not mean that the message doesn't filter down anyway.* By the time it reaches the streets, the decision won't read, "The judgment of the Supreme

Court of Ohio is reversed and the cause remanded for further proceedings."
But it may be translated as "Shit, man, I'm invincible," or "There are no
Kojaks out there."

Either way, the judges themselves are responsible. The judiciary generally likes to limit itself to review by its peers. Most judges feel their primary
responsibility to other judges. If the public is upset about things, then that
just means it "doesn't understand the system." This is nonsense. In self-
government, the public is the system. It is the business of public officials to
make their actions both comprehensible and responsible to the vast majority of the citizenry.

It must be admitted that death-penalty opponents are right when they
say that executing a murderer never really undoes the original crime.
Where they are wrong, however, is in their almost inhumane and bemused
certainty that there is no sense in at least trying to set the world right again.

When I was in college, we were asked to write a paper choosing a line
from *King Lear* to illustrate Keats's famous definition of "negative capabil-
ity." This quality, Keats said, which "went to form Men of Achievement,
especially in Literature," shows itself "when man is capable of being in
Uncertainties, Mysteries, & doubt without any irritable reaching after fact
and reason."

A friend of mine chose a line so perfect that everyone immediately knew
he had written a great paper. The line occurs when Lear returns from the
prison after arriving too late to preventing the murder of his daughter,
Cordelia. Carrying her body in his arms and still speaking to her as if she
were alive, he says:

> I kill'd the slave that was a-hanging thee.

There are several "facts and reasons" that could be "irritably reached
after" here. Was it really the slave's decision that Cordelia should die?
Probably not. Can he justly be held responsible? Not likely. Will killing
him bring Cordelia back? Never.

But Lear kills him anyway. And it is right. It is his last, futile effort to put
the world back together.

Defense attorneys at murder trials often argue that the victim's death
was a "tragedy" but that it doesn't make any sense to "continue the
suffering" by punishing anyone any further.

This is nonsense. Tragedy doesn't occur until the suffering is complete, until justice is done. Oedipus doesn't go off to seek professional counseling. MacBeth doesn't plead diminished capacity. Only when the cycle of crime and punishment is completed can an event properly be dignified by calling it a "tragedy."

Life is not a group therapy session where people make endless appointments to come back next week. It is not a game where people can be given second, third, and fourth chances to "become useful citizens" while climbing over other people's bodies.

Life is lived once, and it is real. The death penalty is our way of reminding ourselves of that.

Part III

The Root Causes
of Crime

CRIME AND BLACKS 19

BLACKS AND Puerto Ricans in New York are in approximately equal economic circumstances. If anything, Puerto Ricans are a little poorer. Yet blacks commit about twice as many murders, three times as many rapes, and five times as many armed robberies.

In San Diego, in the early 1970s, blacks made up about 8 percent of the population, and Mexican-Americans were about 13 percent. Both were equally poor, and Mexicans had a certain reputation for violence. Yet blacks were arrested seven times more often for murder, 4½ times more often for rape, and eight times more often for armed robbery. Almost the same ratios show up in arrest figures from the California Youth Authority.[1]

Nor is high crime necessarily associated with poverty, racial discrimination, or living in segregated communities. Japanese immigrant groups on the West Coast, all originally poor, had crime rates that were lower than the mainstream community. "Chinatowns" were often dominated by "Tong Wars"—rivalries between Mafia-like gangs. But violence was limited to the participants, and levels of random violent crime were usually low. The same pattern of low crime rates is now emerging among immigrant Vietnamese communities in California and Texas.

In 1970, the California Finance Department did a study on crime rates in California's fifty-eight counties. The study involved regression analysis, which compares one variable, crime, to dozens of other variables— poverty, poor housing, urban density, educational levels, unemployment—to see which ones can be most closely tied together.

The results were rather appalling. Of all the possible variables—poverty, housing, jobs, education—the one that most was closely associated with crime rates was *the number of blacks living in a given area.* Moreover, the correlation factor was .70. This means that approximately *70 percent* of the crime difference between two areas can be predicted by measuring the size of the black population.

On the other hand, unemployment, poverty, and overcrowded housing —three factors usually held responsible for higher crime rates—actually correlated weakly or *negatively* in the survey.[2]

We might as well face it. When we talk about crime in America, we are talking largely about black crime. American blacks now commit crimes at an extraordinary rate—probably the highest rate in the world. The crime problem is very much a black problem.

All these statistics are well known in academic circles. But academics find them embarrassing and don't like to talk about them, or else try to disguise their real meaning. One recent book, for example, when confronted with the California figures, decided to define the number of blacks in the population as "inequality." This enabled the author to come to the conclusion that "inequality causes crime." This conclusion, in turn, served as a starting point to argue for better housing, better schools, better jobs, and less discrimination as the "cure" for crime.[3]

One of the few authors who has been willing to face the problem is Charles Silberman. In *Criminal Violence, Criminal Justice,* Silberman wrote:

> The uncomfortable fact is that black offenders account for a disproportionate number of the crimes that evoke the most fear. Whites of good will have shied away from acknowledging this fact for fear of hurting black sensibilities, and both they and blacks have avoided talking about the problem lest they provide ammunition to bigots.
>
> To the extent they do talk about black crime, liberals of both races generally attribute it to the wrenching poverty in which so many black Americans live.[4]

But Silberman is willing to acknowledge that poverty can account for only a portion of black crime.

First of all, he notes, blacks do represent a disproportionate share of the poor. Although composing 12 percent of the population, they comprise 31 percent of the people in poverty. Interestingly enough, blacks also make up exactly 31 percent of the people arrested for non-violent property crimes— burglary, larceny, and auto theft. Recent research by Isaac Ehrlich, who illustrated the deterrence of the death penalty, has also made positive correlations between poverty and the number of property crimes.[5] If we were to equate poverty with a propensity to burglarize, black burglary rates should be just about where they are now.

Unfortunately, with regard to *violent* crimes, blacks are represented beyond all proportion to either numbers or poverty:

> [R]obbery is the prototypical street crime, involving both violence (or the threat of violence) and theft. Injury is frequent—one robbery victim in three is injured nowadays—and robbery always has been a crime committed predominantly by strangers. It is also preeminently a black offense: in 1976, 59 percent of those arrested for robbery were black, and black offenders accounted for nearly three-quarters of the increase in robbery arrests since 1960. Black offenders are disproportionately involved in other violent crimes as well; in 1976, more than half those arrested for murder, nearly half those arrested for rape, and two-fifth of those arrested for aggravated assault were black.[6]

Lest anyone argue that all this is due to racial prejudice, with whites being let off easy and blacks arrested for crimes they didn't commit, Silberman points out this is not so.

Statistics in New York, for example, show that arrests are almost completely race-neutral. About 60 percent of all robbery victims reported that the robber was black, about 60 percent of those arrested were black, and about 60 percent of those convicted were black.[7]

Numerous other studies have reached similar conclusions. Research in several states by the Rand Corporation showed that, while blacks received slightly longer sentences after conviction, *whites* were more often held for prosecution for the same crimes.[8] Concludes another recent commentator: "Police officers do exercise discretion in making arrests. . . . Arrest is more likely when the suspected offense is more serious, when the suspect and the victim are strangers, and when the victim expresses a preference for arrest. Race is not the significant determinant of arrest decision-making that many critics of the criminal justice system believe it to be."[9]

Thus, the disparity in the statistics cannot be laid to discrimination in the justice system. Blacks really do commit more violent crimes.

Why is this so? Silberman is just one of a long line of people who offer an historical explanation. Blacks commit a lot of crimes, he says, because they don't like whites. Blacks have long been oppressed by whites in the American system, both before and after slavery. All this has built up huge reservoirs of resentment. In the 1960s, these resentments finally exploded. In effect, whites are now getting what they deserve. In a famous and oft-quoted passage, Silberman writes:

> The change has come; blacks *have* changed their minds. . . . After 350 years of fearing whites, black Americans have discovered that the fear runs the other way, that whites are intimidated by their very presence; it would be hard to overestimate what an extraordinarily liberating force this discovery is. The taboo against expression of anti-white anger is breaking down, and 350 years of festering hatred has come spilling out.
>
> The expression of anger is turning out to be cumulative rather than cathartic. Instead of being dissipated, the anger appears to be feeding on itself; the more anger is expressed, the more there is to be expressed.[10]

Crime, then, is an expression of black anger against white oppression. There is nothing white people can do except lay low, try to stay out of the line of fire—or start shooting back, presumably.

Along with this, of course, we must continue to eliminate prejudice and discrimination from the system and help black people catch up. On the day all this is over, perhaps, crime may return to normal, acceptable levels.

There is no doubt some truth to this argument. At its core, much black hostility is obviously aimed at white people. Muggings often seem to be mini-melodramas, intended to act out the racial difficulties of the last few centuries. This is one reason why simply handing over your money doesn't always work. The money is not the object. The real aim is *submission.* If the mugging takes on the air of a routine financial transaction, then the mugger has lost some satisfaction. This is when the "senseless" beatings and shootings often enter.[11]

There have also been black fringe groups who clearly preached racial revenge and went around deliberately killing whites. Various groups calling themselves the "Black Liberation Army" killed many white policemen and killed and tortured whites in many parts of the country. In a sense, they have their counterparts in the white-supremacist groups and occasional lone bigots who deliberately aim their violence at blacks.

But as far as *routine* black crime is concerned, the overwhelming obvious fact about it is that *most of it is committed against other blacks.* Black men are 6½ times more likely to be murdered than are white men, and black *women* are 50 percent more likely to be murdered than white *men.* Black women are also four times more likely to be murdered than white women. Even though blacks are only 12 percent of the population, they make up 45 percent of the murder victims. About 85 percent of all homicides involve people of the same race.

So it is, too, with other violent crimes. About 70 percent of rapes against white women are committed by other whites, and 90 percent of rapes against black women are by other blacks. Only armed robbery is an "interracial" crime, with 50 percent being committed by blacks against whites. (Only 8 percent are whites robbing blacks.) At the same time, blacks making between $7500 and $10,000 are twice as likely to be victims of violent crime as whites in the same income category, and blacks making *over* $50,000 are victimized more often than anyone in America, except blacks making under $10,000 and whites making under $7500.[12]

As Claude Brown describes life in Harlem:

> In any Harlem building, whether a tenement or a relatively luxurious high-rise, every door has at least three locks on it. Nobody opens a door without first finding out who's there. In the early evening, or even at midday, you see people—middle-aged men and women—lingering outside nice apartment houses, peeking in the lobbies. They seem to be casing the joint. They are actually trying to figure out who is in the lobby of *their* building. "Is this someone waiting to mug me? Should I risk going in, or should I wait for someone else to come?" ...
>
> In 1950 my grandparents could take a walk in Colonial Park in Harlem at three o'clock in the morning. Today that would be suicide.[13]

In fact, one of the best kept secrets in this country is that *black people are more fed up with crime than white people are.* Black people consistently show a higher concern about crime than do whites in opinion polls. In a *New York Times* survey taken in response to the Bernhard Goetz shooting, 46 percent of blacks said that crime in New York was worse than anywhere else, while only 33 percent of whites felt the same way—an obvious reflection of each group's personal experience with crime.[14]

These voices are constantly raised and constantly ignored. In 1968, the first year that Americans listed "crime" as their major domestic concern, the New York Chapter of the NAACP issued a proclamation against crime, charging that black youths were carrying on a "criminal reign of terror" in Harlem. They demanded that New York City place a uniformed policeman in every apartment building. The author of the report told newspaper reporters, "It is not police brutality that makes people afraid to walk the streets at night, it is criminal brutality."[15]

Only a few years later, A. Phillip Randolph, one of the greatest civil rights leaders of the century, was forced to move out of his Harlem apartment after being repeatedly mugged. About the same time, M. Carl Holman, an Atlanta civil-rights leader and president of the National Urban Coalition, was saying black Americans are tired of being "tricked by the hardened criminal who beats up a seventy-eight-year-old woman and whom someone wants to regard as a political prisoner."[16]

James Q. Wilson says he was lured into the study of crime in 1968 when he did a survey of public attitudes in Chicago and Boston and found that blacks were just as concerned about crime as whites and that only 10 percent of blacks were highly critical of the police. Going back over figures from the Kerner Commission on Civil Disorders, Wilson found that while the figure that one-third of blacks were somewhat critical of police had been widely publicized, the same percentage of blacks were critical of the state and federal governments. Other surveys have shown that a demand for *better police protection* is the heart of black people's complaint, and that crime is almost always regarded as the leading neighborhood problem.

"It is easy to become preoccupied with black criticisms of alleged police abuse," Wilson concluded. "It is easy to forget that there is as much or more black criticism of inadequate police protection and service."[17]

The plain fact is that white people—and particularly white people who profess to be sympathetic to blacks—have rarely been willing to take seriously the debilitating nature of crime in black neighborhoods.

I remember as a young college student in the 1960s sitting in a diner one evening with a middle-aged black man talking about one thing and another. Completely voluntarily, he offered the observation: "You know how you could end the crime problem. You could take all young kids and watch them, and if they start to show any criminal tendencies, you could take them and execute them."

I remember what impressed me most—apart from the draconic nature of his solution—was that he came from a world where crime was regarded as a significant problem. Living in the optimistic flush of the early Kennedy years, and having been raised in a peaceful middle-class suburb, crime seemed to me like a problem from another planet.

There are, of course, few Americans who would still express this sentiment. But it is important to realize that there is still a hard core of enormously influential scholars, intellectuals, and policy-makers who refuse to recognize how seriously crime debilitates black life.

Civil libertarians in particular have always claimed to be representing the interests of black people as they loosened up the system in favor of crime. Unfortunately, the truth may not be quite that simple. Justice Richard Neeley, of the West Virginia Supreme Court, suggests that the real reason the exclusionary rule on searches and seizures was expanded so widely in the 1960s was "so that middle-class people could smoke marijuana in their living rooms."

If black people ask for *more* law enforcement, their voices are ignored, or—more incredibly—not even believed. The most extraordinary moment I had in the entire time spent researching this book was sitting in the office of Burt Neuborne, legal director of the American Civil Liberties Union, and hearing him tell me that Claude Brown's report on the deteriorating situation in Harlem was "a lot of sensationalistic crap."

Why did black people become so violent in American history? And why do black neighborhoods continue to be overrun with crime directed against black people?

The explanation, I think, comes in understanding what *really* happened during the long years of discrimination in Southern history.

Certainly, the root of some of the violence among black people comes from slavery and oppression. It is clear that any people who are confined to a common misery will take out their aggression and frustrations on each other—and finally, if given the opportunity, on their oppressors.

Still, if all this is simply the delayed fuse of slavery and segregation, why, when black violence was exploding against whites in the 1960s, did it explode against blacks even more?

And why, as Silberman himself points out, has black violence become "cumulative?" Why does youthful violence in American cities show no signs of abating, even though racial relations have obviously improved to some degree in the larger society? Why is youthful black crime becoming a separate subculture, driven by its own internal momentum and largely impervious to influences from the outside society?

To answer this question, I think we have to look beyond the historical imperative of black-and-white antagonisms and return to some basic facts about law enforcement.

In 1937, John Dollard, professor of psychology at Yale, completed more than a year of research into the mores of race relations in the South.

He published his findings in a book called *Caste and Class in a Southern Town.*

Looking past the more obvious incidents of lynchings and interracial violence, Dollard noted that the real discrimination in the South's justice system was the failure of the white establishment to treat black-on-black crime as a serious matter:

> It is impossible to see the more violent patterns of Negro behavior in the right perspective unless one understands that there are different standards of justice for the two castes. White persons are held much more strictly to the formal legal code; Negroes are dealt with much more indulgently.... This is true only under one condition, however—when Negro crimes are committed on Negroes; when they are done on whites, the penalties assessed may rather be excessively strict. The result is that the individual Negro is, to a considerable degree, outside the protection of white law, and must shift for himself. This leads to the frontier psychology ... and to its consequent idealization of violence. Indeed, this differential application of the white law is often referred to as a merit of southern white persons; one will be asked to notice that they are lenient and indulgent with Negroes, and that Negroes are not nearly so severely punished as whites would be for the same crimes. It is clear that this differential application of the law amounts to a condoning of Negro violence and gives immunity to Negroes to commit small or large crimes so long as they are on Negroes. It may be indulgent in the case of any given Negro, but its effect on the Negro group as a whole is dangerous and destructive.[18]

In a very real sense, then, blacks have been living in a "vigilante" situation since at least the end of slavery. The heart and soul of racial discrimination in the South lay, not in the relatively infrequent confrontations between whites and blacks, but in the day-to-day "benign neglect" of violence *between* black people. The situation was governed by a simple, cynical equation: "It doesn't matter *as long as they do it to each other.*"

Of course, none of this was expressed openly. Instead, it was done in a series of paternalistic formulas that said that blacks were "by nature" more violent or that it "wouldn't be proper" for whites to intervent or impose their values.

Paula DiPerna found these values all alive and well in the South in 1983 when she witnessed a murder trial where a black man was charged with beating his black wife to death:

> In the murder case, the jury from which all black males had been expunged acquitted the defendant of murder in a 12-0 vote in twenty minutes. They did convict him on the lesser charge of aggravated assault. This lesser charge, the foreman commented to me, the jurors thought was just "a slap on the wrist." But he added, "The state did not prove its murder case." . . . [T]here had been very gory photographs presented to demonstrate the extent of the beating the woman had received and testimony from the couple's eight-year-old daughter that "Poppa was beating on Momma."
>
> I asked the foreman, a white man in his sixties who had had prior jury experience, whether he believed prosecutors tried to keep blacks off juries. He answered that "quite often a black is far harder on another black on a charge like that. The average white . . . would be more lenient. Around here, there still remains some element of that belief they don't really know what they are doing. We ought to be a little kind to them. A paternalistic attitude."[19]

What is remarkable is that this old, patronizing Southern attitude has been lifted bodily out of the South and carried into the rest of the country. In the South, it would be called "racist"—although disguised under patronizing terms like "not interfering," and "being a little kind to them." Today it is called *liberalism* and is couched in patronizing terms like "poverty causes crime" and "criminals are really victims of society."

As Claude Brown wrote in his *New York Times* article:

> Another plausible, not so obvious, explanation for the stupendous wave of violent crime perpetrated by today's young is that many of them were eyewitnesses, at a very tender and impressionable age, to modern-day "Dodge City" shootouts and the broad-daylight slaying so typical of the urban drug wars of the 1970s.
>
> When they were 6, 7, 8 or so, they saw friends, neighbors, relatives and total strangers brutally murdered, and seldom heard of anyone even being arrested for any of the slayings . . .
>
> It is disturbing to consider that murder is the style among young

muggers and that the style among the New York political liberal establishment is anti-capital punishment, and how well the two styles complement each other.[20]

And so we come at last to the supreme irony about blacks, whites, and law enforcement in contemporary American society. The incredible fact is that 95 percent of the time, when blacks are outraged by the police, it is because the police aren't doing enough to *control* crime in their communities. This outrage even extends to the argument that police *corruption* is the reason no one in black ghettos is punished for crime.

Harold is a 35-year-old black from Bedford-Stuyvesant whom I met at a wedding. He is a commercial artist and runs a successful promotion business on the side. He also owns two buildings in Westchester County, where he is a landlord.

Had any of his friends done as well as he had? I asked.

"Most of them are dead," he said. "Either that or in a stupor on heroin."

Had Bedford-Stuyvesant changed much since his youth?

"Oh, sure. Crime has gotten much worse. We used to think it was a big deal to go out and steal a car. Now the kids are into killing each other. Some of these 15-year-olds out here are unbelievable. When they get a new gun, they go out and shoot somebody to try it out, just like you'd drive around the block in a new car."

Had he known anyone on either end of such a killing?

"Oh sure," he said. "Both kids were 19. They got into an argument over a girl or something, and one of them got a gun and shot the other."

Did anything happen?"

"Oh yeah," he smiled knowingly. "The police arrested the guy. But you know, the police and the criminals are just like that." He interlocked his fingers to demonstrate. "That guy was out in about six months. The police don't care. They reduce the charges down to assault, and that's the end of it."

It is only too typical that the police should end up getting blamed for what the criminal courts have done. I would bet the police would be happy to put away such young murderers for 20 years—if only for their own safety. But the system doesn't work that way anymore, especially where young blacks are concerned.

Yet this view of lenient law enforcement as the result of "police corruption" is common in black neighborhoods. For years, Harlem Congressman Charles Rangel has charged that New York City police are receiving payoffs because they won't break up a gathering of drug dealers on a sidewalk. The same rumor often explains why patrolmen won't close down illegal numbers parlors. Yet I know from my own police tours that the average patrolmen would love to break up such places, but aren't allowed to because of concerns that policing these establishments may be "corruption-prone" or will violate civil liberties.

And so—incredibly—after twenty-five years of Constitutional nitpicking intended to "improve the image of law enforcement," the result is a common belief in minority communities that the police are corrupt because they *won't enforce the law.* The wedge driven between the police and the community is nearly complete. While the courts chide the police for being "overzealous," the residents of poor neighborhoods are angry because the police are "unresponsive." It is a perfect double-bind. What better way to produce endless, bitter frustrations?

The reason, then, why blacks are far more violent than other racial and ethnic groups in American society is simple: They have never had effective law enforcement in their communities.

First they were denied it by patronizing Southerners who argued that black violence was only "natural." Now they are denied it by patronizing liberals who argue that black people don't know what they're talking about if they want a crackdown on crime. If average black citizens try to raise their voices to restore law and order to their neighborhoods, they are overridden by civil libertarians—and, it must be admitted, by many black leaders—who only want to talk about "overzealous law enforcement," and "police brutality."

Creating a justice system that is charged with enforcing civilized standards of behavior will produce far more for blacks in this country than it will for whites. It will help them break the cycle of mutual, disintegrative violence that has kept black communities locked in poverty. It will allow civilized behavior to flourish. To deny this is to deny that blacks are capable of leading normal, productive lives.

CRIME AND FAMILIES

20

U NFORTUNATELY, law enforcement alone is not likely to quell the violence in black neighborhoods. The problems have taken very deep root, mainly in that most basic of all human institutions—the family.

Black Americans have been going through a social earthquake over the past twenty-five years that has been unprecedented in history. Their families have been completely unravelling.

In 1960, Daniel Patrick Moynihan, then an assistant secretary of labor, wrote a report entitled "The Negro Family: The Case for National Action." In it, he worried that the level of female-headed, single-parent homes among blacks had grown to an unprecedented level of 20 percent.[1]

What struck Moynihan with particular force was that welfare rates had become uncoupled from unemployment rates. Since 1948, welfare rates and unemployment rates had moved together in almost perfect precision. When unemployment rates went up, welfare rolls went up; when unemployment came down, welfare rolls came down.

But beginning in 1961, things changed. For the first time, the number of people on welfare began to take on a momentum of its own. Unemployment figures had been in a steady decline for five years, but welfare rolls were *climbing*. This did not seem to represent hard times, or the number of women being deserted by their husbands. Instead, it represented an increased number of illegitimate births, particularly among young women. While the actual number of female-headed households among blacks did not rise from 1960-65, the number of reported illegitimate births rose 25 percent.

Borrowing a term coined by sociologist Kenneth Clark, Moynihan worried about a "tangle of pathologies" that was overtaking black neighborhoods. At the heart of this was the female-headed household. A cycle was starting to perpetuate itself. Illegitimacy was rising, and family formation was dropping. Instead of marrying young men and beginning a mutual climb up the ladder, young black women were starting to center their lives around the welfare system. Poverty was becoming institutionalized.

The Moynihan report was heaped with scorn and derided as "racist." Unfortunately, it was all too accurate. If anything, it considerably underestimated the inundation that was about to come.

What the Moynihan report had spotted in 1965 turned out to be only the early swells of a tidal wave. For the next decade, the two lines on unemployment and welfare rates continued to move in opposite directions. In 1968, unemployment among blacks reached an historical all-time low—about 4 percent. Yet welfare rolls went through their biggest explosion in history.

The years 1967 and 1968 marked the birth of the "welfare rights" movement, which started in New York City and spread rapidly to the rest of the country. In 1966 Richard Cloward, whose criminological studies of juvenile gangs were beginning to have enormous impact on the President's Crime Commission, and Frances Fox Piven, both of Columbia University, wrote an article for *The Nation* entitled "The Weight of the Poor: Strategy to End Poverty."[2] In it they pointed out that the welfare laws contained provisions for many special allowances for which most recipients would probably qualify. They urged that poor people apply for these additional funds en masse in order to "cause a financial crisis" that would bankrupt the system.

Cloward and Piven were not advocates of the welfare system. Only a year before Cloward had written critically of welfare, saying: "Our society has preferred to deal with . . . female-headed households not by putting men to work but by placing the unwed mothers and dependent children on public welfare—substituting check-writing machines for male wage earners. By this means we have robbed men of manhood, women of husbands, and children of fathers."[3] Yet they surmised that overloading the welfare system would force Congress into substituting a better program.

Unfortunately, the strategy worked only half-way. Poor people in New York were already organizing "welfare rights" groups, and soon began invading welfare offices, demanding more money. In some cases they terrorized welfare workers, scattered files, and even set fire to one welfare office.[4]

Yet while the Nixon Administration pushed for a guaranteed income, under the direction of Moynihan himself, political opposition blocked the program. Instead, all that happened was that more millions of people ended up on welfare.

In Washington, D.C., for example, the number of single mothers on welfare more than *tripled* between 1961 and 1971. For women over 30, the increase was 140 percent, and for women from 20 to 30, it was 300 percent. But for black *teenagers* the figure rose *800 percent.*[5]

David T. Ellwood, of Harvard's Kennedy School of Government, who has studied the trends extensively, has noted that the birth rates among blacks actually declined during this period. Black women did not start having babies "just to get on welfare."

But what did happen is that, once black women did become pregnant, *they no longer got married.*[6] Instead, they moved onto the welfare rolls as a means of support. Welfare and illegitimacy were "destigmatized" and in many ways became a legitimate way of life in lower-class black neighborhoods.[7]

Today, right across the country from state to state, female-headed households make up an almost perfectly uniform 60 percent of all black households. That figure may represent a high-water mark—although in the poorest sections of Harlem it has reportedly pushed up to 80 percent.

Half of all black babies born across the country today are illegitimate, and half of these children are born to black *teenagers*—meaning 23 percent of all black babies are born to unwed teenagers. Black teenagers now have the highest fertility rate in the industrial world. Half of all black girls have a baby by the time they turn 20, and one-quarter have *two.*

The NAACP and Urban Leagues have become so concerned about the matter that they called a "Summit Conference" at Fisk University, Nashville, in 1984, at which 150 prominent leaders discussed the "Crisis in the Black Family." Both these venerable organizations have since launched campaigns to combat teenage pregnancy.

Things have not always been this way in the black family. The breakup has been a very recent phenomenon. It has nothing to do with the legacy of slavery or segregation.

There is no question that the black family has always been somewhat unstable, particularly among the poor. This pattern was evident in the South in the early part of this century. In ways it was part of the "benign neglect" of Southern paternalism, the way in which blacks were not often pressured to meet certain civic and social standards. In other ways, however, it was typical of the experience of any ethnic or immigrant group living in poverty.

In *Class and Caste in a Southern Town*, John Dollard noted "the weakness of the monogomous family among lower-class Negroes" and felt it accounted for much domestic violence. "Since the Negro cannot hold his woman by force . . . of a strong family institution," he wrote, "he must do it by personal force instead; and jealous aggression is one of the ways in which he expressed his claims." Likewise, "the weak hold of the Negro woman on her man from an institutional standpoint brings forward jealous aggression as a means of claiming possession of the loved object and keeping rivals away."[8]

But despite what Dollard described as "much shifting about of marriage partners," the complete expulsion of the male, with the unwed mother striking out on her own, was not a common phenomenon. In fact, Dollard essentially makes no mention of it.

In his monumental study, *The Black Family in Slavery and Freedom: 1750-1925*, Herbert Gutman showed that the black family survived slavery intact, and that black families remained stable through the early part of this century.[9] A study done on working-class families in Boston around 1900 showed that black families were actually *more* stable than those of Irish immigrants. Broken families among blacks were only about 10 percent at a time when they were running well over 20 percent among the Irish.[10]

The destabilizing trend does not seem to have begun until the 1930s, when the New Deal struck a double blow to black progress. First there was widespread unionization and regulation of the economy, which forced black men out of entry-level jobs. Second, there was the welfare system, which unwittingly offered black women an alternative to family formation.

Although people tend to forget, blacks have been through long periods of relative progress since the Civil War. In nearly every case, though, this advance has eventually met organized resistance from whites.

As Charles Silberman writes:

> From time to time, blacks did fill, and sometimes even dominated, skilled and semiskilled occupations—as railroad locomotive firemen, brakemen, switchmen, and mechanics; carpenters, bricklayers, painters, and masons; waiters and caterers; and a host of other jobs. But

blacks were forced out of these occupations with monotonous regularity—not because they filled them badly, but because white workers wanted the jobs instead. With each wave of immigration from Europe, black workers were displaced by whites. And when jobs were scarce enough, native whites were only too happy to take over Negro jobs, in the process redefining them into white jobs. The growth of trade-unions solidified the process; for many whites the opportunity to monopolize desirable jobs for members of their own race was one of the major attractions of union membership.[11]

Right after the Civil War, for example, blacks held 80 percent of the skilled construction jobs in the South. They were active politically, with white politicians often campaigning for their votes. All this was wiped out in the 1890s, however, by a wave of Jim Crow legislation.

In the 1920s, almost all locomotive firemen in the country were black, partly because the job was regarded as too dirty and exhausting for whites. But the Depression changed this. During the thirties, the Brotherhood of Locomotive Firemen and Engineers, an all-white union, used threats, force, and shootings to drive blacks out of firemen's jobs.[12]

The New Deal is often said to have "saved America by rescuing the Middle Class." This is probably true. The New Deal institutionalized labor unions, legitimized occupational licensing procedures, and generally regulated the economy in a way that insulated businesses from "cutthroat competition" and protected middle-income workers from "cheap labor."

But "cheap labor" essentially meant blacks. All through the early part of the century, black carpenters, painters, plumbers, and contractors were known as the people who would "bid low" on jobs. Blacks competed economically, both as unorganized workers, and as unregulated, un-licensed, small business competitors.

The vast unionizations and business regulations of the 1930s effectively excluded non-unionized, unorganized blacks from the job market. Even today, many construction and trade unions are notorious for their almost-white-only membership. In addition, government regulations give these unions the right to monopolize jobs in a way that prevents entry-level participation by unskilled, unorganized blacks.

New York's Carnegie Hall, for example, is entirely manned by 11 stagehands. Each of these employees makes an average salary of *$90,000 a year*. This is done through monopolization of overtime and holiday pay. All the stagehands are members of the International Alliance of Theatrical

Stage Employees and Motion Picture Operators of the United States and Canada, one of the most notorious father-son unions in New York City.

Construction trades follow many of the same practices. The New York State Investigations Commission recently found a union construction supervisor at the municipally financed Battery Park City who makes $450,000 a year. He was even paid a "gratuity" of $5,000 during one week while he was on vacation in the Caribbean. The Commission said the basic purpose of his salary was to "buy labor peace." These construction unions have never had more than a few black members.

Walter Williams, author of *The State Against Blacks,* has placed emphasis on professional licensing and municipal regulations of small businesses as another source of diminishing opportunity for blacks.[13]

"One of the simplest businesses blacks can enter is taxi-driving," he notes. "All you need is a driver's license and a car. Yet municipal taxi licensing has protected people already in the business and eliminated new entrants. In New York City, a taxi medallion now costs $65,000. Almost all blacks can afford a car and a license, but few can afford the medallion. At the same time, city officials are constantly complaining about a 'cab shortage.'"

In Philadelphia, where taxis are also licensed, Williams points out that only 15 percent of all cabs are owned by blacks. In Washington, D.C., where there are no entry restrictions, 80 percent of cabs are owned by blacks. "You can't tell me that this difference is due to different degrees of racial discrimination in those two cities," he argues.

In addition, Williams cites minimum-wage regulations devastating to unskilled black teenagers. "By forcing these youngsters to price their labor below its actual market value, the government and the unions, working in concert, assure that they will not have any opportunity to work at all."

Altogether, then, the general tightening of regulatory control over the economy has tended to benefit those already established in jobs and hurt people trying to gain entry. Black teenagers have been particularly hard hit, with unemployment rates climbing steadily since the 1950s. In *Losing Ground,* Charles Murray argues that this trend has been exacerbated—and almost institutionalized—by the growing tendency of young mothers to spurn the wage-earning efforts of young men and rely on the welfare system.[14]

Thus, while the New Deal "saved the middle class," it created far more limited economic opportunities among blacks. Although not originally conceived as compensation for these practices, the welfare system has evolved into just that.

Aid to Families with Dependent Children (AFDC)—what we commonly call "welfare"—was originally only one segment of a four-part program adopted under the Social Security Act of 1936. Especially needy people in four specific categories were to receive supplementary social payments. These four categories were: the elderly, the handicapped, the blind, and "widows and orphans."

AFDC was originally conceived as a small subsidy for children under 16 who had lost a parent through death. Support for children of divorced parents was assumed to be covered by strict enforcement of alimony payments.

At first, the program worked well. In 1940 the age was raised to 18, but there were no other changes. It was not until 1950 that the parent was also given a small allowance. Outlays were low, and the program made up only a small portion of the welfare budget.

During the 1940s, however, it was realized that many people were starting to use the system as a substitute for alimony. Since there were still strict standards of financial need, this was regarded as "cheating." The Truman Administration passed a law requiring states to tighten up on efforts to find missing husbands and force them to pay alimony.

In 1950, there were 651,000 families on the program nationwide, receiving total assistance of $556 million. Over the next five years, the number of families "on welfare" actually declined to 602,000 as the country prospered. By 1960, the recession had pushed the figure back up to 803,000, but the figures were still not alarming.

It was only after 1960 that people began to worry that the welfare system might be acting as an incentive for couples to split up or—worse yet—never to bother getting married in the first place. This tendency was beginning to appear among lower-class blacks. The Kennedy administration expressed concern and amended the law to allow families to go on welfare when the husband was unemployed. However, this section is rarely used, and "unemployed-father" families still constitute only 2 percent of all welfare cases.

By the late 1960s, the tidal wave that the Moynihan report had spotted was arriving. From 1965 to 1970, welfare roles almost doubled, and from 1969 to 1970 they rose 30 percent in one year. All this was in the midst of a booming economy. From 1960 to 1975, outlays in constant dollars rose almost *10 times,* from $1.1 billion to $9.2 billion.

This situation is entirely unique to the United States. All other industrial democracies have developed "family allowances" that make payments to intact families solely on the basis of income requirements without requiring one parent to be unemployed or missing. Efforts to introduce similar plans here have never gained much headway, however.

Thus, from modest and unassuming beginnings as a "widows and orphans" program, "welfare" has become the nation's "family allowance." The only difficulty is that most people break up their families—or never bother to form them—in order to qualify. Welfare has become a subsidy for illegitimacy and broken families.

What this means for crime in America is almost too staggering to contemplate in one chapter. It probably deserves an entire book. But let me try to take a sketchy look at some of the major points.

First, we are dealing with a situation that is completely unprecedented in history. There has never been a human society in which 60 percent of the children were sired by couples who did not settle down and form families.

The genius of human evolution has been in harnassing the energies of men to raising families. This occurs *nowhere else in nature.* There is no other species where males regularly stay around to care for children past the point of birth and dependency. The key to human evolution has been that the male aggression that usually goes to status-competition or the predatory life is channeled into taking care of the family. The contemporary breakup of black families has reversed this development. It has been, essentially, an evolutionary regression.

Second, the lack of a father in the household eliminates a key part of cultural continuity. The female role is well-defined in nature. Mothers have children, nurture them, love them, and raise them until they reach independence. In basic biological terms, human females are not much different from other females in other species.

The male role, however, is much more a cultural creation. It requires a great deal of learning, most of it taking place in juvenile and adolescent years. Without a father present, males have no one to learn from, and no defined role to emulate within the family.

Much of the complexity of the human personality seems to result from our having two parents instead of one. It is something like the "good-cop, bad-cop" routine—one parent as the sympathetic supporter and the other as the disciplinarian. Traditionally, fathers play the disciplinarian, but the roles are easily reversed. The important thing is that both roles are necessary, and it is difficult for one parent to play both at the same time.

True, many black women, through almost superhuman efforts, are learning to play the roles of both the mother and the father. But as admirable as these efforts may be, they hardly serve as the basis for a stable culture. In particular, lone mothers are often unable to handle their male children once they reach adolescence. As a result, teenage black males— with no experience in male discipline and no visible role model to emulate—have two alternatives. Either they can drive their male aggression inward in a neurotic fashion. Or they carry their aggressions into the streets.

I worked in the South during civil-rights efforts of the 1960s and met many stable, close-knit black families. One of the most common sights in Alabama and Mississippi around July and August is cars with Michigan and Ohio license plates filled with kids and dogs coming back down South for family reunions. These gatherings often include dozens of people from several generations centered around a single set of elderly grandparents.

While I was working in the South, I heard one story that became so familiar that I eventually decided it must be part of the general folklore. It was always told by an adult male who was raising his own family, and it always went like this:

"When I think back on my growing up, I think the thing that probably turned me around more than anything was one time when I must have been—oh, about 12 or 13 or so—and I did something that got my daddy mad at me. And he took me back behind the house and I swear before God, he must have whupped me within an inch of my life. And I can tell you, I didn't like it too much at the time. But looking back, I would say that, from that day to this, that was the thing that turned me around and got me up to where I am today."

A generation raised on Dr. Spock, of course, is likely to be appalled by this corporal punishment, and lament that such people can't be taught to be more gentle and persuasive in rearing their children. But that may be part of the problem. One of the major impediments black people have encountered over the past 25 years, I think, has been their "adoption" by a well-educated, upper-middle class that was more permissive in its social attitudes, and more interested in spending its social capital than accumulating it.

It is obvious that black urban males growing up today feel a penetrating sense of loss at not being raised by their fathers. As Claude Brown poignantly puts it:

> Admittedly, a significant percentage of this country's young black men are too bitter, too cynical or, for various reasons, too intractable. And some are definitely incorrigible. Yet most of them possess a hunger for guidance and advice so profound it would be too humiliating to express it even if they could.[15]

Urban blacks and Puerto Ricans interviewed by Ken Auletta virtually said as much:

> I asked Ramon Lopez if he feels that kids who grow up in a home without a father suffer more than kids who grow up in a home with two parents.
> "The problem in our community is that we let a woman have maybe seven kids, you know?" Ramon says. . . . "[A]nd the mother just stay home, maybe let the kids go out, do what they want to do. Nobody tells them right or wrong because today nobody tells nothing. And the kids grow up doing wrong. Nobody to guide him."
> Why doesn't the mother guide him?
> "Mother might guide him in the house, you know," says Ramon. "But out of the twenty-four hours, he might be in the house two, three hours. Might just come to eat and go right back out. So he grows up to whatever he sees other kids doing. . . . He grows up listening about people mugging other people; that's what he might do because he has no guide. Nobody, you know, to take him to the park, take him to the baseball, take him to the swimming pool. He's all by himself, you know. Got nobody to teach him anything. He got no school. He just do nothing; just stays around and does whatever he wants to. That kid might grow up doing things that are bad. Mother have too many kids, maybe. More than she can handle."[16]

Another young black told Auletta about how his friends had envied him for having a father who beat him:

> Leon Harris says that young males rarely fear their mothers. "It's hard for a lady to ever fill a man's shoes. I have friends who were brought up by their mother—and when we was younger, my father

used to beat me. They used to get accidentally beat also, because they was with me. . . . I used to say to my friend, 'Man, what's wrong with you? You got it made. You want a father to whup you?' And he'd say, 'Yeah, 'cause I miss it. I never had a man to hit me, to make me know that I'm doing wrong.'"[17]

Such comments, of course, are likely to bring howls of anguish from upper-middle-class feminists who insist that women can be both a mother and a father, raise children, jog, bake zucchini, and run a small corporation all at the same time. But common sense tells us that it is easier for two parents to raise a family than it is for one. If anything, this is even more true in the age of the "two-income family."

Thus, an historical mistake has turned into a social disaster. As the perverse incentives of AFDC have taken hold of black culture, the average black family has turned into a woman, her assorted children, and a welfare check. The welfare system has not simply withheld poor blacks from the chance to progress economically. It has deprived them of the basic tools of cultural continuity.

All this is bad enough. But I am afraid I have saved the worst news for last.

Unfortunately, it seems very clear that a great deal of what we call the "criminal personality" is the result of men being raised exclusively, or under the predominating influence, of women.

Several psychologists who have studied criminals have noted this. Alfred Adler writes:

> Among criminals there is a large proportion of orphans; . . . In a similar way there are many illegitimate children. . . Unwanted children often take to criminal practices . . .
>
> The other type is the pampered child; and I have frequently noticed, in the complaints of prisoners, that they assert "The reason for my criminal career was that my mother pampered me too much."[18]

Stanton Samenow makes some of the same observations:

> A tattoo saying "mother" frequently seen on criminals reveals their deepest sentimentality. In most cases, mother has believed in the criminal, bailed him out of trouble, and never abandoned hope. On the

one hand, he adores her, but on the other, he makes her life hell, cursing her when she opposes something he wants to do, stealing from her, threatening her, and causing her sleepless nights. Yet mother remains forgiving, always willing to help him pick up the pieces of his life.[19]

In her book, *The Feminized Male,* psychologist Patricia Cayo Sexton makes a very similar observation:

> Murders are usually committed by quiet and gentle men, "nice guys." Sirhan and Oswald, both reared under the maternal shadow, grew to be quiet, controlled men and dutiful sons . . . whose normal male impulses (were) suppressed or misshapen by overexposure to feminine norms.[20]

The etiology of this "criminal personality" seems to be this: Anyone who has ever raised children knows that most children go through a period of severe indiscipline around two years old—the "terrible twos." They throw tantrums, fight over the most insignificant things, and are pretty unmanageable for an extended period. This is also the time when they begin to make sharp differentiation between their parents. They cling to their mothers, and are often very hostile to their fathers for short periods—Freud's "Oedipus complex."

Gradually, however, they grow out of it. Freud asserted that boys eventually come to identify with their fathers, while girls remain identified with their mothers. Children learn better ways to assert their will over the world and give up their tantrums.

What seems to happen with the criminal personality, however, is that such children *never grow out of their "terrible twos."* Repeated observations in children who develop abrasive, antisocial personalities, has shown that this war-against-the-world usually begins by the time they are two and three years old.

Almost all these children are boys, and it seems likely that the driving force is once again aggression, derived from the male hormone, testosterone. In solitary animals, this aggression drives mating and territorial behavior. In the more social animals, it expresses itself through peer-group competition. In baboons and chimpanzees, for example, male-dominant hierarchies are constantly shifting under aggressive pressures, while female hierarchies are relatively stable.

The human family, however, is unique. Almost at the dawn of our emergence as a species, male aggression seems to have been curbed and channeled into family behavior. *We have always had fathers.* Human beings did not simply evolve as a gaggle of tribal animals and then start pairing off into married couples somewhere around the eighteenth century, as is sometimes supposed. The eight-million-year-old human footprints recently discovered in an African lava bed by Mary Leakey, show a man and woman walking side-by-side. Leakey thinks they were actually holding hands. In the father's footprints, walking directly behind him, are the footprints of a small child.

We entered human evolution as a family.

All this has meant that, since the dawn of time, male children have been constantly exposed to adult males during their upbringing. This early encounter with male discipline seems to be what curbs and directs male aggression—what keeps us from turning into "wild animals."

Of course, there have always been boys who grew up without fathers, but there have been many mitigating factors that have kept these individuals civilized.

First, single mothers can raise boys normally simply by encouraging a male identity. Although they may have been widowed or divorced, single mothers have always belonged to a two-parent *culture.* Mothers can encourage identification with other male family members—grandfathers, uncles, older brothers—or other adult males outside the family. Or, a male child can often find these role models for himself.

What is happening among blacks, however, is that the role of "adult family male" is being lost as a *cultural* identity. Without a stable role model in the home, young black males have two choices—the home environment ("the crib," as it is often called), where women are a dominating influence and male identities are scarce; or the street, where peer culture reigns supreme. From a criminological viewpoint, it is hard to tell which is worse. The choice seems to be between what might be called a "pathological" kind of development, or an environment where crime could almost be considered natural and healthy.

The "smothered male" is one of the most common criminal types. Particularly if the child is physically strong and has decisive masculine tendencies, a smothered male child can often end up a wild bundle of contradictions. He can have extremely circumscribed aggressions that have no natural outlet channels. This can make him habitually anti-authoritarian, self-indulgent yet violent. In other words, he takes on the "criminal personality."

All this explains one of the most puzzling aspects of criminal development—why criminal personalities often arise out of families that are perfectly normal and intact. The reason is this. Very often a child can come to be very closely identified with one or the other parent, *even though both parents are present.* Because of the various political lineups within families, children often end up getting very strongly attached to one parent or the other.

Thus, it is possible that a male child can remain very strongly attached to his mother, even though the father is present. Such a development does not *automatically* lead to criminal tendencies. But it often does. The "pampered son" is one of the most common among old-type juvenile offenders.

Many of the recent "serial murderers" and "serial rapists" show exactly this pattern. These men are often handsome, stable, and normal-*appearing,* but nonetheless plagued with difficulty in establishing a stable male identity. For example:

— Ted Bundy, who is suspected of murdering more than forty young women, was an illegitimate child whose parents separated shortly after he was born. He was raised entirely by his mother until he was 10 years old. His mother eventually married a man whom Ted considered his mental inferior. Ted continually outsmarted his stepfather and taunted him unmercifully.

Although he was handsome and clever, Bundy had terrible trouble with girls. He had a peculiar boyishness that seemed to make it impossible for him to establish a stable adult relationship with women.

Shortly after entering college, Bundy went through a series of personal crises. He changed colleges and majors several times, started drinking a lot, and became an inveterate shoplifter, often walking off with thousands of dollars worth of merchandise. He also started a career as a Peeping Tom, frequently following women home at night.

After college he made an attempt to find his real father, but was unsuccessful. Shortly after, he started killing young women.

Bundy always had a peculiar fascination for women's bodies. One of his girlfriends—who eventually became very suspicious of him—said she awoke one night to find Bundy under the sheets examining her body with a flashlight. After killing his last victim, a 12-year-old Florida junior-high student, Bundy may have torn the flesh off her lower torso with his teeth. He was sentenced to death partly on the basis of teeth-marks left on the body of another of his victims.[21]

— Randy Woodfield, the "I-5 Killer," was convicted of killing two women, and suspected of killing as many as eight others. A handsome "golden boy" and talented athlete, he starred in football and had a brief tryout with the Green Bay Packers before his athletic career ended with an arrest for indecent exposure.

Woodfield, the youngest child, with two older sisters, had obvious problems with sexual identity:

> His mother was usually the one to mete out the discipline—not physically painful, but humiliating to Randy because he felt that he had disappointed her. He was torn early on between his desire to please his mother, to be a "good boy," and his anger at her because it seemed impossible to meet what he considered to be her expansive and unrealistic goals for him. Still, as an adult, he would recall that his relationship with his mother was "real good. I'm closer to my mother than I am to my father."[22]

Like Bundy, Woodfield was a handsome fellow who had a terrible time with women. When he was thirty, he was still running after 16- and 17-year-olds, and even they often found him "too immature." As Ann Rule wrote:

> Fellow employees [at his bartending job] were puzzled that Randy seemed fixated on young girls. . . Although his co-workers found him easygoing and a "pretty nice guy," they wondered why all his close friends were women. One of the other bartenders describes Randy as "having an eighteen-year-old level of conversation. He was kind of a dumb-blond type—except that he was a man." . . .
> Randy's approach to women was so frenzied that he turned most of them off, and they rolled their eyes at each other when he wasn't looking and called him a "weirdo" in giggling whispers. He skipped vital steps in forming relationships.[23]

Despite his physique, he was kicked off another job as a bouncer because he could not act authoritatively. Shortly after, he began killing women.

— Christopher Wilder, a successful Florida building contractor worth hundreds of thousands of dollars, killed at least nine young women in a cross-country rampage in 1984, before committing suicide as he was being apprehended by a New Hampshire state policeman. Once again, he was a handsome, successful man in his thirties who had a string of girlfriends, but seemed unable to establish a mature relationship with one woman. He began a voyeuristic sideline of taking pictures of young girls. Soon he began molesting them, and was arrested in 1977 for raping a teenager. The psychiatrist who examined him reported: "He was raised in an intact family consisting of parents, three younger brothers, and himself.... Father was the boss and the disciplinarian. Defendant was closer to the mother who was warm, too easy and gave them whatever they wanted."[24]

— Fred Coe, from Spokane, Washington, was another all-American boy. Dynamic, good-looking, ambitious, he came from a household completely dominated by his mother, a lethally self-centered woman. Coe had beautiful girlfriends and ambitions about becoming a millionaire. While living with a girlfriend, however—and running up huge debts—he was pulling a series of brutal nighttime rapes in the Spokane area. He was finally caught, prosecuted, and convicted. His mother, Ruth Coe, was later convicted for trying to hire someone to kill the prosecutor and judge who had presided over the case.[25]

Thus, the "smothered son" syndrome can be the lethal outcome of a failure to establish a strong male identity. It occurs more or less randomly in isolated instances among stable, middle-class families. In the "broken families" of the welfare culture, however, it is becoming a social institution.

Black male teenagers are "smothered" to a great degree in that they live in a home environment dominated by women, where there are no visible male roles to play. But they have an alternative. They can "learn their manhood in the streets."

In a recent story in *New York* magazine, Michael Daly described the recent emergence of "wolf-packs"—gangs of black teenagers, some no more than 12 or 13, who congregate in predatory packs, up to forty- to fifty-strong, to prey on victims in the streets and subways.[26]

After a Diana Ross concert in Central Park in 1983, a whole army of teenagers descended on Manhattan's Upper West Side for an orgy of chain-snatchings, robberies, and muggings. A few years ago, Harlem gangs armed with two-by-fours ambushed a bicycle race in Central Park, knocking contestants to the ground and stealing their bicycles. In 1985, a March of Dimes Walkathon in Central Park was overrun by hundreds of black teenagers who stole money, radios, and jewelry. Recently, a single elderly man was attacked by a gang of thirty-five teenagers in Times Square. Other cities have had identical incidents. Mobs of black teenagers have gone on rampages in recent years in Detroit and Philadelphia. In 1983, huge crowds leaving the October Riverfront Festival in Cincinnati were ambushed by hundreds of black teenagers in the downtown area, and dozens of people were robbed and beaten.

Let us be frank about all this. No justice system is ever going to control such a social phenomenon. Putting hundreds of people in jail—even building large concentration camps—would not put an end to this savagery. What we are witnessing is a broad-scale regression into primitive, predatory behavior.

There was once a time when the criminal urges of these teenagers were at least kept under control by *older* criminals. Today, Claude Brown writes, "The neighborhood Fagins, so characteristic of the Harlem of my youth, are mostly absent. Contrary to what any sane observer might assume, these Dickensian scoundrels inadvertently exerted a restraining influence on the junior hoodlums. . . [T]hey gave patient instruction in the commission of rational crimes."[27]

Now, Brown writes, these older mentors no longer have any effect. Many older black criminals—older than 21, that is—are intimidated by this subculture of violence and casual homicide. Interviewed by Ken Auletta, one 21-year-old—a dropout with a history of violence and a long criminal record—said he was afraid to walk home at night. "Even I walk soft in the ghetto," said another experienced black burglar. "Some of those kids out there are just crazy."

If criminologists are still looking for "root causes" of crime, I think we have found one. The family disintegration among blacks over the past 25 years has turned loose forces that spell the unravelling of what we know as human culture.

In describing one group of young muggers brought into a Manhattan police station, Michael Daly reported the following exchange:

> The big juvenile was named Derriah. He said that he had a prior arrest for attempted murder. He also announced that he was the father of two children.
>
> "How old are they?" [a policeman] asked.
>
> "Three and two," Derriah answered.

"How old are you?"

"Fifteen."

At a nearby desk, Sheridan [another cop] was on the telephone to Derriah's mother. Sheridan hung up and said, "She says his being arrested is a blessing. She doesn't want him, and she doesn't like him." Derriah said, "If my mother slap me, I hit her back." The rest of Derriah's posse laughed. A fourteen-year-old named Thomas said, "Me too. Someday, I'm going to have to snuff her."[28]

Eliminating the exclusionary rule, restricting appeals, enforcing the Seventh Amendment, or expanding the power of juries—none of these will come within a seven-mile radius of dealing with antisocial forces. Nothing is going to begin curing this sort of crime in this country until we start putting the black family back together.

First and foremost, we have to overhaul the welfare system totally. Unfortunately, the issue has set off a nasty academic debate, with embattled liberals—embarrassed by the disastrous results of their altruism—still saying that welfare really isn't the problem. I'm not arguing that welfare is the *whole* problem. But anyone who won't admit that welfare is *part* of the problem is either dishonest or doesn't deserve to be thinking about public issues.

I would suggest two steps:

— First, no welfare payments should be made *except* to intact families. As long as we are going to subsidize something, let's subsidize the human two-parent family.

— Second, no welfare payments should be made for a child born before the mother turns 21. Give black teenagers a chance to grow up before signing them up for a lifetime in the welfare culture.

We also have to start deregulating the economy to give blacks a better chance economically. All this will cut into the many, many vested interests created by government regulations—labor unions, licensed cab drivers, licensed beauticians, licensed roofing contractors, and on and on down the line. All this may bring howls of protest. But the choice is simple—it's either deregulation or welfare, economic opportunity or crime.

Harsh as these measures may seem, I see no reasonable alternative to undoing the combined incentives of limited economic opportunity and the welfare program that have unravelled the black family. The present direction is leading us to a social and moral catastrophe.

Many welfare specialists, driven into a corner, have tried to redefine the issue as the "feminization of poverty" and argued it can be solved once again by *increasing* welfare benefits.

It may be conceivable that we could make welfare payments generous enough so that female-headed households could be "lifted out of poverty." The costs would be stupendous, and such efforts would probably only encourage women to have more children at an earlier age.

But there is one thing that is always forgotten. Even if we concentrate all our efforts on the mother-and-children complex and try to "lift them out of poverty," black men are not going to go away. They are going to be right there in the neighborhood and on the streets with *absolutely nothing to do,* and absolutely no stake in the society.

If they are completely read out of the family by "public policy-makers," black men will simply become an internal proletariat that will destroy whole blocks, whole neighborhoods, and eventually threaten the whole society.

There is no alternative. The only way we are ever going to cure this kind of crime in America is to start putting the black family back together.

COMMUNITY AND CRIME

21

THE PEOPLE'S Alliance was founded in 1984 in Brooklyn's Bedford-Stuyvesant. Despite its radical-sounding name, it is made up of merchants and community leaders organized to fight crime in their neighborhood.

In its first few months, the Alliance has achieved some success in obtaining more police patrols along Flatbush Avenue. The big complaint —as in many areas of New York—was illegal gambling parlors and "smoke shops." The former duplicate the New York State Lottery but offer bigger prizes, while the latter offer retail prices on marijuana. Both tend to collect crowds of restless, unemployed men who harass passers-by, driving away customers from nearby stores. The People's Alliance was started, in part, by some of the people who run those other stores.

The problem occurs all over New York and any other major city. A shopping avenue in my neighborhood has a terrible problem with smoke shops. The neighborhood newspaper, which usually has at least one article about conditions in South Africa or the efforts to defeat the Reagan Administration's budget cuts, also complains loudly about the conditions. One recent story reported favorably on "'sledgehammer searches' and 'clumsy cops' who literally wreck numbers parlors and so-called smoke shops" in the course of "investigating" them. Unfortunately, "community leaders testified to seeing carpenters repairing the damage done by the police officers . . . within hours."

Since my neighborhood is largely gentrified, no one raises any objections to these things, and in fact they are enthusiastically supported. In a black neighborhood, however, there would probably be charges of "police brutality" and "racial prejudice."

On the night I attended the meeting of the People's Alliance, a whole panel of government officials had made an appearance—a good sign for any fledgling organization. Although there were no more than 100 people in the room, almost all black, two New York City Councilmen, a state senator, a member of the State Liquor Authority, two members of the Federal Immigration and Naturalization Service, and a police captain whose picture I had seen in the paper were sitting ready to answer questions.

Bill Birdsong, one of the co-founders whom I had met at my own precinct council meeting, presided. He is thin and wiry, about 35, with a Jamaican lilt to his voice. "The People's Alliance was organized a year ago to fight crime in our community," he told the gathering. "We are good people, and we want to live in peace. We don't want our community overrun with crime.

"Now we're going to start the meeting with a prayer from Dr. Lewis," he said.

Dr. Lewis turned out to be a fairly heavy-set woman in her sixties. She began what turned out to be a rather lengthy prayer. "Bless our discussions here tonight, oh Lord, and let them be fruitful. Bless these men who have come here tonight to discuss our problems with us. May we work together to find a resolution to the difficulties we all face."

That was only the beginning. After running down the present situation for a while, she swung back into the Old Testament. She mentioned a few of the prophets by name and compared their deeds to the tasks that awaited the gathering. Then it was into the New Testament for a while. Jesus was looking down on us. Finally, she brought things back to the rostrum, where she again mentioned some of the speakers, blessing them and describing the tasks they had before them. Like a good courtroom attorney, she was seeding her case with the jury.

As Huck Finn would have said, she went on for a powerful long time. I was starting to wonder what she was a doctor of. Finally, she wound up, finishing with another quote from the Bible. The sermon had taken a full five minutes.

Birdsong came back to the rostrum and introduced the speakers individually. Each of them gave a politician's salute to the polite applause.

"Thank you very much," said Birdsong. "And now I know everyone has a lot of things they would like to discuss tonight. But first, Dr. Lewis would like to take a minute to make a few opening remarks."

And so, once again, up came Dr. Lewis. "My friends, I am one of the oldest residents in this neighborhood," she began proudly. "I've seen a lot of changes. Some of them have been good. But I'm afraid most of the ones we're here to talk about tonight have been bad."

It turned out that she lived only a few doors away from a place that was on everybody's mind—a bar called the "Boom-Boom Room." "The other night the noise was absolutely unbearable," she said. "I simply could not sleep. I had to call the police and ask them if they could come and get me so I could go down there and get some rest. My friends, I had to spend the night in a police station. Now, how do you think it feels to be driven out of your own home and to have to go to a police station to get a good night's sleep?"

Everyone seemed to have a good idea of how it felt, but people were getting pretty restless. The meeting was already a half-hour old and only one person had spoken.

Suddenly, a wonderful thing happened. After a few more minutes, everyone burst into applause. Dr. Lewis was quite flattered, then realized it was a polite way of asking her to leave. Slowly she retired from the rostrum, a fixed smile on her face. The audience didn't stop clapping until she was back in her seat.

As it turned out, just about everybody had a story to tell about the Boom-Boom Room. Every night was filled with noise, fights, drinking, and gambling. Rumors circulated involving drugs and prostitution. The representative of the State Liquor Authority was there to announce that this agency was beginning steps to revoke the liquor license. The state senator modestly volunteered that he was responsible for the effort.

"How long will it be before the place is actually closed down?" someone asked.

"Maybe about a year," said the State Liquor Authority representative. Nobody took credit for that.

Next, a sergeant from the Brooklyn Narcotics Unit announced "operation close-down" on Nostrand Avenue. "We've had 34 felony drug sales and 152 arrests altogether," he said.

Still, the audience was skeptical.

"What happens after an arrest?" someone asked.

"They pay the fine and they're back on the street the next day," the sergeant said candidly. "It's basically a cost of doing business."

"Can you send these people to jail?"

"The jails are full already."

Enoch Williams, a popular City Councilman, tried to rescue the situation by explaining how the police department is using its new "padlock law" to close down illegal numbers operations. "If there's three arrests, the landlord can't rent the premise for a year," he said.

"What happens if they move next door?"

"Well, I guess we have to go back and start the whole thing over again.

"You know, I think we've all got to look into ourselves a little bit on this," Williams continued. "I hear some people who are the pillars of the community complaining about these numbers places, but then the next day I see the same people stopping off to place a dollar bet before they get on the subway in the morning."

There was appreciative laughter.

"I also hear people complaining about all the stealing that goes on, and the next thing you know they're buying stolen goods from somebody."

Nobody laughed at that.

"If we don't protect our own turf here, nobody is going to do it for us."

He received a nice round of applause.

Another middle-aged woman rose to speak about her experiences with street crime. "You know, there are a lot of bad people out here," she said. "If you make a complaint, there can be repercussions."

"You'll just have to trust us," said the police captain. "We'll do everything we can to protect you."

"But how can we know you'll be able to protect us?"

"You'll just have to trust us, ma'am. We can't do anything without your help."

Sylvester Leeks, a member of the school board, took the microphone. He was an erect man of about 50, broad-shouldered with a bullet head. "Let me just say one thing here. No matter if we have a precinct house on every block, the problems will only be solved when we solve them ourselves. The Italians don't have crime problems—they take care of things themselves. The Jews don't have a drug problem. They don't allow their kids to do those things. We've got to look to ourselves here, and take care of our own.

"We've got to organize—if you'll pardon my language here—an ass-kicking squad to get the pimps and the prostitutes and the antisocial element out of the community." Enthusiastic applause. "That is the only kind of language they understand."

"You know, I just want to say one more thing. Until our black men take responsibility—I look around the room here and I see mostly women. At an Italian neighborhood meeting, you don't see all women. You see mostly men.

"We've got to get our men involved, and we've got to take control of our community again. We've got to picket bars. We've got to sit in at bars until they close down. There are ways."

At this point, a small, well-dressed white man who had been sitting on the side of the room hurried up and said a word to the state senator. There was some whispering and he was allowed to speak next.

"You know, I've been listening to things here tonight, and there's just something I've got to say. Crime is not a cause. It's only a symptom. You see, I'm a defense attorney, so I deal with these things. Now I hear a lot of talk tonight about 'these people' and 'those people.' I just want to tell you, 'these people' are not strangers or aliens. They are us. They are you and me.

"The Catholic bishops just came out with their position paper on poverty. And they said something in there that I'd like to quote here. They said, 'They have taken from the needy and given to the greedy.' Now I think that's the problem with our system, and it's because of these problems that we have crime today.

"Now I don't know what causes crime . . ."

"How do you stop it!" someone shouted from the audience.

". . . I don't know what causes it, but I do know this. In order to stop it, we are going to have to effectively acquire power. All of us are going to have to take control of the system. That's what I'd like to leave you with tonight." He sat down to only tepid applause.

The man he had jumped ahead of was about 30, a tall, nervous black man, obviously worked up about something. He was wearing worn dungarees and a pair of motorcycle boots, and hadn't shaved in about a week. When his turn finally came again, he grabbed the microphone, swaying back and forth as he talked.

"Listen, I've heard people talking here tonight about drugs. Now there's something I've got to say here. I mean, we've got to get together and wipe out drugs, forever. I mean *forever*. These kids today don't know what they're getting into. We've got to get out there and tell them what this stuff is really about."

It was painful to listen to him—and painfully obvious that he was speaking about himself. He rambled on a bit more, until Birdsong finally asked if they could go on to the next speaker.

Not yet ready to give up the microphone, the man lurched toward the panel, dragging the microphone with him. "Now wait just a minute," he said, "wait just a goddamn minute." He turned around to address the audience. "Now goddamn it, I've got something I've been thinking about here, and I'm going to say it! I don't care how long it takes." Several uniformed men began stirring around the room.

"Please be advised that the sergeant-at-arms is going to escort anyone from the hall who cannot act properly," said Birdsong calmly. "Everyone is going to be asked to limit their remarks to one question."

Finally, the man was persuaded to give up the microphone. He left the hall and the meeting went on.

Next came a man in a dashiki. He couldn't have been more than five-foot-six, about 35 years old, wearing the red, green, and black colors of African unity.

"I don't think anything being said here tonight is making any sense," he began. "You people aren't talking about the right issues. Black people must seize power. We've got to talk about things that make sense. One of the things we must ask ourselves is whether it is natural for us to have people of another race coming in here educating and policing us."

There was a certain tension in the room, but everyone listened politely. He continued for a few minutes and then sat down. That was it.

Finally, the discussion started focussing on a methadone clinic run by Kings County Hospital right in the neighborhood. The doctor who administered the program had arrived late, but as soon as he spoke, it seemed this was what everyone wanted to talk about.

"Can't you do anything to control those people! They are robbing and stealing from the community," someone said angrily.

"We're doing everything we can," said the doctor. "We have security personnel at the clinic. But we can't police the entire neighborhood."

"You're taking addicts in from all over New York and bringing them in here to prey on us," someone else shouted. "They're driving us out of our homes."

"I'm sorry," said the doctor, trying not to sound too condescending. "But our records show that all of our patients are right from the neighborhood. We're not allowed to service clients from outside a one-mile radius."

"They lie about their addresses," a woman shouted. "They come in here to get methadone, and then they go back and sell it in Manhattan."

The doctor politely disagreed.

Gradually it became clear that just about everybody in the room had some story to tell about being robbed or burglarized.

One man, about 30, solidly built with a neat mustache, was livid.

"That clinic is an abomination," he shouted from his seat. "I've been robbed dozens of times. I've had $12,000 worth of things stolen from my house. I work three jobs and there's nothing I can do to protect myself. Those junkies sit on my porch, talking and playing their radios all day and all night. My children are terrified. They can't sleep. I'm a decent man raising a decent family, and you're ruining our lives!"

The doctor shook his head sadly but said nothing.

At the close of the meeting, a tall, dignified woman got up to make some final remarks. She was regal. "This is our community," she said. "We've got to make it work. This business of linking poverty with crime—I *will* not accept it. It's no excuse. Our kids quit school because they think they can do better for themselves in a life of crime. We cannot tolerate that. We must challenge our young people.

"We've got to stop offering our children excuses. We pat them on the heads and say, 'Poor little thing, you're poor, you're black, there's nothing you can do about it.' We've got to stop doing that. I *will* not accept that."

She received a huge final round of applause.

One woman had caught my attention during the meeting, although she hadn't spoken. She was about 50, small and slim, and wearing a spotless white robe. On her head was a bishop's hat about two feet tall.

After the meeting, I introduced myself. She said her name was Sister Elizabeth and handed me a flyer. It was an advertisement for a small church she ran, with "readings and advice," plus regular services. Her conversation was lively and intelligent. "We've got some *bad* people around here," she said earnestly. "You wouldn't believe some of the stuff that goes on out there."

She seemed so fragile, yet charismatic, that it was hard to imagine anything bad could ever happen to her.

Have you ever had any trouble, I asked.

"Sure!" she said genially. "They broke into my house, robbed me, beat me, and tied me up for four hours. And I'm a woman who doesn't even chew gum."

When I left, the ex-addict was outside in the hall, still pacing the floor. He didn't seem quite so dangerous now, actually a little pathetic, with an earnest, lost look in his eye.

"Hey man, I know I acted bad in there, but like I know what I'm talking about," he said. "You know, I'm just trying to help. These kids need someone to guide them."

He made me think of what Claude Brown had written: "Admittedly, many black men may be bitter and intractable. Yet most of them possess a hunger for guidance and advice so profound it would be too humiliating to express it even if they could."

I was going to ask if he had kids of his own, but thought better of it.

"You know, man, somebody comes along and offers them some stuff and says, 'Try this,' and before they know it their whole life's wasted. They don't know what they're getting into."

I asked him if he tried talking to kids himself.

"Sure, man, but you know they won't listen to you. They think they know it all. It's hard to make 'em listen."

I told him I thought he could probably be of help and then we shook hands. I wished him luck, knowing he will be needing it.

I have been to dozens of such meetings around the country. The participants are almost always the same. They are never terribly verbal, bright, or knowledgeable. They tend to be older rather than younger, and many of them are elderly. Often there is something distinctly pathetic about them. They are usually neighborhood-bound—people who have grown up where they live, have never moved, and never done anything very extraordinary.

They are people who, when you ask them to describe themselves, will probably use the word "decent." They are not the pillars of the community, but they are its backbone. They are people who do not feel that they are at war with society. But more and more they feel that society is at war with them. The one thing they always say is that their neighborhood is not as safe as it used to be.

Their opinion is not often articulately expressed in the media. It lacks the flamboyance of criminality—the vicarious excitement that interests people whose lives are rarely touched by violence. Their everyday needs would be impossible to define in terms of "Constitutional rights." As James Q. Wilson says, these are the people who look up to the courts and the policy-makers one day and say, "Those people don't care about us anymore."

They are also the people who hold the key to restoring an America, safe from crime.

Edward Campana, a senior research associate at the URSA Institute, in San Francisco, has spent many years working in poor neighborhoods, exploring ways to help people restore order to communities that are overrun by violence.

"For an ordinary person growing up in a suburb it's hard to believe the kind of conditions these people can live under," said Campana. "We've been going around trying to do interviews on how people feel about crime, and one of the most difficult things is just getting into their apartments. These people are often terrified of strangers and won't even talk to you through the door.

"If you do finally get inside, they're extremely suspicious of you. They can't believe that you simply want to ask them about crime. They think it's a trick by someone to set them up for retaliation. They're terrified that you're going to betray them.

"Sometimes they don't even think of these things as crimes. We'll say to someone, 'Have you ever been the victim of a crime?' and they'll say 'No.' Then we'll say, 'Have you ever had your purse snatched?' 'Oh sure.' 'Have you ever had your car broken into?' 'All the time.' They don't even think of these things as crimes. They're just normal everyday events.

"When they finally tell you about their fears, though, it's unbelievable. These people often feel they are risking their lives to run to the grocery store at night. Whole streets are in possession of drug dealers, and there are fights and shootings continuously. Everybody knows who's doing it, but no one feels they can do anything about it."

To control crime in this country is going to mean "taking back" such communities—all communities. It is going to have to be done in a *nonviolent* way. Shooting and carrying out personal vendettas—vigilantism—will only make things more violent and unpredictable.

What we need is a "vigilance of the majority"—a civilized effort to restore justice and domestic tranquility through the social institutions that were created for that purpose.

New community efforts are constantly sprouting up, an everlasting indication of people's willingness to do something about crime.

For many years, neighborhoods have been forming "crime patrols"— citizens' groups that ride regular routes through neighborhoods, usually in radio contact with the local police station. They are not armed and do not try to intervene in situations, but they are clearly identified and report crimes. They serve as the "eyes and ears of the police."

Toledo police sponsored such groups for several years although they eventually created some problems. "They tended to attract cop buffs and people who wanted to do a little more than just report crime," said Captain Larry Armstrong, commander of community affairs. "We tended to get a vigilante type."

Instead, like many other cities, Toledo police have now been emphasizing "blockwatchers." These are more passive organizations of neighborhood residents who simply agree to "keep their eyes and ears open" and call police if they see anything suspicious. One out of every six homes in Toledo is now a "blockwatcher," and in some neighborhoods more than half the homes participate.

"It's a way of crossing the threshold of concern," said Captain Armstrong. "People feel they're participating in a common effort, and it makes them feel safer. Unfortunately, it tends to work better in the neighborhoods where it isn't needed as much."

A more direct effort in Toledo has come from NUBIA—the New Union of Blacks in America, a volunteer organization founded by Delmond Smith, a former high school administrator. Since 1977, NUBIA has engaged in a broad range of programs to improve community order and steer children out of a life of crime.

Smith got the idea after making the rounds in the homes of problem students and realizing that most of their educational problems were well-grounded at home. He eventually set up an after-school tutorial program to create an environment where children could concentrate on their schoolwork. NUBIA now tutors 500 students a year, with another 500 on waiting lists.

"Education was one thing, but it wasn't long before we realized we were going to have to deal with the whole community," said Smith. "There was so much crime and drugs out there, we knew we had to give the kids better examples."

NUBIA has formed its own radio patrols and crime-watch programs and has its own garbage trucks that are continually cleaning up the community. "We are convinced that crime will only stop when the community rises up in righteous indignation and says, 'We've had enough.'" said Smith. "We've learned from our door-to-door canvassing that most people really care about crime—they just feel it's too big a problem for them to make a difference. Once they see we're doing something, they want to join."

In 1985, NUBIA quelled a series of disturbances by black youths on Toledo city buses. "We found out who the kids were and went down to confront them," said Smith. "Once those kids saw myself, the president of the NAACP, and the head of the school board—once they realized it was the *community* that is outraged and not just the police—they quit right away. Some of those kids are now doing volunteer work on our anti-blight efforts."

Relations with the Toledo Police have been uniformly sound. "We have a beautiful relationship," said Smith. "They've been fabulously cooperative, and we respect their responsibilities by recognizing that law enforcement is their job, not ours." At the same time, NUBIA's colorfully uniformed patrols have become a constant symbol of community resistance to crime.

The effort recently received national attention—including a letter of commendation from President Reagan—and has inspired similar efforts in Chicago and several other large cities.

In Oakland, block-watch groups—called "Home Alert"—have halted outbreaks of burglaries and cleaned up parks. In one neighborhood of East Oakland, drug pushers had almost completely pushed children out of a playground area. "It was ridiculous," said Officer Donna Masters of the community services division. "There were traffic jams of buyers trying to get in to see their dealers."

With the help of police, Home Alert organized a walkie-talkie patrol that helped drive the pushers out of the park neighborhood. Oakland Parents' Alert has also started "Just Say No," an organization that warns schoolchildren about the pitfalls of drugs.

In Atlanta, similar efforts organized in poor neighborhoods have tremendously improved relations with police. "It's wonderful to drive through a neighborhood and see kids waving to you," said Captain Howard Baugh of the crime-prevention bureau.

In Washington, D.C., youngsters have formed patrols to police housing projects. In Dallas, store owners have organized a "buddy system" to prevent robberies. In Chicago, volunteer radio patrol cars still prowl the streets near the University of Chicago.

"This is not a vigilante system," said Charles H. Asher, a certified public accountant who helped organize the Chicago patrols. "I'm an ACLU member myself, and the last thing I want to see is an infringement of civil liberties. But we've got to have community participation if we're going to stop crime."

Indeed, Americans seem to have a vast, untapped potential for law-abiding behavior. Community restoration means more than just achieving "togetherness." It means creating ideals, upholding commonly held values, and letting the weight of community opinion fall on the side of reasonable standards of acceptable public behavior.

"We see ourselves as the direct descendant of the civil rights movement," said Delmond Smith of Toledo's NUBIA. "Our enemies are crime, violence, ignorance, illiteracy, and neighborhood decay. We feel that's a battle in which everyone can emerge a winner."

None of this, of course, is going to mean anything without leadership from the courts in upholding commonly accepted standards of behavior. But the public is waiting.

Indeed, it often seems as if some people would rather die than live with fear and unjustice. Why else do they fight in wars? Why do they risk their lives for something they believe is right?

Peggy Coughlin, of the Northwest Bronx Community and Clergy Coalition, has worked with community groups for the past ten years. She says she is continually amazed at the courage and determination people show in trying to rid their communities of crime.

"We'll have a public meeting with the police in the basement of an apartment building and the drug dealers will come right down to the meetings and listen to people complaining about them. I remember telling one woman, 'Look, I really feel I should warn you for your own safety, you'd better be careful what you say in front of these people.'

"She said to me, 'I don't care. I've had it. I'd rather die than live with this much crime.'"

EPILOGUE

I AM WALKING through my neighborhood to the subway stop on the way to attend a preliminary hearing for Emmanuel Torres in his trial for killing 23-year-old Carolyn Isenberg.

As I pass the first corner, I am approached by an elderly West Indian man who starts giving me a long story about how his car has broken down and he has to get to New Jersey. I think he is asking me to help him with his car, but it finally emerges that he is panhandling for money. I give him the 50 cents I have just collected from saving empty bottles for two weeks, and am on my way again.

In another moment a young black man, about 27, falls in step beside me. "Guys like that are really sad," he says. I give him a noncommittal answer. "My brother's just like that. He's 35 years old now. I keep telling him, 'You got to get out and get yourself a job. You're getting to be an old man.' But he don't care. 'I'm doin' alright, man,' he says. 'I just want to have my fun.' All he cares about is his dope."

He is about 5-foot-8-inches, scruffily dressed, with a scraggly growth of beard. Strangely enough, he bears a striking resemblance to Emmanuel Torres, the dark-skinned Puerto Rican who I am going to see put on trial for life in prison.

"You wanna get somewhere in this world, you've got to work for it," he continues earnestly. "I'm just coming back from work right now. I got to get up and catch a few hours sleep so I can go to my other job this afternoon."

As we continue to talk, it emerges that he commutes all the way over to Secaucus, New Jersey, every night, where he is a supervisor on a truck-loading dock. "You've got to be fair about things," he explained. "I don't try to work my guys too hard. I tell them, 'Look, this is the job we've got to

345

do. If you want to take it slow, we can work straight through to six o'clock. If you want to hustle, we can quit at four o'clock and have a few beers.' Some guys even catch a little sleep."

How long has he been working over there?

"A long time, man. I worked my way up. You start out and watch things, you know, and pretty soon you learn how everything gets done, see? Then pretty soon you can start telling other people how to do it."

Is he married?

"Oh yeah. My wife works too. She'll just be getting up by the time I get home. She works up at the hospital. She's been working her way up, too. They're going to make her a supervisor."

Does he have kids?

"That's my little girl," he says proudly. "She's the one who makes it all worth while. She's six years old now. I'm just taking her over to my mother's house. See, she takes care of her while I work, and I take care of her while she works. Then my mother takes care of her while we both work. I've been with the same woman for ten years now, and we still get along real good. They say if you work hard, eat right, and have a good woman, you'll live a long time."

We have walked about five blocks, and although I want this conversation to go on for hours, our paths finally separate.

What are his plans for the future? I ask.

"Man, I figure I'm going to keep working and save a lot of money, and then I'm going to retire around 60. I figure by that time I'll have enough saved so me and my wife can go out and have a really good time."

What does he want to do?

"Oh, you know. Take a vacation down in the Caribbean somewhere. Buy a little place, maybe. Get a boat. Really enjoy life.

I want somebody to erect a statue of him in the park. I want to hire him to speak before all the welfare bureaucrats who insist that nobody can make it without their help. I want him to tell his life story to all those people who argue that poverty justifies crime.

He has all the wild, naive, irrational faith in the future that criminals always lack. There is something so utterly foolish in the idea of a vigorous, 27-year-old planning for the day 40 years down the road when he can retire and have a little fun. He could be dead at 45. Even if he makes it, he may be so old and pained that the idea of enjoying himself may only be a dim memory. Why not go for it all now? Why not forsake responsibility and try for that "big score" that every criminal always believes will "set him up for a lifetime."

Then I realize he's already got it made. He's already set up for a lifetime. He's hit his big score.

We shake hands, say goodbye, and part. I wish him luck, knowing he won't be needing it.

CHAPTER NOTES

1—Vigilante

1. Myra Friedman with Michael Daly, "My Neighbor Bernie Goetz," *New York,* February 18, 1985.
2. Mike Royko, "They Deserved It, Sure As Shooting," *New York Daily News,* January 16, 1985.
3. Lars-Erik Nelson, "Goetz in Light of Jefferson and Lincoln," *New York Daily News,* January 18, 1985.
4. Stanley Crouch, "I the Jury," *Village Voice,* March 12, 1985.
5. Andrew A. Karmen, "Vigilantism," *Encyclopedia of Crime and Justice.* (New York: The Free Press, 1983), pp. 1616–17.
6. Alexis de Tocqueville, *Journey to America.* (Garden City: Doubleday/Anchor, 1971), pp. 102–3.
7. "Education: New Prospects, Old Values," *Time,* June 17, 1985.
8. Alexis de Tocqueville, *Democracy in America, Vol. 1,* (New York: Vintage Books, 1954), pp. 126–27.

2—America's Crime Wave

1. Bill Reel, "No Hiding Place in New York City," *New York Daily News,* February 3, 1985; also, personal communication, Mrs. Beatrice Karp.
2. President's Commission on Law Enforcement and the Administration of Justice, *The Challenge of Crime in a Free Society,* Introduction by Isidore Silver, (New York: Avon Books, 1968), p. 17.
3. Sidney Zion, "The Police Play a Crime Numbers Game," *The New York Times,* June 12, 1966.
4. James Q. Wilson, *Thinking About Crime,* (New York: Vintage Books, 1977), pp. 6–7; Thomas Sowell, *Knowledge and Decisions,*

(New York: Basic Books, 1980), pp. 275–75; Charles Silberman, *Criminal Violence, Criminal Justice,* (New York: Vintage Books, 1977), pp. 3ff.

5. Silberman, *op. cit.,* p. 41.
6. Wilson, *op. cit.,* pp. 14–19.
7. Arnold Barnett, Daniel J. Kleitman, and Richard C. Larson, "On Urban Homicide," Working paper WP-04-74 (Operations Research Center, Massachusetts Institute of Technology, March, 1974); *Criminal Victimization in the United States, 1982,* Bureau of Justice Statistics, U.S. Department of Justice.
8. Sandra Evans, "A Crime Victim's Story," *Washington Post,* February 3, 1985.
9. "Interview: Walid Jumblatt," *Playboy,* June, 1984.
10. Thomas Hanrahan, "A Talk-Show Call Saves Tailor from Youth Gang," *New York Daily News,* November 12, 1984.
11. Wilson, *op. cit.,* pp. 14–15.
12. Silberman, *op. cit.,* pp. 4–5; *Criminal Victimization in the United States, 1982,* U.S. Department of Justice, Bureau of Statistics, 1984; "Rapists and Victims: Some Facts," *Newsweek,* May 20, 1985.
13. Claude Brown, "Manchild in Harlem," *The New York Times Sunday Magazine,* September 16, 1984.
14. *Ibid.*
15. "The Curse of Violent Crime," *Time,* March 23, 1981.
16. "A Goetz Backlash?" *Newsweek,* March 11, 1985.
17. "Images of Fear," *Harper's,* May, 1985.
18. Harry E. Figgie, *The Figgie Report on Fear of Crime,* (New York: New American Library, 1983).
19. Gordon Tullock, "The Welfare Costs of Monopolies, Tariffs, and Theft," in Tullock, James Buchanan, and Robert Tullison, *Toward a Theory of the Rent-Seeking Society,* (College Station: Texas A & M University Press, 1981), pp. 39–50.

3—New Ideas About Crime

1. Karl Menninger, *The Crime of Punishment,* (New York: Penguin Books, 1982), pp. 14–15.
2. *Ibid,* p. 5.
3. Richard A. Cloward and Lloyd E. Ohlin, *Delinquency and Opportunity,* (New York: The Free Press, 1960).
4. Lloyd E. Ohlin, "Report on the President's Commission on Law

Enforcement and the Administration of Justice," (Paper presented to the American Sociological Association, August, 1983), p. 26.

5. Wilson, *Thinking About Crime,* pp. 194; 184.
6. Thomas Sowell, *Knowledge and Decisions,* (New York: Basic Books, 1980), p. 280.
7. Howard S. Becker, *Outsiders,* (New York: The Free Press, 1963), p. 14.
8. Kai T. Erikson, "Notes on the Sociology of Deviance," in Howard S. Becker, *The Other Side: Perspectives on Deviance,* (New York: The Free Press, 1964).
9. Becker, *op. cit.,* pp. 33–34.
10. Menninger, *op. cit.,* pp. 30–31.
11. *Ibid.,* p. 68.
12. *Ibid.,* p. 153.
13. *Ibid.,* p. 9.
14. Ann Landers, "The Crime of Punishment," *New York Daily News,* March 28, 1985.
15. Menninger, *op. cit.,* pp. 88–89.
16. Bruce Jackson, *In the Life,* (New York: Holt Rinehart Winston, 1972), p. 19.
17. *Ibid.,* pp. 41–42.
18. Silberman, *op. cit.,* p. 101.
19. *Ibid.,* p. 103.
20. Daniel Glaser, *Strategic Criminal Justice Planning,* (Rockville, Md.: National Institute for Mental Health Studies in Crime and Delinquency, 1975), pp. 79-80.
21. Jan M. Chaiken, Michael E. Lawless, and Keith A. Stevenson, *The Impact of Police Activities on Crime: Robberies in the New York City Subway System,* Report No. R-1424-NYC, (New York: Rand Institute, 1974), p. 65.
22. Wilson, *op. cit.,* p. 195-96.
23. *Ibid.,* p. 196.
24. Seymour Wishman, "Evidence Illegally Obtained by Police," *The New York Times,* September 21, 1981.
25. Wilson, *loc. cit.*
26. John Allen, *Assault with a Deadly Weapon,* (New York: Pantheon Books, 1977), pp. 50–53.
27. Ted Morgan, "They Think, 'I Can Kill Because I'm 14,'" *The New York Times Sunday Magazine,* January 19, 1975; Nicholas Pileggi,

"Inside the Juvenile Justice System: How Fifteen-Year-Olds Get Away With Murder," *New York,* June 13, 1977.

28. Ken Auletta, *The Underclass,* (New York: Vintage Books, 1983), p. 93.

29. Silberman, *op. cit.,* pp. 560–61.

4—The Courts and Justice

1. Stephen Gillers, *Getting Justice: The Rights of People,* (New York: New American Library, 1971), p. 17.

2. William J. Brennan, Jr., "Address to the 79th Annual Dinner of the American Jewish Committee," May 2, 1985.

3. Raoul Berger, *Government by Judiciary,* (Cambridge: Harvard University Press, 1977).

4. Richard Neeley, *Why Courts Don't Work,* (New York: McGraw-Hill, 1983), p. 26.

5. Majority opinion of Justice James C. McReynolds, quoted in Fred Rodell, *Nine Men: A Political History of the Supreme Court of the United States from 1790 to 1955,* (New York: Vintage Books, 1955), p. 201.

6. Rodell, *op. cit.,* p. 22.

7. Robert Nozick, *Anarchy, State, and Utopia,* (New York: Basic Books/ Harper Torchbooks, 1974).

8. *State v. McKnight,* 52 N.J., 35, 52–53, 243 A2d.240, 250 (1968).

9. Donald Horowitz, *The Courts and Social Policy,* (Washington: Brookings Institute, 1977), p. 1.

10. Laurence M. Friedman, *A History of American Law,* (New York: Simon and Schuster, 1977), p. 316.

11. Roscoe Pound, *The Formative Era of American Law,* (Boston: Little, Brown, 1938), p. 45.

5—Search and Seizure

1. *United States v. Leon,* 82 L Ed 2d 677.

2. Preliminary draft to the opinion written by clerk for Justice Potter Stewart, quoted in Bob Woodward and Scott Armstrong, *The Brethren,* (New York: Avon Books, 1979), pp. 135–36.

3. Richard Morgan, *Disabling America: The "Rights Industry" of Our Times,* (New York: Basic Books, 1984), p. 170.

4. "Lawyers in Poll Divide on Issue," *The New York Times,* July 6, 1984, p. B6.

5. *United States v. Leon, op. cit.*
6. Dan Morain, "State High Court Reverses Four Death Penalty Cases," *Los Angeles Times,* June 7, 1985; Philip Carrizosa, "Death Sentences In Four Cases Are Upset by Justices," *The Los Angeles Daily Journal,* June 7, 1985.

6—Confessions

1. Joseph McNamara, "The Detective's Downfall," *New York Daily News,* May 5, 1985.
2. Henry N. Pontell, *A Capacity to Punish,* (Bloomington, Ind.: University of Indiana Press, 1984), pp. 55–60.
3. Wilson, *Thinking About Crime,* p. 231.
4. Dr. Sydney Smith, quoted in Menninger, *The Crime of Punishment,* p. 239.
5. "Confession, Guilt, and Responsibility," *British Journal of Law and Society, Vol. 6, No. 2,* Winter, 1979.
6. *Ibid.,* p. 232.

7—Habeas Corpus

1. *Ex Parte Hawk,* 321 U.S. 114 (1944).
2. *Townsend v. Sain,* (1963) 372 U.S. 293.
3. Macklin Fleming, *The Price of Perfect Justice,* (New York: Basic Books, 1974), p. 25.
4. Alan Dershowitz, *The Best Defense,* (New York: Vintage Books, 1983), p. xv.
5. *Ibid.,* pp. xiv; xvi.
6. Julian Hawley, "What Hath Habeas Corpus Wrought?" *New York State Bar Journal,* October, 1974.
7. *Engle v. Isaac,* 50 United States Law Week, 4376 (April 5, 1982).
8. Edward Bennett Williams, "There's Been a Terrible Breakdown in Criminal Justice," *U.S. News & World Report,* March 16, 1970.
9. Report to the Association of the Bar of New York City, 1970, quoted, Fleming, *op. cit.,* p. 27.
10. *McKay v. United States,* 401 U.S. 667 690–91 (1971), quoted, Patrick M. McGuigan and Randall R. Rader, *Criminal Justice Reform,* (Chicago: Regnery/Gateway, 1983), p. 144.

8—The Bill of Rights and the Constitution

1. Morgan, *loc. cit.*

2. James Madison, "Federalist X," in Alexander Hamilton, John Jay, and James Madison, *The Federalist*, (Garden City: Anchor Books, 1961), p. 22.
3. Madison, "Federalist XIV," *Ibid.*, p. 26–27.
4. Broadus Mitchell and Louise Mitchell, *A Biography of the Constitution*, (New York: Oxford University Press, 1964), p. 199.
5. Judge Robert Jackson, dissenting, *Brown v. Allen* (1953), 344 U.S. 443 540.
6. Madison, "Federalist XIV," op. cit., pp. 27–28.

9—Cooperation

1. Raymond J. Michalowski, *Law, Order, and Society*, (New York: Random House, 1985), p. 47.
2. *Ibid.*, p. 48.
3. Lloyd Ohlin, "Report on the President's Commission on Law Enforcement and the Administration of Justice," p. 26; Henry N. Pontell, *A Capacity to Punish*, p. 112.
4. Robert Axelrod, *The Evolution of Cooperation*, (New York: Basic Books, 1984).
5. *Ibid.*, p. 174.
6. Thomas Sowell, *Knowledge and Decisions*, (New York: Basic Books, 1980.
7. "Blackboard Jungle," reprinted from *Presidential Biblical Scorecard*, Biblical News Service, *Harper's*, March, 1985.
8. Michael Daly, "Hunting the Wolf-Packs," *New York*, June 3, 1985.
9. Wilson, *Thinking About Crime*, p. 3.
10. Brian Kates and Patrick Clark, "A Jekyll & Hyde Life—Bosket's Death Stuns Pals," *New York Daily News*. March 10, 1985.

10—What Is Crime?

1. G. Newman, *Comparative Deviance: Perception and Law in Six Cultures*, (New York: Elsivere, 1976).
2. Donald R. Cressy, *Theft of the Nation: The Structure and Operation of Organized Crime in America*, (New York: Harper Torchbooks, 1969).
3. Russell Kirk, "Criminal Character and Mercy," in McGuigan and Rader, *Criminal Justice Reform*, p. 217.
4. Herbert Spencer, *The Man Versus The State*, (Indianapolis, Ind.: Liberty Press, 1981).

5. "Wife-Beating—The Silent Crime." *Time,* September 1983.

11—Criminals

1. Alfred Adler, "The Roots of the Criminal Pattern," *The Police Journal,* Vol. XVII, No. 7, April, 1930.
2. *Ibid.*
3. *Ibid.*
4. *Ibid.*
5. Menninger, *The Crime of Punishment,* p. 86.
6. Ann Landers, *New York Daily News,* February 8, 1985.
7. Stanton Samenow, *Inside the Criminal Mind,* (New York: Times Books, 1983), p. 95.
8. *Ibid.,* p. 41.
9. *Ibid.,* p. 87.
10. Quoted, Auletta, *The Underclass,* p. 115.
11. Samenow, *op. cit.,* p. 115.
12. John Allen, *Assault with a Deadly Weapon,* p. 102.
13. Bruce Jackson, *In the Life,* pp. 224ff.
14. Wilson, *Thinking about Crime,* p. 189.
15. Roger Starr, "Crime: How It Destroys, What Can Be Done," *The New York Times Sunday Magazine,* January 27, 1985.
16. David Kelly, "Stalking The Criminal Mind," *Harper's,* August, 1985.
17. *Ibid.*
18. Samenow, *op. cit.,* p. 114.
19. St. Clair McKelway, *Tales from the Annals of Crime and Rascality,* (New York: Modern Library, 1951), pp. 319–20.
20. John Allen, *op. cit.,* pp. 106–7.
21. Jackson, *op. cit.,* pp. 7; 26.

12—The Victims

1. Bella English, "Survivors Serve Life Term," *New York Daily News,* February 14, 1983.
2. Peter Martin, *The Yale Murder,* (New York: Berkley Books, 1983).
3. Willard Gaylin, *The Killing of Bonnie Garland,* (New York: Penguin Books, 1982), p. 11.
4. Justice Charles T. Weltner, "The Criminals Are Winning," *Reader's Digest,* November, 1982.
5. Steven Phillips, *No Heroes, No Villains: The Story of a Murder Trial,* (New York: Vintage Books, 1978).

6. Dominick Dunne, "Justice: A Father's Account of the Trial of His Daughter's Killer," *Vanity Fair,* March, 1984.
7. Murray Weiss and Arthur Browne, "A Trial Witness Is Slain," *New York Daily News,* November 17, 1983.
8. Nicholas Pileggi, "The Last Liberals," *New York,* September 13, 1982.
9. Scott Paltrow, "New Anti-Crime Law in California Is Helping Some Accused Felons," *Wall Street Journal,* November 26, 1982.
10. Andy Stack (Ann Rule), *The I-5 Killer,* (New York: New American Library, 1984), p. 191.
11. *Ibid.,* p. 210.

13—The Police

1. George Kirkham, "A Professor's 'Street Lessons,'" *FBI Law Enforcement Bulletin,* March, 1973.
2. *Ibid.*
3. James Q. Wilson and George L. Kelling, "Broken Windows," *The Atlantic Monthly,* March, 1982.
4. *Ibid.*
5. *Ibid.*
6. Robert Trojanowicz, "An Evaluation of the Neighborhood Foot Patrol Program in Flint, Michigan," (East Lansing: Michigan State University).
7. "Images of Fear," *Harper's,* May, 1985.
8. Peter Shaw, "John Hinckley—A Face in the Crowd," *Commentary,* September, 1981.
9. John Serra and Micki Siegel, "My 11-Year Search For My Daughter's Killer," *Good Housekeeping,* March, 1985.

14—Prosecution versus Defense

1. Alan Dershowitz, *The Best Defense,* pp. xiv; xix.
2. Dominick Dunne, *op. cit.*
3. Seymour Wishman, *Confessions of a Criminal Attorney,* (New York: Penguin Books, 1982), p. 10.
4. *President's Task Force on the Victims of Crimes,* (Washington, D.C.: U.S. Government Printing Office, 1982), p. 99.
5. Dershowitz, *op. cit.,* p. xv.
6. *loc. cit.*

7. Gerry Spence, *Of Murder and Madness,* (Garden City: Doubleday, 1983).
8. Tracy Kidder, *The Road to Yuba City,* (Garden City: Doubleday, 1974), p. 63.

15—Power to the Jury

1. "Judge Nixes Testimony in Trial of Ex-Athlete," *Las Vegas Review-Journal,* April 2, 1985.
2. Isak Dinesen, *Out of Africa,* (New York: Vintage Books, 1972), p. 101.
3. Paula DiPerna, *Juries on Trial,* (New York: December, 1984), p. 119.
4. *Ibid.,* p. 126.
5. *Ibid.,* p. 131–32.
6. *Ibid.,* p. 147.
7. *Ibid.,* p. 134.
8. *Ibid.,* p. 235.
9. *Ibid.,* p. 133.
10. Edward Bennett Williams, "There's Been a Terrible Breakdown in Criminal Justice," *U.S. News & World Report,* March 16, 1970.

16—Punishment and Prison

1. Michel Foucault, *Discipline and Punish: The Birth of the Prison,* (New York: Vintage, 1979), pp. 32ff.
2. Frank Carrington, *Neither Cruel or Unusual,* (New Rochelle: Arlington House, 1979), p. 37.
3. *Ibid.,* p. 33.
4. Nealy, *Why Courts Don't Work,* p. 96.
5. Silberman, *Criminal Violence, Criminal Justice,* p. 401.
6. Robert Martinson, "What Works—Questions and Answers About Prison Reform," *The Public Interest,* Spring, 1974.
7. William Raspberry, "Probation—More Harm Than Good," *New York Daily News,* February 12, 1985; Joan Petersilia, Susan Turner, James Kahan, and Joyce Peterson, *Granting Felons Probation: Public Risks and Alternatives,* (Santa Monica: The Rand Corporation, 1985).
8. Jeffrey Shedd, "Making Good(s) Behind Bars," *Reason,* March, 1982.
9. Silberman, *op. cit.,* pp. 534–35.
10. *Ibid.,* p. 547.
11. *Ibid.,* p. 548.

12. *Ibid.,* p. 537.
13. Kathleen Engel and Stanley Rothman, "Prison Violence and the Paradox of Reform," *The Public Interest,* Fall, 1983.
14. *Ibid.,* p. 100.
15. W. G. Stone and I. Hirliman, *The Hate Factor: The Story of the New Mexico Prison Riot,* (New York: Dell, 1982), p. 71.
16. *Ibid.,* p. 75.
17. James Webb, "What We Can Learn From Japanese Prisons," *Parade,* January 15, 1984.

17—The Insanity Defense

1. Bruce Bower, "Not Popular By Reason of Insanity," *Science News,* October 6, 1984.
2. Menninger, *The Crime of Punishment,* p. 107.
3. Silberman, *Criminal Violence, Criminal Justice,* p. 108.
4. Stephen G. Michaud and Hugh Aynesworth, *The Only Living Witness,* (New York: New American Library, 1983).
5. George Groh, "What Doctors Think of the Insanity Defense," *MD,* November, 1983.
6. Bower, *op. cit.*
7. Samenow, *Inside the Criminal Mind,* pp. 10–11.
8. Alfred Adler, *What Life Should Mean To You,* (New York: G. P. Putnam's Sons, 1980), pp. 204; 208.

18—The Death Penalty

1. Edward Koch, "Death and Justice," *The New Republic,* April 15, 1985.
2. Isaac Ehrlich, "The Deterrent Effect of Capital Punishment—A Question of Life and Death," *American Economic Review,* June, 1975.
3. Mary Ann Giordono, "There Will Never Be Another Tommy," *New York Daily News Sunday Magazine,* February 17, 1985.
4. Koch, *op. cit.*
5. "I Choked Coed to Death in Cemetery," *New York Post,* May 10, 1985.
6. "The Random Killers," *Newsweek,* November 26, 1984; Robert Lindsey, "Officials Cite Rise In Killers Who Roam U.S. for Victims," *The New York Times,* January 19, 1984.
7. Lindsey, *Times, op. cit.*
8. *Ibid.*

9. Gerold Frank, *The Boston Strangler,* (New York: New American Library, 1967); *Newsweek, op. cit.*

10. *Newsweek, op. cit.*

11. Hugo Adam Bedau, "The Death Penalty in America," *Federal Probation,* 35 June, 1971, pp. 32–43.

12. Wilson, *Thinking About Crime,* p. 211.

13. William J. Bowers and Glenn L. Pierce, "Arbitrariness and Discrimination under Post-*Furman* Capital Statutes," *Crime and Delinquency,* 26 (October, 1980), 635–53.

14. Earnest van den Haag, *Punishing Criminals,* (New York: Basic Books, 1975).

15. Edward Bennett Williams, "There Has Been a Terrible Breakdown in Criminal Justice," *U.S. News & World Report,* March 16, 1970.

19—Blacks and Crime

1. Silberman, *Criminal Violence, Criminal Justice,* p. 162–67.

2. Henry N. Pontell, *A Capacity to Punish,* pp. 70ff.

3. *loc. cit.*

4. Silberman, *op. cit.,* p. 160.

5. Isaac Ehrlich, "Participation in Illegitimate Activities: A Theoretical and Empirical Investigation," *Journal of Political Economy,* May-June, 1973, pp. 521–65.

6. Silberman, *op. cit.,* p. 161.

7. *op. cit.,* pp. 616–17.

8. Joan Petersilia, *Racial Disparities in the Criminal Justice System,* (Santa Monica: The Rand Corporation, 1983).

9. Samuel Walker, *Sense and Nonsense About Crime,* (Belmont, Cal.: Brooks/Cole Publishing, 1985), p. 207.

10. Silberman, *op. cit.,* p. 208.

11. Stanley L. Saxton, "Explaining Variations in the Fear of Crime," paper presented at the Academy of Criminal Justice Sciences Annual Meeting, 1985.

12. "Violent Crime By Strangers," *Bureau of Justice Statistics Bulletin,* April, 1982.

13. "Images of Fear," *Harper's,* May, 1985.

14. Robert D. McFadden, "Poll Indicates Half of New Yorkers See Crime as City's Chief Problem," *The New York Times,* January 14, 1985.

15. Wilson, *Thinking About Crime,* p. 115–16.

16. Silberman, *op. cit.,* pp. 218–19.

17. Wilson, *op. cit.,* p. 115.
18. John Dollard, *Caste and Class in a Southern Town,* (Garden City: Doubleday Anchor, 1949), pp. 279–80.
19. DiPerna, *Juries on Trial,* pp. 159–60.
20. Claude Brown, "Manchild in Harlem," *The New York Times Sunday Magazine,* September 16, 1984.

20—Families and Crime

1. Daniel P. Moynihan, *The Negro Family: The Case for National Action,* (Washington, D.C.: Office of Policy Planning and Research, Department of Labor, 1965).
2. Richard Cloward and Frances Fox Piven, "The Weight of the Poor: Strategy to End Poverty," *The Nation,* May 2, 1966.
3. Richard Cloward, "The War On Poverty—Are The Poor Left Out?" *The Nation,* August 2, 1965.
4. Charles R. Morris, *The Cost of Good Intentions: New York City and the Liberal Experiment,* (New York: McGraw-Hill, 1980); also, Blanche Bernstein, *The Politics of Welfare: The New York City Experience,* (Cambridge: Abt Books, 1982).
5. Wilson, *Thinking About Crime,* p. 16–17.
6. David T. Ellwood and Mary Jo Bane, "The Impact of AFDC on Family Structure and Living Arrangements," Harvard University, March, 1984.
7. Charles Murray, *Losing Ground: American Social Policy 1950–1980,* (New York: Basic Books, 1984).
8. Dollard, *Caste and Class in a Southern Town,* pp. 270–71.
9. Herbert G. Gutman, *The Black Family in Slavery and Freedom, 1750–1925,* (New York: Vintage Books, 1977).
10. Stephen Thernstrom, *The Other Bostonians,* (Cambridge: Harvard University Press, 1973).
11. Silberman, *Criminal Violence, Criminal Justice,* pp. 175–76.
12. *Ibid.,* p. 176.
13. Walter Williams, *The State Against Blacks,* (New York: McGraw-Hill, 1982).
14. Murray, *op. cit.*
15. Brown, "Manchild in Harlem," *op. cit.*
16. Auletta, *The Underclass,* p. 82.
17. *Ibid.,* p. 83.
18. Adler, *What Life Should Mean To You,* pp. 208–9.

19. Samenow, *Inside the Criminal Mind,* p. 166.

20. Patricia Cayo Sexton, *The Feminized Male,* (New York: Random House, 1969), pp. 3–4.

21. Michaud and Aynesworth, *The Only Living Witness.*

22. Andy Stack (Ann Rule), *The I-5 Killer,* p. 45.

23. *Ibid.,* pp. 85–86; 93.

24. Quoted, Bruce Gibney, *The Beauty Queen Killer,* (New York: Pinnacle Books, 1984), p. 200.

25. Jack Olsen, *Son: A Psychopath and His Victims,* (New York: Dell, 1983).

26. Michael Daly, "Hunting the Wolf-Packs," *New York,* June 3, 1985.

27. Brown, "Manchild in Harlem," *op. cit.*

28. Daly, *op. cit.*

BIBLIOGRAPHY

Adcock, Thomas Larry. *Precinct 19*. Garden City: Doubleday, 1984.

Allen, Harry E.; Friday, Paul C.; Roebuck, Julian B.; and Sagarin, Edward. *Crime and Punishment*. New York: Free Press, 1981.

Allen, John. *Assault With a Deadly Weapon*. New York: Pantheon Books, 1977.

Auletta, Ken. *The Underclass*. New York: Vintage, 1983.

Bailey, F. Lee. *The Defense Never Rests*. New York: New American Library, 1971.

———. *For the Defense*. New York: New American Library, 1976.

Barlow, Hugh D. *Introduction to Criminology*. Boston: Little, Brown, 1984.

Bayley, David H. *Forces of Order: Police Behavior in Japan and the United States*. Berkeley: University of California Press, 1976.

Becker, Ernest. *Escape From Evil*. New York: Free Press, 1975.

Becker, Gary S. *The Economic Approach to Human Behavior*. Chicago, University of Chicago Press, 1976.

Becker, Howard S. *Outsiders: Studies in the Sociology of Deviance*. New York: Free Press, 1963.

———. *The Other Side: Perspectives in Deviance*. New York: Free Press, 1964.

Becker, Theodore L. *Comparative Judicial Politics: The Political Functioning of Courts*. Chicago: Rand McNally, 1970.

Bedau, Hugo Adam, ed. *The Death Penalty In America*. New York: Oxford University Press, 1982.

Berger, Raoul. *Death Penalties: The Supreme Court's Obstacle Course*. Cambridge: Harvard University Press, 1984.

———. *Government by Judiciary*. Cambridge: Harvard University Press, 1977.

Berns, Walter. *For Capital Punishment: Crime and the Morality of the Death Penalty.* New York: Basic Books, 1979.

Bickel, Alexander M. *The Supreme Court and the Idea of Progress.* New Haven: Yale University Press, 1978.

Blau, Zena Smith. *Black Children / White Children: Competence, Socialization, and Social Structure.* New York: Free Press, 1981.

Bloch, Herbert A., and Geis, Gilbert. *Man, Crime, and Society.* New York: Random House, 1962.

Bortner, M. A. *Inside a Juvenile Court.* New York: New York University Press, 1984.

Campbell, Anne. *The Girls in the Gang: A Report From New York City.* New York: Basil Blackwell, 1984.

Capaldi, Nicholas. *Clear and Present Danger: The Free Speech Controversy.* New York: Western Publishing, 1969.

Caplan, Lincoln. *The Insanity Defense and the Trial of John W. Hinckley, Jr.* Boston: David R. Godine, Publisher, 1984.

Carlen, Pat, ed. *Criminal Women.* Oxford: Polity Press, 1985.

Carrington, Frank. *Crime and Justice: A Conservative Strategy.* Washington, D.C.: Heritage Foundation, 1983.

————. *Neither Cruel Nor Unusual.* New Rochelle, N.Y.: Arlington House, 1979.

————. *The Victims.* New Rochelle, N.Y.: Arlington House, 1977.

Chevigny, Paul. *Police Power: Public Abuse in New York City.* New York: Vintage, 1969.

Clark, Ted. *The Oppression of Youth.* New York: Harper & Row, Pub., 1975.

Cloward, Richard A., and Ohlin, Lloyd E. *Delinquency and Opportunity: A Theory of Delinquent Gangs.* New York: Free Press, 1960.

Cohen, Albert K. *Delinquent Boys: The Culture of the Gang.* New York: Free Press, 1955.

Cressy, Donald R. *Theft of a Nation: The Structure and Operation of Organized Crime in America.* New York: Harper Colophon, 1969.

Curzon, Sam. *"Legs" Diamond.* Derby, Conn.: Monarch Books, 1962.

David, Rene, and Brierley, John E. C. *Major Legal Systems in the World Today.* New York: Free Press, 1978.

Dershowitz, Alan M. *The Best Defense.* New York: Vintage, 1983.

DiPerna, Paula. *Juries On Trial.* New York: Dembner Books, 1984.

Dollard, John. *Caste and Class in a Southern Town.* Garden City, N.Y.: Anchor Books, 1947.

Donahue, William A. *The Politics of the American Civil Liberties Union.* New Brunswick, N.J.: Transaction Books, 1985.

Dostoevski, Fëdor. *Crime and Punishment.* Middlesex, Eng.: Penguin, 1966.

———. *The House of the Dead.* New York: Dell Pub. Co., Inc., 1959.

Down, Thomas. *Murder Man.* New York: Dell Pub. Co., Inc., 1984.

Duster, Troy. *The Legislation of Morality: Law, Drugs, and Moral Judgment.* New York: Free Press, 1970.

Eidelberg, Paul. *The Philosophy of the American Constitution.* New York: Free Press, 1968.

Ericson, Richard V. *Making Crime: A Study of Detective Work.* Toronto: Buttersworth, 1981.

Evan, William M., ed. *The Sociology of the Law.* New York: Free Press, 1980.

Feeley, Malcolm M. *Court Reform on Trial: Why Simple Solutions Fail.* New York; Basic Books, Twentieth Century Fund, 1983.

Fleming, Macklin. *The Price of Perfect Justice.* New York: Basic Books, 1974.

Forer, Lois G. *Criminals and Victims: A Trial Judge Reflects on Crime and Punishment.* New York: W.W. Norton & Co., Inc., 1980.

Foucault, Michel. *Discipline and Punish: The Birth of the Prison.* New York: Vintage, 1979.

Frank, Gerold. *The Boston Strangler.* New York: New American Library, 1967.

Fribourg, Marjorie. *The Bill of Rights: Its Impact on the American People.* New York: Avon, 1967.

Friendly, Fred W., and Elliot, Martha J. H. *The Constitution: That Delicate Balance.* New York: Random House, 1984.

Gaylin, Willard. *The Killing of Bonnie Garland.* New York: Penguin, 1982.

———. *The Rage Within: Anger in Modern Life.* New York: Simon & Schuster, 1984.

Gellhorn, Walter. *American Rights: The Constitution in Action.* New York: Macmillan, 1960.

Genet, Jean. *The Thief's Journal.* New York: Grove Press, 1964.

Gibney, Bruce. *The Beauty Queen Killer.* New York: Pinnacle Books, 1984.

Gillers, Stephen. *Getting Justice: The Rights of People.* New York: New American Library, 1971.

Golden, Sandy. *Driving The Drunk Off The Road.* Washington, D.C.: Acropolis Books, 1983.

Goulden, Joseph C. *The Benchwarmers: The Private World of the Powerful Federal Judges.* New York: Ballantine, 1974.

———. *The Superlawyers.* New York: Dell Pub. Co., Inc., 1972.

Graham, Fred P. *The Self-Inflicted Wound.* New York: Macmillan, 1969.

Hamilton, Madison, and Jay. *The Federalist Papers.* New York: New American Library, 1961.

Hayek, F. A. *Law, Legislation, and Liberty:* Vol. 1, *Rules and Order.* Chicago: University of Chicago Press, 1973.

Hazelrigg, Lawrence, ed. *Prison Within Society.* Garden City, N.Y.: Doubleday/Anchor, 1969.

Horowitz, Donald L. *The Courts and Social Policy.* Washington, D.C.: The Brookings Institute, 1977.

Jackson, Bruce. *In the Life.* New York: Holt, Rinehart & Winston, 1972.

———. *Law and Disorder.* Urbana: University of Illinois Press, 1984.

Jacoby, Susan. *Wild Justice: The Evolution of Revenge.* New York: Harper & Row, Pub., 1983.

Jenkins, Philip. *Crime and Justice: Issues and Ideas.* Belmont, Calif.: Brooks/Cole, 1984.

Johnson, Robert, and Toch, Hans, eds. *The Pains of Imprisonment.* Beverly Hills: Sage Publications, Inc., 1982.

Kadish, Sanford H., ed. *Encyclopedia of Crime and Justice,* Vols. 1–4. New York: Free Press, 1983.

Karmen, Andrew. *Crime Victims.* Belmont, Calif.: Brooks/Cole, 1984.

Kinder, Gary. *Victim: The Other Side of Murder.* New York: Dell Pub. Co., Inc., 1982.

King, Harry. *Box Man: A Professional Thief's Journey.* New York: Harper & Row Pub., 1972.

Kornhauser, Ruth Rosner. *Social Sources of Delinquency.* Chicago: University of Chicago Press, 1978.

Lauder, Ronald S. *Fighting Violent Crime in America.* Dodd, Mead, 1985.

Leith, Rod. *The Prostitute Murders.* New York: Pinnacle Books, 1983.

Levine, Richard M. *Bad Blood: A Family Murder in Marin County.* New York, New American Library, 1982.

Lewis, Anthony. *Gideon's Trumpet.* New York: Vintage, 1966.

Liebow, Elliot. *Tally's Corner: A Study of Negro Streetcorner Men.* Boston: Little, Brown, 1967.

Lynd, Robert S., and Lynd, Helen Merrell. *Middletown: A Study of*

Modern American Culture. New York: Harcourt Brace Jovanovich, 1956.

Maas, Peter. *The Valachi Papers.* New York: Bantam, 1972.

Magee, Doug. *What Murder Leaves Behind: The Victim's Families.* New York: Dodd, Mead, 1983.

Mann, Kenneth. *Defending White-Collar Crime.* New Haven: Yale University Press, 1985.

Mayer, Martin. *The Lawyers.* New York: Harper & Row Pub., 1966.

McCloskey, Robert G. *The Modern Supreme Court.* Cambridge: Harvard University Press, 1972.

McGuigan, Patrick B., and Rader, Randall R. *Criminal Justice Reform.* Chicago: Regnery/Gateway/Free Congress Research and Education Foundation, 1983.

McKelway, St. Clair. *The Tales From the Annals of Crime and Rascality.* New York: Random House, 1951.

McNamara, Joseph D. *Safe and Sane: The Sensible Way to Protect Yourself, Your Loved Ones, Your Property and Possessions.* New York: The Putnam Publishing Group, 1984.

Mellen, Joan. *Privilege: The Enigma of Sasha Bruce.* New York: New American Library, 1982.

Menninger, Karl. *The Crime of Punishment.* New York: Penguin, 1968.

Meyer, Peter. *The Yale Murder: The Fatal Romance of Bonnie Garland and Richard Herrin.* New York: Berkley Books, 1983.

Michalowski, Raymond J. *Order, Law, and Crime.* New York: Random House, 1985.

Michaud, Stephen G., and Aynesworth, Hugh. *The Only Living Witness.* New York: New American Library, 1983.

Miller, Arthus Selwyn. *The Supreme Court and American Capitalism.* New York: Free Press, 1968.

Mitchell, Broadus, and Mitchell, Louise. *A Biography of the Constitution of the United States.* New York: Oxford University Press, 1962.

Mitford, Jessica. *Kind and Usual Punishment.* New York: Vintage, 1974.

Moquin, Wayne, ed. *The American Way of Crime.* New York: Praeger Publishers, 1976.

Morris, Norval. *Madness and the Criminal Law.* Chicago: University of Chicago Press, 1982.

Murphy, Patrick T. *Our Kindly Parent—The State.* New York: Penguin, 1978.

Nash, Jay Robert. *Murder Among the Mighty: Celebrity Slayings That*

Shocked America. New York: Delacorte Press, 1983.

National Advisory Commission on Civil Disorders. *U.S. Riot Commission Report.* New York: Bantam, 1968.

National Advisory Commission on Criminal Justice Standards and Goals. *A National Strategy to Reduce Crime.* New York: Avon, 1975.

Neely, Richard. *How Courts Govern America.* New Haven: Yale University Press, 1981.

———. *Why Courts Don't Work.* New York: McGraw-Hill, 1983.

Nelson, Rick. *The Cop Who Wouldn't Quit.* New York: Ballantine, 1983.

Newman, Graeme. *Just and Painful: A Case for the Corporal Punishment of Criminals.* New York: Macmillan, 1983.

New York State Special Commission on Attica. *Attica.* New York: Bantam, 1972.

Niederhoffer, Arthur. *Behind the Shield: The Police in Urban Society.* Garden City, N.Y.: Anchor Books, 1969.

Nizer, Louis. *My Life In Court.* New York: Pyramid Books, 1962.

Olsen, Jack. *Son: A Psychopath and His Victims.* New York: Dell Pub. Co., Inc., 1983.

Oppenheim, Felix E. *Dimensions of Freedom.* New York: St. Martin's Press, 1961.

Padover, Saul K., ed. *The Living U.S. Constitution.* New York: New American Library, 1983.

Parsons, Talcott. *On Institutions and Social Evolution.* Chicago: University of Chicago Press, 1982.

Petersilia, Joan, Greenwood, Peter W., Lavin, Marvin. *Criminal Careers of Habitual Felons.* Santa Monica, California: The Rand Corporation, 1977.

Petersilia, Joan; Turner, Susan; Kahan, James; and Peterson, Joyce. *Granting Felons Probation: Public Risks and Alternatives.* Santa Monica, Calif.: The Rand Corporation, 1985.

Peterson, Mark A., and Braiker, Harriet B. *Who Commits Crimes: A Survey of Prison Inmates.* Cambridge: Oelgeschlager, Gunn & Hain, Publishers, 1981.

Phillips, Steven. *No Heroes, No Villains: The Story of a Murder Trial.* New York: Vintage, 1978.

Piven, Frances Fox, and Cloward, Richard. *Regulating the Poor: The Functions of Public Welfare.* New York: Vintage, 1971.

Platt, Anthony, and Cooper, Lynn. *Policing America.* Englewood Cliffs, N.J.: Prentice-Hall, 1974.

Pontell, Henry N. *A Capacity to Punish.* Bloomington: University of Indiana Press, 1984.

Posner, Richard A. *The Federal Courts: Crisis and Reform.* Cambridge: Harvard University Press, 1985.

President's Commission on Law Enforcement and Administration of Justice. *The Challenge of Crime in a Free Society.* New York: Avon, 1968.

President's Task Force on Victims of Crime. *Final Report.* Washington, D.C.: U.S. Government Printing Office, 1982.

Radin, Max. *The Law and You.* New York: New American Library, 1948.

Radzinowicz, Sir Leon, and Wolfgang, Marvin E. *Crime and Society,* Vol. I-III. New York: Basic Books, 1977.

Rembar, Charles. *The Law of the Land: The Evolution of Our Legal System.* New York: Simon & Schuster, 1980.

Rodell, Fred. *Nine Men: The Political History of the Supreme Court of the United States from 1790 to 1955.* New York: Vintage, 1955.

Rosenblatt, Stanley M. *Trial Lawyer.* Secaucus, N.J.: Lyle Stuart, 1984.

Rossum, Ralph A. *The Politics of the Criminal Justice System.* New York: Marcel Dekker, 1978.

Ryan, William. *Blaming the Victim.* New York: Vintage, 1976.

Samenow, Stanton E. *Inside the Criminal Mind.* New York: Times Books, 1984.

Schlesinger, Steven R. *Exclusionary Injustice: The Problem of Illegally Obtained Evidence.* New York: Marcel Dekker, 1977.

Schubert, Glendon, ed. *Judicial Decision-Making.* New York: Free Press, 1963.

Scigliano, Robert. *The Supreme Court and the Presidency.* New York: Free Press, 1971.

Senzel, Howard T. *Cases: A Courthouse Chronicle of Crime and Wit.* New York: Viking, 1982.

Serge, Victor. *Men in Prison.* London: Writers and Readers Cooperative, 1969.

Simon, Rita James. *Women and Crime.* Lexington, Mass.: Heath, 1978.

Skolnick, Jerome H., director, Task Force on Violent Aspects of Protest and Confrontation of the National Commission on the Causes and Prevention of Violence. *The Politics of Protest.* New York: Ballantine, 1969.

Sowell, Thomas. *Ethnic America.* New York: Basic Books, 1981.

———. *Knowledge and Decisions.* New York: Basic Books, 1980.

Stack, Andy. *The I-5 Killer.* New York: Signet, 1984.

Stephen, Otis H., Jr. *The Supreme Court and Confessions of Guilt.* Knoxville: University of Tennessee Press, 1973.

Stone, W. G., and Hirliman, G. *The Hate Factory: The Story of the New Mexico Penitentiary Riot.* New York: Dell Pub. Co., Inc., 1982.

Sutherland, Edwin H., and Cressy, Donald R. *Principles in Criminology.* Philadelphia: Lippincott, 1966.

Thompson, Hunter. *Fear and Loathing in Las Vegas.* New York: Warner Books, 1971.

Toch, Hans. *Living in Prison: The Ecology of Survival.* New York: Free Press, 1977.

de Tocqueville, Alexis. *Democracy in America.* Vols. 1 and 2. New York: Vintage, 1945.

_____. *Journey to America.* Garden City, N.Y.: Anchor Books, 1971.

Trojanowicz, Robert. *An Evaluation of the Neighborhood Foot Patrol Program in Flint, Michigan.* East Lansing: Michigan State University, 1984.

Tullock, Gordon. *Economics of Income Redistribution.* Boston: Kluwer-Nijhoff Publishing, 1983.

Unger, Roberto Mangabeira. *Law in Modern Society.* New York: Free Press, 1976.

van den Haag, Ernest, and Conrad, John P. *The Death Penalty: A Debate.* New York: Plenum, 1983.

van den Haag, Ernest. *Punishing Criminals.* New York: Basic Books, 1975.

von Hirsch, Andrew. *Doing Justice: The Choice of Punishments—Report of the Committee for the Study of Incarcerations.* New York: Hill and Wang, 1976.

Walker, Sam. *Sense and Nonsense About Crime.* Belmont, Calif.: Brooks/Cole, 1985.

Wilkenson, Fred T. *The Realities of Crime and Punishment: A Prison Administrator's Testament.* Springfield, Mo.: Mycroft Press, 1972.

Willwerth, James. *Jones: Portrait of a Mugger.* New York: M. Evans and Company, 1974.

Wilson, James Q., ed. *Crime and Public Policy.* San Francisco: Institute for Contemporary Studies Press, 1983.

_____. *Thinking About Crime.* New York: Vintage, 1977.

Wilson, James Q., and Hernstein, Richard J. *Crime and Human Nature.* New York: Simon & Schuster, 1985.

Winslade, William J., and Ross, Judith Wilson. *The Insanity Plea: The Uses and Abuses of the Insanity Defense.* New York: Scribner's, 1983.

Wishman, Seymour. *Confession of a Criminal Lawyer.* New York: Penguin, 1981.

Wolfgang, Marvin E.; Savitz, Leonard; and Johnston, Norman. *The Sociology of Crime and Delinquency.* New York: John Wiley, 1962.

Woodward, Bob, and Armstrong, Scott. *The Brethren: Inside the Supreme Court.* New York: Avon, 1979.

Zimring, Franklin E. *The Changing Legal World of Adolescence.* New York: Free Press, 1982.